Politics and Society in the Third World
Second Edition

Peter Calvert and Susan Calvert

PEARSON
Longman

Harlow, England • London • New York • Boston • San Francisco • Toronto
Sydney • Tokyo • Singapore • Hong Kong • Seoul • Taipei • New Delhi
Cape Town • Madrid • Mexico City • Amsterdam • Munich • Paris • Milan

Pearson Education Limited
Edinburgh Gate
Harlow
Essex CM20 2JE
England

and Associated Companies throughout the world

Visit us on the World Wide Web at:
www.pearsoned.co.uk

First published 2001

ISBN 0 582 43724 5

British Library Cataloguing-in-Publication Data
A catalogue record for this book is available from the British Library

Library of Congress Cataloging-in-Publication Data

Calvert, Peter.
  Politics and society in the Third World / Peter Calvert and Susan Calvert.-- 2nd ed.
     p. cm.
  Susan Calvert's name appears first on the earlier edition.
  Includes bibliographical references and index.
  ISBN 0-582-43724-5
  1. Developing Countries--Social condition. 2. Developing countries--Politics and
  government. I. Calvert, Susan. II. Title.

  HN980 .C325 2001
  306'.09172'4--dc21

                                                              2001016446

10 9 8 7 6 5 4 3
08 07 06 05 04

Typeset by 35 in 10/12pt Sabon

Printed in Malaysia, LSP

IN MEMORIAM
IRENE CALVERT
1909–2000

Contents

List of tables and maps

Tables

Maps

List of plates

Plate 1   Anti-capitalist, anti-American politics, Uruguay

Plate 2   Transport, Brazil

Plate 3   Drying fish, Sri Lanka

Plate 4   Street scene, Sierra Leone

Plate 5   Avellaneda Bridge: declining traditional industry, Argentina

Plate 6   Where South meets North, Istanbul, Turkey

Plate 7   Traditional lifestyles, Iran

Plate 8   Husking coconut, Sri Lanka

Plate 9   Voters registration drive, Toluca, Mexico

Plate 10 Globalisation, Chile

Plate 11 Hydroelectric power, Paraguay

Plate 12 Vegetable cultivation, Cuba

Plate 13   Green and other politics, Uruguay

Preface to the Second Edition

The first edition of this book was published four years ago. Since then, sadly, three of the trends we emphasised have become more evident. Despite a great deal of talk about relieving the debts of the poorer countries, little has been done and the debts of the poorest continue to drain their resources. In fact those resources have been depleted by the terms imposed by their creditors: devaluation, privatisation and the opening up of their economies to foreign competition. Increasing pressure from migrants desperate for jobs has been met by the advanced industrialised countries constructing both legal and physical barriers to try simply to keep them out. The 'pulling apart' of the Third World has also continued, so that the gap between rich and poor has become wider, both between and within individual countries.

If there is not enough money for basic needs, there always seems to be enough for war and civil war. The UN peacekeeping mission has run into the sand and the optimism of the early 1990s has faded. The United States has only agreed to pay part of the cost of peacekeeping if in return it gets a rebate on its basic contribution to the running of the world organisation. If the former world powers seem less and less willing to intervene, new actors have taken their place. Ethiopia, once again facing famine, has somehow found the resources to invade and occupy a large part of its neighbour Eritrea. China, in search of oil, is helping the government of Sudan suppress the long-running movement for autonomy in the South. Keeping track of these and many other developments is a full-time task in itself.

The moral imperative of the alleviation of these glaring inequalities has led to the suggestion that the leading powers to give computers to the Third World. Without sufficient clean water, available food, primary health care and educational infrastructure but with only a few hours of electricity on a good day, it is hard to see computers as the immediate priority for the poorest nations.

The problem for many in the richer countries, on the other hand, is not a shortage of information, but how to make sense of the flood of knowledge that is readily available. The purpose of this book is to provide an introduction to the Third World, its political institutions and issues of social and economic development. The approach is interdisciplinary. Three key issues recur: 'environment', 'development' and 'democratisation'. As will become clear, on all three counts, there are still some grounds for optimism, but with each year these diminish.

Chandlers Ford

August 2000

Acknowledgements

The publishers are grateful to the following for permission to use copyright material:

Table 2.1 from *South America, Central America and the Carribean 2000*, Europa Publications, London (West, J. 1999).

Table 10.1 from *Third World Guide 93/94*, Instituto del Tercer Mundo, Uruguay

List of abbreviations

AIDS	acquired immune deficiency syndrome
ANC	African National Congress
AOSIS	Association of Small Island States
ASEAN	Association of South East Asian Nations
BBC	British Broadcasting Corporation
CAP	[European Union] Common Agricultural Policy
Caricom	Caribbean Community
CBI	Caribbean Basin Initiative
CERDS	[UN] Charter of Economic Rights and Duties of States
CFCs	chlorofluorocarbons
CFA	Communauté Française Africaine
CFF	[IMF] Compensatory Financial Facility
CIS	Commonwealth of Independent States
CITES	Convention on International Trade in Endangered Species of Wild Fauna and Flora
CNN	Cable News Network
CPP	Convention People's Party [Ghana]
Danida	Danish Ministry of Foreign Affairs
DDT	dichlorodiphenyltrichloroethane
ECLA	[UN] Economic Commission for Latin America
ECOSOC	[UN] Economic and Social Council
ECOWAS	Economic Community of West African States
EPZs	Economic Processing Zones
EU	European Union
Exmibal	Exploraciones y Explotaciones Minerías Izabal
EZLN	Zapatista National Liberation Army
FAO	Food and Agriculture Organization
FIS	Front Islamique de Salvation
FPR	Rwandan Patriotic Front
GATS	General Agreement on Trade in Services

GATT	General Agreement on Tariffs and Trade
GDP	gross domestic product
GNP	gross national product
G7	Group of Seven nations
HDI	Human Development Index
HEP	hydroelectric power
HIPCs	heavily indebted poorer countries
HIV	human immunodeficiency virus
HKSAR	Hong Kong Special Administrative Region
HYVs	high yield varieties
IBRD	International Bank for Reconstruction and Development
IBM	International Business Machines
IFIs	international financial institutions
IGOs	intergovernmental organisations
IMF	International Monetary Fund
imr	infant mortality rate
INC	[UN] Intergovernmental Negotiating Committee
ios	international organisations
IPCC	Intergovernmental Panel on Climate Change
IPKF	Indian Peacekeeping Force
ISI	import-substitution-industrialisation
ITA	International Tin Agreement
ITT	International Telephone & Telegraph
JVP	Janatha Vimukti Peramuna [People's Liberation Front, Sri Ianka]
KLM	Koninklijke Luchtvaartmaatschappij [Royal Dutch Airlines]
LDCs	less developed countries
LTTE	Liberation Tigers of Tamil Eelam [Sri Lanka]
MNR	National Revolutionary Movement [Bolivia]
MPLA	Movement for the Liberation of Angola
NAFTA	North American Free Trade Agreement
NAM	Non-aligned Movement
NGOs	non-governmental organisations
NICs	newly industrialising countries
NIEs	new industrial economies
NIEO	New International Economic Order
NPFL	National Patriotic Front of Liberia
NRC	National Reformation Council [Sierra Leone]
NPRC	National Provisional Ruling Council
OAS	Organization of American States
OAU	Organization of African Unity
ODA	official development assistance
OECD	Organization for Economic Cooperation and Development
OPEC	Organization of Petroleum Exporting Countries
PACD	[UN] Plan of Action to Combat Desertification
PEMEX	Petróleos Mexicanos

PNC	People's National Congress [Guyana]
PNP	People's National Party [Jamaica]
PNR	Mexican Party of the National Revolution
PPP	People's Progressive Party [Guyana]
PRI	Institutional Revolutionary Party [Mexico]
PT	Workers' Party [Brazil]
R & R	Rest and Recreation
RPF	Rwandan Patriotic Front
SAARC	South Asian Association for Regional Cooperation
SAPS	structural adjustment packages
SIDS	small island developing states
SLFP	Sri Lankan Freedom Party
SPC	South Pacific Commission
SPF	South Pacific Forum
SPLA	Sudanese People's Liberation Army
SSA	[Africa] South of the Sahara
Swapo	South West People's Organization
TB	tuberculosis
TNCs	transnational corporations
TRIMS	[GATT] investment measures
TRIPS	[GATT] intellectual property rights
TV	Television
U5MRs	under-five mortality rates
UFCo	United Fruit Company [Honduras]
UK	United Kingdom
UN	United Nations
UNCED	United Nations Conference on Environment and Development
UNCTAD	United Nations Conference on Trade and Development
UNDP	United Nations Development Programme
UNEP	United Nations Environment Programme
UNESCO	United Nations Educational, Scientific and Cultural Organization
UNFPA	United Nations Population Fund
UNHCR	United Nations High Commission on Refugees
UNICEF	United Nations (International) Children's (Emergency) Fund
UNITA	National Union for the Total Independence of Angola
US	United States'
USA	United States of America
USAID	United States Agency for International Development
USSR	Union of Soviet Socialist Republics
WCED	World Commission on Environment and Development
WHO	World Health Organization
WTO	World Trade Organization
WWF	World Wide Fund for Nature
YPF	Yacimientos Petrolíferos Fiscales

PART I

The Third World

CHAPTER 1

What is the Third World?

Introduction

This book is intended as an overview of the Third World and as a guide to its political and social problems. It is interdisciplinary, because the subject is so large. No one academic specialism poses all possible questions, let alone gives all possible answers to the main themes with which we shall be concerned: environment, development and globalisation. All three are very much current issues and much of the material on which we draw, therefore, comes from current sources: newspapers, magazines and TV and radio programmes. The principal task is to bring all this material together in a series of topic areas that make sense in themselves and also relate to one another. Before turning to the way in which the book is structured, however, we should first define its subject: the Third World.

What is the Third World? We cannot get away from the fact that there is no consensus on how it should be either defined or categorised. This lack of agreement is increasing with time and already many specialists prefer to use a different term or to avoid it entirely; but the term is so widely known and so convenient that it is still used and therefore still has meaning (Thomas 1999). Nor would most writers have any difficulty coming to a broad agreement as to which regions of the world and which countries within those regions the concept covers. Chapter 2, therefore, deals with the physical structure of the Third World and the way in which geography and climate have shaped it. Yet many important questions remain.

'Third World' is frequently seen as having been coined by the French demographer Sauvy in 1952. It is believed to derive from the French term, the 'third estate', which was used to signify the commoners as against the aristocracy and the clergy. But this is perhaps looking for a degree of precision in the term's origins that is somewhat suspect. The idea of some kind of third alternative to the rapidly developing post-war division between East and West does not really require much explanation. For example General Juan Domingo Perón in Argentina had before 1948 identified what he saw as the extremes of exaggerated individualism and state collectivism that called for the pursuit of a 'middle way', and by the following year the 'Third Position' between capitalism and communism had become a central plank of his doctrine of 'Justicialism'. As Perón anticipated, during the cold war the problems of definition were somewhat simpler in that the very idea of non-alignment suggests a three-way division.

The 'Third World' has evolved into a concept of development (Worsley 1967). However this is problematic for different reasons. There are different sorts of development and levels of development vary so much, hence the term has different meanings to different people and organisations; different institutions use different indicators of different types of development. In any case it is unlikely that any two states will exhibit comparable levels of development on all indicators. Second, to use the term 'developing world' instead is to accept unchallenged the claim that it is in fact developing.

To define the Third World in terms of poverty is even more problematic. It is true that even the least developed country of western Europe, Portugal, is better off in terms of per capita income than any country in Latin America. But this is a single indicator, and there are many people in Latin America who have lifestyles that the poor of Portugal – or indeed of an advanced industrialised country such as Germany or the United States – would envy.

Increasingly those who are advantaged by our global system are recognised as a minority, with an expanding, marginalised and insecure 'Third World' in all states, whether they be First World or Third World (Cox in Thomas 1999). The global poor, wherever they live, have even been identified as a 'fourth world', but the more usual use of this term is that of the World Bank, which has since 1978 talked of a 'Fourth' World of the very poorest countries. At the same time the World Bank has taken some of the oil-rich Middle East out of its Third World category. A different problem is posed by the relatively well-developed but still poor and still Third World newly industrialising countries (NICs), many of them knocked back firmly into that category by the East Asian crisis of 1998. Despite the diversity of states included in the category, international organisations and commentators such as Thomas (1999) see the Third World as expanding as a consequence of the process of globalisation (Smith 1992).

Certainly the Third World shares problems, though the same ones do not necessarily apply in all the countries of a region, let alone worldwide. Among these are geography (Bangladesh), lack of infrastructure (Burkina Faso), war/famine (Somalia), and a burgeoning population in some areas without economic growth to compensate for the additional demands this makes on the economy (Africa South of the Sahara generally). Third World states may be seen to share economic dependency and vulnerability to the impact of factors beyond their control. They are socially and economically disadvantaged. As Clapham says: 'What distinguishes the third world is its peripherality.

Economic peripherality has meant separation from, and subordination to, the dominant industrial economies which have developed especially in Europe and North America' (Clapham 1985: 3).

Such economies are part of the global economy but they became part of it in the first instance through the supply of primary products, and the global system they joined was created by and is sustained by the (post-)industrial economies. Development in the Third World thus depends on access to First World technology and this actually enhances the gap between the developed and the developing worlds. The NICs were successful both in obtaining this access and in making use of it, which is not by any means the same thing. But their steep rise was cut short and for the rest of the Third World the big question is: where will investment come from – will it be just displaced pollution or market access investment?

Colonisation

Inheriting a colonial economy determines the pattern of infrastructure available to a newly independent state. Since 1945 there has been an increase in the number of independent countries in the world from around 50 to nearly 200. Naturally this complicates the idea of a single category to embrace some two-thirds of the states, but at the same time this process has made consideration of this group of countries and their histories more vital than ever.

Nearly all Third World states are former colonies. Three exceptions are China, Thailand and Iran, each of which was subject to considerable pressure from colonising powers but ultimately maintained its independence as a result of conflict between two or more potential colonisers. A fourth, Ethiopia, escaped colonisation in the nineteenth century only to fall victim to the imperial ambitions of Mussolini.

However the historical experiences of colonisation in different parts of the Third World are in fact very different. They vary with:

- The stage at which colonisation took place and with the economic development of the colonial power involved.

- The different policies and practices of the colonial powers. French colonial rule emphasised cultural superiority while British rule stressed racial superiority. Once colonies adopted French culture they became part of France, and one in particular, Algeria, was actually incorporated as part of metropolitan France. Britain's ideology of superiority clearly would not permit such incorporation, but on the other hand made rejection easier to take. When the French left Sekou Touré's Guinea they smashed everything that they could not take with them.

- The nature of indigenous societies. In much of Latin America there has been a far longer period of independence and there was much less traditional society to supersede and/or absorb. In Asia colonial rule was shorter, independence more recent and colonial absorption of existing political systems was much more variable and sometimes much less complete. 'Protectorates' such as Egypt, Morocco, Vietnam, and parts of Malaysia, Nigeria, etc. were least affected.

However, common features of the colonial experience might include:

- The establishment of arbitrary territorial boundaries, notably in the interior of Africa, which was penetrated late and then not for settlement, which was mainly coastal.

- The imposition of a political and administrative order ultimately based on force though often legitimised locally by superior technology and the mystique of power.

- Centralised, authoritarian administrative systems. All colonial rule, even that of a democratic country like the United States of America, which was the colonial power in the Philippines and (briefly) Cuba, is authoritarian.

Independence

Most of Latin America became independent at the beginning of the nineteenth century, much earlier than the rest of the Third World. Thus Argentina was effectively independent in 1810 and formally so after 1816, though it was not recognised as such by Spain until 1853.

Independence came to the rest of the European empires much more recently. The Second World War destroyed the myth of invincibility that helped make colonial rule acceptable and it encouraged the growth of nationalism in the Third World. Invariably such nationalist movements were led by western-educated individuals such as Kwame Nkrumah in the Gold Coast (Ghana). After 1945 the will to hold the colonies no longer existed amongst large sections of the elite of the exhausted western powers: Britain, France, the Netherlands and Belgium. At this point there was much less contradiction than there had been previously between the values of the colonial power and the ideal of independence. With independence, however, these perceptions were to change rapidly, as the new state's identity was defined.

However in all cases the institutions created by the colonial power for its own purposes became a state at independence. This made the newly independent state at once strong and weak. It was strong insofar as it was intact, functioning, and usually centralised. Only Argentina, Brazil, Mexico, India and Nigeria emerged into independence as true federal states and in each case the struggle between federal and state governments has gone on ever since with varying outcomes. This independent state was weak in that it was inflexible and subject to nationalist criticism that its forms were inappropriate. It was associated with a small ruling clique and not with society as a whole, and so lacked legitimacy. This lack of legitimacy fed corruption that in turn contributed to the lack of legitimacy.

Westernised elites, who saw themselves as heirs to colonial overlords, sought to milk the state for all it is worth. This distorted development. Government did not plan for development and in any case could not pay for it. The benefits accruing from control of the state so far exceeded those available from other sources that desperation to control the state resulted in at best an undignified scramble that undermined its already tentative legitimacy and, at worst, in the suppression of opposition and the use of clientelism to reward political supporters. The illegitimate state often cannot build legitimacy slowly through evolution. Rather there is a tendency to frequent changes of constitutions and other superficial attempts to enhance its legitimacy.

Internal insecurity goes hand in hand with external insecurity, which may be summarised as vulnerability due to lack of autonomy. Such weaknesses would exhibit themselves in the world market and also in the lack of power in institutions such as the International Monetary Fund (IMF). US domestic policy can hit Third World states, as in the 1980s when interest rates were at historically high levels. But the same vulnerability has indirect effects too and Third World states are also much more susceptible to natural disasters, as is evident from the very different capacity to manage flooding in Bangladesh and the Netherlands, for example.

Cold war rivalries

The term 'Third World' gained acceptance quickly since it reflected the dilemma facing the newly independent states in an era characterised by two power blocs. The earliest tentative moves towards the establishment of the Non-aligned Movement (NAM), notably the Bandung Afro-Asian Solidarity Conference in 1955, included states on the basis of their independence, not their ideological leanings. Cuba, despite its strong cold war alliance with the former Soviet Union, became a leading member of the NAM, as did Pakistan, despite its clear pro-western orientation. But both could conveniently be grouped together with others as neither being part of the First World (the advanced industrial economies) nor Second World (the command economies of eastern Europe and China).

During the cold war the Third World became an arena for conflict, for two reasons. First, despite the apparently overwhelming power of both the USA and the Soviet Union each sought to influence the world balance of power by winning allies and friends amongst the uncommitted. Some, such as India, made a particular point of asserting their independence of either power and so made particularly desirable friends. Second, the nuclear stand-off made the prospect of war between the two superpowers so dangerous that the conflict between First and Second Worlds was played out by proxy in the Third – Korea, the Congo, Vietnam. Clandestine support to insurrectionary movements by both the Soviet Union and the USA added another zone of conflict.

The 'end of history' and the Washington consensus

The more mundane arguments surrounding the impact of the collapse of the Soviet Union on the continuing relevance of the concept of a Third World are twofold:

1.   The most obvious point is that the term's literal meaning ceases and, without a second world, the term is obsolete.

2.   If it is to be retained its use is complicated by the liberation of the former Second World states from that category and their varied and sometimes ambivalent relation to the remaining categories of First and Third Worlds. Where do the Central Asian republics fit, the Ukraine or Russia? If they do fit in, will it be where they feel they belong, with the developed countries, or as part of the new Third World? Certainly over the past decade the circumstances of the former Second World have changed so much that some authors extend the Third World category to embrace the former communist economies (see Thomas 1999). The assertion that the liberal democratic state is the ultimate form of human social organisation (e.g. Fukuyama 1992) is reminiscent of the unwarranted optimism of early modernisation theories, which were shaped on an implied long-term blueprint based on western industrial capitalism. Today the salvation of the Third World is seen as achievable through the operations of the global marketplace and the benevolence of the Group of Seven (G7) nations.

A number of points may be raised to counter such arguments:

1.   There is the pragmatic argument that the discipline of the cold war and its alliances may have been a stabilising force. This now removed makes the Third World a far more important area of study and concern, since it now constitutes in many ways a greater threat to the apparent stability of international relations.

2. There is a sense in which the collapse of the eastern bloc might be seen as concentrating the Third World, in that there ceases to be anywhere else to go. There are no alternatives to being poor in a western-dominated global system and, insofar as the Third World ever was polarised into two ideological camps, a division of the Third World has disappeared.

3. On the other hand the end of the cold war does not really make much difference to the concept of a Third World, in that the term was at least in part one of self-definition for poorer states whether they were within the ambit of one of the main power blocs or not.

4. Most importantly, as the emphasis on self-definition suggests, those common elements that gave rise to the term Third World remain valid as indicators despite the end of the cold war. The operations of global markets may enhance the opportunities for some Third World states as First (and elite Third) World investors are attracted by potential profits from 'emerging market' funds. Thus the economic diversity of the Third World may be increased. But free markets will not end global poverty and the evidence thus far (see NICs, Chapter 4) is that prospective escapees have proved susceptible to speculation and other external constraints imposed by the 'Washington consensus'. By this phrase its inventor, John Williamson of the Institute for International Economics, meant the model of development which claims that there is only one road to prosperity and that it lies through the operation of the free market impeded as little as possible by national boundaries. As Thomas (1999) points out, the term stresses the extent to which the liberalisation of trade and the free market have become hegemonic values not just for US policy makers but also for international institutions, including financial institutions. In Gramscian terms, it has achieved hegemony.

The case of China

China presents a genuine anomaly. First of all its economy is so large that it ranks globally [seventh] among world economies. Second, however, its population is so vast that it ranks very low in per capita gross national product (GNP) ($860), though this now makes it a lower middle income country, and in real gross domestic product (GDP) per capita it now ranks 98th out of 174 countries. In this sense China has still far more in common with the Third World than with the First that it seeks to emulate. Third, it retains the political forms and the authoritarian style of the former Second World at a time when many Third World countries have already taken major steps along the road to democratisation. Yet it pays lip-service at least to the principles of free trade and a free market, suggesting that its leaders see no necessary connection between the economic and the political.

Table 1.1   GNP per capita of selected states 1992

RANGE	Population 1992 (millions)	GNP per capita 1992 (US$)	Growth 1980–92 (%)	Life expectancy (years)	Adult illiteracy (%)
LOW INCOME	3,191.3	390	3.9	62	40
1 Mozambique	16.6	60	–3.6	44	67
18 India	883.6	310	3.1	61	52
21 Nigeria	101.9	320	–0.4	52	49
27 Ghana	15.8	450	–0.1	56	40
28 China	1,162.2	470	–	69	27
32 Sri Lanka	17.4	540	2.6	72	12
37 Indonesia	184.3	670	4.0	60	23
LOWER MIDDLE INCOME	1,418.7	2,490	–0.1	68	–
43 Côte d'Ivoire	12.9	670	–4.7	56	46
44 Bolivia	7.5	680	–1.5	60	23
68 Jamaica	2.4	1,340	0.2	74	2
75 Thailand	58.0	1,840	6.0	69	7
80 Turkey	58.5	1,980	2.9	67	19
85 Chile	13.6	2,730*	3.7	72	7
UPPER MIDDLE INCOME	477.7	4,020	0.8	69	15
80 S. Africa	39.8	2,670	0.1	63	–
92 Brazil	153.9	2,770	0.4	66	19
99 Mexico	85.0	3,470	–0.2	70	13
100 Trinidad & Tobago	1.3	3,940	–2.6	71	–
102 Argentina	33.1	6,050	–0.9	71	5
107 Greece	10.3	7,290	1.0	77	7
108 Portugal	9.8	7,450	3.1	74	15
109 S. Arabia	16.8	7,510	–3.3	69	38
HIGH INCOME	828.1	22,160	4.3	77	–
110 Ireland	3.5	12,210	3.4	75	–
112 Israel	5.1	13,220	1.9	76	–
116 Australia	17.5	17,260	1.6	77	a
117 UK	57.8	17,790	2.4	76	a
124 France	57.4	22,260	1.7	77	a
127 USA	255.4	23,240	1.7	77	a
131 Japan	124.5	28,190	3.6	79	a
132 Switzerland	6.9	36,080	1.4	78	a

a = UNESCO data, illiteracy less than 5%
* = revised upwards from 2,510
Source: World Bank (1994)

One thing is clear: China certainly cannot yet be regarded as an advanced industrialised country and statistically it is so significant that it can hardly be categorised on its own. China, therefore, will be treated here as a Third World country, although for some purposes it will be necessary to consider it separately.

Social and other indicators

Since many concepts used routinely in political discussion, such as development, are very complex, social scientists are used to employing indicators of various kinds to measure them. Thus it has long been traditional to measure economic development in terms of a single indicator, per capita GNP, that is to say the GNP of a country divided by its population. In Table 1.1 selected figures for 1992 are given. They show not only how wide is the gap between the most developed nations and the rest but, more worryingly, how it is tending to open up as the Third World itself is 'pulling apart'. In 1992 there was no real difference between the highest low income country, Indonesia, and the lowest middle income country, Côte d'Ivoire. By 1997, however, Indonesia ($1110) ranked as a lower middle income country and well ahead of Côte d'Ivoire ($710). Chile ($4820), a lower middle income country in 1992, had moved further ahead of South Africa ($3210), while Ireland ($17,790), like Israel ($16,180) had nearly twice the GNP per capita of the lowest high income country, Slovenia ($9840). At the other end of the scale, the Democratic Republic of the Congo ($110), Mozambique ($140), Sierra Leone ($160) and Rwanda ($210) remained among the poorest countries in the world (World Bank 1999) (see Table 1.2).

In recent years, however, there has been increasing dissatisfaction with the crudity of this measure. First, comparisons of per capita GNP were rendered very difficult indeed by wide variations and fluctuations in exchange rates. Second, the indicator in itself does not show how the economic resources generated are actually used. Unless they are being channelled back into investment or social welfare they will not necessarily generate further development. To give a clearer picture of what is going on, therefore, more indicators are required. Economic indicators include the actual purchasing power of the currency in terms of daily necessities, the rate of saving, the level of investment in industry and inequality of income and wealth. Social indicators include life expectancy, infant mortality rate (imr, meaning the deaths of children under one year per 1000 live births), the number of persons per doctor, the proportion of children in school and the percentage of adults who are able to read and write. Political indicators include governmental instability, the frequency of elections and the tendency to military intervention.

In 1990 the United Nations Development Programme (UNDP) published the Human Development Report, which used for the first time the Human Development Index (HDI). This ranked countries by a single measure derived from a small number of carefully selected indicators. The most important difference from older measures was to reject the use of fluctuating and frequently misleading exchange rate conversions in favour of purchasing power parities. There are four basic indicators: life expectancy, adult literacy, mean years of schooling and average income. From 1994 the comparisons between countries made on the basis of the HDI are made more realistic by fixing maxima

Table 1.2 GNP per capita of selected states 1997

RANGE	Population 1997 (millions)	GNP per capita 1997 (US$)	Growth 1996–97 (%)	Life expectancy (years)	Adult illiteracy (%)
LOW INCOME	2,036	350	3.9		
207 Mozambique	17	140	10.5	45.2	59.5
191 Nigeria	118	280	2.8	50.1	40.5
177 India	962	370	4.3	62.6	46.5
173 Ghana	18	390	1.7	60.0	33.6
154 Côte d'Ivoire	14	710	4.3	46.7	57.4
LOWER MIDDLE INCOME	2,283	1,230	6.2		–
148 Sri Lanka	19	800	5.9	73.1	9.3
145 China	1,227	860	7.4	69.8	17.1
141 Bolivia	8	970	1.4	61.4	16.4
135 Indonesia	200	1,110	2.6	65.1	15.0
119 Jamaica	3	1,550	–2.9	74.8	14.5
95 Russia	**147**	**2,680**	**0.6**	**66.6**	**a**
94 Thailand	61	2,740	–2.1	68.8	5.3
UPPER MIDDLE INCOME	574	4,540	0.6		
91 Turkey	64	3,130	6.8	69.0	16.8
89 S. Africa	41	3,210	–0.4	54.7	16.0
81 Mexico	94	3,700	6.3	72.2	9.9
76 Trinidad & Tobago	1	4,250	7.0	73.8	2.2
73 Brazil	164	4,790	1.9	66.8	16.0
72 Chile	15	4,820	5.7	74.9	4.8
64 S. Arabia	20	7,150	–1.4	71.4	26.6
57 Argentina	36	8,950	6.7	72.9	3.5
HIGH INCOME	927	25,890	1.9		
52 Portugal	10	11,010	4.3	75.3	9.2
49 Greece	11	11,640	0.7	78.1	3.4
32 Israel	6	16,180	–0.6	77.8	4.6
28 Ireland	4	17,790	7.3	76.3	a
23 Australia	19	20,650	–0.6	78.2	a
22 UK	59	20,870	3.7	77.2	a
15 France	59	26,300	3.2	78.1	a
10 USA	268	29,080	2.8	76.7	a
4 Japan	126	38,160	1.5	80.0	a
3 Switzerland b	7	43,060	2.5	78.6	a

a = less than 1%
b = no state is ranked 1 or 2!
Source: World Bank (1999) *World Development Indicators*, Table 1.1: Size of the economy;
http://www.worldbank.org/

Table 1.3 HDI of selected states 1997

RANGE	Life expectancy	Educational attainment	Adjusted real GDP/cap	HDI	GNP/cap minus HDI rank
LOW H/D	50.6	0.45	982	0.416	
174 S. Leone	37.2	0.32	410	0.254	0
169 Mozambique	45.2	0.35	740	0.341	−2
161 Guinea	46.5	0.34	1,880	0.398	−37
146 Nigeria	50.1	0.58	920	0.456	15
MEDIUM H/D	66.6	0.72	3,327	0.662	
133 Ghana	70.5	0.58	1,640	0.544	−1
132 India	71.2	0.54	1,670	0.545	−1
112 Bolivia	60.5	0.79	2,880	0.652	−4
101 S. Africa	68.7	0.87	7,380	0.695	−47
98 China	73.3	0.78	3,130	0.701	6
90 Sri Lanka	66.7	0.82	2,490	0.721	22
86 Turkey	65.8	0.76	6,350	0.728	−22
82 Jamaica	62.2	0.78	3,440	0.734	15
79 Brazil	62.4	0.85	6,480	0.739	−16
78 S. Arabia	68.7	0.83	10,120	0.740	−37
67 Thailand	68.8	0.83	6,690	0.753	−7
65 Libya	70.0	0.82	6,697	0.756	−6
46 Trinidad & Tobago	73.8	0.87	6,840	0.797	11
HIGH H/D	77.0	0.95	21,647	0.904	
39 Argentina	72.9	0.91	10,300	0.827	1
28 Portugal	75.3	0.91	14,270	0.858	3
27 Greece	78.1	0.91	12,769	0.867	8
23 Israel	77.8	0.90	18,150	0.883	3
12 Switzerland	78.6	0.92	25,240	0.914	−6
11 France	78.1	0.97	22,030	0.918	4
10 UK	77.2	0.99	20,730	0.918	9
7 Australia	78.2	0.99	20,210	0.922	15
4 Japan	80.0	0.94	24,070	0.924	5
3 USA	76.7	0.97	29,010	0.927	0
1 Canada	79.0	0.99	22,480	0.932	12

Source: United Nations Development Programme (1999)

and minima for each variable range (UNDP 1994a). Adult literacy cannot exceed 100 per cent, and 98.5 per cent is probably a more realistic maximum. Life expectancy is unlikely to attain 85 years in any country in the foreseeable future, nor is it likely to fall below 25. Mean years of schooling vary between 0 and 15. Such refinements reflect the growing awareness that economic growth, changes to the productive sectors and increased per capita income do not necessarily bring benefits to whole societies (UNDP 1994a).

Some general conclusions emerge very clearly from Table 1.3, which is based on figures from 1996. Comparison with Table 1.1 shows how with the effects of exchange rates taken out the differences within countries can be seen to be as important as, if not more important than, the differences between them. The percentage in poverty is highest in South Asia and Africa South of the Sahara. South Asia has 30 per cent of the world's population but nearly half the world's poor. Average life expectancy is 77.7 years in the developed world, 62.7 years in South Asia, 48.9 years in Africa South of the Sahara – a figure that has actually declined since 1988. Moreover these effects are reflected in wide disparities within Third World states – in Mexico (where average life expectancy in 1997 was 72.2 years) life expectancy for the poorest 10 per cent is 20 years less than for the richest 10 per cent (UNDP 1999).

Globalisation

Globalisation has been defined as the 'intensification of world-wide social relations which link distant locations in such a way that local happenings are shaped by events happening many miles away and vice versa' (Giddens 1990: 64). There is widespread agreement that globalisation is happening; there is less certainty, however, about precisely how and where it is happening and what its consequences are. Again, most writers seem to agree that globalisation has already resulted in:

- **a greater integration of peoples** – people, wherever they live, have a greater awareness of one another and more in common than they used to;
- **the shrinking world** – transport has speeded up travel and communications are now virtually instantaneous;
- **the blurring/disappearance of boundaries** – banking and investment, trade and commerce, radio and television, human rights and the causes of conflict, pollution and environmental change all transcend the boundaries of the nation state as it has been known since 1648;
- **technocratic dominance** – in the new globalised world there are a great many specialists who understand how things work in a way that governments and politicians do not.

Globalisation, however, is tending to preserve and not eradicate many of the differences between the advanced industrialised countries and the Third World. The effects can be divided conveniently into the cultural, the economic and the political.

The cultural effects are so obvious that it is easy to overlook the rest. Europe has succumbed to the modern as has everywhere else; those who dislike it have termed the new world style 'Americanisation' or, worse, 'Cocacolonisation'. With the arrival of moving images on screen the image of the good life as lived in Hollywood, USA, has spread worldwide. Supermarkets, 'long-haul' tourism, satellite television and the Internet have all in turn boosted global brand recognition and the power of the vast transnational corporations to set new standards of consumption. It is true that not all the new images are from the USA, and neither baseball nor American football has become a world sport. It was the World Cup of 1990 that first established the existence of a truly global TV audience for football and every four years since new viewing records have been set. What makes it global is not the game, however, but the apparatus of marketing and publicity that surrounds it.

Post-Marxist writers stress the economic effects of globalisation. These include the reassertion of the world capitalist system, governed (if at all) through Bretton Woods institutions (see Chapter 4). These new world financial/trade institutions have the power to control national spending by setting terms for treasuries and central banks (conditionality). They are the International Monetary Fund, the World Bank and the World Trade Organization (WTO). Together with the US government and 'all those institutions and networks of opinion leaders centred in the world's de facto capital' they enforce they so-called Washington consensus (Krugman 1995).

Within this network of assumptions, the bipolar world of the cold war has given way to a tripolar world dominated by the USA, Japan and Europe, with economic rather than political centres of power, characterised by the exercise of economic power across fading national boundaries by transnational corporations (TNCs). At the same time the distinction between centre and periphery has blurred (as neo-liberalism encourages the emergence of multiple centres and peripheries). New regional economic groupings emerge strengthening regional hegemonies. Indeed the periphery itself is differentiated, e.g. by the emergence of 'dependent development', and three areas/regions are exceptional in at least some respects:

1. the oil-rich Middle East
2. the 'Asian Tigers' and their imitators
3. small island developing states (SIDS).

The *political* effects of globalisation are in many ways the most disturbing. The real centres of power now lie outside the nation state and in most cases lie beyond its control. Neo-structuralism (see Chapter 4) argues that the nation state can no longer control its own economy, and hence is subject to the unpredictable play of market forces. It is therefore restricted in what it can do, and control of the old centres of political power no longer carries with it the ability to change things. In turn, interest groups, political parties and legislatures have to come to terms with their own powerlessness but seek to avoid the consequences of it.

If this is so democracy, previously challenged by the cold war, superpower dominance and the national security state, has arrived at a new level of acceptance, only (paradoxically) to have to meet the new threat posed by the

Table 1.4   Arguments for and against the validity of the concept of a Third World

FOR	AGAINST
Economics	
Lower per capita income, higher percentage living in poverty, lower life expectancy, higher imr, less access to education and other social services	Massive disparities both within Third World and within states, even if oil-rich states taken out and Fourth World of poorest created. Vague concept that obscures more than it illuminates – all societies contain their own 'fourth worlds'
Geography	
Location in 'south', climatic disadvantages not accompanied by the economic/technological means to resolve them	Very diverse in advantages/disadvantages of location – compare rich grasslands of Argentina and semi-desert regions of Ethiopia
History	
Few exceptions to colonial experience, resultant distortions in economies, national boundaries, etc. Cold war location outside main power blocs, despite possible alliances; hence self-definition, e.g. Group of 77 and NAM, but subject to consequences of superpower struggles e.g. Somalia	Experiences totally different, not only in different colonising powers' agendas but also variations in how and when independence was achieved. Variations in perceived strategic importance. Different local traditions and attitudes of national leaders resulted in very diverse experience of the Cold War
Marginality	
Peripheral position in the global economic system created and sustained by the industrial economies	Economic system constantly changing, e.g. rise of NICs, 1980s' pulling apart of Third World with massive gains in East Asia, some gains in South Asia, some loss of development in Latin America, disaster for many countries of Africa South of the Sahara

neo-liberal paradigm of the 'Washington consensus', which threatens to render its victory meaningless. However this pessimistic view is challenged. Scholars broadly agree that there is no evidence as yet of a clear relationship between democracy and economic development.

We can summarise the arguments for and against the question of whether the concept of a Third World is any longer valid as follows (see also Table 1.4).

Those who believe that it is point first and foremost to general social indicators. Third World countries, for them, are those that have a lower per capita income, a higher percentage living in poverty, lower life expectancy, higher imr and less access to education and other social services. Geographically they are located in the 'south', and suffer from climatic disadvantages not accompanied by the economic and/or technological means to resolve them. Most but not all have undergone colonisation and have become independent quite recently.

During the cold war however they were located outside the main power blocs despite possible alliances and the risk of superpower intervention. Hence they have exhibited the tendency to self-definition in terms of a 'third bloc', e.g. the so-called Group of 77 and NAM. The Group of 77 is an economic grouping of developing countries actually made up of 133 members. All countries of the South except China are members. They retain a peripheral position in a global economic system created and sustained by the industrial economies.

Critics of the notion of a Third World point first to the massive disparities within the Third World and within states. Geographically they are also very diverse in advantages/disadvantages of location – compare the rich grasslands of Argentina and the semi-desert regions of Ethiopia. Historically their experiences were totally different, not only in different colonising powers' agendas but also in variations in how and when independence was achieved. Different local traditions and attitudes of national leaders resulted in very diverse experiences of the cold war. See Plate 1.

Perspectives

An optimistic view of the future of the Third World tends to be associated with a political perspective that might generally be considered 'right wing'. Central among such thought is the liberal or neo-classical school that gave rise to the Washington consensus. Many who hold neo-liberal or neo-classical views of economics believe that the operation of the global 'invisible hand' will eventually advantage the Third World, enabling it to break out from its present impoverished position.

'Disadvantage' theories, often known as 'cumulative disadvantage' theories, hold that disadvantage compounds disadvantage, though better results can be obtained, at least in part, by better understanding of the process of development, including the judicious use of interventionist measures by Third World governments, often part of policies of import substitution. These measures were, of course, the developmental solutions advocated by some early dependency theorists (notably Raúl Prebisch).

The free operation of markets thought by neo-liberals to be the means to overcome the rigidities holding back the Third World is viewed as pessimistically by the left now as it was in the 1960s before the ascendancy of the neo-liberal school. (Thus an anti-free trade position is both initiative and response in relation to the neo-liberal position.) The problem remains the same for nations not advantaged during the nineteenth century. Free markets create unequal exchange and advantage the most powerful. A social-democratic or reformist position accepts these difficulties but argues that they can be overcome by a combination of self-imposed limitations by the advanced industrialised countries and concerted action by the UN and other agencies.

Table 1.5 Perspectives compared

	Liberal/neo-classical	Disadvantage	Structural/dependency	Social democratic/reformist	Ecological-green	Religious world view	Feminist
PROPONENTS	Rostow, OECD*	Myrdal	Baran, Amin, various schools	Brandt; UNCTAD†	Brundtland, Greenpeace	John Paul II; the Ayatollahs	V. Shiva; E. Boserup, etc.
OPTIMISTIC/ PESSIMISTIC	Optimistic – trickle-down	generally pessimistic	degree of pessimism varies, non-Marxist most	cautiously optimistic	generally pessimistic	millenarian	generally pessimistic
EMPHASIS ON	the operation of markets; equilibrium	development economics	world capitalist system; global class structure	North–South division; basic needs	sustainable development	personal salvation	role of women in development process
VIEW OF TNCs	transfer advantages	good for thriving region, not others	exploit Third World	advanced industrial countries need to control	destructive beyond redemption	foreign, therefore suspect	male, therefore suspect
VULNERABLE GROUPS	will eventually benefit	Third World generally	peripheries	South	ultimately all living things; immediately the world's poor	poor, meek, downtrodden	women
DEVELOPMENT SOLUTION	break-out is inevitable	possible escape with overflow from advantaged countries	structural inequality; escape only possible with: a) fall of capitalism; or b) in dependent form	North–South dialogue; concerted action by UN agencies	restrict growth; control pollution; encourage return to pastoral state	God	women
ENVIRONMENTAL PROBLEMS	irrelevant – the market will resolve when the time is right	exported pollution from developed countries	by-product of capitalism; remedy social revolution	tends to rely on technological 'fix'	supreme crisis of humanity in one lifetime	the Lord will provide	created by men

* = Organization for Economic Cooperation and Development
† = United Nations Conference on Trade and Development

Others argue that free trade will not, as hoped, eventually overcome poverty and enable comparative advantage to equalise the situation, because the rich countries have 'weighted the dice'. They did not and will not themselves rely on the free play of the market and risk losing those advantages. Such an argument is sometimes labelled 'structural'. In some ways this term is as misleading as terms such as neo-liberal or orthodox, because all market arguments stress some structure or another, sometimes that of world trade, sometimes of global capitalism. Usually 'structuralism' is a term specifically applied to the Marxist/neo-Marxist school and dependency theories, which can be both Marxist/neo-Marxist and non-Marxist.

The way forward for the Third World and what development is is differently perceived by the different schools, but so is how to achieve it. For neo-liberals the main rigidities or obstacles to development are the deadweight of traditionalism and state interference that function to limit the dynamic forces of personal initiative and competition. There are echoes here of the theories of Talcott Parsons and Seymour Martin Lipset, US sociologists who sought to identify specific characteristics of traditional and modern society.

Most schools accept industrialisation as what development is. Only radical schools question it. Amongst these we can single out, for their originality and special interest, the 'greens' and feminist thinkers, though they question it for very different reasons. The greens want smaller-scale, less damaging technologies and are forced by the logic of their own argument to question the assumption of growth itself. Feminist writers distrust the very nature of industrial society as it currently exists. They reject its masculine values and they see no possibility of balanced development without the full participation of women in the development process. Again we can sum up the various positions of the rival schools in tabular form (see Table 1.5), provided we do not take them too rigidly as definitions.

Themes of the book

The three themes of this book, therefore, are environment, development and globalisation. Environment has shaped, and is continuing to shape, the politics and society of the Third World. At the same time the impact of development is increasingly changing the environment in ways that look likely to test to the limit the human capacity to adapt.

Third World countries generally see industrialisation as the key to development, and with good reason – it is what the advanced industrialised countries have to a degree that they do not. But times have changed and the capital for development will come from abroad, thus in the 1980s China encouraged foreign investment in industrialisation. The disadvantage of this is the extent to which it will simply mean some limited development *in* a Third World country rather than the development *of* that country, since development of a country holds little interest for foreign companies investing there. Effective development must incorporate some genuine improvement in the quality of life for the majority of a country's population and not just for a western-oriented elite. Those countries that have been most successful at development in recent years are precisely those in which wealth is spread most widely. For reasons that will be discussed later the quality of development must include all its aspects: political, social and environmental as well as economic. Displaced First World pollution or continuing western-supported authoritarian rule cannot be seen as development.

In the rest of Part I, Chapter 2 looks at the natural environment, the shape and structure of the Third World and the geographical factors that give it a distinctive identity. In Chapter 3 the nature of the crisis that confronts the Third World will be examined in more detail.

In Part II we turn to the human environment and the economic (Chapter 4), social (Chapter 5) and cultural (Chapter 6) context of Third World states and their decision makers will be examined in turn.

Part III deals more specifically with the politics of the Third World, with the problem of state building (Chapter 7), democratisation (Chapter 8), the special role of the armed forces (Chapter 9) and the international pressures that shape Third World life and society (Chapter 10).

Last, in Part IV we return to policy issues: the right to development (Chapter 11), the role of women in a developing world (Chapter 12), the international politics of the environment and the growing North–South divide (Chapter 13).

CHAPTER **2**

The shape of the Third World

Physical location

Christopher Clapham defines the Third World, as usually regarded, as comprising 'the Americas south of the United States; the whole of Africa; Asia apart from the Soviet Union, China and Japan; and the oceanic islands apart from Australia and New Zealand' (Clapham 1985: 1). This does not make for a neat conceptual package in geographical terms. The Third World is not a geographical unit, but a state of mind.

Yet some kind of division has to be made and the rival term, 'the South', is no less misleading in the geographical sense. As can be seen from Map 2.1, which illustrated the Brandt Report and familiarised many people with a non-Mercator projection for the first time, the line that demarcated 'the South' meanders across the northern hemisphere before plunging southwards to exclude Japan, Australia and New Zealand.

There are also more specific questions that could be raised about the definition as it stands. Even in 1985 the inclusion of South Africa in the Third World was a little odd. China is not included because it was part of that Second World that was perceived to exist before the collapse of the USSR. As suggested in Chapter 1, its size makes it virtually impossible to ignore, but its inclusion (or exclusion) may distort our view of other Third World countries. (Similarly generalisations about South Asia are distorted by the sheer human weight of India.)

In 2001 we need to differentiate the different parts of the former Soviet Union if trying to apply Clapham's definition: economically Estonia ranks as an upper middle income country, Belarus, Kazakhstan, Latvia, Lithuania, the Russian Federation, Ukraine and Uzbekistan rank as lower middle income countries and Armenia, Azerbaijan, Georgia, the Kyrgyz Republic, Moldova, Tajikstan and Turkmenistan as low income countries (World Bank 1997) Last but not least, the meaning of 'the oceanic islands' is far from clear, and is

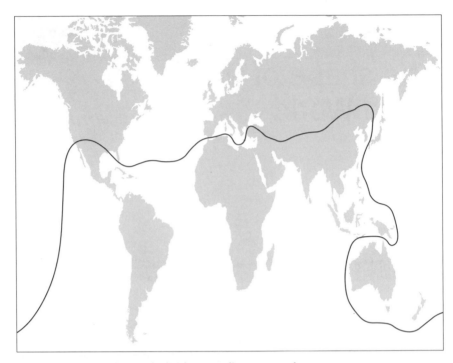

Map 2.1   The North–South divide according to Brandt

certainly not the same as the islands of Oceania, which is what most people
would probably expect it to mean.

As regards map projections, Mercator's, used in Europe since the sixteenth
century, exaggerates the relative size and hence the visual impact of the North.
Only at the Equator is latitude correct in relation to longitude. The distortion
becomes infinite at the poles, turning the Antarctic into a white smudge round
the bottom of the map. The effect is even more dramatic with a polar projection such as that on the flag of the UN itself. Exaggeration has its value – a cir-
cular map of the world centred on New Zealand places Antarctica in the near
foreground, which says much about the relationship between the two territories. But it transforms Spain and Portugal into a thin brown line round the
edge. The currently favoured Peters Projection (used by Brandt), which dis-
tributes the distortions between the equator and the poles, renders more accurately the proportions between the more and less densely inhabited parts of the
Earth. It is more appropriate than older projections, therefore, to enable the
viewer to understand the relative importance both of the Third World as a
whole and of individual countries within it. Unfortunately it would be of little
or no use in helping you to get from one part of the Third World to another,
unless you wanted to go due North–South or East–West (see Map 2.1).

Redrawing the map of the world to reflect in terms of relative area non-
geographical variables such as wealth or political power is, unfortunately,

impossible without distorting spatial relationships to a point at which they become completely unrecognisable. However any map of the world that differentiates countries by, say, their place in the World Bank classification by per capita income is a useful corrective to the simple North–South model (see Map 2.2). Sadly many of the oil-rich countries of the Middle East are very small, or the map would show up very clearly the secondary concentration of wealth in the region (World Bank 1999).

Main geographical features

Climate

The term 'South' does not imply it, but most Third World countries do lie in the tropical and/or subtropical zones. However both Chile and Argentina, which are truly southern, span the entire range of climates from subtropical to sub-Antarctic. Outer Mongolia, and much of China, falls within the northern temperate zone.

In tropical countries there is little division between hot and cool seasons, but there are other very important climatic differences between countries and between regions. For example, West/Central Africa has a hot wet equatorial climate, very heavy rainfall and a rapid rate of evaporation. East Africa has a wet tropical or dry savannah climate owing to its mountain and plateau features. The Horn of Africa is arid, though many of its problems are exacerbated by human action (or inaction).

The fact is that a vertical separation of climate zones is often more important for most purposes than a horizontal one. In Latin America, whether in Mexico, Central America or the Andean countries, the traditional division is made between the *tierra caliente*, below 1000m, which is low lying, hot and humid; the *tierra templada*, lying at a moderate altitude, between 1000 and 2000m, which is cooler and so capable of growing temperate zone crops; and the *tierra fría*, the zone that lies between 2000 and 3000m and which is mountainous, cold and subject to frost. Above that lies an alpine zone stretching from 3000m to the snowline over 4500m. In both Mexico and Colombia snow remains on the highest peaks all the year round.

Altitude is the key to the nature of human settlement in such regions. It is essential to the growing of cash crops such as tea and coffee. Not only do these crops need cooler conditions but the height – preferably with forest cover – is required for reliable precipitation. This is just one of the ways in which mainland Central and South America gains geographically over the Caribbean islands, where production of almost anything is more difficult and thus expensive. Of course, if cost is no object, production at the margin is often considered to be of the highest quality. This is said of Caribbean bananas; it is

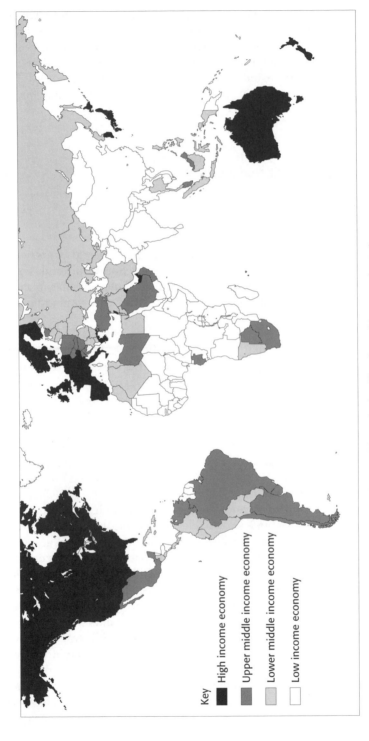

Map 2.2 Map of countries according to the World Bank classification of income (1999)

Key

High income economy

Upper middle income economy

Lower middle income economy

Low income economy

indisputably true of Jamaican Blue Mountain coffee. Low-lying Caribbean islands lack moisture and many of the smaller ones are uninhabited in consequence. The Bahamas rely on imported water.

Within the tropical zone the shifts in prevailing winds bring the monsoon, seasonal winds that carry large quantities of moisture with them; hence local reliance as in the Western Ghats of India or in Sri Lanka on the storage of water from the monsoon in 'tanks' to use during the dry season. The complexity of the patterns involved even in a small area like Sri Lanka is shown by the fact that the north-east (mid-October to mid-February) and south-west (April to June) monsoons affect different parts of the island; part of the island, notably the main city Colombo, gets both, and other parts get neither and are arid.

If a country uses less than 10 per cent of its annual renewable water resources it is unlikely to experience shortages of water. China and most of southern Asia use more than this, but not more than 20 per cent so shortages, when they do occur, happen on a regional rather than a national basis. However in the North China Plain there are already acute water shortages, as demand outstrips supply. By 1990 20 countries were already 'water scarce', that is to say they had less than 1000 cubic metres of renewable fresh water per person per year and by 2025 at least ten more will be in the same position, even on the most optimistic projections of population growth (National Council for Science and the Environment 2000). Access to water resources is likely to become more problematic and further subject to international disputes in the very near future (Thomas and Howlett 1992).

Relief

There are major geological fault lines under both developed (Japan, the western USA, Iceland, Greece, New Zealand) and Third World countries (Iran, Indonesia, Philippines, Peru, Colombia, Mexico). The relative geological stability of much of the USA, Canada, northern Europe and northern Asia is undoubtedly an asset to economic and social development, though Japan, a model for much of today's world, is spectacularly unstable and experiences on average 700 earthquakes a year. However, as we shall see later, where the incidence of natural disasters is the same their impact is much less in developed states.

The massive block of the Himalayas determines much of the geography as it does much of the climate of a sizeable section of the Third World. It is high enough to interrupt the circulation of winds in the Indian Ocean such as takes place in the Pacific, and the result is the monsoon. In South America the Andes, the highest and longest major cordillera of young fold mountains, are geologically extremely active. Extensive trough faulting gives stepwise topography and volcanoes and earthquakes attest to continuing upward movement of strata. The Andes, like the Himalayas, are a major climatic barrier, and it is now thought that the formation of both ranges was responsible for ending the relative warmth of the Tertiary era and bringing about the onset of the ice ages.

Today mountains still have a great importance for human beings. They establish political boundaries, structure communications, source major rivers, yield important minerals and provide temperate foothills and low uplands where human settlement is safer and more comfortable than on the plains. Even smaller mountain ranges have a regional/local significance. The only frontier between the First and Third World that consists of no more than a line on a map is that between the USA and Mexico. Otherwise the Mediterranean, the Dardanelles, the Caucasus Mountains and other features act as natural barriers.

Mountain-building (orogenic) processes continue under water. A celebrated under-water fault line encloses the Caribbean, stretching from the Virgin Islands by way of Puerto Rico to the Dominican Republic, where west of the Cordillera de Cibao it forks, giving to the north the northern peninsula of Haiti, the Sierra Maestra of Cuba and the Cayman Islands, and to the south the southern peninsula of Haiti and Jamaica.

Though relatively quiet at present the volcanic origin of the Lesser Antilles has been accompanied by dramatic evidence of its continuing importance, notably the eruption on Montserrat beginning in 1997, which rendered four-fifths of the island temporarily uninhabitable and continued to interfere with air traffic in 1999. Vulcanism in both Indonesia and the Philippines, similarly, has had a regional and indeed global significance.

Rivers

Great river basins have everywhere been the seat of the earliest known human civilisations, both in the Middle East (the Nile and the Tigris–Euphrates) and in East Asia (Yangtze, Hoang Ho, Mekong). Great rivers have formed the major routes both into and out of new areas in Europe and North America (St Lawrence, Mississippi–Missouri, Rhine, Danube) in the era before wheeled land travel became a reasonably convenient alternative to transport by water. The celebrated amber route from the Baltic to Byzantium ('Middlegarth' to the northerners) followed the rivers. In Asia the Jordan, Tigris–Euphrates, Indus, Ganges–Brahmaputra, Irrawaddy, Salween, Mekong, Yellow and Yangtze have all helped shape the distribution of human settlement.

In North America the two great navigable river systems account for the growth of and still serve Canada and the USA. Mexico has to share the waters of the Colorado and the Rio Grande with the United States of America. Neither is navigable and heavy use has reduced the Rio Grande to a muddy trickle. Most of Mexico's rivers flow directly but seasonally from the Sierra Madre to the sea.

In South America, on the other hand, the situation is very different. The Magdalena, Orinoco, Amazon, and the Parana, which with its tributaries and the Uruguay flows into the estuary called the Rio de la Plata, are all navigable, while others, the Tocantins and São Francisco in Brazil, and the Colorado, Negro and Chubut in Argentina, fulfil other important local needs.

In Africa, apart from the Nile, the Zambesi, Orange, Congo–Zaire, Niger and Senegal rivers have similarly acted as traffic routes since well before the age of colonial penetration. Of all the major regions of the world only Oceania fairly obviously lacks major river systems, with the rather doubtful exception, perhaps, of the Murray River in Australia.

The value of navigable river systems lies, above all, in their connection with the sea. However the sea not only links navigable rivers, but coastal and island civilisations, e.g. Japan, China, Korea, Taiwan. The sea has the distinctive property of joining all coastal points on the globe with one another, without the need for the navigator to go through territory controlled by others.

The sea is the great motor of climate. Now that they can be measured more accurately and over the entire world's surface, changes in sea temperature are known to have massive effects on regional climates. It had long been known that 'El Niño' affected the flow of the cold Humboldt Current northwards along the west coast of South America, causing the fish harvest to fail. Only in the last few years has it become clear that the shift in this current, which has its beginning in the positioning of some relatively small islands some 3000km out in the Pacific, has much wider implications. The episode that began in February 1997 brought torrential rain to Peru and Ecuador and exceptional heat in North America in 1998. It was also associated with heavy storms in China, hurricanes of record strength in the Pacific and a delayed onset for the monsoon in India (National Council for Science and the Environment 2000).

The question of whether the increasing frequency of El Niño is a natural variation or an aspect of the process of human-induced climate change is disputed. The present authors accept the weight of evidence in favour of the latter view (see Chapter 13). Global warming poses a serious threat to the Third World, especially where, as we shall see, the effects of drought are amplified by the degradation of the land through overuse. Drought in turn causes changes in river use. The controversial Sardar Sarovar dam on the Narmada River in India was designed to cope with the droughts in Gujarat occasioned by the failure of the monsoon (Vajpeyi 1994). But human action has the greatest impact on river systems. The most recent human use of rivers is for the generation of hydroelectric power. This is quite possible even where rivers are not navigable, as in the case of the Bumbuna Falls project in Sierra Leone.

Boundaries

Frontiers are influenced by and in turn influence geography. In some parts of the world, notably in Europe, international boundaries have not only been agreed but are formally demarcated by the placing of posts, fences or checkpoints. In Third World countries this is often not the case.

The major influence on present day international boundaries in the Third World has been colonial expansion. Time and again the frontiers between colonial empires were settled via diplomatic conferences by people who had no first-hand knowledge of the areas and features to which they were referring. In addition, only occasionally were they formally demarcated. Hence unless they follow the lines of rivers they often cut across the territories of indigenous peoples or tribes. A classic example of this is in West Africa, where British settlements in The Gambia, Sierra Leone, Ghana and Nigeria adjoin states that were formerly part of French West Africa. Prescott quotes a Yoruba chief in Dahomey (now Benin), separated by the colonial frontier from the majority of his tribe in Nigeria, as saying: 'We regard the boundary as separating the French and the English, not the Yoruba' (Prescott 1965: 63). The same may be said of East Africa, where Uganda exemplifies the arbitrary nature of colonial boundaries. An even odder example is to be found in southern Africa, where Namibia's boundaries are extended eastwards into the narrow Caprivi Strip running between Angola and Botswana to Barotseland in what is now Zambia. This illogical feature was originally intended to allow the former colonial power, Germany, to build a railway to link their East and West African territories.

The potential for boundary disputes is great and is not helped by the fact that many colonial period treaties did not refer to identifiable physical features but assumed the existence of a boundary that was well known to all concerned at the time.

Agricultural activity

Land tenure and production

Inequality in land ownership is not confined to the Third World. Australia, an advanced industrial country, has one of the most unequal land distribution ratios in the world as measured by the Gini index, the standard measure of land inequality. However the Third World is distinguished by the survival of traditional cultivation, even if this is now often under threat. It is important to distinguish between peasants, cultivators who have traditional rights to land, and plantation workers on large estates, who work for wages.

Peasants have a) access to land, b) family labour, c) small-scale technology and d) ability to generate surplus in a cash economy. Even small-scale technology requires cash for purchase and maintenance. Peasants make up some 80 per cent of farm workers in the Third World.

Traditional peasant cultivation was balanced between the need to produce for subsistence and exchange and the need to conserve. The key requirement is production for subsistence, which is conditioned by the nature of the crops available. There are three major variants based on:

- wheat (subtropical, temperate) Europe, North-west Africa, Middle East, 'Southern Cone' of South America;
- rice (tropical, humid) South, South-east and East Asia, West Africa;
- maize (subtropical, dry) Americas, East Africa.

Production for subsistence is based on traditional knowledge and understanding of the needs of the soil. It is therefore resilient and because of its varied nature and limited expectations forms the best possible protection to the poor against the possibility of famine. The big problem with it is that as population expands the land areas cultivated are subdivided until production is often barely adequate, implying that large sectors of the population must be malnourished. Because peasants are producing large-bulk, low-value crops in the main they are also not very productive in monetary terms, which leads their contribution to be underestimated by those in the so-called 'modern' sector of the economy.

With rising population too many people in the Third World are working too little land. There are two possible 'solutions': land reform by redistribution, which is politically difficult with the vested interests involved, and land colonisation. The latter is of course only possible where land is available. Increases in the 1970s in the land area cultivated in Latin America, China, South and South-east Asia have been considerable though at the cost of damage to marginal land and its fragile ecosystems. The 'carrying capacity' of the land, that is to say the number of people a given area can support, has also been increased at least temporarily as a result of the so-called 'green revolution', involving the use of high-yielding strains and chemical fertilisers. On the other hand there has been a marked decline in the production of both wheat and maize in Africa, despite (or because of) the increase in production of cash crops for export, such as tobacco and cotton.

Estates vary a great deal. They have existed in their present form in Latin America since the sixteenth century, and Brazil has experienced three successive 'boom' periods in sugar, rubber and coffee respectively. In South Asia plantations have been established since the nineteenth century, producing tea and cotton. In tropical Africa, plantation agriculture dates often only from the beginning of the twentieth century, and crops produced include cocoa, peanuts and palm oil. Of course a considerable part of plantation production is consumed within the Third World itself (e.g. before the Gulf War Iraq was the major consumer of Sri Lankan tea). Nor are all plantation crops necessarily in direct competition with local food production. Tree and shrub crops such as tea and coffee usually occupy a relatively small part of a country's cultivated land. Even bananas, which as a cultivated crop are very wasteful of land, are largely grown for consumption within the Third World.

Land colonisation has a detrimental effect on the land where, as it usually does, it results in permanent land clearance. Initially the methods are very similar to that of traditional 'slash-and-burn' agriculture. This is still practised, usually in tropical rainforest, sometimes in savannah. The main locations that have been significant in recent years are: Central America, Western Amazonia, West/Central/East Africa, Philippines, Malaysia, Indonesia. A fresh site is selected, trees are cut down, larger tree stumps left in place and then branches, twigs and bushes are burnt, leaving the charred landscape covered with a layer of wood ash, which acts as a fertiliser. Intercropping of species is normal and the system, which was devised for local crops, such as manioc and cassava, has successfully assimilated crops introduced from elsewhere.

However when intensively practised the results are very different. Slash-and-burn cultivation can be used successfully over very long periods provided not too much is asked of the land. But the fertility of the thin forest soils falls off rapidly and yields in the third year are normally only half that of the first. The success of the method therefore depends on cultivation of relatively small patches which are shifted every two to three years. One or two years of crops in Brazilian/West African/South-east Asian rainforest is followed by periods of fallow varying between 8 and 15 years during which secondary vegetation is re-established and the forest begins to regenerate. It is impossible to accelerate this cycle without damage, but this is in effect what the new settlers are trying to do. Land clearance opens up areas to permanent settlement. Population growth leads to reduction in fallow periods. Global demand leads to the sale (or usurpation) of the land by large landowners or corporations, followed by intensive cultivation by mechanical and chemical means, and attempts to realise increased profit, in particular by the introduction of ranching after the initial decline in fertility. The result is the permanent degradation of the land, resulting over time in a general decline of its carrying capacity in face of rising demand. The UN Food and Agriculture Organization (FAO) has identified a number of 'critical zones' where land resources were already inadequate to feed their 1975 populations. Most of these were areas subject to severe land degradation, where the natural carrying capacity of the land was already seriously impaired, and their total population was in excess of a billion (Higgins et al. 1982). In 1998 30 developing countries were facing food emergencies (Oneworld 1998).

Marketing and supply

The development of towns was initially the result of grain cultivation and the need for protected storage. Towns soon found themselves forced into alliance or conflict with local big landowners for political power. Towns need a rural hinterland to ensure their feeding. The long-term trend everywhere has been first the expansion of towns and then the urbanisation of the countryside. The concentration of wealth in the towns made them a tempting target, and an alliance with local landowners offered them necessary protection for their markets in return for a considerable profit for the landowners. The growth of populations was accelerated by irrigation and the development of wet rice farming where this was possible.

Getting products to market however implies some element of food preservation. The traditional methods developed in the neolithic era were drying (pulses, tubers, meat), smoking (meat, fish) and the use of salt or brine (fish, meat). Canning uses more modern technology, but still does not rely on the availability of a power supply for storage. Refrigeration, first developed in the mid-nineteenth century but much extended in the past 40 years, opened up the possibility of marketing high quality products. The success of the application of preservation and marketing techniques to agriculture, or 'agribusiness' as it is now often known, is that it creates added value in the end product and ensures its marketability. Bananas and other soft fruit depend for almost all their very high value in the shops on the measures that have been taken to get them there.

Speeding up transport makes the preservation and marketing of food much easier. Since the traditional overland routes from Europe to the east were blocked by Turkish expansion, first the Portuguese and then the Spaniards sought a way to the east by water. The Portuguese empire was built on the spice trade, and though later disputed by Dutch and English traders it had, when Macau reverted to China in 1999, lasted just over 500 years. Fast clipper ships brought tea to Britain in the nineteenth century; in the twentieth the steamship made tropical produce available widely for the first time. In recent years it has become possible for Third World produce to be sold in the advanced industrial countries competitively even at the time of year at which their own produce is in season, while even a slight variation of the harvest season enables Mexican fruit to be sold in the USA when direct competition with Florida and California might make this seem impossible. Many Third World countries' dependence on an external market is reflected in the nature and orientation of their communication links, by land or water.

Mining

If the Portuguese empire was built on the spice trade, the main motivating factor in Spanish colonial expansion was the search for gold and silver. However by the end of the 1980s the major producers of gold were two oddly matched but relatively developed states, South Africa and the former Soviet Union. In the meanwhile Third World states had been the scene of colonial and postcolonial rivalries over access to a whole variety of mineral deposits, and the latest gold rush has been taking place in the northern part of Brazilian Amazonia.

As in the development of the Soviet Union under Stalin, but with less drastic methods, early attempts to develop Third World countries were based on the traditional 'smokestack' industries of coal and steel. Hence in Brazil primacy in the 1930s went to the creation of an indigenous steel industry, centred on the massive Volta Redonda project. In China during the 'Great Leap Forward' an attempt was made to substitute labour for investment by encouraging the creation of 'backyard' blast furnaces. What metal these succeeded in

Table 2.1   World aluminium production 1997 (leading producers other than USA)

Countries	Bauxite, crude ore, '000 tonnes, 1997
Australia	44,065
Guinea	16,500
Brazil	12,300
Jamaica	11,875
China	8,000
India	5,800
Venezuela	5,084
Suriname	4,000
Russian Federation	3,350
Guyana	2,502
World (excl. USA)	122,764

Source: Jacqueline West (ed.), *South America, Central America and the Caribbean, 2000*
(London, Europa Publications Ltd, 8th edn, 1999), 788.

producing, however, proved to be of such poor quality that the experiment was allowed to lapse, though not, unfortunately, before it had created considerable environmental damage. More recently competition from the NICs and from Japan has driven down the world price of steel to the point at which there is now a substantial oversupply of basic steel products.

Though there is much less demand for steel than there was, it still remains central to successful industrialisation. In the developed world for a variety of uses it has been superseded by aluminium (see Table 2.1). Aluminium is one of the commonest elements in the earth's crust and in the form of bauxite is found throughout the world. However it is such an active chemical element that its separation from the ore involves a very high input of electrical power. Hence only where there is a very considerable surplus of power available at low cost, as in developed countries such as Canada that have considerable quantities of bauxite, is aluminium production economic. An additional problem is that the fabrication of aluminium alloys involves relatively expensive techniques if it is to be successful, thus limiting the spread of technology from the advanced industrialised countries into the Third World.

The result is that only a quarter of world production comes from the Third World, from Guyana, Jamaica and Suriname. In the case of Jamaica, it is the island's sole mineral resource and in 1980 Jamaica was still forced to sell most of its unprocessed bauxite for a relatively meagre return (Dickenson et al. 1983: 136–7). In Sierra Leone bauxite is mined by Sieromco, part of Alusuisse of Switzerland. The effect of mineral extraction there has been to create huge areas of devastation.

The high bulk and low value of most minerals exported in this way means that some of the abundant mineral resources of the Third World have not been exploited at all. Those deposits most readily accessible by river or sea have generally speaking been opened up first and certainly remain most competitive on the world market; for example the copper of Chile or Peru, or alluvial tin in Malaysia and Indonesia. However world economic conditions can change rapidly, as mining from a country such as Chile demonstrates, and the ability of TNCs to switch production from one part of the world to another makes the negotiating strength of Third World governments much weaker than their nominal sovereignties would suggest. The collapse of the world price of copper has dealt a severe blow to the economies of Zaire (now Democratic Republic of the Congo) and Zambia.

The fate of Guatemala's dealings with International Nickel over its subsidiary Exploraciones y Explotaciones Minerías Izabal (Exmibal) is instructive. No sooner had the government of the day realised that the nickel ore was there than it hastened to 'renegotiate' Exmibal's 1968 contract, giving the government a 30 per cent share in the proceeds. However with oil accounting for one-third of the cost of production Exmibal's nickel plant at Chulac-El Estor in Guatemala did not begin operations until 1977 and never worked at more than 20 per cent of capacity until production was suspended in 1981 in adverse world economic conditions (Calvert 1985: 150–2).

The situation does not seem to be much better for a small Third World country that happens to have a really unusual resource. Sierra Leone is not just a producer of bauxite, it is also one of the few places in the world where there are substantial deposits of rutile, the black sand from which the space age metal titanium is extracted. Since 1983 Sierra Rutile Ltd, a subsidiary of the US multinational Nord Resources Corporation, has extracted 150,000 tons of rutile worth more than $80 million each year. Sierra Rutile is the country's largest employer, but wages are still meagre. Conditions are even worse than before Nord Resources moved in. Often mining gives rise to other infrastructural developments. This has not been the case for Sierra Leone. Representatives of the mining companies blame the corruption of the Sierra Leone government and the people for not throwing the rascals out, and not the terms of trade that they have had to accept. Successive IMF structural adjustment packages (SAPs) have failed. The government agreed to float the leone, which devalued 25,000 per cent against the dollar, and to cut subsidies on fuel and food. Sierra Leone was virtually bankrupt, even before half its national territory was occupied by rebel forces from Liberia.

Human settlement

Population

One person in four in the world lives in China. Three out of four live in the Third World. Over the past 40 years the population of the Third World has grown exponentially, leading some (including, notably, the Chinese and Indian

Table 2.2 Most densely-populated countries 1997

Country	Population density (persons/km²) 1997	Percentage below poverty line
Singapore	4991	–
Bermuda	1242	–
Bangladesh	935	35.6
Bahrain	868	–
Barbados	615	–
Mauritius	559	10.6
South Korea	461	–
Netherlands	457	–
Aruba	452	–
Puerto Rico, USA	426	–
Lebanon	399	–
Japan	334	–
India	318	35.0
Belgium	310	–
Sri Lanka	283	35.3
El Salvador	280	48.3
Israel	276	–
Rwanda	273	–
Haiti	266	65.0
Trinidad & Tobago	253	21.0
Burundi	245	36.2
United Kingdom	243	–
Philippines	241	54.0
Germany	235	–
Jamaica	234	34.2
Vietnam	232	50.9
United States	29	–
China	130	6.5
Russia	9	30.9

Source: World Bank (1999)

governments) to place control of population at the centre of their strategy to achieve a reasonable standard of living for their people. The United Nations Population Fund *State of World Population Report* (1992) called for 'immediate and determined action to balance population, consumption and development patterns: to put an end to absolute poverty, provide for human needs and yet protect the environment'. Certainly many states in the Third World have very high population densities by world standards (see Table 2.2).

But what is a balanced population? First of all, a note of caution. Censuses even in the First World can be controversial. Accurate information about the size of families and the ages of family members may be even harder to obtain elsewhere, especially where the majority of the population is illiterate.

According to the *Report*, world population in mid-1992 was 5.48 billion. It would reach 6 billion by 1998, by annual increments of just under 100 million. Nearly all of this growth would be in Africa, Asia and Latin America. Over half would be in Africa and South Asia. In the event, these figures proved to be somewhat pessimistic, and the population of the world reached 6 billion officially in October 1999.

Asia is more than four times as heavily populated as any other part of the Third World. With a population of 3.58 billion in 1998 its density of population ($113/km^2$) is eight times that of North America excluding Mexico: 304.7 million ($14/km^2$). It also includes seven of the ten largest countries by population: the largest, China (1220.2 million), the second largest, India (929 million), Indonesia (197.5 million), Pakistan (136.3 million), Japan (122.6 million) and Bangladesh (118.2 million). Of these only Japan is an advanced industrialised country.

Latin America is relatively sparsely populated. With a total population in 1998 of 503.5 million it includes another country, Brazil, that has a population of more than 100 million (159 million) and Mexico which, with 91.1 million in mid-1995, was getting near it. But as the fifth largest country in area in the world after Russia, Canada, China and the USA, Brazil is not at all densely populated, and the only country on mainland America that approaches European standards in terms of population density is tiny El Salvador, in Central America (with a population of 5 million). Many Latin Americans quite reasonably regard their countries as being underpopulated. Argentine public policy, for example, still favours 'peopling the pampas'.

Africa too is sparsely populated ($25/km^2$). However, though population statistics for its poorest countries are notoriously unreliable and overall estimates therefore have to be approached with care, its estimated 748.9 million population is growing at an average rate of 2.4 per cent a year. This has fallen since the early 1990s and may not seem much, but it would lead to the population of the continent being nearly three times as great by 2025. The second largest country by area in Africa, Nigeria, has the largest population. This is currently (1995) estimated at 111.5 million. However as the results of the 1962, 1963 and 1973 censuses had to be set aside owing to political unrest there is considerable doubt as to whether these more recent figures are in fact correct.

Oceania, by contrast, has accurate statistics but is the most sparsely populated region. Apart from developed Australia and New Zealand (20.3 million), only some 29 million people are scattered over its vast area. Many of them live on very small island states where the distinctions we make elsewhere between town and countryside are of relatively little use (UNDP 1998).

As a result of population pressure in the Third World increasing numbers of migrants are crossing national boundaries in search of work. In the 1980s an average of 603,000 immigrants entered the United States of America legally every year, and an equivalent number went to Canada and Australia. In Europe politicians played on the fears of voters to push through legislation restricting legal immigration, and the former British colonial government of Hong Kong forcibly repatriated Vietnamese who were described as 'economic migrants', not political refugees.

Of the 57 countries in the world that by 1990 had passed laws to reduce immigration no fewer that 43 were themselves developing countries. Until 1982 Nigeria, the largest country in Africa, enjoying an oil boom, welcomed migrant labourers. With the recession in 1983 its military government summarily expelled a million Ghanaians, who were left to make their way back to their own country on foot, by bus or by car, as best as they could.

Refugees: the case of Rwanda

In 1994 the world was shocked by news of the large-scale massacres in the tiny Central African state of Rwanda. Before April 1994 Rwanda was the most densely populated country in Africa with more than 6 million people farming the fertile land. But the country was divided between two antagonistic ethnic groups: the Tutsi, traditionally the warrior class, and the Hutu, traditionally the labourers, and many Tutsi had been forced out of the country soon after independence in the 1960s. In 1979 they formed the Rwandan Patriotic Front (RPF) in exile in Uganda and in 1993 at Arusha, Tanzania, a peace agreement was signed. The spark that ignited the new conflict was the death of the country's Hutu President Habyarimana (1973–94) when his aircraft was shot down as it was landing at Kigali. Within hours government forces and accompanying militias had begun to slaughter Tutsis. The RPF retaliated, but by deliberate state policy the slaughter continued, leaving half a million people dead, and up to a million Hutu and Tutsi languishing in refugee camps in Zaire, Tanzania and Burundi. The French government, which had its own agenda, sent in troops two months after the start of the slaughter and tried to establish a safe area within the country and deliver humanitarian aid, but soon withdrew. By the end of August Rwanda was looted and large areas deserted.

Having failed as a peacekeeper, the UN faced formidable difficulties in mounting a successful relief effort; in the end most of the work was done by non-governmental organisations (NGOs) under the general direction of the United Nations High Commission on Refugees (UNHCR). The refugee camps were hardly able to cope with such a massive displacement of humanity: in Zaire the water supply was polluted by corpses and the volcanic ground was too hard to dig graves, while in Tanzania refugees deforested the landscape in search of fuel, and the resentment of the local population was only just kept under control (Toma 1999).

Refugees: the case of East Timor

At the collapse of the Portuguese empire in 1975 the territory of East Timor was occupied by Indonesia, of which West Timor was already an acknowledged part. The world community did not accept Indonesian occupation of East Timor, but it did not organise any effective opposition to it, and the Australian government in 1989 even signed a treaty with the Indonesian government, then under the control of General Suharto, to exploit off-shore oil resources in the Timor Gap. Oil production began there in July 1998 and was expected to yield its 29 million barrels of light, low-sulphur crude in only four years (Australian Broadcasting Company 1998).

Resistance to the occupation continued, however, and with the fall of General Suharto in 1999 his successor, President Habibie, agreed to release its leader, Xenana Guzmao, to permit a referendum on the future of the territory and to abide by the result. Unfortunately only a small group of UN observers was sent to oversee the referendum and the security of the poll was left to the Indonesian army. Once the votes had been counted and it had become evident that the result had been heavily in favour of independence local commanders conspired with so-called 'militias' to sack the towns and villages and to drive the bulk of the population out of the territory into West Timor, where many continue to live in fear, concerned that if they express a wish to return home they may be killed before they can get there.

Traditional rural settlement

Despite urbanisation, traditional rural society remains and is indeed essential to the survival of the Third World. The duality of many Third World economies is well recognised. The modern formal sector can be contrasted with the traditional informal sector, and the urban with the rural. However the distinctions are neither clear nor separate. The one depends on the other.

Standard poverty measures ignore subsistence production. Hence it is very difficult to determine accurately levels of poverty in rural areas, though it is clear that they are generally poorer than urban areas – hence the direction of migration. Lower levels of participation in the economy, whether as producer or as consumer, are found amongst the poor in all parts of society, but especially amongst the rural poor.

It is said that the degree of rural inequality in India is declining. This is questionable though evidence from Indian government surveys does show increasing diversification of the rural economy. India's overall economic growth is impressive (c.4.3 per cent p.a. in 1996–97) and it is now the seventh largest economy in the world. However its growth is mainly urban and consists largely of the secondary production of consumer durables for the urban elite. There is, though, one major achievement in rural development: self-sufficiency in cereal production was achieved during the 1980s. Nevertheless, at the same time, in many rural areas population is growing rapidly, agricultural production is stagnant, unemployment is high and consumption is down. Inequality in landholding, as measured by the Gini index, has increased and, more critically, so has the proportion of holdings that are too small to be viable.

Among regional variations, it is in the South and East that there has been the slowest growth in agricultural output. The Central, South and East regions also record the highest proportions of rural poor, and the highest mortality rates are to be found in the Central region and the East. By contrast, urban poverty has been declining as a proportion in urban areas, though it is still growing in absolute terms (Ghosh and Bharadwaj in Bernstein et al. Johnson 1992: 140–6).

The survival of the traditional rural sector was seen in the nineteenth century by classical liberals as an obstacle to development. It is still seen as such by neo-liberals today, though at the same time the greens offer a sharply contrasting interpretation, arguing that traditional rural lifestyles are the way forward to sustainable development.

Land reform

Land reform is one means by which the state can act to help the poorest sectors of society by the redistribution of property. It can take various forms, the three most common of which are:

1. the distribution of land to the landless poor
2. legislation limiting the size of estates, forcing the sale of 'surplus holdings'
3. rent control.

Land reform is often opposed (especially by landowners) on the grounds that it will lead to a fall in production. In the state of Kerala in India, because of the second kind of land reform, there is a much greater degree of equality in landholding, however, than there is in semi-feudal Pakistan, and production levels are high.

However land reform is far from easy to carry out. The power of existing landowners to resist any serious land reform by political pressure and legal obstruction is frequently reinforced by the inclusion within their ranks of senior army officers. In Latin America major land reform programmes have either followed or been accompanied by high levels of violence. In Mexico land reform was made possible by the alliance forged between rural interests and the leaders of the Mexican Revolution (1910–40). In Bolivia it followed the revolution of 1952 that placed the National Revolutionary Movement (MNR) in power, and in Cuba it was a consequence of the Cuban Revolution of 1959. But in Chile between 1970 and 1973 the government of Salvador Allende was unable to overcome a strong alliance between the local landowners and the armed forces, supported by the United States of America, and land reform in the Dominican Republic, though pressed by the Carter administration in an attempt to avert revolution, was successfully killed by military opposition.

Even where a government has the strength to carry out land reform the technical problems are immense. First, land is by no means a homogeneous commodity that can be shared out at will. Its varying quality, the availability `of water and transport and its nearness or otherwise to the market all affect its utility. Second, it is not always easy to agree who should get access to land. Those who already work it regard themselves as having a prior claim. But what of the needs of the landless? Should those who have worked the land be made to share their good fortune with strangers? In the Mexican case serious conflict between the competing claimants played into the hands of the traditional owners.

Collectivisation seems at first sight to be an ideal solution. In Latin America, where land had been traditionally regarded as the property of the state, the pioneering experiment was that of Mexico, where limits were placed on the size of estates that could be held, and in the 1930s cooperatives (*ejidos*) were endowed with the land that had been expropriated, which was declared inalienable. Working practices varied, the earlier *ejidos*, broadly speaking, being divided into equal-sized plots worked by separate families and the later worked in common by all the families settled on them. These *ejidos* were strongly criticised by their political opponents as inefficient and unproductive, but the evidence is that, having regard to the nature of the land in each case, they were as efficient as privately owned land. Not until 1992 did a Mexican government actually challenge the nature of the land reform carried out by its predecessors.

In Africa land has not normally been expropriated as private holdings. Tanzania from the beginning saw collective ownership as traditionally African as well as socialist. Critics of the Tanzanian experience, however, remark that after some 30 years of a socialist economy it remains one of the poorest countries in the world. A different problem, however, has arisen in Zimbabwe, where the independence settlement guaranteed the rights of existing white settlers to much of the best land in the country. In 2000 President Mugabe, finding himself increasingly unpopular, tried to divert hostility towards the former colonial power. When the ruling Zanu-PF sponsored occupations of white-owned land he refused to enforce a legal decision ruling the occupations unlawful. His supporters then succeeded in mustering a majority in Parliament to amend the constitution to allow expropriation of the lands without compensation while systematic attacks were launched on white farmers to force them to yield (Dorman 2000, *Financial Times* 8/9 April 2000).

Communists and some socialists regard such measures as half-hearted. Disputes over ownership, for them, can be simply resolved by the state assuming ownership of all land. It is then for the state to create collective institutions by which individual farms can be managed by those who work them. However after the initial impetus given by mechanisation, and despite the social benefits of community centres, health clinics and the rest, Soviet collective farms proved to be unable to meet their country's needs for basic foodstuffs, while in the Third World the record has been similarly ambiguous. In China collectivisation after 1949 led to a level of production sufficiently high to reduce hunger but it failed to provide additional funds for industrialisation. In Cuba attempts at diversification and industrialisation failed and after 1970 the country returned to its traditional dependence on the large-scale production of sugar, though for the Soviet rather than the US market.

Table 2.3 The world's largest cities

Rank	Name	Metro area population (millions)	City population
1	Tokyo, Japan	27.3m	7,967,614
2	Mexico City, Mexico	24m	8,235,744
3	São Paulo, Brazil	22m	10,017,821
4	New York, NY, USA	19.8m	7,380,906
5	Mumbai, India	16.6m	9,925,891
6	Shanghai, China	16.2m	8,214,384
7	Los Angeles, USA	15.3m	3,553,638
8	Beijing, China	13.3m	7,362,426
9	Jakarta, Indonesia	12.8m	9,112,652
10	Kolkata, India	12m	4,399,819
11	Seoul, S. Korea	12m	10,231,217
12	Tianjin, China	11.6m	5,855,054
13	Buenos Aires, Argentina	11.2m	2,965,403
14	Osaka, Japan	10.6m	–
15	Rio de Janeiro, Brazil	10.1m	5,606,497

Urbanisation

The most striking feature of Third World countries is rapid urbanisation. In 1950 only 29 per cent of the world's peoples lived in cities; in 1990 three times as many people did so, and the proportion had risen to 43 per cent. But, more strikingly, in 1950 only about half the world's urban population was in Third World cities. By the year 2000 the population of cities in the Third World was expected to outnumber that in the rest of the world by more than two to one: 2251.4 million to 946.2 million (Hardoy et al. 1992: 29).

However Hardoy et al. identify three inaccurate assumptions about urbanisation in the Third World that tend to be repeated, namely that: 'most of the problems (and much of the urban population) are in huge mega-cities'; 'the high concentration of population and production is a major cause of environmental problems' and that these problems are accurately documented in the existing literature (Hardoy et al. 1992: 31).

It is hardly surprising that in the First World people tend to think of urban areas in the Third World as megacities (see Table 2.3). In 1950 there were only two cities, London and New York, with a population of more than 8 million. In 1990 there were 20 such giant cities, and 14 of them were in the developing world (UNFPA 1992: 16). However it is also true that in 1990 only a third of the urban population of the Third World lived in cities with more than 1 million inhabitants. In fact in many of the smaller and/or less populous countries half the urban population lived in cities with populations of less than 100,000.

Such smaller cities have also grown very rapidly in recent years, and it is this rapid growth, rather than the overall size of the cities, that is associated with the problems of urbanisation. These problems do not stem solely from the overall level of urbanisation, which varies a great deal from one region to another. The most urbanised part of the developing world is Latin America (73.7 per cent), which is comparable with Europe (73.3 per cent), but has some way to go before overall it reaches the level of North America (76.1 per cent). Other parts of the Third World are much more rural: East Asia is only 36.1 per cent urban, Africa 33.8 per cent and South Asia 28.4 per cent, but this is not likely to last long (UNDP 1994). Bangladesh is rural and has only 17.7 per cent of its population living in cities. But it has in fact a higher population density ($935/km^2$) than the Netherlands ($457/km^2$), the most densely populated country in Europe, which has 88.9 per cent of its population living in cities (World Bank 1999). What is most worrying, undoubtedly, is that countries that have the fastest rate of population growth overall also tend to have the fastest rates of growth of urban populations.

The main features of Third World cities are:

1. One large 'primate' city, which is usually but not necessarily both the capital and the main commercial centre, predominates, containing anything up to a quarter of the entire population. The disproportion can be striking. The extreme case is the city-state of Singapore (100 per cent urban). But Montevideo, capital of Uruguay, contains half the country's people; Buenos Aires, capital of Argentina, some 23 per cent. The feature is equally marked in Africa, where it is often attributed to colonialism, but this can hardly be the case in Latin American states that have been independent for a century and a half. Dependency theorists would argue that the size of cities is linked to their role as a point of contact with the world economic system, but this seems rather to understate the role of government. Occasionally there are two large cities of roughly equal size, such as Rio de Janeiro and São Paulo in Brazil, Ankara and Istanbul in Turkey, Cape Town and Johannesburg in South Africa, Beijing and Shanghai in China. Where this happens one either is or has been the capital, the other the major commercial centre (Gamer 1976: 131–9). Three major exceptions to the primate city model exist: China, Japan and India.

2. Other cities are surprisingly small. In Mexico, Mexico City is some ten times as big as the next largest city, Guadalajara. Traditionally migration has taken place over relatively short distances, owing to the difficulty of transport, though disentangling these flows is problematical because in the Third World as in the First there is of course also a substantial amount of movement from one city to another in search of work. Hence these smaller, regional centres act as 'way stations' for migration to the capital/largest city, and indeed at one time this may have been the case everywhere. However in modern times evidence is that in Latin America at least the main migration flows are direct from the countryside to the largest city.

3. Third World cities are swollen by heavy recent immigration. China is an
    exception, probably only because until recently movement from place to
    place was rigorously controlled by the authorities. In Africa and Asia the
    cities attract an excess of young men in search of work, while women often
    stay in their villages and keep their farms or plots going for subsistence.
    In Latin America and the Caribbean young women predominate in the
    burgeoning cities and towns. In both cases many migrate as part of an
    existing family unit.

4. Migration places the maximum strain on the infrastructure (roads, trans-
    port, housing, utilities, education, health, other public services). However
    city governments tend to spend very little on housing or other services for
    the poor, partly because they do not want them to come in the first place,
    partly because they do not get much from them in the way of taxes. In all
    but the most favourable times much of the urban area of Third World
    cities consists of shanty towns.

5. Shanty towns, perhaps unexpectedly, are not always very densely popu-
    lated, and many of the worst urban conditions develop in older-type prop-
    erties that have been allowed to fall into disrepair and are then subdivided.
    In Brazil these overcrowded tenement slums are called 'beehives'. Living in
    them consumes the greater part of a new immigrant's resources and offers
    little in the way of services. It is not very surprising therefore that people
    soon move out into the shanty towns. By definition shanty towns seldom,
    if ever, have reasonable mains services, though some Brazilian *favelas* have
    been established for so long that they do have some laid on. The absence
    of piped water and sanitation for such areas would be a dangerous com-
    bination in any circumstances, but shanty towns tend to congregate in the
    least favoured areas, and there are more immediate dangers when a shanty
    town locates close to factories or other sources of employment. Hundreds
    died in February 1984 when petrol (gasoline) leaking out of a fractured
    pipe exploded under a shanty town at Cubatao in Brazil, but this was only
    the most spectacular evidence of an environment so heavily polluted by
    unchecked industrial development that children had to go to hospital daily
    to breathe unpolluted air (Hardoy et al. 1992: 85–7). Though some effort
    has been made to clean up Cubatao since this incident more recently a
    similar leak into sewers destroyed several blocks in Mexico's second city,
    Guadalajara, in a series of explosions over three days. Three thousand
    were killed by toxic gas and 200,000 were evacuated following a release of
    methyl iso-cyanate from a chemical plant at Bhopal in India (Hardoy et al.
    1992: 92). Despite this cities are, by contrast with the countryside, seen as
    favoured places to live, especially by young people.

6. Above all, in Third World cities, industrial activity is unable to provide
    jobs for all the immigrants. Production is dominated by TNCs who by the
    standards of the society are capital intensive and employ relatively few

people. The main job opportunities come in the disproportionately large services sector, in which government employment predominates. Much of the population therefore is unemployed or underemployed. Links with the home village are maintained therefore as much out of economic necessity as out of family loyalty. This is quite the opposite of what is usually intended, as for example in Africa, where tribal identity is very strong and urban workers send remittances to their families, expecting in due time to return to the village.

Provided that urban areas are well governed they have important advantages. It is much easier and cheaper to deliver efficient public services where distances are short and costs relatively low. Properly planned transport systems can not only make it easy for citizens to get to work but also to enjoy a good range of recreational and other facilities – the rich have always liked to live in cities. Policy makers are urban dwellers and in their decisions they tend to favour what they know best. It is, of course, in the city that democratic politics originally evolved and there is widespread agreement that a satisfactory environment can only be attained in Third World cities by the empowerment of those directly affected.

Communications

The impact of air travel

In some ways the new ease of air travel in the age of the jumbo jet, which has compressed space and time, has helped widen, not close, the gap between the First and the Third World. It has done so perhaps to a greater extent between the more developed countries of the Third World, where infrastructure is sophisticated, and the poorer countries, where it is often virtually non-existent.

Because of the special conditions of Latin America – its size and the obstacles to travel by land – air travel was taken up with particular interest and enthusiasm. Avianca, Colombia's flag carrier, is the second oldest airline in the world. This is no coincidence. Owing to the incredibly broken terrain Colombia's surface transport network remains fragmented and inadequate and air freight has played and continues to play a significant role in its economic development (Hilling in Mountjoy 1978: 91). Air travel has also helped make possible a degree of unity in Malaysia, Indonesia and the Philippines. Otherwise it is an expensive luxury for a Third World country to have its own airline, particularly when, as with Pluna in Uruguay, it had 4000 employees and only one aircraft. But not many ruling elites have been able to resist the temptation. In recent years some have been seeking to divest themselves of the expense through privatisation, only to find that there are relatively few players willing to buy. Such is the internationalisation of the air industry that in the holiday season you can easily find yourself travelling from Buenos Aires to Montevideo on an aircraft chartered from Royal Jordanian Airlines.

Railways

Transport systems developed during the colonial period (or in Latin America during the early national period) were very basic. Given the limits of technology there was little difference between those for local use and those oriented towards export. It was the application of steam power to locomotive propulsion that turned railways into both a practical means of transport and an instrument of colonial expansion, particularly in its last phase, the scramble for Africa. Cecil Rhodes' dream of a 'Cape to Cairo' railway was never realised, but an African transcontinental railway was eventually completed, although the engineers who surveyed it were lucky enough to arrive on the scene only a few days after the end of the Ashanti Wars. It was the railway that made a united India possible. Railways remain a significant means of transport in East, South-east and South Asia.

Once the infrastructure is in place railways are easy to maintain: even if a bridge is washed away by floods it is much easier to replace it for a train than for road transport. Against this, of course, there is the problem of inflexibility: goods have to be trans-shipped to train or lorry for eventual delivery to their destination. Such inflexibility often reflects the purpose for which Third World countries were originally linked into the global economy. Railways built to serve the transport needs of colonial or semi-dependent production are quite often no longer in the right place for modern centres of population. Examples of this can be found in the radial pattern of the railways on the pampas of Argentina and in the short railways feeding the hinterland from a variety of ports in West Africa. Many of these have proved useless for modern conditions and have been closed.

More generally, from the 1960s onwards, rail has had to contend with an unfavourable political climate. Increasingly for long-distance passenger travel, not least by politicians and the staffs of development agencies, trains have been superseded by aircraft. Cheap motor vehicles became available in large numbers, and for people in the Third World offered a freedom of movement they had never previously enjoyed. Four-wheel drive vehicles offered a reasonable ride on the worst of surfaces. The high cost of building and maintaining roads was borne, not by the passenger, but by the state. So rail networks were run down and in some countries disappeared altogether.

This had significant social consequences, as an example will show. Some colonial railways did come to benefit the independent nations. Though built originally with strategic defence of the Protectorate in mind, the Sierra Leone Government Railway had since its opening become a major factor in knitting together the country's many tribes and providing employment. Its closure was the price paid by the Siaka Stevens government for IMF support. Today few signs of it remain and at Magaburaka, once an important centre but now lying off the main road, it is almost impossible to trace the outlines of what was once the station yard. The only railway in the country is a recently constructed mineral line carrying iron ore from the mines down to the harbour at Port Loko. Being electrified (in a country where parts of the capital only get four hours electricity a day!) it employs very few people, and having no other function it makes no useful impact on the surrounding countryside. Instead both passengers and freight have to contend for space on the country's few roads, even fewer of which have anything that might be termed an all-weather surface. Not surprisingly, anyone who can afford it, or can get someone else to pay for it, drives a Mitsubishi Pajero (Shogun).

Road

Much of the traffic of West Africa is still carried by the so-called 'mammy lorry', an improvised bus on a truck chassis. Many if not most of these are brightly painted with surprising but sometimes all too appropriate slogans, often with a religious flavour. Similar improvisations, notably the ubiquitous 'jeepney' in the Philippines, are to be found with local variations in many other Third World countries. However the enthusiasm for these picturesque vehicles often shown by First World visitors should be tempered with a greater realisation of their environmental disadvantages. In the countryside these may not be so apparent. But badly tuned diesel engines are one of the biggest problems of Third World cities. They pump out vast quantities of toxic fumes that constitute the major element in polluting the atmosphere in cities as far removed as Calcutta, Cairo, Lagos or Mexico City and overall increase the concentration of greenhouse gases and contribute to global warming.

Roads of a sort are not hard to build and they have the great advantage that improvements can be phased in as funds or labour becomes available. In addition road building is labour intensive and requires relatively simple skills. It makes therefore an important input into a developing economy. However good roads are expensive to build and difficult to maintain. In West Africa heavy rains can bring flash floods that can wash away whole sections of surfaced road. Not surprisingly Africa is very short of surfaced roads; in fact Africa and Latin America together have only 7 per cent of the world's surfaced roads. At least a third of all World Bank loans have consistently been for road projects and in June 1971 the UN Economic Commission for Africa took the initiative to set up a permanent bureau to construct a Trans-African Highway, to stretch 6393 km from Mombasa to Lagos, linking a number of existing 'growth areas' and using for the most part existing roads that were to be upgraded to an approved standard by their respective national governments (Hilling in Mountjoy 1978: 88–9).

The military government of Brazil (1964–85) placed the building of access roads at the centre of its strategy to open up Amazonia. The move of the capital to Brasília in 1960 had been accompanied by the building of an access road from Belem to Imperatriz and thereafter up the valley of the Tocantins, opening up a large sector of Eastern Amazonia. In the mid-1960s Rondônia was opened up by a new road from Cuiabá to Pórto Velho, again linking with the highway from Brasília via Goiana. But the centrepiece of its National Integration Programme of 1970 was the Transamazonian (Rodovia Transamazônica), a massive project to connect the coast to Humaita and thence to Porto Velho, while at the same time facilitating land colonisation along a 10 kilometre strip on either side of the proposed route (Hilling in Mountjoy 1978: 90). See Plate 2.

The work of 'opening up' Amazonia was to be continued subsequently by the building of an even longer strategic road, the Rodovia Perimetral Norte, round Brazil's northern frontier, connecting up with feeder roads into all the neighbouring countries of the Amazon basin. Such alarm has been created at the environmental implications of effectively unrestrained logging, and the impact this has had on Brazil's Indian communities and the wildlife of the area, that most of the original plan remains on the drawing board. However the northern section has been constructed to link up with the road northward from Manaus and work is currently about two-thirds complete on a link road from this down the Essequibo valley towards Georgetown in Guyana.

Small island developing states

While transport across the enormous distances of the continental Third World remains a central problem, some parts of the Third World exhibit very different needs. The global problems of climate change and the potential rise of mean sea level has, at least for the moment, called attention to the special problems faced by small island developing states (SIDS).

There are two major areas in which such states are to be found: in the Caribbean, in close proximity to larger mainland states, from which they owe their independence to the accidents of colonial rivalry; and in the Pacific, where their isolation gives them a natural geographical identity. At Barbados in 1994 under UN auspices an Association of Small Islands States (AOSIS) was formed to defend their common interests.

1. SIDS are particularly vulnerable, owing to their small size and frequent dependence on a single export crop, to natural and environmental disasters. In the long term their extremely limited supplies of land are easily exhausted. In what is now the Republic of Nauru mining for phosphate in the colonial period had left one-third of the small island state a waste of dead coral, with its 5000 population crowded into the part that remains. Biological diversity on the remaining land is minimal. Though as points of

access to our maritime environment the islands offer particular advantages, their capacity to absorb significant increases in tourism, their only obvious source of additional revenue, is very limited. As a result of the need to import food, etc. for tourist consumption, the island state of St Vincent in the Caribbean actually loses money on its tourist industry.

2. The dependence of SIDS on fishing makes their immediate maritime environment particularly sensitive to disturbance. Their traditional habit of discharging wastes into the sea therefore has to be superseded as a matter of urgency by effective management of wastes and care of irreplaceable coastal and marine resources. This is at once a threat from the tourist influx and a threat to the attractions that bring them. Chief among these are the living corals of which many of the Pacific islands are composed.

3. Many of them are low lying and depend on infrequent rains for fresh-water supplies.

4. Their geological structure, rising from the deep seabed, means that for energy resources they are for the present extremely dependent on the import of fossil fuels, though in the long run the harnessing of solar, wave and wind power are all practical 'renewable' alternatives.

5. Some SIDS are so remote that they are totally dependent on the outside world for transport and communication.

The balance sheet: assets and problems

To sum up, therefore, Third World countries other than the SIDS mostly have a complex balance of assets and problems. Let us consider their assets first.

On either side of the tropics there is plenty of sunshine and a generally reliable and predictable climate pattern, though in the tropics themselves mist and haze can persist well into the morning, lowering the overall temperature but raising humidity. In the subtropical zones there is generally a considerable annual surplus of rainfall. In conjunction with the great rivers as sources of irrigation this has enabled these regions, through the wet cultivation of rice, to develop some of the world's largest concentrations of population and, though there is considerable argument about how far the earth's capacity to produce food can be extended, some expansion at least does appear to be a reasonable possibility, though in the case of rice by extending the area cultivated and not by increased productivity.

The tropical rainforest, if it survives, offers the most spectacular possibilities for the development of new and valuable products from its rich biodiversity. But the amount of information that has to be gained first is so great that conservation is of vital significance if this asset is ever to be realised.

Many Third World states have significant mineral deposits, some of which are still unexploited. Yet owing to the development of satellite sensors the location of key minerals can now be made by those having access to space technology, which means, in practice, a small handful of advanced industrialised countries and the TNCs they shelter. Third World governments that can get access to this information and can bargain effectively could, if the companies are willing to let them, plough back the proceeds of these irreplaceable resources as Venezuela initially did and Kuwait (until the Gulf War) continued to do with their oil, either into infrastructure or long-term investment, or both. With their large populations Third World states also have vast human resources. Many of their citizens have already to be very resourceful simply to survive. But countries, such as those which are termed the East Asian 'powerhouse' (see Chapter 4), that set out systematically to unlock the potential of their citizens by promoting education, particularly for women (see Chapter 12), are likely to find that their investment is very well spent in terms of the general betterment of society.

On the other side, however, there are also deep-rooted and persistent problems.

Poverty is the root of many of the most persistent problems of the Third World. Floods, drought and hurricanes all threaten human life and pose serious challenges to governments. However people are much more vulnerable to these emergencies if they live in inadequate shelter and lack the economic resources to protect themselves against them.

Population growth may not of itself be a problem, but population growth coupled with the compelling pressure to achieve First World standards of living undoubtedly is. A child born today in an advanced industrialised country will, it is estimated, consume around 40 times the natural resources that a Third World child will consume before its reaches adulthood. This contrast is not only unethical but unstable.

The pessimists who have warned of the coming exhaustion of land and mineral resources have so far generally been shown to be wrong (though mineral deposits can and do run out and the dire state of Bolivia's tin industry is there to prove it). However mineral deposits are not infinite and agricultural land once lost, whether to neglect, to urbanisation or otherwise, cannot easily be replaced, if indeed it can be replaced at all. So it would be prudent to assume that at some stage shortages will act in a way not at present predictable to check development in some if not all Third World countries.

CHAPTER 3

The crisis of the Third World

Poverty and basic needs

One billion people in developing countries – or one in five of the world's population – live in poverty. Their basic needs remain to some degree unmet. While the manner of organising to meet them varies with circumstances, basic human needs are universal:

- clean water
- good food
- proper sanitation and health facilities
- reasonable housing
- education.

Where basic needs are not met the effects can be devastating. For example, a major world effort is needed to break into the cycle of infection and reinfection that in recent years has led to millions of deaths in countries in Africa South of the Sahara (SSA). In 1995 an outbreak of the Ebola virus in Zaire led to headlines throughout the developed world featuring its terrifying consequence, acute haemorrhagic fever leading in over 80 per cent of cases to death through the dissolution of the victim's internal organs.

Generally speaking, where population is high relative to the resources available to sustain it, the basic needs are most difficult to meet and the most marked forms of poverty and vulnerability are likely to occur. Aspects of material poverty as experienced in the Third World include undernutrition, malnutrition, ill health and low levels of education. However a complicating factor is that poverty is not experienced by whole countries. Even in very poor countries (as measured by GDP per capita) there is a rich elite, though elite lifestyles vary also. Moreover the relative importance of the different factors making for poverty (physical, national past and present, international past and present) varies over time and from place to place.

Stressing the need to meet basic needs as the primary driving force towards development, sometimes imaginatively termed the 'basic needs approach', emphasises that health and education are motors for productivity and that the basic needs of all sectors must be met. This approach was expressed in the ideological framework of UN conferences in the early 1970s, when it confronted the older emphasis on the eventual trickling down of the benefits of development and the 1960s' development agenda stressing employment and income distribution. In other words this new approach saw qualitative change as the vital first step, not as something achievable through initial quantitative change. Such an approach was not then and is not now universally accepted.

In First World countries the 1970s saw the emergence of ideas associated with neo-liberalism and by the 1980s these had been adopted in most parts of the Third World. Neo-liberals have argued that, for example, emphasising the meeting of basic needs slowed down growth in Sri Lanka in the 1960s/1970s, impeded the development of Jamaica in the 1970s (as witness the fiasco of the sugar industry there) and proved detrimental to that of Tanzania, still, after several decades, one of the poorest countries in Africa.

Despite this ideology of non-intervention the fact remains that the meeting of basic needs depends for many on the continued provision of funding, and that the only way this can be done with certainty is by a system of financial transfers from the better-off to the poor at international, national and subnational levels. Third World countries, however, tend to lack internal transfers as safety nets for the poorest sectors. Shifting resources to the poor is a cost to the non-poor, and it is they who are likely – all other things being equal – to have a greater say in political and economic decision making. In an extreme case, the wealthy backed by the armed forces were able to prevent the introduction of income tax in Guatemala until the early 1970s. When, finally, it was introduced, the top rate was only 4 per cent.

On the other hand it is always difficult to target benefits on the poor. First of all the poor often have an all too well-founded suspicion of government. Censuses do not pick up all of the poor. Officials are always suspect and census workers are no exception. Non-governmental organisations are better at targeting aid to the poor than are governments, but they often lack the resources. Most effective may be a process of self-selection, that is to say making available benefits of no interest to those who are not poor, such as low-paid public sector employment. However economic orthodoxy frowns on creating employment in this way, no matter how socially desirable it might be, and governments that have got into financial difficulties may find themselves compelled to cut the size of the public sector regardless of the inevitable social consequences.

Water

Basic needs are, of course, interrelated, but the most important of all is clean water. Fresh water is less than 3 per cent of the world's water and is not evenly

Table 3.1 Water-scarce countries 1950, 1990, 2025 (est.)

Water-scarce countries in 1955	Additional water scarce by 1990	Additional water scarce by 2025 under all UN growth assumptions	Additional water scarce by 2025 under med/high UN assumptions
Malta	Qatar	Libya	Cyprus
Djibouti	Saudi Arabia	Oman	Zimbabwe
Barbados	UAE	Morocco	Tanzania
Singapore	Yemen	Egypt	Peru
Bahrain	Israel	Comoros	
Kuwait	Tunisia	South Africa	
Jordan	Cape Verde	Syria	
	Kenya	Iran	
	Burundi	Ethiopia	
	Algeria	Haiti	
	Rwanda		
	Malawi		
	Somalia		

Source: Sustaining water: population and the future of renewable water supplies, Washington, DC, Population Action International, 2000.
http://www.cnie.org/pop/pai/water-14.html.

distributed. The majority of Third World populations live in rural areas where only some 15 per cent have access to clean water. Even in urban areas of the Third World most households do not have running water. In India, for example, it is estimated that as much as 70 per cent of all surface water is polluted. The *World Development Report* (World Bank 1992) suggests that globally 1 billion (one thousand million) people are without access to clean water and 1.7 billion do not have proper sanitation. The combination of in-adequate water supply and no sanitation is a guaranteed recipe for the rapid spread of water-borne illnesses. The World Health Organization (WHO) says that the number of water taps per thousand population is a better indicator of health than the number of hospital beds.

Not only is clean water scarce in the Third World but it is getting scarcer (see Table 3.1). Growing population, increasing urbanisation (which lowers quality through sanitation problems as well as increasing demand), rapidly ris-ing demands from industry and the increasing pollution of watercourses by both solid and liquid wastes (Postel 1989), all combine to make potable water a rarer and therefore more valuable resource. Indeed water is also required for a variety of purposes other than drinking: washing and cleaning, irrigation for crops and, in more recent years, the generation of hydroelectric power (HEP). The world's food production must double over the next 40 years. There is no realistic way this can be achieved except by continuing to expand the wet cultivation of rice.

Food

In the 1930s Third World countries collectively exported some 12 million tons of grain. By the late 1970s they were importing some 80 million tons.

However these figures conceal two paradoxes. World food production overall was sufficient even in the 1990s to feed all the people in the world to a reasonable standard and FAO projections are that 3600 calories per person is practicable (see also UNFAO 1999). Despite global needs, however, in 1972 the US government paid farmers $3 billion to take 50 million hectares out of production while millions starved in the Sahel for want of a harvest (Bradley 1986) and under the EU's Common Agricultural Policy (CAP) land is being 'set aside' to keep prices up. Further, there are increasingly severe grain shortages in the Third World at the same time that a growing proportion of world cereal production is being diverted to animal feed. In 1972 the heavy sales of wheat to the Soviet Union that helped raise the world price went to the production of meat. By the end of the 1970s in Mexico more basic grains were eaten by animals than by 20 million peasants (*International Herald Tribune*, 9 March 1978, quoted in Frank 1981).

About 30 per cent of the world's land is potentially arable, about half of which is under cultivation. Half of the land under cultivation is in the Third World but it is inhabited by three-quarters of the world's population, and the disproportion is even more marked in individual countries. Inequality of land distribution contributes to overfarming and underproduction. Some 80 per cent of the land in Latin America is held by less than 10 per cent of the population. The environmentalist George Monbiot (1992) cites the case of Brazil where farmland extending to the size of India lies uncultivated because it is held by its owners as an investment. Brazil's richest 1 per cent own 15 times as much land as the poorest 56 per cent. Under Brazilian law land idle for more than five years may be legally occupied by any of Brazil's 10 million landless peasants. Landowners, not surprisingly, have a variety of means to resist such occupations. They are quite prepared to use violence if necessary.

At present one-quarter of the earth's population is not getting enough food. More than 500 million people are seriously malnourished. Malnutrition is not just an evil in itself – it lowers resistance and so exacerbates the problem of disease. These problems begin before birth: poor nutrition in mothers causes underweight babies and low birthweights are increasing in some areas. Some 60 per cent of children in rural Bangladesh are underweight. Low birthweight is the factor most strongly correlated with later health problems. Directly or indirectly malnutrition causes the death of 40,000 children under five every day. In Africa SSA deaths of the under-fives contribute between 50 and 80 per cent to the total mortality of the population, compared with 3 per cent in Europe.

Undernutrition has been exacerbated by the tendency of some Third World countries to cease to be self-sufficient in staples and to become importers of food they used to produce. Africa SSA was a food exporter until 1960. According to Shiva (1988) the region was still feeding itself as late as 1970. But by 1984 140 million out of 531 million Africans were being fed with grain from abroad. This is a common phenomenon in Africa, due to urbanisation, changing consumption and production patterns and the 'demonstration effect' fostered by the mass media. Even Mexico, where maize probably originated, is no longer self-sufficient in the basic staple of its diet. In fact it now exports fruit and vegetables to the United States of America and imports wheat in return. When Third World countries get into financial difficulties their plight is often because of the need to maintain a high – some would say excessive – level of imports of grain and other basic foodstuffs. Importing food and food products increases Third World vulnerability anyway, because of the need to deal in scarce convertible currency, but the imposition of austerity measures, along with currency devaluation, hits imports of all kinds, food included.

Much was made at the time of the so-called Green Revolution that from 1940 onwards did so much to increase world food production. But the 'miracle' seeds of the Green Revolution (financed by the Rockefeller Foundation in the 1940s and the Ford Foundation in the 1960s) were HYVs (high yield varieties) which, as they were intended to, produced massive increases in marketable surpluses, especially of wheat and rice. There were two problems for Third World farmers. The new seeds were hybrid. They did not breed true and new supplies had to be bought each year, thus making the farmer dependent on cash purchases. They also needed huge volumes of water and high levels of chemical fertilisers, pesticides and fungicides. These things consumed scarce foreign exchange, increasing the national debt in the process and adversely affecting water supplies. Hence the benefits of the Green Revolution, and there were many, were in practice skewed to the wealthier sectors because they were only easily available to larger landowners. They therefore inadvertently helped increase the serious disproportion in access to land and wealth in Third World societies.

There are important domestic consequences too. Agribusiness is 'modern'; it seeks to gain efficiency by mechanisation and it is the best arable land that is easiest to subject to this. The occupation or purchase of these lands displaces settlers on to marginal lands. Hence it is, ironically, often the free market in land rather than population pressure that creates refugees and/or hunger. In the case of the Philippines marginal workers have been driven into the forests, where they in turn displace indigenous peoples, with disastrous consequences for the environment and lost lifestyles.

The most severe form of food deficit is famine, which differs from under-nutrition in its acuteness and in the accompanying increase in deaths associated with the crisis. Famine is high profile through First World television appeals but it should not be forgotten that the greatest achievements in surviving famines are local, the result of community and family efforts in the affected areas. Famine is not simply a natural disaster and it is no accident that it is currently associated with Africa SSA and especially with the Sahel region and the Horn.

Famine was also commonplace in India historically (Weiner 1962). However the most recent famine in India was the Bengal Famine of 1943, during the Second World War, when both government and the transportation network were strained to the limit. There has been none in India itself (as opposed to neighbouring Bangladesh) since independence in 1947, thanks to a public food distribution system, although chronic hunger persists in India and claims many lives as a matter of course. On the other hand, China has since the Revolution greatly reduced chronic hunger as a routine condition of the population, but has nevertheless suffered famine, most notably at the end of the 1950s during the turmoil of the Great Leap Forward. The fact is that the cause of famine is not usually a lack of food but rather whether food gets to those who need it – the question of the difference between availability and entitlement.

As Dreze and Sen point out: 'it has to be recognized that even when the prime mover in a famine is a natural occurrence such as a flood or a drought, what its impact will be on the population depends on how society is organized' (1989: 46). Even in a country stricken with famine most sectors do not suffer famine as such; Sen estimates only 2–3 per cent do. Most sectors have entitlement based on their capacity to produce their own food, to trade some other product for food or to earn a wage with which to buy food. The rich do not go hungry even in famine. Urban areas tend to draw resources from marginal areas, as was the case in Ethiopia, where government food purchases for the cities contributed to rural famine. In 1988 it was a time of reasonable food availability in Somalia, and the famine that shocked the world was the result of human agency. In the civil war crops had been burnt, resulting in a flood of refugees without reserves or mutual support networks and no 'entitlement' to food. In 1994 in Rwanda the flood of refugees was so massive that in only three weeks a major disaster was created (see also Wijkman and Timberlake 1984).

Climatic factors are not the causes of famine in any real sense, therefore. Rather, like wars and political crises they are trigger factors. Droughts have occurred year after year in Africa SSA in the past but have not necessarily been accompanied by famine (see Schmandt 1994). Much of the USA is arid but it does not suffer from famine, as it has the complex infrastructure to ensure that in emergencies resources are more equitably distributed. This infrastructure is vital to reduce vulnerability. But in their former colonies traditional defence mechanisms were often dismantled by European colonisers, as Gita Mehta describes in *Raj* (Mehta 1990). Famine therefore emerged as an unintended consequence of the ways in which local economies were restructured to meet the needs of the colonial powers. The most productive land was taken for settlement or plantations, reducing land available for production to meet local needs. Competition frequently destroyed local artisan production that could have earned funds for times of food shortage. See Plate 3.

Food aid can make things worse. Critics have particularly targeted the sending of infant feeding formula as part of aid packages, as there is evidence that both this and the aggressive marketing of artificial babymilk powder to Third World mothers by companies such as Nestlé is resulting in many unnecessary deaths. The formula itself is not the problem, but it has to be made up with clean water in sterile equipment and, even where mothers understand the need for hygiene, the facilities are often inadequate. More often the formula is made up with dirty water and diluted to make it go further, so that if the child fails to contract gastroenteritis or dysentery, he or she is of low body weight and so less well equipped to resist other challenges to his or her immune system. Breast feeding is by far the safest method for Third World babies, particularly since it conveys a degree of immunity against local diseases. In Sierra Leone, where 170 children per 1000 die before the age of one and a quarter (males 277 per thousand, females 248) of all children die under the age of five, babies often thrive until weaned.

Unhappily food aid, though an essential humanitarian response to short-term crisis, can very easily be exploited as a political weapon. In 1974, for example, US government disagreements with Bangladesh led to a reluctance to release food aid in a time of famine. Even when food aid arrives at its intended destination, as in Somalia in 1993, it may be hijacked by local warlords or power blocs and used by them to reward their own political supporters. Last, the availability of free food drives down the price of staples on the local market. If the supply of aid goes on too long, therefore, the incentive to plant for the new season is eliminated and the cycle of deprivation is set to continue. In this way food aid has ironically and tragically acted to prolong the effects of drought in Ethiopia.

Sanitation and health

Clean water and sanitation are functional, they are not just luxuries. From 1992, beginning with Peru, South America experienced its first cholera epidemic for more than 100 years. The cost of the Peruvian cholera epidemic in terms of lost tourism and agricultural exports exceeded by far what it would have cost to avoid the problem.

The estimate of the number of cholera infections each year is enormous, some 6 million. Cholera breeds in the gut and is spread by contaminated food and water. It hits hardest at the weak, the old and the young. Convulsions, vomiting and diarrhoea produce dehydration that can kill in four hours. Yet years of neglect made Peru highly susceptible to this disease. For Peru it is an artificial, not a natural, disaster. Cholera was brought by boat to Chimbote in 1990–91, where the Peruvian preference for raw fish and the absence of simple sanitation (communal latrines and contaminated water supplies) combined to pave the way for an epidemic. Chimbote should be a prosperous place with an adequate infrastructure for the general health of its population. It is the world's largest fishmeal producer. But the European-descended elite who control the profits from fishmeal do not get cholera. They do not invest in infrastructure, arguing that this is the government's job and its absence the government's failure. Like their counterparts in other Latin American countries the Peruvian elite prefers to keep its money abroad in more stable countries.

Within weeks the epidemic had spread to five neighbouring states and it is now again endemic in South America. Mountain villages have been hit by cholera too, although they might have been assumed to be healthier places, because their rivers (which are their main source of water) are also their sewers. The main exception was in areas controlled by the guerrilla movement Sendero Luminoso. Where the building of latrines was ordered by Sendero, and those who did not use them were threatened with death, there was no cholera (*Assignment*: 'Peru in the Time of the Cholera', BBC Television 1993).

One good thing has come out of this – schools are now teaching basic hygiene for the first time, but most such education and other assistance has been left to the aid agencies. Peru's hospitals were totally overwhelmed, but it does not take an epidemic to overwhelm Third World hospitals. Poverty has the same effect, if more slowly.

Poverty is the main reason for poor health. Health improved dramatically in Europe in the nineteenth century by the provision of public water supply and sewerage, and this long before there were significant advances in the ability of medicine to cure illness. Many diseases in the Third World today were once as common in the now developed world but public expenditure solved the problems that gave rise to them. Economic development in its fullest sense, therefore, is the quickest and surest way to better health for all.

However aid agencies have continued in recent years to seek to increase economic growth through large-scale industry and agribusiness, knowing full well that this would primarily benefit the health of the already fairly healthy higher income sectors. The touching belief remained that the benefits of this development would in time 'trickle down' to the poorer sectors of society. But in practice the health gap between rich and poor continued to widen. In 1978, therefore, the 134 countries which attended the WHO conference of that year agreed on behalf of their peoples to seek as a conscious goal the target of 'Health for All'. In 1981 health was identified by WHO as a fundamental human right and the year 2000 was set as the achievement date for 'Health for All' (Thomas 1987: 106).

Primary health care was identified as the main means through which the target could be met. Social indicators were to be used for monitoring the success of health programmes, which would stress accessibility, participation and health education in their design. The main policy initiatives were to be in the areas of adequate food, safe water, family planning, immunisation, the provision of essential drugs and the treatment of common injuries and illnesses.

By 1985 it was clear that the achievements in health care varied enormously and the early optimism had waned. At this point the Rockefeller Foundation published *Good Health at Low Cost*, an investigation into the successes of China, Sri Lanka, Costa Rica and, perhaps most notably, the state of Kerala in south-western India. In all of these areas residents had life expectancies of more than 65 despite the fact that, as their low per capita GDPs demonstrated, these areas were all very poor indeed by world standards. Four factors were found that reduced the infant mortality rate sufficiently to raise life expectancies to developed country levels:

1. an ideological commitment to equity in social matters
2. equitable access to and distribution of public health care provision
3. equitable access to and distribution of public education
4. adequate nutrition at all levels of society.

The logic is clear. Malnutrition aggravated by infectious diseases spread by poor sanitation and polluted water supplies causes the bulk of Third World mortality, especially in children under five. Of the 15 million unnecessary infant deaths each year 4 million are from one or more of six cheaply immunisable diseases and a further 5 million result from diarrhoea preventable by oral rehydration therapy, the salts for which cost next to nothing. The cost of just three weeks of what the world's governments spend on arms would pay for primary health care for all Third World children, including ensuring access to safe water and immunisation against the six most common infectious diseases.

Infant mortality rate varies strikingly between the major regions of the world. The world average in 1998 was 57 per thousand. This compared with, on the one hand, Europe, where the average was 21 (a figure that had actually risen from 16 in 1988), and Africa, where it was 91. These figures also conceal striking variations within regions. Likewise imrs are always higher in rural areas that are less likely to have the same levels of access to medical services, female education, potable water and proper sanitation or indeed the incomes necessary to achieve adequate levels of nutrition. Malnutrition has a serious effect on the unborn child and can lead to irreversible impairment. Surveys in East Africa and South Asia show that children under five are moderately malnourished in some 15–30 per cent of cases and the same percentage of children have low birthweights indicating probable malnourishment during pregnancy. At the same time poor hygiene and unsafe storage conditions make food poisoning a serious danger for both children and adults.

Where urban conditions are grimmest and overcrowding most marked the differences between urban and rural imrs still exist but they are less pronounced. At the beginning of the 1990s the world's highest imr was for Sierra Leone, at 180, but the rate for Equatorial Guinea was almost as bad. Since many more small children die after the age of one, there is an increasing tendency amongst agencies involved in development to prefer under-five mortality rates (U5MRs) to imrs as indicators. Using these rates the United Nations Children's Fund's (UNICEF's) 1998 figures (WHO 1999) suggest that currently Mali has the worst rate (244 for boys, 227 for girls) after Sierra Leone. Such statistics are not surprising for the poorest countries of Africa, but what is perhaps most interesting and hopeful is the significantly lower rates now

Table 3.2 Children's health, under-5 mortality rate, per 1000 live births 1998; 20 poorest states by per capita GNP rank 1997

Rank GNP per capita 1997	Country	U5MR Males 1998	U5MR Females
209=	Ethiopia	193	174
209=	Congo DR	148	130
207=	Burundi	189	168
207=	Mozambique	193	173
206	Sierra Leone	277	248
205	Niger	125	119
202=	Tanzania	138	123
202=	Rwanda	213	191
202=	Malawi	223	217
201	Nepal	110	124
198=	Eritrea	154	137
198=	Guinea Bissau	214	192
198=	Chad	184	164
196=	Madagascar	123	110
196=	Burkina Faso	176	166
193=	Mali	244	227
193=	Angola	217	199
192	Yemen	112	114
191	Nigeria	154	140

Source: World Health Organization, Basic Indicators for all Member States: http://www.who.int/whr/1999/en/annex.1.htm

being achieved by some still very poor countries. India now has U5MRs of 82/97, China 43/54 and Sri Lanka 22/20, while Cuba, at 13/10, is comparable with many wealthy First World nations (e.g. Italy's 9/8). A high infant mortality rate is the main reason for low life expectancy at birth (see Table 3.2). In most parts of the Third World, if you survive childhood, you have a fair chance of living almost as long as people do in Europe or the USA. Again, because of the high infant mortality rate, many of the worst life expectancies are to be found in Africa SSA. These figures are usually broken down by gender, since almost invariably women live longer than men, and in some societies, Japan being the most obvious example, there is such a wide a gap that it calls for explanation. Male/female life expectancy gaps do tend to be smaller in poorer countries, though, and the gap is non-existent in Bangladesh. Today only the Maldives (female 63, male 66) and Nepal (female 56, male 57) have a lower expectancy of life for women than for men (Afghanistan no longer reports – see below). For Africa some representative figures for 1998 were:

Angola: 46.5: female 48, male 45
Chad: 47.2: female 49, male 46
Guinea: 46.5: female 47, male 46.

In Sierra Leone, devastated by civil war, the 1998 figures were the worst in the world: 37.2 overall (female 39, male 36). It is true not all low life expectancies are to be found in Africa, but the exceptions are few. Afghanistan (where the estimated female life expectancy of 43 was less than the male of 44) was the lowest in Asia while it still reported. But a more representative figure is that for India, which in 1998 had has a life expectancy of 63 years for women and 62 years for men compared with 53 and 53 years respectively in 1988 (WHO 1999).

Although when things go wrong there is no substitute for good medical help, the least important factor in general good health is the provision of good medical services. Medical solutions tend to be rich-world solutions, they are generally expensive and involve technology. They would include vaccination, which is relatively cheap and simple to administer, and, while poverty may be the factor most intimately bound to the health of the population, levels of immunity to infectious diseases are important to public health also. However while in the UK 99 per cent of one-year-olds are fully immunised against tuberculosis and 95 per cent against measles, the corresponding figures for Zambia are 81 per cent and 69 per cent and Zambia had 481.8 cases per 100,000 of tuberculosis in 1996 compared with 10.3 for the UK (WHO 1999).

Paradoxically one of the growing problems of the Third World is not the unavailability of drugs, but that there are too many of the wrong kind. Some 30 major companies control some 50 per cent of the world pharmaceutical trade. External regulation of them by Third World countries is often weak, since they lack both the resources and the expertise to control what is sold. Pharmaceutical companies are big foreign exchange earners so restrictions in their home countries in the developed world may not be too tight either. The market is very competitive – the merger of Glaxo Wellcome with SmithKline Beecham in January 2000 would have created the world's largest drug company, but still accounted for only 9 per cent of the world market. The World Health Organization itself is only an advisory body and its advice is not always followed. It is frequently found to be the case that drugs banned in the developed countries are either tested in developing countries or left on sale in developing countries long after they have been withdrawn from sale elsewhere.

Drug companies need to make money to recoup development costs as well as to keep shareholders happy. To do this they want to sell, not generic drugs from which the returns are relatively low, but specific branded products over which they can claim right of 'intellectual property'. Through heavy advertising they promote the sale of branded drugs where generics would do. Prices are high and Third World health budgets low but what is purchased may have virtually no additional therapeutic value, except possibly to the elite in the main urban centres. WHO has identified 200 cost-effective, tried and tested drugs seen as basic and indispensable to any country's health needs, but in the name of free trade the developed countries can offer strong and successful resistance to any attempts to limit provision in this way.

However drug regulation legislation has been proven to decrease reliance on expensive imported drugs. Sri Lanka established a national formulary as early as 1959 and in 1972 the government of Mrs Sirima Bandaranaike established the Sri Lanka Pharmaceutical Corporation to produce generic drugs at low prices. Following independence in 1975 Mozambique established a central purchasing organisation and an effective national formulary, though the circumstances of the country did not allow it (as had been hoped) to establish its own national drugs industry. In 1982 Bangladesh replaced its 1940 Drugs Act with a detailed National Drug Policy, banning many branded drugs altogether and establishing tight controls over the activities of TNCs in the country. Though this policy had strong support in the region the US government threatened reprisals on grounds of free trade regardless of the ethical implications of forcing high-cost products on the population of one of the poorest countries in the world (Thomas 1987: 106–14).

At best, the power of the international drug companies can mean that Third World markets are flooded with branded cough medicine while penicillin and other key drugs are unobtainable. Generally it can mean the widespread availability of suspect products banned in the USA and Japan. At worst, it means that a flourishing black market in prescription drugs grows up and, through their overuse, valuable antibiotics and anti-malarial drugs cease to be effective because germs and parasites develop resistance to them.

Health care in the Third World is often disproportionately used by the wealthy. As elsewhere, the rural poor are the group least likely to have access to it. Not only is it more difficult for logistical reasons to provide reliable health care in rural areas, but Third World governments, in health as in other aspects of provision, often prefer to put their limited resources into large visible expenditures on urban hospitals rather than devote it to primary health care, still less to essential health education.

While circulatory diseases are the main killers in the First World, infectious gastroenteric and respiratory diseases are more important in the Third World. It is however the rural populations who still suffer disproportionately from largely preventable infectious diseases (Danida 1989). For example:

- Over 400 million people in the world suffer from malaria.

- At least 225 million have hookworm (infestation by parasitic roundworms of any of several species of the genus Nematoda).

- 200 million are sick with schistosomiasis (infestation by blood flukes).

- 20 million suffer from sleeping sickness (trypanosomiasis, an endemic disease caused by a protozoan parasite carried by the tsetse fly).

- 20 million are afflicted by 'river blindness' (onchocerciasis, prevalent in West Africa, in which a water-borne filiaral parasite enters the skin, usually in the lower body. It migrates through the body to the eyes, ultimately destroying the optic nerve, resulting in irretrievable loss of sight). Other preventable causes of blindness in tropical countries include trachoma, chronic infection of the conjunctiva by the bacterium *Chalmydia trachomatis*, and xeropthalmia, loss of sight through a simple deficiency of Vitamin A.

- 1.5 million children under five die each year from measles, a condition that is rarely fatal in the developed world, though it can and occasionally does lead to serious complications.

Case studies

Malaria

One of the worst of these scourges is malaria. It is also one that could be relatively easily addressed, if sufficient resources could only be delivered to the task on a coordinated basis. The figures speak for themselves, though reporting is patchy among the poorer countries, and of the countries discussed here neither The Gambia nor Cambodia reported in the latest year available. In 1995 there were 15,594.3 cases per 100,000 people in Kenya, 21,054 in Papua New Guinea, 30,030.2 in the Comoros, 30,269.5 in the Solomon Islands and 32,867.5 in Zambia. Of these both Kenya and the Comoros are popular long-haul holiday destinations.

The tiny West African state of The Gambia, until the 1994 coup an increasingly popular 'long-haul' tourist resort, was ever known to sailors as the Graveyard Coast, and with good reason. In their villages Gambians can expect an average of three bites per night from malaria-bearing mosquitoes. Mosquito nets would be considered an expensive luxury by most Gambians. Nor can most Gambians afford imported malaria preventives; if they reach adulthood they build up resistance. However malaria is a real problem for children, who have not yet had time to develop resistance. Cerebral malaria, the kind found in The Gambia, attacks and destroys the brain. Hence not only do a million children under five die in Africa from malaria each year, but those who do not die may still suffer irreversible mental impairment. That malaria may soon become virtually untreatable is a real prospect in the year 2000. New, at present untreatable forms are developing and new drugs are not being developed as quickly as they were.

Early work by WHO in the 1950s was mainly an attack on the carriers, the mosquitoes. DDT was extensively used until it was banned, but it turned out to be unnecessary. Simply covering stagnant water with a thin film of paraffin was enough to deter the mosquito from breeding. The campaign therefore was very successful. For example, the number of cases in Sri Lanka was reduced from thousands to an average of only 17 a year. Sadly, the campaign was not carried through to its logical conclusion. Residual cases remained and from these malaria parasites were transmitted again with greater frequency once the mosquitoes had become immune to the pesticides being used against them and resources were no longer devoted to spraying the ponds and lakes. By the 1970s the war was lost. Ninety per cent of malaria cases today occur in Africa where over 200 million people get it each year. Attacking the vector itself rather than trying to immunise or cure people is cheap and effective. Peruvian research may be on the verge of producing a cheap and straightforward alternative means: coconuts are being used to incubate a bacillus that will kill the mosquito larvae (*New Internationalist*, 322, April 2000: 6).

It is not only in Africa that drug resistant forms are re-emerging and presenting a formidable challenge to the resources of the major drug companies. Along the Thai/Cambodia border amongst prospectors the strains are virtually untreatable. The Thai operate mobile clinics along the border, but parasite resistance is encouraged by the abuse of anti-malarial drugs. The problem is the availability of drugs in Thailand, where malaria is under control, and their use as prophylaxis in Cambodia, a country that had been dislocated by 20 years of war, where they promote resistance. Already the effects of chloroquine are diminishing. Aid workers have been seriously concerned at the absence of medical advice when Cambodians buy malarial treatments. As a result this area now has the most virulent form of malaria in the world.

The problems presented by malaria are not only medical but social. People move much further than mosquitoes, and in great numbers too in an area with refugees such as Thailand/Cambodia. The dispersal to the rest of the world of the 22,000 UN troops formerly in Cambodia, many of whom will have been sent from malarial areas, has not helped either as they have taken resistant strains home with them. But US military interest in developing malaria preventions is diminishing as it is now much less likely that US troops will be sent in large numbers into South-east Asia. Instead malaria is losing out in the competition for funds. Since the victims of malaria are generally from poor countries there is no money in tropical medicine and the big drug companies do not even bother to send their representatives to international conferences on tropical diseases – WHO does all the cajoling, but often to little effect (*Assignment*: 'Fatal Latitudes', BBC Television 1993).

Three out of five Third World governments spend more on arms than they do on health. Although there are marked variations, the *World Development Reports* suggest that this tendency is actually stronger in the low-income developing countries than it is in others. Two-and-a-half hours is all the time it takes for world military spending to consume the equivalent of the entire annual budget of WHO. The cost of eradicating smallpox worldwide was only $83 million, the same as the cost of just one strategic bomber. But work against malaria was delayed due to 'shortage of funds' and the battle was lost.

AIDS

The toll of lives from malaria is more than 20 times greater than deaths from acquired immune deficiency syndrome (AIDS). AIDS is the acute form of a viral infection spread by sexual contact or the interchange of body fluids, for example by intravenous drug abuse using shared needles. There is as yet no cure for AIDS once it has developed and people in developing countries cannot afford even to be tested for human immunodeficiency virus (HIV) let alone treated with the expensive 'cocktail' of drugs used to arrest the development of the virus in patients in the advanced industrialised countries. Hence the disease has shown an alarmingly rapid spread in Third World countries. In 1997 Japan had 1.2 cases of AIDS per 100,000 people, the UK 25.9, Canada 50.4 and the USA 225.3; but Zimbabwe had 564.4, Zambia 530.1 and Malawi 505.4 (WHO 1999). These figures, unlike those for other diseases, are cumulative. Worldwide 33.4 million people were infected with HIV/AIDS at the end of the century (*The Guardian*, 1 January 2000).

Individual countries most severely affected are Barbados and the Bahamas. However it is not too much to state that the incidence of HIV/AIDS in Africa SSA is so great that the actual survival of many societies is threatened. AIDS is already out of control in Eastern and Central Africa, nurtured by a deadly combination of migrant work patterns, macho attitudes towards sex and unwitting spread by truckers and prostitutes. Since no conventional cure is so far available the position has been worsened by resort to a variety of dubious treatments at the hands of traditional curers.

Tuberculosis

The most recent epidemic to reappear, after several decades during which it had been possible virtually to ignore it, is tuberculosis (TB). The disease is caused by a bacillus that is spread by the persistent characteristic cough; it attacks and progressively destroys the lungs. The overcrowding characteristic of poverty favours its spread. According to WHO (1993) the number of people infected with TB in Africa is 175 million, in Latin America 115 million and South-east Asia 420 million. Again, the worst incidence of the disease is in Africa SSA. Worst affected in 1996 were Djibouti with 503.5 cases per 100,000, Zambia 481.8, Botswana 439.9, Swaziland 433.3, Namibia 427.8, the Philippines 395.3 and Zimbabwe 323.5. Despite its relatively high level of economic development South Africa reported 240.2 cases per 100,000.

Tuberculosis is still treatable, but the treatment has to be administered over a period of time to be effective and if the sequence is broken resistance develops to almost all known antibiotics. The proportion of population with access to treatment in Africa is only 25 per cent, in Latin America 42 per cent and in South-east Asia 45 per cent. Eight million new cases are reported every year. Since in the 1990s the disease has been spreading like wildfire in the big cities of the USA, among the population deprived of welfare services by the free market philosophy of the Reagan years and after, there is, ironically, some hope that in the end something may be done about it. Dr Arati Kochi of WHO's TB programme has said: 'Tuberculosis is humanity's greatest killer and it is out of control in many parts of the world. The disease, which is preventable and treatable, has been grossly neglected' (quoted in *The Guardian*, 4 May 1993).

Housing

Two main aspects of this problem are important: the quality of housing and its location. For the first, 100 million people have no shelter at all and a further 1 billion are inadequately housed. For the second, most of the world's population still live in rural areas. However many of them are landless, or nearly so, and hence have little to hold them there. Their natural course is to migrate to the big cities.

In 1950 only New York had more than 10 million inhabitants; by 1970 two Asian cities, Tokyo and Shanghai, had grown that large. Two decades later, in 1990, 13 urban agglomerations had at least 10 million residents, and that number of urban agglomerations is projected to double by 2010. All but one of the new cities are in the less developed regions. Nine of the 13 largest urban agglomerations in 1990 were in the less developed regions; the proportion is expected to increase to 21 of 26 in 2010 (UNDP 2000).

It is already difficult adequately to describe the extent of the pollution in downtown Mexico City. The air is thick with photochemical smog generated by cars, diesel engines and industrial machinery. Since the city was built on a dried-up lake bed the city centre has sunk by some five metres and sewage has to be pumped uphill to get it out of the way. With such serious problems of pollution the future could be horrendous. It is even possible to contract hepatitis 'A' in Mexico City from the windblown faecal dust from the city's sewage farms.

In rural areas poverty facilitates the spread of sicknesses often unknown to the urban dweller. Thus in rural Argentina dirt floors allow the spread of Chagas disease, a tick-borne parasitic illness. However overcrowding, most likely in urban areas, enormously increases the spread of air-borne diseases such as TB and diphtheria.

Education

At first sight, education might not appear to be as essential a need as water, food or shelter. However education plays a vital role in enabling human beings to become part of and work within modern society. It is of course inseparable from health issues, in particular family planning and thus population growth. As a British trade union slogan has it: 'If you think education is expensive, try ignorance.'

The availability of education is measured in various ways: by the percentage of children who attend school, by the mean number of years schooling they receive, by the proportion of government expenditure devoted to education and, above all, by 'literacy' – the percentage of the population that can read and write, though this is not an easy figure to determine accurately.

In the developing world 30 per cent of children aged 6–11 and 60 per cent of youngsters aged 12–17 do not attend school. However, much depends on the policies pursued by national and state governments. Thus in the State of Kerala in India there is 87 per cent adult female literacy, compared with only 29 per cent for India generally, and 94 per cent adult male literacy, which is much higher than in any other low-income region or country. In middle-income Brazil, where only 3 per cent of government expenditure goes on education, less than a quarter of primary school entrants successfully complete their courses. This compares very unfavourably with a much poorer country such as Sri Lanka that spends a far greater proportion on educating its children and where nearly 9 out of 10 successfully complete their primary school courses. Hence in Sri Lanka literacy rates are much higher than they are in Brazil and this is reflected in Sri Lanka's far better performance on all the social indicators (see Table 1.3, p. 13 and Table 3.3).

Table 3.3 World's lowest literacy rates 1990

Country	Per cent literate	Men %	Women %
Djibouti	12		
Solomon Islands	15		
Somalia	17	27	9
Burkina Faso	18	28	9
Sierra Leone	21	31	11
Benin	23	32	16
Guinea	24	35	13
Nepal	26	38	13
The Gambia	27	39	16
Sudan	27	43	12
Niger	28	40	17
Afghanistan	29	44	14
Chad	30	42	18
Mali	32	41	24
Yemen	32		
Mozambique	33	45	21
Mauritania	34	47	21
Bangladesh	35	47	22
Cambodia	35	48	22
Pakistan	35	47	21

Population growth

In April 1992 a UN report saw population growth as the greatest threat to humanity. This view was shared by many of the world's leaders, notably the Prince of Wales, who said that same month: 'we will not slow the birth rate much until we find ways of addressing poverty; and we will not protect the environment until we address the issues of population growth and poverty in the same breath'.

Leaders from the First World were unsuccessful in their efforts to make population control a central theme of the Earth Summit. Their argument stemmed from the Malthusian view, which had become received wisdom in the western industrial nations, that increased population will at some stage confront finite world resources. But this was publicly resented by much of the Third World, and a great deal of time was wasted on a sterile debate about whether Third World population or First World consumption was a more serious threat. Since the two are not mutually exclusive the debate as such cannot have an outcome.

Population growth is highest in the countries of the Third World, as the figures for average population growth 1995–2000 by continents shows: Africa 2.4 per cent per year, North America 0.8 per cent, South America 1.5 per cent, Asia 1.4 per cent, Europe 0.0 per cent (UNDP 1998). Population growth places serious strains on the ability of Third World countries to feed, clothe and house their populations. But population is also a resource: where capital is scarce, labour is cheap (Boserup 1981). So the balance from a purely economic point of view is not clear cut. But two much more immediate reasons for population control that are usually cited in Malthusian lines of argument are harder to dispute. Population control directly acts to raise the quality of women's lives. By facilitating the spacing out of families it indirectly also contributes to the better health of children.

Population growth in the South is an issue in the North because it threatens northern lifestyles through environmental pressures. Perhaps more seriously, it promotes a fortress mentality in response to refugees' desire to escape, whether from persecution or from poverty.

There has in recent years been a vigorous debate as to whether poverty stimulates population growth. However recent evidence is that, although birth rate drops dramatically once imr is reduced, it is not poverty as such, but the availability at a reasonable cost of means of artificial birth control, that has the most immediate relevance to population growth. Thirteen (rich) nations have already achieved zero population growth. But 4.3 billion people or 78 per cent of the world's population were already living in developing countries in 1995, and on current trends there will be 5.9 billion or 82 per cent by 2015 (UNDP 1998). The Third World has 90 per cent of the world's population growth. Hence the world population, growing by 100 million people a year at present, is expected to rise by 2050 to around 9 billion. Without natural disaster or human intervention or both it will probably not level off until it reaches 14 billion, nearly three times today's level.

Interpreting the consequences of this growth, however, is more problematic. The present rate of population growth in the Third World alone would mean a 75 per cent increase in Third World energy consumption by 2025, even at present inadequate per capita levels. It is also possible to argue that population is only a problem in relation to use of the world's resources. Since the Third World currently only uses about 20 per cent of these, it is if anything underpopulated, so population is not an issue. The population of the Third World is not expected to grow enough to consume as much as the North in the foreseeable future. Hence population will probably never have the equivalent environmental impact of Northern consumption as the South's consumption is not increasing at a sufficient rate to do so.

If we look at contribution to global toxicity, then we find that the population of rich countries is contributing some ten times the per capita municipal/industrial waste of that of the developing countries. It has been suggested that if I = impact on the environment, P = population, A = affluence, T = technology, then $I = P \times A \times T$ (*New Internationalist*, September 1992, p. 8). Although the linear equation may seem simplistic at first glance it does seem reasonable to suppose that affluence and technology operate as multipliers, because consumption increases with affluence and because increased access to advanced technology increases the use of natural resources.

On the other hand, up to a point, affluence can increase the carrying capacity of land; that is to say, the numbers which can be supported without threatening an area's capacity to do so in the future. So its absence exacerbates the problems of population increase to much of the Third World. Population increase is a problem in Africa SSA because the carrying capacity of its land is low, not because population density is particularly high – in the region population density is less than 20 persons per square kilometre, while that of the Netherlands is more than 400 persons per square kilometre. However the case of Africa SSA is illuminating also because it demonstrates that the question of population distribution is vital to any consideration of the matter. Africa SSA has overpopulated regions where carrying capacity is less than the population seeking a living there, especially in its vast and growing cities, in crowded coastal areas and in the most marginal highland ecosystems. At the same time there are enormous uncultivated and underpopulated fertile tropical areas with as yet underutilised carrying capacities. Despite this Africa has long been the most deprived area of the world (Thrift 1986, Timberlake 1985) and all the signs are that matters are going to get much worse.

A number of factors can be shown to reduce population growth:

- urbanisation, which raises the cost of childrearing at the same time as reducing the pressure for child labour
- health care (inc. family planning)
- female literacy

- more earning opportunities for women, which tend to delay marriage as well as giving incentives to have smaller families
- reduced infant mortality rate, especially when resulting from better access to clean water.

Only 30 per cent of couples in the developing world outside China who wish to use artificial methods of birth control have access to contraceptives. In China the regime has tried to enforce in urban areas a single child policy, with various sanctions against couples who produce two children. However this has created a new social problem, that of over-cossetted offspring and the potential problem of later dependency ratios.

PART II

Social and economic contexts

CHAPTER 4

The economic context

Introduction: competing ideologies

Agricultural earnings traditionally form the basis of Third World export economies. The most important thing about them, however, is that they rest on so few products and that these show a strong regional concentration. For example, two-thirds of the exports from Africa South of the Sahara are coffee and cocoa. Nearly three-quarters of all exports from Latin America consist of three crops: sugar, coffee and soya beans. The situation is even worse for certain individual countries, whose reliance in extreme cases may be on a single crop: in the case of Cuba, sugar, and of Bangladesh, jute.

The drive to find and exploit crops for export has resulted in a worldwide move from the growth of foodstuffs for subsistence to the production of cash crops for export. Such cash crops now occupy more than a quarter of the cultivable land of the Third World. This shift has serious consequences. First of all it increases people's vulnerability to famine because personal reserves of food no longer exist (see Chapter 3). Second, for the individual family, it introduces a new kind of vulnerability, dependency on macroeconomic changes. The periodic fall in commodity prices, which previously would have affected only a few, now acts to reduce the country's foreign exchange earnings and hence its capacity to buy staple foodstuffs that are no longer locally produced in sufficient quantities.

There are even more serious long-term environmental consequences, the full effects of which are only just beginning to be recognised and have yet to be addressed by governments. The move into cash crops takes up much of the best, most fertile land and subjects it to intensive cultivation of a single crop. Traditional patterns of crop rotation, which have kept the land in good condition for decades, if not for centuries, are abandoned. To compensate for the resulting deterioration the land is subjected to heavy doses of fertilisers and pesticides. Since these have to be imported, as does much farm machinery and the equipment for irrigation, the new agriculture consumes much of the country's scarce foreign exchange. Meanwhile the soil suffers serious and potentially irreversible environmental damage, as in the case of the desertification of Iraq, Ethiopia and the Sahel. Turning Third World products into commodities (commodification) has indisputably linked the countries of the Third World to the global economic system, though how this linkage works, what the impact is of unequal relationships and what the prospects are for the future all remain vigorously disputed.

The conservative tradition: modernisation theory

The cold war resulted in the USA taking a direct interest in some parts of the world almost for the first time, especially but not exclusively to fill the gap left by the dismantling of the European colonial empires. Its initial approach was based on the notion of modernisation.

The attraction of the United States of America for the rest of the world was that it represented modernity. There was little initial resistance, therefore, to the US belief that the rest of the world was destined in time to follow its example. Indeed this view has, in the longer term, turned out to be at least partly true.

What was termed 'modernisation theory', though, derived from two influences: the structural–functionalism of Talcott Parsons, based on the work of Herbert Spencer and Emile Durkheim, and Max Weber's work on values and attitudes. McClelland and Inkeles concentrate on values and take up the theme of evolution in their tendency to see growth towards equilibrium. Some of the early work of the structural–functionalists now seems almost naive in its touching belief in stability and pluralist consensus. Almond's work combines elements of Parsonian social theory and David Easton's political system analysis.

The best-known example of the school is the work of the US economist W.W. Rostow (Rostow 1971). Rostow's five stages of development – traditional society, preconditions for take-off, take-off, sustained growth, mass consumption – represent stages in the process of development in the USA (Rostow 1960, 1971). As with Clark Kerr et al., *Industrialism and Industrial Man* (1960), this was seen as a unilinear process leading to an end-state akin to that of the USA in the 1950s. For these writers modernity implied liberal-democracy and pluralism. Hence political development was virtually synonymous with modernisation. It was a concept largely sustained by Ford Foundation finance and it expired with the grant in 1971.

The early modernisation theorists saw traditionalism and modernity as two poles and in zero-sum relationship with one another, though it was recognised that there were political problems with economic development (Staley 1954).

Later material acknowledges the survival of the traditional alongside the modern. The persistence of ethnic distinctions, clientelism, etc. would exemplify the survival of traditional patterns, likewise the continuing importance of caste in Indian elections. Traditional, however, did not necessarily mean static. Traditional culture was not internally consistent and traditional societies were not necessarily homogeneous in social structure, nor were they always in conflict with modern forms and therefore liable to be destroyed by change.

The failure of the first, optimistic modernisation theories results in more sophisticated 'modernisation revisionism'. Huntington, who coined the term (1965, 1976), stresses the importance of indigenous social structures but also the need for strong government. Unlike early modernisation theory, which was optimistic in an era of assumed progress, modernisation revisionism exuded a new pessimism and saw modernisation itself as a force for the breakdown of order and the development of praetorianism. The process of development mobilises social groups previously neglected or ignored and temporary disorder must be contained until institutionalisation restores stability.

Ensuring order during the development process rests on strengthening the government and state. Its techniques often include repression, co-option and ideological penetration. Huntington himself laid a strong emphasis on the value of the military as modernisers. Some modernisation revisionists, e.g. J.J. Johnson, take the role of the military one step further. They argue that the military is a substitute for an effective middle class as an agent of developmental change (Johnson 1964).

More recent neo-liberal interpretations of development return to the older-style optimistic approach to modernisation. The benefits of development will trickle down to the less developed countries (LDCs) because the market will ensure that production relocates to where costs are cheapest and therefore advantage moves from region to region ensuring the distribution of global resources. No action is necessary.

Developmentalism

Alternatively there is a perspective that is broadly associated with the social reformist tradition of thought, which acknowledges the present inequity, but sees it as redeemable through First World action. Such ideas are found in the Brandt Commission Report (Brandt 1980) and are therefore sometimes called a North–South model. Benefits could and should be redistributed in favour of the Third World. This could be done through restructuring trading relationships, through aid and investment. There are, though, obstacles to its success that must be addressed; problems such as protection of First World economies, repatriation of profits and interest on debts.

The radical tradition: dependency

An economic emphasis characterises work in the 'dependency' school whether it be of the UN Economic Commission for Latin America (ECLA) derived dependentista type (see Prebisch 1950) or André Gunder Frank's 'development of underdevelopment' (1966). The dependency thesis originated with the Marxist analysis of Third World economies by Paul Baran (1957). It was Baran who first distinguished Third World economies as being on the periphery of the world economic system, whose centre was in Europe and North America.

As the Spanish term 'dependentista' would suggest, the dependency thesis was developed and popularised in Latin America by a variety of writers, not all of whom were Marxists (Jaguaribe 1967, Dos Santos 1969, 1970, Sunkel 1969, Furtado 1970, Cardoso[1] 1972, Ianni 1975, Cardoso and Faletto 1979 (first published 1969)), and in a very similar version has since been widely adopted in other regions of the Third World (Amin 1990a, b). The term is derived from the view that because Third World economies are on the periphery of the world capitalist system they have become *dependent* on the advanced industrialised countries. It rejects the developmentalist view that Third World states can in time undergo the same form of development as the existing industrialised states, for at least as long as the capitalist system exists in its present form. The reason, its adherents argue, is that the 'centre' (the advanced industrialised countries) sets the terms on which the system operates. As a result the terms of trade are unfavourable to Third World countries and the flow of capital is asymmetrical, tending to flow from the periphery towards the centre. This outflow is a structural constraint that ensures that the states of the 'periphery' are weak, open to penetration from the centre and with little or no scope for autonomous action (Bonilla and Girling 1973).

Most of these authors as well as the relevant international institutions and non-dependency theorists would accuse early modernisation theorists of stressing the political to the exclusion of the economic and would charge revisionists with ignoring the international dimension, and these are the key elements of dependency theory.

Dos Santos (in Bernstein 1973) writes:

> [underdevelopment] is a conditioning situation in which the economies of one group of countries are conditioned by the development and expansion of others. A relationship between two or more economies or between such economies and the world trading system becomes a dependent relationship when some countries can expand through self-impulsion while others being in a dependent position can only expand as a reflection of the expansion of the dominant countries.

---

[1] Cardoso made a long, slow journey rightwards and, after a spell as Senator from São Paulo, became President of Brazil in January 1994.

The duality of coexistent modern and traditional sectors found in modernisation revisionism made life easier for the development of dependency theory but it has its roots in two sources:

1. **The non-Marxist nationalism of Latin American structuralism.** This school was exemplified by the ECLA and its best-known representative, Raúl Prebisch. ECLA, established in 1949 at the request of the Latin Americans, who wanted 'a Marshall Plan for Latin America', criticised the theory of comparative advantage. The ECLA theorists divided the world into centre and periphery and argued that the oligopoly of markets in the centre leads to a long-term tendency towards declining terms of trade and to the concentration of industrial production in the centre and, in turn, to Latin American dependence on imports. As a result sustained development depends on the nationalist bourgeoisie promoting industrialisation – at first through import-substitution-industrialisation (ISI).

2. **Marx's distinction between core and periphery.** Though Marx saw the exploitation of the Third World as part of the inevitable development of industrial capitalism, he argued also that imperialism breaks up traditional societies and creates new markets for industrial goods. Baran, Frank, and Cardoso and Faletto were all influenced to some extent by this argument, but pointed out that things did not go thereafter entirely as Marx had envisaged. The fact was that capital did not accumulate in the Third World to be invested *in situ* to the benefit of the state. Instead it was repatriated to the centre, thus accentuating its dominance in terms of capital formation.

The notion of the development of underdevelopment is associated particularly with the work of André Gunder Frank (1966, 1967, 1969). Frank argues that developed countries were formerly 'undeveloped' but they have never been 'underdeveloped'. Underdevelopment for Frank is a process of structural distortion. The economies of underdeveloped countries have been partially developed, but in a way that enhances their economic value not to their own citizens, but to the advanced industrialised countries. In this process he, in common with other dependency writers, ascribes a special role to two agencies. The first is what he terms the 'lumpenbourgeoisie', otherwise generally known as the national bourgeoisie or, for the Maoists, the *comprador* bourgeoisie (from the Portuguese word for a merchant – Frank 1970, 1974). The ruling classes in peripheral states actively encourage the outflow of wealth from their countries by using their 'control of state power to protect the interests of multinational capital' (Kitching 1982). It is they who find their economic interests best served by an alliance with the second agency, the foreign corporation, to exploit their own fellow-countryfolk.

Thus for Frank development in metropolis and underdevelopment in its satellites are two sides of the same coin. The metropolitan centres were once undeveloped but never underdeveloped. It is capitalist penetration that causes underdevelopment and development in the satellites is only possible when they break away from their metropolitan exploiters. This is rarely possible and only takes place in moments of major crisis, such as war or severe economic depression.

Hence for Frank differing levels of development are not the product of different historical stages of development but of the different functions the areas concerned perform in the international system. Production in colonies was determined not by the needs of those colonies (except for colonial settlers 'needing' luxury goods) but by the needs of the colonial power. Hence unequal power relations have developed and continue to be maintained both between First and Third World countries (metropolis and periphery) and within Third World countries (city and 'camp', elite and mass). The worst off are the masses of the Third World since they suffer from 'superexploitation' by both their own elite and that of the metropole. Such inequality is known as 'structural heterogeneity' and stems from the fact that the local political elite are the agents of the international class and the state is their instrument.

Dependent economies are subjugated to the needs of the world economy by foreign (metropolitan) control of markets and capital, as well as by ownership of concerns that have competitive advantages over local firms leading to the further continued outflow of capital. This has two causes: the need for capital-intensive foreign technology and imported capital goods on the one hand, and endemic balance of payments problems on the other. It is the reliance on the export of primary products hit by fluctuating prices that leads to balance of payments problems and thus to reliance on foreign direct investment and aid. The repatriation of profits, technological dependency and the dominance of multinational corporations all serve to undermine sovereignty. Tied aid and loans are examples of capitalism's need to continue its penetration of the Third World.

The third subdivision usually distinguished within the dependency school – Wallerstein's world systems analysis – also lays stress as would be expected on economic factors. Wallerstein's world systems model assumes that a peripheral position in the world economy by definition means a weak state, whereas being part of the core means having a strong state (Wallerstein 1974). However this is just not true. Wallerstein's argument is reversed by those who see late industrialisers as developing under the protection of a strong state. Late industrialisers such as Japan have been able to develop through the leadership of a strong state bent on the objective of economic development. The case of the NICs is still controversial and will be discussed in a later section.

In recent years there have been a variety of criticisms made of the dependency/dependentista school. The most important is that its theories do not fit the historical facts. As Laclau (1977) points out, Frank's historical analysis of the origins of capitalism is not accurate. Smith (1979) describes dependency theory as 'theoretically logical but empirically unsubstantiated'. The next most important criticism is that national differences are neglected or even ignored altogether. Dependency theory does have a tendency to ignore differences between states. The global economy is the key and national characteristics such as political parties, military establishments are, if not incidental, at least very secondary. Dependency theory was developed to 'explain' the case of Latin America and is not really relevant elsewhere.

If there are strong criticisms from the empirical point of view there are equally strong criticisms of the theoretical concepts employed by dependency writers. Their work fails adequately to define 'development' and their use of terms such as 'class' is inconsistent. It relies on 'latent conspiratorial assumptions' (Kamrava 1993) rather than a realistic perception of how business executives and politicians actually think. Much of the debate within the dependency school has been an internal Marxist squabble about the past that offers no hope for the future.

However, not all dependency theory is Marxist (see Chilcote 1978: 61; see also Chilcote and Edelstein 1974) and dependency theorists are no longer as simplistic or depressing as they have been in the past. They would not now accept a simple core–periphery split but would want to introduce intermediate categories such as semi-periphery (a category that would include a large and powerful state such as Brazil) and submetropolis. Cardoso and others recognise internal forces as agents, making choices and decisions that impact on development though their options are limited by external factors, this is 'national underdevelopment' (Cardoso and Faletto 1979: 21). Some internal groups wish to maintain dependent relations; others oppose them. So dependency is not simply an external variable.

These writers have moved on from the early work of André Gunder Frank in seeing some kind of development as possible within capitalism even if it is dependent development. Thus they may be seen to take some account of the emergence of the NICs.

Class and state

Those concerned with the role of the state in the process of development have stressed either political or economic aspects. 'Class/state politics' (for further details see Randall and Theobald 1985: 137–78) stresses both. This may occur within either:

a) a Marxist framework, such as is to be found in the writing of Roxborough (1979). His frequent stress on 'modes of production' shows in the choice of term the Marxist base and the use of the plural indicates the importance of individual national histories and states that are of course essentially political; or

b) a non-Marxist schema such as that found in the works of Stepan (1973, 1978), Schmitter (1979) or O'Donnell (1988).

Later neo-Marxist post-dependency explanations make class alignments within dependent states and the relative autonomy of the state central to their analysis. More emphasis is placed on examining indigenous structures. Obviously class formations are central, but so too is the political role of the state, not just as a representative of the dominant class but as a participant in its own right. Pre-existing (i.e. pre-capitalist) modes of production survive in peripheral economies subjected to the capitalist mode (this idea is found in the work of Laclau). Indeed several modes of production may coexist and the role of the state is vital in determining the role of the national bourgeoisie (e.g. Roxborough 1979).

By comparison with old-fashioned Marxism these explanations are flexible. Maoist influence can be seen in the fact that peasants are recognised as being a potentially revolutionary force (see also Colburn 1994). However, those they seem to have in mind are not peasants in the true sense, who remain a very conservative stratum, but those who constitute a 'peasantariat' such as the plantation workers for TNCs such as Del Monte.

Conversely, there is a belated recognition that, far from being a powerful force for change, the industrial proletariat may constitute a small privileged elite in the Third World, as, for example, in Mexico, where the trade union sector forms one of the three pillars maintaining the dominance of the Institutional Revolutionary Party (PRI). On the other hand nitrate and copper miners in Bolivia and Chile were left wing, while the urban working class in Brazil and Argentina followed Vargas, Goulart and Perón, populist figures of the centre-left.

The view that the state is not simply part of the superstructure and an instrument of the dominant class has obvious sources within Marxist thought, especially the work of Gramsci. The state is seen as above squabbles by fractions of the ruling class pursuing their own short-term interests. There is a non-Marxist emphasis on the state from those, such as Stepan and Schmitter, who see an authoritarian stage as an historic necessity, not actually desirable but something that unfortunately cannot be avoided at a critical stage of development.

O'Donnell developed the widely used concept of 'bureaucratic authoritarianism' to describe the situation when in a post-populist society constrained by the limits of industrialisation civil and military technocrats ally with foreign capital to demobilise or repress popular movements. However O'Donnell's model is not only not generally applicable to Latin America, but fits very narrowly the specific case of Argentina between 1966 and 1973. For this reason 'military developmentalism' may be a more broadly acceptable term to describe the common features of the repressive military regimes of the 1960s and 1970s.

There is also a Marxist form of modernisation theory. Although most Marxists are critical of it, some think that development is possible but will be of a distorted kind. This is progress, they believe, in that it takes the Third World a stage closer to eventual socialism. These ideas are associated with Bill Warren, and Nigel Harris, *The End of the Third World?* (Harris 1986).

Warren believes Marx made it clear that capitalism is a transitional stage between feudalism and socialism that cannot be avoided. It is therefore inevitable (and even desirable) that the Third World will become enmeshed in the capitalist system. For Warren capitalist imperialism functions to drag the Third World with it, thus promoting economic development (Warren 1977). Harris's is a globalisation model with a single interdependent global economic system with TNCs moving freely around it. The nation-state is increasingly irrelevant and nationalism is destined to decline. Thus it is impossible to maintain a separate category of countries termed the Third World (Harris 1986; see below Harris on the experiences of NICs).

Newly industrialising countries

The possibility of a successful late start to development was first exemplified in Japan, Germany and the former Soviet Union. In the period since 1945 the dramatic growth of these economies and, more recently, the rise of the NICs has certainly exacerbated the many problems of conceptualising the Third World (Dicken 1986). The problem of Third World variety requires us to take account of the varying degrees of economic autonomy that may be possible within the global economy.

The term newly industrialising countries already has a slightly dated look. The new term that seems to be coming into vogue is 'new industrial economies' (NIEs), which is in any case more accurate since the 'core group' of NICs always includes Hong Kong (now the Hong Kong Special Administrative Region of China (HKSAR)), which is not a 'country'. South Korea, Taiwan and Singapore are perceived as having already 'made it' from the Third World to fully industrialised status and along with Hong Kong they constitute what was initially termed the 'Gang of Four' or the 'Asian Tigers'. Thailand, Indonesia, Malaysia, Argentina, Brazil and Mexico have been seen as on the same track, possibly to be followed by the Philippines and Mauritius. However there is less agreement on which other countries should be included in this category. Different institutions and different authors express different opinions about what constitutes a NIC. Further the East Asian crisis of 1997 clearly illustrates the vulnerability of many of these emergent economies, though there is a case for arguing that in a globalised world the vulnerability does not stop there, as the evidence of Japan shows.

Specifically the question arises whether the NICs are a symptom of the changing order that signifies what Harris has called 'the end of the Third World'. As he points out (Harris 1986: 102), as recently as 1960 North America and western Europe had 78 per cent of the world's manufacturing output. By 1981 their share had fallen to only 59 per cent. At the same time manufacturing output of the NICs and other middle-income countries had risen from 19 per cent to 37 per cent, while that of low-income countries, including Africa South of the Sahara, had remained virtually the same.

However the impact of development is sometimes glaringly obvious even on the simplest of indicators. For example, in 1967 Indonesia was much poorer than India in terms of per capita income. In 1970 60 per cent of the population of this vast, sprawling archipelago lived in what the World Bank defined as 'poverty'. By 1990 this figure had dropped to 15 per cent. Asia is the most significant area when it comes to dramatic economic growth precisely because of the huge numbers of human beings involved. Between 1970 and 1990 the number in absolute poverty more than halved despite rapid population growth. There can be no more dramatic evidence of the massive market expansion in that region, which has accompanied its rapid industrialisation.

It is hardly surprising that the relatively advantaged and diversified middle-income countries should seek to increase their share of global markets, but only a small proportion of them have done so. The NICs represent *the* most important blurring of the Third/First World division to date, as they have set out successfully to challenge the developed nations, both on their own traditional bases of industrialisation, e.g. iron, steel and heavy industry, and also in the new consumer markets.

This can be seen by closer examination of the recent economic histories of the 'core' NICs – those on which there will be general agreement. South Korea and Taiwan will be taken as examples.

South Korea

The country was hard hit by the Second World War and the division of the peninsula between east and west. Korea had developed a significant manufacturing sector before the First World War but most of its industry was located in the North. Hence despite the flight of many North Korean entrepreneurs to the South, South Korean industry had to establish itself with few resources and a dense population dependent on what it could produce. However, although manufacturing in 1945 constituted less than 10 per cent of the South's output, and exports and the savings rate were both low, native enterprise initially benefited from the distribution of confiscated Japanese property. Then came a major setback, the Korean War (1950–53), which devastated the country and caused major hardship. The war, however, marked a turning point, since US aid, given to maintain a strategic ally in the cold war, was used to pay for infrastructure, spent on roads, railways, ports, communications, power supplies, etc.

South Korea met the first oil shock by borrowing oil surpluses from private commercial banks. Its overall borrowing in the 1970s and 1980s was already high. However this borrowing was not wasted, as so often occurs, but was put to work for developmental purposes. There was a strong emphasis on education. There were strict if not harsh labour laws, but popular disaffection with growth at the cost of poor conditions and low pay did not really surface until the military lost control in the wake of President Park's assassination in October 1979. The land reform that was part of liberation had led to the emergence of much small-scale rural enterprise. The period from the late 1960s to the end of the 1980s was one of high real per capita growth, averaging more than 6 per cent per annum. This period, initially characterised by high savings and investment rates, gave way to one of artificially suppressed interest rates that attracted low domestic savings. This further stimulated borrowing abroad. Debt prompted the seeking of a World Bank structural adjustment loan and IMF encouragement, along with US pressure based on that country's desire for reciprocity of markets, led to liberalisation.

Everywhere the role of the state was apparent, at least until this liberalisation in the 1980s, and the interplay of government policy along with a culture of work and saving is often seen as the source of South Korean development. Initially export-led development of labour-intensive manufactures was given every possible assistance, with exports from the new industries protected by subsidies, and the use of selective tariffs and protective quotas against imports to develop a home market for indigenous goods. Foreign exchange manipulation was employed to retain an export advantage. It is true that the 1970s saw the beginning of the liberalisation of the South Korean economy. However, far from this process liberating hitherto unrecognised potential, it is in fact not yet complete. The South Korean economy still exhibits many of the features of its early origins. Wages are still low, hours long, working conditions poor and strikes are common. Structural weaknesses are its overdependence on a few products and especially on the US market for them, the dominance of the powerful chaebol and the reliance on internal borrowing, both between these powerful corporations and from Japanese banks that in 1997 proved themselves to be dangerously overextended.

Harris points out that neo-classical explanations will not do for South Korea. The importance of the role of the state is far too clear. But nor will explanations based on the massive civil and military aid from the USA. Accelerated growth came after the period of high input of aid and was in part the result of attempting to compensate for its loss. Foreign investment tended to concentrate in certain sectors only, to follow rather than precede growth, and was in any case less than that enjoyed by many other places that did not experience comparable levels of growth (Harris 1986: 44–5).

Taiwan

Taiwan had been colonised by Japan from 1895 to 1945, a much longer period than South Korea. It was densely populated and to this it added in the 1950s émigré Chinese nationalists, many of them entrepreneurial in ideology, who ruled it virtually as a colony in the name of the government of nationalist China. In 1949 it was poorer than the mainland, though it did have a small established industrial base dating from the 1930s. Between 1949 and 1955 land reform limited the size of individual holdings though generous compensation was given to the larger landowners who used the funds to start their own businesses. High interest rates encouraged high domestic savings and foreign borrowing was unnecessary.

However because of its strategic location Taiwan did get an enormous amount of US aid, which again was used for infrastructural development and education. Given its military orientation Taiwan came naturally to adopt a model of state-led economic growth. The authoritarian, and effectively colonial government undertook the largest industrial enterprises and used high levels of tariff protection for its infant industries (though this was being reduced by the 1980s). It also controlled exchange rates.

Taiwan, having been less indebted, was in some respects more successful than South Korea. Exports showed massive growth to some 60 per cent of GNP and much of that was heavy industrial. However there was a downside. Despite egalitarian income distribution conditions for labour remained poor and Taiwan's overreliance on the US market made it vulnerable to shifts in US policy. Again Harris is clear that neo-classical explanations fail in the case of Taiwan's accelerated growth; government action, especially in keeping down labour costs, is seen as too important to the process. For Taiwan: 'The invisible hand was more of an iron fist' (Harris 1986: 53).

What both South Korea and Taiwan along with the other Asian Tigers have achieved is a specialised role in the world economy. They have done so from different starting points with different resources available to them and by way of different policy decisions. (For further economic details of 'the modernisation of Asia' down to 1993, including a wealth of comparative figures and graphs, see *The Economist*, 30 October 1993.)

It can be seen that, unlike Japan, many NICs were originally penetrated economies. There are therefore four ways NICs could encourage development in the wider Third World:

1. as an example to others
2. as suppliers of technology and skills
3. as a market for Third World goods
4. as providers of development capital.

The NICs are seen by some as indicative of a genuine shift of economic power away from the First World. They are the first Third World countries to make the transition to fully developed status. China, with what the World Bank has recently begun to call the eight 'high performing economies' – Japan, Taiwan, Hong Kong, South Korea, Singapore, Malaysia, Indonesia and Thailand – and possibly Vietnam, have now developed to the point at which they are no longer strongly affected by fluctuations in the US economy, though they do remain vulnerable to the decisions of other global economic players such as financial speculators. In the recession of 1991–93, when most of the OECD economies were static, the economies of all the NICs but Japan continued to grow strongly.

Certainly the OECD countries (less Turkey) are no longer overwhelmingly dominant in the world economy. By local exchange rates they still account for 73 per cent of world output, as against less than 18 per cent for the developing countries and only 2 per cent for China. But by assessing the relative strength of economies by purchasing power parities the IMF has placed the relative strength of the OECD and the Asian Tigers in a very different perspective. By this measure the OECD countries (less Turkey) account for only 54 per cent of world output as against 34 per cent for the developing countries and 6 per cent for China, making the Chinese economy in absolute terms the third largest in the world after the United States of America and Japan.

But there are many questions still to be answered. Having made it, will the NICs be more sympathetic to their former companions of the Third World or will they simply join the rich world clubs (OECD, WTO, IMF, World Bank) in accepting the burdens they lay on the less fortunate? Moreover, they made the transition in specific circumstances, with in each case a good balance of payments situation at a crucial moment, with closed markets and (often though not always) authoritarian regimes. Nor can independent states hope to replicate the unique circumstances of the former British colony of Hong Kong.

By joining the rich world the NICs accepted – at least on paper – the prevailing ideology of market liberalism. However their reactions to the 1997 East Asian crisis suggest that they may now be having second thoughts. The crisis was precipitated by heavy speculation against the Thai baht, but in fact the Thai economy had been overheating for some time and no action had been taken to counter it. In the case of Hong Kong, the government of the HKSAR took immediate action to prop up the stock market. Malaysia went further still. Blaming the crisis on a western conspiracy, the government of Dr Mahathir effectively suspended the convertibility of the ringgit and forced investors wishing to repatriate their profits to accept government bonds in lieu of cash – always the last resort of a desperate government.

The effects of the Asian economic meltdown are felt in a variety of ways. *New Internationalist* (320, January–February 2000: 25) cites higher school drop-out rates owing to rises in fees in Thailand, declining real wages and rising unemployment in South Korea, an accelerating bankruptcy rate in Malaysia and a massive increase in poverty in Indonesia, where subsidised food had to be distributed in a vain attempt to stave off political unrest. Moreover, under the World Trade Organization, all these countries will be expected to comply with the terms of the Uruguay Round by ending systems of export incentives, upholding intellectual property rights protection, guaranteeing foreign investment, eliminating tariffs and non-tariff barriers to trade and liberalising government procurement policies, services and exchange rates. It remains to be seen how far in practice they will comply with these standards and, if they do, what effect it will have on their ability to compete. For, up to now, the most striking thing about them is what the World Bank terms 'pragmatic flexibility', combining government support for infrastructure and heavy industry; directed credit for specific industries, especially in the field of new technologies; free enterprise in manufacturing and distribution; and (contrary to prevailing models in the developed countries) a policy of promoting rapid wage growth to create a strong internal market as a basis for export success.

Existing NICs had advantages of cheap labour giving a potential for surplus, but not too many other costs to prevent such a surplus being accumulated and therefore dissuade investors. It is precisely the advanced nature of many NICs and the size of their internal markets, especially in Latin America, that has attracted investment from the outside world, including the NICs themselves. However the Mexican peso crisis of 1994–95 demonstrated that, despite the advantage of cheap labour, capital could equally as well flow out again should there be any loss of confidence in the strength of the existing order.

Other LDCs hope that manufacturing costs will now rise for NICs as they get richer and that others will be able to take their places at the top of the Third World pile. They expect that their capital accumulation will, as with the industrialised countries, be limited by their need to distribute to a more demanding labour force with raised expectations. The present NICs would then become the markets for the kind of LDC product that they grew rich on while moving on to more high-tech, capital-intensive production themselves.

The opinion is however widespread that the NICs' export success is unlikely to become much more general in the Third World. Moreover, if it did, the response of the developed countries might be protectionism. In any case who would buy the quantity of manufactured products produced by all the other countries of the Third World if they were in a position to export at the rate of the existing NICs? The price in terms of environmental degradation could also be unsustainable. As noted above, the sort of free trade envisaged by the makers of WTO would work against the kind of advantages existing NICs enjoyed during their period of most rapid growth. Circumstances today are not only different, but they are very different for different regions. The ability to generate manufactured exports seems to have been vital to the success of all the NICs. Yet less than 10 per cent of all LDC manufactured exports come from Africa South of the Sahara. Where will Africa SSA begin to find the money for the levels of infrastructural investment it needs? On paper, thanks to the use of flags of convenience, Liberia is one of the great maritime nations of the world. In practice it is an extremely backward country devastated by civil war. Nobody is going to invest in Liberia after its recent dismal history. It will take too many years for malnourished, ill-educated generations to be replaced by healthy and bright successors. The ruling military elite has neither the ability nor the means to achieve these changes.

Debt

Developing countries generally made social and economic progress relative to developed countries between 1945 and 1975. Then there was a decline, followed by a world recession lasting from 1980 to 1983, after which the developed countries have been pulling away again, despite a further decline and plunge into another recession, led by the United Kingdom in 1989 (see also Hayter 1983, Adams 1993). Recovery in the early 1990s was accompanied by accelerating liberalisation of economies, which further advantaged the already strong.

The impressive growth in almost all Third World countries between the 1950s and the late 1970s was accompanied by a decline in the proportion, though not the numbers, of Third World populations living in absolute poverty. Agriculture was modernised to some extent almost everywhere by the so-called Green Revolution. Public health and educational provision improved.

However the boom ended as dramatically as it had begun. The trigger was the first 'oil shock' of 1973–74. The sudden increase in the price of oil hit Third World countries as well as the advanced industrialised ones. Unlike the industrialised countries they were in a weak position to meet the challenge. By the early 1970s private capital flows had far outstripped aid to the Third World and amounted to nearly 70 per cent of the net bilateral flows from industrialised to developing countries. This reflects the growth of transnational corporations as well as the involvement in the process of recycling the oil revenues of more than 500 private banks including the very largest in the USA, Japan, Germany, France and the UK. As a result the 1980s saw net debt transfers of some $40 billion per year from developing to developed countries, a figure in excess of colonial repatriation and more than Third World spending on health and education (Adams 1991).

Foreign investment did encourage some modernisation that was sometimes extended through linkages to the rest of the economy – though it more often promoted the development of 'enclaves' of advanced technology. These limited gains had to be set against outflows in the form of profits, fees and royalties, payments for imported inputs and losses due to transfer pricing by TNCs.

Geographical catastrophes added to economic crisis for some of the Third World. There was drought in Africa and hurricanes in the Caribbean. First World greed and incompetence certainly helped cause the devastating impact of the 1980s' downturn on the Third World. But so too did unrealistic hopes and expectations as well as corruption and incompetence in the Third World itself, leading to a massive burden of debt (see Table 4.1).

Dollar surpluses from oil had been loaned to the Third World. They were all too often spent either, as in the case of Mexico or Venezuela, on producing oil (the price of which then collapsed) or, as in the case of Argentina or Nigeria, on arms. Between 1975 and 1985 military expenditure accounted for 40 per cent of the increase in debt. By the end of the 1980s annual world military expenditure was of the order of $1000 billion. Of this 15 per cent was being spent in the Third World, where average military spending was 30 per cent more than expenditure on health and education. Often these massive expenditures were being incurred by military governments that had never been elected by their people. For many people this raises an important ethical question.

Table 4.1   Total external debt of selected states, US$m 1992

RANGE	External debt	Debt per capita
LOW INCOME		
1 Mozambique	4,929	298
18 India	76,983	87
21 Nigeria	30,959	303
27 Ghana	4,275	270
28 China	69,321	59
32 Sri Lanka	6,401	367
37 Indonesia	84,385	457
LOWER MIDDLE INCOME		
43 Ivory Coast	17,997	1,395
44 Bolivia	4,243	565
68 Jamaica	4,303	1,792
75 Thailand	14,727	253
80 Turkey	54,772	936
85 Chile	19,360	1,423
UPPER MIDDLE INCOME		
80 S. Africa	–	–
92 Brazil	121,110	786
99 Mexico	113,378	1,333
100 Trinidad & Tobago	2,262	1,740
102 Argentina	67,569	2,401
107 Greece	–	–
108 Portugal	32,046	3,270
109 S. Arabia	–	–
HIGH INCOME		
110 Ireland		
112 Israel		
116 Australia		
117 UK		
124 France		
127 USA		
131 Japan		
132 Switzerland		

Source: World Bank (1994)

It is morally wrong to ask people who had nothing to do with the contracting of the debts to repay them – debt is not a national problem for debtor countries, but rather a burden that falls disproportionately on the poorest and weakest sections of Third World societies (see the section on the IMF below and Chapter 12).

In 1981–82 Argentina's military government postponed its debt service. However debt did not really become a big issue and the term 'debt crisis' did not appear until in August 1982 the two biggest debtors (Brazil and Mexico) suspended interest payments with the risk that in time they might actually default. It was this possibility that shook the stability of the world economy. In 1982, within two days of Mexico's announcement that it could not service its debt, the US government was already putting in place emergency measures. The government of Mexico almost at once agreed to terms that enabled it to reschedule. Financial support came through the IMF with the backing of the US government, worried about the political and financial stability of its southern neighbour. IMF support however was supposed to be backed by long-term adjustment through 'reforms' proposed by its technical advisers in consultation with the Mexican government of President Miguel de la Madrid.

These measures included: the devaluation of the peso; import liberalisation to force local prices down; and 'stabilisation', that is to say cutting the endemic budget deficit that had led to printing money and therefore to inflation. As in other cases, the IMF recommended that the government balance its books more by reducing expenditure than by increasing revenue, with the rationale that tax rates had to be kept low to encourage compliance and reduce the burden on the most 'dynamic' sectors. However the Mexican government for political reasons baulked at the advice that subsidies (on water and electricity) were not targeted and therefore could be safely reduced and a more limited safety net put in place to support the very poorest sectors. Nor initially did they welcome the advice to embark on a far-reaching programme of privatisation, starting with the most obvious assets, the state airlines.

This package became the model for dealing with subsequent cases, in most of which, as in Mexico, governments found themselves able to comply with only part of the strict conditions laid upon them. However the anxiety of the world financial community was such that when this happened further adjustments were made and new packages agreed, though inevitably with further costs. Some 25 countries were in arrears a year later but through the cooperation of the debtor nations the creditors had already achieved 15 renegotiations. The process did not always go easily. The new civilian government in Argentina signed a deal with the IMF in 1984 but proved quite unable to meet its targets. In 1985 the incoming government of Alan García in Peru refused to pay more than 10 per cent of its export earnings. Brazil for a time suspended payment to force debt relief but did not get it. And, given the weakness of many Third World economies, it was often unrealistic to expect them to pay off their debts without help. So the debts continued to mount (see Table 4.2).

On the other hand, this case-by-case handling prevented the debtor countries cooperating with one another, still less, as the banks feared, forming a 'debtors' cartel' (Roett 1985). The fact is that debt empowers creditors, *not* debtors – unless they are very large debtors and act in concert (see Table 4.3). Individual debtor countries did call for debt relief, but did not combine to challenge creditors as they wanted to keep contacts with the world financial system in order to be able to arrange new loans. Most of all, they did not want to be pariah states denied all access to outside funds and so forced to borrow internally in their own currency. (The only country that has an advantage in this respect is the United States of America itself. From 1986 on net US debt was

Table 4.2 Debt as percentage of GNP, selected states, US$m 1992

RANGE	External debt	Debt as % GNP
LOW INCOME		
1 Mozambique	4,929	494.8
18 India	76,983	25.9
21 Nigeria	30,959	108.4
27 Ghana	4,275	39.1
28 China	69,321	12.8
32 Sri Lanka	6,401	41.0
37 Indonesia	84,385	61.9
LOWER MIDDLE INCOME		
43 Ivory Coast	17,997	191.0
44 Bolivia	4,243	61.2
68 Jamaica	4,303	131.7
75 Thailand	14,727	35.2
80 Turkey	54,772	47.8
85 Chile	19,360	48.9
UPPER MIDDLE INCOME		
80 S. Africa	–	–
92 Brazil	121,110	31.2
99 Mexico	113,378	34.1
100 Trinidad & Tobago	2,262	45.7
102 Argentina	67,569	30.3
107 Greece	–	–
108 Portugal	32,046	39.0
109 S. Arabia	–	–
HIGH INCOME		
110 Ireland		
112 Israel		
116 Australia		
117 UK		
124 France		
127 USA		
131 Japan		
132 Switzerland		

Source: World Bank (1994)

the largest in the world, but this debt was in its own currency, so overseas creditors did not have the same power to ensure that it could be repaid.)

Weaknesses in commodity markets coincided with the effects of tight monetarist policies in the industrialised countries and net resource flows were reversed. Africa South of the Sahara was most heavily indebted and hardest hit by interest rate rises. Most of the 26 most severely indebted nations were in that region. The G7 Toronto Protocol allowed rescheduling for these countries and the IMF had similar arrangements, but repayments were still massive in proportion to resources. To make matters worse, half of them were the

Table 4.3   Total identified external debt in excess of US$20b 1986, 1992

Country	1986	1992
Mexico	108.3	113.1
Brazil	106.3	121.1
South Korea	57.7	43.0
Argentina	49.9	67.6
Indonesia	37.2	84.4
Egypt	37.0	40.0
India	36.4	77.0
Venezuela	29.3	37.2
Israel	28.8	na
Philippines	28.6	32.5
Greece	24.9	na
Turkey	23.8	54.7
Chile	22.3	19.4
Portugal	21.6	32.0
Algeria	21.8	26.3
Malaysia	21.5	19.8

Source: World Bank, *World Debt Tables* (March 1987), and *World Development Report* (1994)

francophone countries hit by French withdrawal of financial support and consequent forced devaluations in January 1994.

The consequences were drastic. Africa may have lost as much as 30 years of development. For Latin America the 1980s were a 'lost decade'. Net transfers had been positive for Latin America (i.e. new funds borrowed exceeded debt repayments) until 1983, but the 1980s saw inflation without growth in most of the region. South Asia had borrowed heavily but repayments were more manageable in proportion to their growing economies. Some East Asian countries, on the other hand, enjoyed favourable balance of payments situations, and were largely unaffected by the crisis until the mid-1990s. The debts remain. In 1997 the external debt of countries with a per capita income of $1500 or less was $2 trillion or $400 per head (*New Internationalist*, 312, May 1999: 18). Servicing them continues to place an immense burden on many of the states of the Third World. In six of the eight years 1990–97 inclusive external debt payments (servicing and capital receipts) exceeded receipts from new loans. It is not surprising that the UN Conference on Trade and Development, NGOs and other groups sought to mark the new millennium with a debt moratorium for the most heavily indebted nations (see Table 4.4).

Debt has many adverse consequences. It contributes to the pulling apart of the Third World, focuses attention on big debtors to the exclusion of small ones (Costa Rica was unable to get rescheduling on its small debts and was summarily ordered to pay up or face the consequences), and results in a vast increase in poverty. Other factors acting against a satisfactory resolution of the debt problem as far as the Third World is concerned include the policies of TNCs, the growing cost effectiveness of labour-saving manufacturing

Table 4.4   World's most indebted states, US$ 1992

Country	Total external debt as % exports	Total external debt as % GNP
22 Nicaragua	3,161.7	750.3
1 Mozambique	994.5	494.8
12 Guinea Bissau	6,414.2	200.5
43 Ivory Coast	473.7	191.0
3 Tanzania	784.4	177.7
56 Congo	327.6	166.0
60 Jordan	203.1	163.2
31 Mauritania	342.4	158.4
4 Sierra Leone	574.0	158.3
68 Jamaica	148.9	131.7
66 Bulgaria	202.6	124.5
13 Madagascar	649.4	116.8
21 Nigeria	232.5	108.4

Source: World Bank (1994)

technology, the bias of the world trading system against primary products, protectionist measures by developed countries and the policies of the IMF and World Bank, through which creditor countries may intervene in debtor economies to ensure debts are serviced. The IMF's Heavily Indebted Poorer Countries (HIPCs) Initiative, begun in 1976, required the 40 countries identified as in need of debt relief to meet all the IMF's requirements for six years before any relief would be granted. Since 1996 the debts of HIPCs have increased and by 2000 only one of them had received relief.

The ultimate irony was that private banks boosted profits for several years in the mid-1980s and have already been repaid many times over, not least because the money loaned often returned to the lending banks on deposit from the Third World elites to whom it had been lent. Their lending was irresponsible, as borrowers were not necessarily elected by their people, but the money was loaned to a country with the assumed security that implied and much of the money was squandered or purloined by the borrowers.

As Susan George (1993) points out, it is also 'bad news' for all but a few people living in the creditor countries. The general population of the creditor countries gives tax relief to private banks on their bad debts and finances tax concessions when they write off debts. A further economic cost to the North is the unemployment consequent upon the loss of sales to Third World countries that cannot afford to buy as many First World products. There are social costs too, notably drugs, which are a major foreign exchange earner for heavily indebted countries. Not only does this have serious social consequences for the developed countries, but in financial terms it again hits the developed country taxpayer. George leaves us with the sobering thought that since 1982 the North has received the cheapest-ever raw materials from the South. Who then is the real debtor?

Bretton Woods

Rightly or wrongly, many attributed the failure of peace in the inter-war years to the defects of the world financial system. Hyperinflation in Germany, Austria and Hungary destroyed middle-class savings and made the victims eager recruits for fascism.

In 1944 the United Nations established what became known as the Bretton Woods System. The two key institutions of the new order were the IMF and the International Bank for Reconstruction and Development (IBRD – now commonly known as the World Bank). The timing of its creation reflected the perception that amongst the causes of the war was economic nationalism. Hence the free market principles that from the beginning underlay the work of the IMF.

Today even many free marketeers would argue that markets operate less efficiently in conditions of poverty and that theories of markets and movements to equilibrium are not entirely appropriate for application to the Third World. However in 1944 the majority of the present-day Third World states did not exist as sovereign entities and had to fit in later with a system not designed for their benefit. It was a system essentially designed to help the industrialised countries avoid the problems they had faced pre-war.

The main objectives of the Bretton Woods System therefore were: 1) to promote stable exchange rates, and 2) to encourage the growth of world trade and facilitate international movements of capital. As far as the developed countries were concerned, it has long been generally believed that it was successful. However this view has come under attack from Sir Alec Cairncross, who has written:

> The popular idea that Bretton Woods accounted for the prosperity of the post-war years has little substance. Throughout its first 10 years the International Monetary Fund did very little and the World Bank contributed only a small part of the total flow of capital into international investment. The international monetary system was managed, not by the IMF, as was envisaged at Bretton Woods, but by the United States. (Cairncross 1994)

The fact was that most of the so-called evils of the pre-war system – devaluations, inconvertible currencies, exchange controls, trade restrictions – proved very resilient and lingered throughout the classical period of the Bretton Woods System, which ended with the devaluation of the dollar in 1971.

The International Monetary Fund

The purpose of the IMF is to assist countries in maintaining stable exchange rates – it is not primarily intended to promote economic growth and in practice it often does not do so. It is particularly important to the very poorest countries in the same way that the World Bank extends most of its loans to those countries that do not receive commercial bank loans.

The IMF began with 29 members but by 2000 had 182. It is a mutual assistance society or club. The amount paid in by members is determined by a formula that broadly reflects their relative positions in the world economy. These quotas also determine the number of votes the country concerned can exercise and its maximum potential borrowing. The USA, UK, Germany, France and Japan together have 41 per cent of the votes. With the other two members, Italy and Canada, thrown in, G7 control over 50 per cent. Although the US quota is now down to 20 per cent this is enough (given the large sums that it pays in) to ensure that the US government always has considerable influence. It is the only country that commands enough votes to be able to veto the key decisions that require 85 per cent majorities.

The theory behind the IMF – and in particular its Compensatory Financial Facility (CFF), which was set up in 1963 to give support during foreign exchange crises – is that borrowing temporarily can help a government to resolve the problems of deficits, by giving it a breathing space in which to carry out adjustments to its economy. If this were the case it would be very convenient for Third World states, as it would enable them to make adjustments without surrendering their control over their economies.

Unfortunately in practice Third World relations with the IMF have not been happy ones. The IMF, rightly or wrongly, is not perceived as enhancing Third World security. Third World states see themselves as lacking influence within the IMF. At the same time the IMF is seen as imposing on them an economic orthodoxy that is against their interests and indeed violates their sovereignty through the conditions it attaches to loans ('conditionality'). In 1980 African states meeting at Arusha in Tanzania expressed their frustration and called in the Arusha Declaration for the creation of a new system.

The problem is that the ideology of the IMF favours orthodox economic explanations of the need for stabilisation. Those who work for the IMF think of it as being an organisation that is concerned only with the technicalities of maintaining that system. Consequently to borrow from the IMF countries have to take measures that will as far as possible free up world trade regardless of the consequences for themselves. They will be faced with the following specific requirements:

1. to reduce budget deficits through an immediate reduction in public expenditure
2. to eliminate all forms of price and wage control including the removal of subsidies on basic foodstuffs
3. to control the money supply
4. to devalue the currency in order to promote exports and reduce imports
5. to remove tariffs and quotas that protect infant Third World industries.

These requirements are collectively referred to as structural adjustment packages (SAPs).

The shared resources of the IMF are in theory available to all members with increasingly stringent conditions. The first and second tranches are available unconditionally but amount only to taking out again some of the membership fee paid in. For many Third World countries it is the subsequent loans which are paid out in hard currency, and therefore have to be repaid usually over a period of three to five years in the same form, that are the ones on which they have come to rely. The IMF sees its role as technical (relating to short-term, non-structural economic problems) and argues that where the effects of structural adjustment fall is an internal political decision. What it has only recently come to recognise, at least in part, is that its free market orientation is political too.

The austerity measures, which are an inevitable requirement of loans in excess of 50 per cent of quotas, are supposed to boost exports, reduce imports, (usually through devaluation) and lower government expenditure by constraining wages and welfare. Thus they tend to increase unemployment and to make the domestic working class pay for what is often a problem deriving from changes in world terms of trade. Such international fluctuations in any case hit the poorest sectors and disadvantaged groups hardest (see Chapter 12). Primary producers are more at the mercy of the international system than those who produce exportable manufactured goods, so countries that rely heavily on primary exports are most likely to get into balance of payments difficulties and therefore have to resort to IMF help. But at the same time they are the countries least likely to have the resources to be able to meet the welfare needs of their people.

Conditionality is part of the ideology of stabilisation. But the IMF resists rescheduling of debts for the same reason, that its system of loans is supposed to be short term and repayments need to be available to be reloaned elsewhere. Third World countries wanted IMF principles to stress Third World development specifically. However the USA and the UK argued this was the role of the World Bank, not the IMF, and hence development in all member states was given equal consideration. They were of course right that this was the original objective, but even for the World Bank the reconstruction of Europe and Japan came first. With the IMF in its present form short-term loans to rectify balance of payments problems and the equal treatment of unequal members simply combine to produce circumstances that favour industrialised nations.

The IMF will help fund debt purchase by Third World countries. However if those countries have already accepted SAPs and then defaulted their past default will give them little prospect of future loans. Worst of all, the IMF's position as banker of last resort means that if the IMF will not lend to them then no one else will either.

The effects of the debt crisis, in fact, were to lead to some enhancement of the role of the IMF. The first response was the development of special facilities requiring detailed programmes of reform. These were rejected by India and

China, and almost all the Africa SSA countries, where the drying up of funds resulted in increased harshness of conditions. There were riots at the proposed austerity measures in Bolivia, Brazil, Egypt, Venezuela and Zambia, and governments ousted partly for dealing with the IMF included those of both Ghana and Nigeria. On the other hand the failure to deal with the IMF or to meet its conditions were to lead to defaults by the governments of Liberia, Somalia, Peru, Sierra Leone and Zambia, amongst others.

The World Bank

The World Bank has since its foundation been seen as the main source of multilateral lending to countries for individual capital projects. Its initial mandate was to fund the revival of post-war European economies but its role was later extended to the developing countries. It established the International Development Association in 1960 to give 'soft' loans (loans on easy terms) to the poorest countries, and certainly since 1973 the World Bank has distinguished between relative and absolute forms of poverty at personal and national levels, has stressed investment in the poor, and funded projects concerned with small-scale production.

However in the same year that the then president of the World Bank, Robert McNamara, said 'it is clear that too much confidence was placed on the belief that rapid economic growth would automatically result in the reduction of poverty', the 1977 World Bank (IBRD) Report on Africa said that aid should only be given where subsidies were abandoned, even if this meant food riots.

The evident failure of the IMF to deal with the problems of Third World debt has led the World Bank, too, to offer SAPs to specified countries. One of their attractions originally was that there was no cross-conditionality, for example, a World Bank loan to Argentina has been unsuccessfully opposed by the IMF. But during the 1980s an informal or tacit 'cross-conditionality' became increasingly evident.

GATT and WTO

The General Agreement on Tariffs and Trade (GATT) was never intended to be permanent. It was an interim measure proposed by the advanced industrialised countries in 1947 at the First (Geneva) Round of trade talks, to fill the gap left in the Bretton Woods System when the US Congress refused to ratify the Havana Charter. The original idea had been to establish an international trade organisation, with the goal ultimately of securing universal free trade. However owing to the onset of the cold war the USA finally abandoned the idea in 1950. GATT remained, extending its scope through a series of Rounds. These took longer and longer to complete, and it was only after five years of negotiating at the Eighth Round, which began in Punta del Este, Uruguay, in 1986, that a Draft Act was agreed, and three more years before it was signed (15 April 1994). Hence it was not until 1 January 1995 that the World Trade Organization (WTO) finally came into existence, and then without agreement between the 81 (now 134) member states on a secretary-general.

GATT was not designed to deal with Third World countries' problems. For example, balance of payments disequilibria are to be dealt with by pressure to adjust on the countries that are in deficit, not those that are in surplus. The outcome of such adjustments would appear to favour the countries of the North and their transnational corporations. Where they have not liked GATT principles the developed countries have simply established trade barriers against them. Such groups as textile manufacturers, industrialists and farmers are well organised and powerful in the developed countries. Whatever they profess to believe, they resist trade liberalisation that could favour less-developed countries.

GATT was and WTO is based on three assumptions, that:

1. Trading results in higher living standards.
2. Free markets as the basis of international trade promote the greatest benefits.
3. The distribution of such benefits is of secondary importance. It is a technical issue and is for the market to decide rather than for political solution.

Pessimists have taken the view that, on the contrary, there can only be limited growth in world demand for primary products, that LDCs therefore have inherent balance of payments problems because imports are more elastic than exports, and hence that their fragile economies need protection in a way that stronger ones do not. Optimists reply that the less developed countries have comparative advantage in cheap labour and thus low unit costs. They will benefit from the opening up of their economies to world trade as this will result in diversification, which in turn will protect them from reliance on primary products and food crops that can fail.

Overall the optimists got their way in the most recent GATT negotiations. This was to be expected as it responded in large measure to growing protectionism and bloc building in the developed world. The Uruguay Round liberalises and dismantles barriers but the Third World loses protection. GATT Rounds of the 1950s and 1960s opened up new markets and thus facilitated the growth of transnational corporations to the advantage of the developed nations on whose territory these companies are located (and taxed), but some semblance of balance was maintained. GATT rules allowed LDCs to use quotas to defend themselves against balance of payments problems. Under the Seventh (Tokyo) Round (1979) and earlier Round rules, the industrialised countries were not permitted to subsidise manufactured goods or minerals, though limited subsidies to agricultural products remained. Less developed countries were allowed to continue to use export subsidies in the short term but with the rather open-ended proviso that these must not do any damage to any other signatory. Some LDCs approaching the Uruguay Round thought that industrialised countries should deliver on agreements from previous Rounds before embarking on more negotiations.

This Eighth (Uruguay) Round began with background negotiations in 1982. Though it formally assembled for full negotiations in Uruguay it then moved to Geneva, where the bulk of the debate took place. It was eventually concluded at the end of 1993. Altogether 117 countries were involved in the negotiations but, as this number shows, many LDCs were not then members. Others had only very recently joined, such as Mexico, which had joined the organisation in 1986 after years of declaring the intention of determining its own trade policy. This Round brought new areas under international jurisdiction: agriculture, services (such as telecommunications, banking and transport through the General Agreement on Trade in Services – GATS), intellectual property rights (TRIPS) and investment measures (TRIMS) being the most important.

The OECD estimated that the conclusion of the Uruguay Round would add $270 billion to world output by 2002. However this is equivalent to an increase in global GDP of only $40 per capita. Moreover it is clear that the benefits, such as they are, will not be evenly distributed. Some two-thirds will accrue to the developed world, and especially to the European Union (EU). The effects on the Third World will broadly be:

- South America gains $8 billion, of which Brazil alone will gain $3.4 billion.
- India gains $4.6 billion, as much as the whole of South America less Brazil.
- The Asian Tigers gain $7.1 billion between them.
- Africa will lose some $2.6 billion, with Nigeria bearing the brunt of the loss to the tune of $1 billion.

This astonishing negative impact the new WTO regime is expected to have on Africa is due to the loss of trade preferences in the European market and in particular the consequences of the dismantling of the Lomé Convention. Africa SSA in particular simply does not have any alternative products with which it can take advantage of the liberalisation in world trade. In summary, GATT will contribute to the 'drawing apart' of the Third World as one-third of benefits expected to go to the Third World will go to the wealthier parts of it and to China. See Plate 4.

Pessimists argue that the Uruguay Round deal did not address the problems of debt and low commodity prices, that it serves the interests only of some sections of the industrialised countries and more particularly of transnational corporations. Deregulation of trade is seen as enhancing the power of international capital and giving active encouragement to the global search for cheaper labour. Thus pessimists expect negative impacts on the standard and quality of life in the Third World and for poorer sections of the First World. The environment is also threatened as investment and jobs move to areas offering the lowest production costs. Low costs often reflect the lack of environmental protection legislation in such areas with serious consequences for especially fragile ecosystems. Not surprisingly proposals to start a new Round in Seattle met with such concentrated hostility from demonstrators that the meeting had to be abandoned.

In addition, LDCs must now deregulate, and this means removing restraints on transnational corporations such as the existing limits imposed on profit repatriation. Services that constitute some 20 per cent of world trade – including transport, tourism and construction – are brought under the ambit of WTO for the first time. This is thought to present another problem for the Third World, in that it undermines the indigenous development of services without advantaging those less developed countries that do not export services. As regards financial services, LDCs that are members of WTO must now open their markets up to US banks and insurance companies. The predictable consequence is that nascent financial services sectors in these countries will be destroyed as they face unconstrained competition from northern transnational corporations such as American Express. A third consequence is that they must implement patent protection laws that will hit indigenous industries and in particular make the production of vital drugs in a generic form problematic. They will have to pay royalties on such developmental necessities as seeds and technology. Non-compliance will mean retaliatory action under the rules of the World Trade Organization, for the new trade body has the power (which did not exist at before) to police and regulate international trade in the same way that the IMF regulates international borrowing.

Optimists argue that the South will get much more in return. They claim that northern markets will be opened up to LDCs and that more investment will flow South. They also take the view that the alternative was far worse. To save their advantages the northern states could have imposed high tariffs and other protectionist measures that would have hit the Third World particularly hard. See Plate 5.

Case study

Bananas

Small producers on their family-run farms in the Windward Islands, Jamaica and Belize could not compete without some form of protection. They could not produce bananas as cheaply as the low-paid workers on the plantations of Central and South America. In fact 'dollar bananas' cost only half as much to produce, and one Central America plantation can grow as many bananas as 20,000 growers in the Caribbean island states. The problem is an historical one. Although the islands were not very suitable for banana cultivation Britain encouraged the growing of bananas in its Caribbean dependencies because it wanted guaranteed prices in the financially problematic post-war years and the islands' sugar production was in decline. There is little scope for diversification in the islands. Tourism is growing but some form of agricultural production is vital, and whatever is grown will cost more to produce than elsewhere (see also Grugel 1995).

Bananas and other soft fruit depend for almost all their very high value in the shops on the measures that have been taken to get them there. In other words the economic value of a product such as a banana comes almost entirely from the situation of the producing country within the world market, and this means the ability of large transnational corporations that control the infrastructure within which bananas are marketed.

The producers of so-called dollar bananas, especially the three big US transnational corporations, Del Monte, Chiquita and Dole, want to increase their sales to Europe, where they already have 60 per cent of the market. The TNCs established themselves throughout Central America by the 1920s. Refrigeration gave them the technology they needed and they soon had turnovers bigger than the countries in which they were operating. They were notorious for their interference in local politics. The involvement of the banana companies in local politics has many unsavoury aspects, ranging from unsecured personal 'loans' to dictators (such as the $1 million paid to Jorge Ubico in Guatemala to get a reduction in corporation taxes) to the fact that in all countries they held much land idle to prevent competition developing while they paid minimal taxes and export duties.

Honduras is the archetypical 'banana republic'. The United Fruit Company (UFCo), now Chiquita, cynically exploited the unlimited access its weak government allowed. The banana plantations form a vast enclave in the north-east of the country, on the shore of the Caribbean and well away from the centres of Honduras's small population. There whole towns were built by UFCo, linked to each other and to the company ports by company-owned railways. Both workers and other local inhabitants use company stores, hospitals and schools.

By contrast Costa Rica, the second largest banana producer in the Caribbean, has avoided becoming a banana republic and is a democratic and politically sophisticated country. However its prospects now confront the interests of its banana growers. Ecotourism is very important to Costa Rica, but the country has recently doubled the acreage given over to bananas. A chemical-free banana production system is possible, but agribusiness 'needs' take precedence over the environment. Conservation groups are very concerned. Pesticides seep into drainage systems and are threatening Costa Rica's national parks. The coral reef is dying. In addition, Costa Rica has the highest rate of deforestation in Latin America (*Assignment*, 'Banana Wars', BBC Television, 1993).

However the new World Trade Organization had hardly been established when agitation began for the US government to use it to end the preferential treatment of bananas sold by the Caribbean island states in the EU. This was resisted fiercely by the leaders of the smaller island states, and in a meeting in Washington on 13 September 1995 the prime minister of Jamaica, Percival J. Patterson, sought and received assurances that the US government would not pursue its case against the EU.

Despite this, on 28 September 1995, the US government went ahead and filed a complaint against the EU's banana regime on behalf of Chiquita Brands. It claimed that the Lomé system favoured imports from African, Caribbean and Pacific states over those from Central America and that in consequence Central American exports had suffered. Shortly afterwards, on 6 October, the European Commission decided to permit the importation of an additional 98,800 tonnes of bananas from Latin America on the grounds that hurricane Luis between 5 and 7 September had damaged crops in the Leeward Islands and so reduced supplies. The WTO ruled in favour of the United States of America and the EU modified the banana regime to comply with the ruling. However on 7 April 1999 a WTO arbitration panel held that the EU's banana import policy, which had come into effect on 1 January, still failed to comply with earlier WTO judgements, and authorised the imposition on EU countries of unilateral US sanctions. With the banana dispute still unresolved efforts continued in Belize to expand citrus production, and shrimp farming was developing rapidly, but the situation on the islands of Dominica and St Lucia looked bleak.

Conclusion

In economic terms what Third World countries have in common is a tendency to be exploitable and thus exploited, though the extent to which this actually happens varies a great deal. Interpretations of why this is and how it might be changed have dominated theories of development. The changing position of the NICs and the extent (and impact) of Third World indebtedness remain key issues in the current debates about the economic prospects for Third World nations.

CHAPTER 5

The social context

Introduction

The impact of the process of, first, colonisation and, then, development on Third World social structures may vary a great deal in form, but will always be a key to understanding those societies.

At its most basic level this impact affects the most fundamental of social factors, the size of the population. The act of colonisation often meant a sudden catastrophic population fall as new infectious diseases were introduced. This was conspicuously the case in Spanish America and has continued to be a problem until recently in very isolated communities with only sporadic contacts with the outside world, notably Easter Island. In modern society the introduction of public health measures such as clean water and sanitation has meant rapid population increase as fertility remains relatively high and mortality falls sharply. Goldthorpe (1975: 23) notes however that there have been considerable differences between actual societies.

Impact of development on disadvantaged groups

Development, suggesting as it does social aspects such as increasing welfare provision and decreased inequality, should be expected to have a particular and positive impact on groups such as children, the aged and indigenous peoples.

Development should lead to increased possibilities of education and the opening up of a greater variety of life chances. However there are problems. In the first phase of development rapid population growth means a greatly increased burden on the financial resources available for education, particularly in rural areas, and the urban–rural divide in provision widens. There can

Table 5.1   Literacy rates below 50%, 1995

Country	Both Sexes	Male	Female
Niger	14	21	3
Burkina Faso	19	29	4
Nepal	28	41	14
Sierra Leone	31	45	9
Mali	31	39	9
Afghanistan	32	47	15
Senegal	33	43	12
Burundi	35	49	12
Ethiopia	35	46	14
Guinea	36	50	11
Benin	37	49	10
Bangladesh	38	49	26
Liberia	38	54	11
Mauritania	38	50	19
Pakistan	38	50	24
Gambia	39	53	12
Ivory Coast	40	50	14
Mozambique	40	58	12
Bhutan	42	56	28
Haiti	45	48	42
Djibouti	46	60	18
Sudan	46	58	17
Chad	48	62	19

Source: UNESCO (2000), http://unescostat.unesco.org

be considerable resentment in rural communities at state educational provision being directed towards the concerns of the town and thus remote from the needs and interests of the rural sector.

Inequalities between the rich minority and the poor majority are of course much more marked. Only 11 per cent of global educational spending goes on the 75 per cent of the world's children who live in developing countries; 23 per cent of them do not attend school at all, compared to less than 1 per cent in the developed world. But, as ever, there are glaring disparities within the Third World, resulting in the most massive wastage of talent where it is most needed, in the very poorest countries. In Africa SSA 47 per cent of children do not attend school, that is 35 per cent of the world's 125 million out-of-school population. This latter percentage is expected to exceed 75 per cent by 2015.

Lack of education is 'bad news' for individuals, their families and their societies. At the individual level most of the countries of Africa SSA and several elsewhere in the Third World have literacy rates below 50 per cent (see Table 5.1). This denies them access to social, economic and political power. The empowering quality of education is illustrated by the fact that women with secondary education in Bangladesh are three times more likely to take collective political action than those without it. At the family level, lack of education is associated with poverty. In countries as far apart as Peru and Vietnam, for example, two-thirds of families living in extreme poverty are headed by an adult with no education. At the societal level, it is estimated that raising the average time in school by only one year adds 23 per cent growth to the GDP of developing countries.

In 1990 the world's governments promised 'education for all' by the year 2000. It would have cost some $6 billion to put every child in the world in school, less than 1 per cent of global military spending. Worse still, the continuing repatriation of debt service charges has in some cases hit domestic resources otherwise available for the provision of services such as education. In Tanzania in 1997–98, for example, debt repayments were four times the investment in primary education (*Guardian Education*, 11 April 2000).

Development also presents different opportunities to those who might in First World countries be in secondary or tertiary education. Integration into the world culture of film and television has presented Third World societies with an almost unattainable image of the good life, as lived in penthouse apartments in Los Angeles or New York. Young people are likely to feel most keenly the disparity between their ideal and their actual circumstances. This and the pressure of population drives youngsters to seek work in the town, joining the tide of migration.

For the aged, development also offers the possibility of better medical care; access to wider horizons through public transport, radio and television; and some labour-saving devices. Migration to towns and splitting up of families however either takes the elderly away from their village community where their skills are of use or leaves the elderly a charge on rural relatives who by definition are less likely to be able to carry the burden.

Indigenous peoples are most vulnerable to the impact of development, not least because many governments intent on rapid development see their traditional lifestyles as a drag on progress and modernity.

Ethnic cleavages

All societies are stratified, though in the most homogenous societies divisions remain those of gender and age sets, membership of the latter often being determined by the particular batch of initiates into adulthood with which a young man or woman shared the appropriate tribal rituals. Stratification implies a horizontal division, which is registered in the power structure in the form of superordination vs. subordination. However one can differentiate between *horizontal* and *vertical* systems of stratification. In the former other characteristics are spread across each band in a way that cuts across the main axis of stratification; in the latter they tend to form the basis of stratification (Horowitz 1971). These are ideal types – in practice several different criteria usually work together. Hence we must also differentiate between *rigid* and *flexible* systems of stratification.

Ethnic differences are usually thought of as being obvious and clear cut. However this is not always the case: where physical differences are not evident they may well be expressed in terms of religion, language or shared common culture. Most areas subject to colonisation were in fact already inhabited. Hence from first encounter there arose a sense of ethnic differences. The annexation of land created new class structures. Local inhabitants were used to work the land, and where they were insufficient or failed to survive the rigours of forced labour new workers were brought in. Slavery made a deep impact both in Africa and after 1517 in the Americas, but a century after emancipation both in Brazil and Cuba the experience has become historical and old divisions have had time to be eroded. It is worth remembering that slavery was not formally abolished in Mauritania until 1980, and that involuntary servitude in various forms is still prevalent in the Middle East and is believed to have been on the increase throughout the 1990s.

Wherever ethnic differences are conspicuous the tensions generated by them remain socially significant and where they are of more recent origin conflict can be considerable. In a number of territories once part of the British Empire such tensions have been generated by the importation of Indian contract labourers, whose descendants today constitute a significant minority. In 1968 the government of Kenya deported the Asian minority who had contributed a disproportionate share to the government and entrepreneurial skills of the country. In 1972 President Idi Amin of Uganda did the same, attracting much international criticism. Their absence has had such negative economic effects that by the end of the 1990s their return was being actively sought.

Fijians today still share their island with the descendants of Indian indentured labourers, a minority that is almost as big as the majority. But they do so on their own terms since they bitterly resent pressure for equal access to power. When an Indian-backed party won political power it was excluded by force and Fiji withdrew from the Commonwealth rather than accept the right of the descendants of immigrants to take power.

In Guyana the descendants of Indian labourers form about 50 per cent of the population. Those of African descent account for a further 30 per cent and the division between these groups is the major social cleavage. Since 1957 the country's first ruling party, the People's Progressive Party (PPP) has been dominated by the Indo-Guyanese. But serious communal violence in 1963–64 led to the adoption of the proportional representation system that had the effect of transferring power to non-Indians in the form of the People's National Congress (PNC), led first by Forbes Burnham and subsequently by Desmond Hoyte. When Hoyte lost the presidential election of 1997 the PNC continued to exploit racial feelings among the one-third of the country's population of Afro-Guyanese origin and to do everything they could to reverse the verdict of the electorate. It took a great deal of pressure from the United States of America and other neighbouring states to get Hoyte to accept even a restricted term for his elected successor, President Janet Jagan, who was forced to resign in 1999 because of illness.

The existence of a substantial minority however does not of itself mean that they will be politically, as opposed to socially, significant, and not all importations of indentured labour have led to conflict. One such exception is the island state of Mauritius. In Sri Lanka the so-called 'Indian Tamils' form an encapsulated society in the tea-growing central highlands and remain largely apart from the struggle between a Tamil separatist movement, the Liberation Tigers of Tamil Eelam (LTTE), and the Sinhalese-majority government. The Tamil Tigers, as they are generally known, represent the aspirations of elements among the so-called 'Sri Lankan Tamils', who have lived in the Jaffna Peninsula and in other parts of the north and east of the island at least since the eleventh century.

Similar hostilities have been directed at the Chinese minority, descendants of traders and settlers, who can be found throughout South-east Asia, notably in Myanmar, Indonesia and the Philippines, and against the Vietnamese in Thailand. In the former British colony of Singapore, founded in 1824, they form a majority. Tension between this Chinese majority in Singapore and the Malay ruling establishment of Malaysia led to Singapore's peaceful secession from the federation.

Most Third World countries contain significant ethnic minorities of indigenous origin. In some countries, e.g. Burma (Myanmar), they are so numerous as seriously to call into question the central government's ability to control outlying areas. In others, ethnic differences have been fanned by populist leaders and the result has been large-scale social conflict and open civil war. Examples in Africa have included Burundi (1966–72 and 1994), Chad (1966–84), Nigeria (1967–70), Angola (1975–84) and Rwanda (1993–). In yet others, such as Laos and Vietnam, ethnic differences have been targeted by external powers as a way of influencing national politics.

Class and state

The colonial state maintained the structure of class dominance/subordination. Significantly, pre-revolutionary Ethiopia, which was not effectively colonised, retained the indigenous semi-feudal structure, which elsewhere had to a greater or lesser degree been modified by the colonial experience. However it is important not to see the concept of class in the Third World through the prism of Marxist concepts, which were based on Europe at a particular stage of historical development. Class structures are endogenous – they arise from the particular nature and circumstances of the country concerned. And in Third World states they remain largely traditional, with the impact of industrialisation, etc. being in the main accommodated to existing patterns of dominance and

subordination. Thus in post-colonial Senegal politics continued to be dominated by noble and freeborn families, while the descendants of slaves continued
to be effectively excluded from power (Crowder 1967: 110). Though in India
the former ruling families have been deprived of their traditional powers, both
there and in Pakistan and Bangladesh (to say nothing of Sri Lanka) they have
used their social standing to pursue the democratic route to power as a very
successful alternative.

There are instances where the colonial experience exacerbated and distorted traditional relationships in a way that would prove disastrous later. The
Rwandan case (discussed in Chapter 2: 23) illustrates this. The Belgian colonial administration played on ethnic rivalries in asserting its political control,
making the Tutsi dynastic aristocracy the tax collectors and administrators of
justice. The obvious tensions in such a situation were exacerbated by demo-
graphic pressures. They exploded in the most brutal fashion following the
collapse of the coffee market in 1993, reliance on which was the legacy of the
colonial export economy, and the subsequent macroeconomic return required
by the IMF (Chossudovsky 1994).

The impact of settlement varied a great deal and it is difficult to generalise
about it. Countries where settlement supplanted almost all traces of the indigenous populations include Argentina and Uruguay as well as First World
countries such as Australia, Canada and the USA. Countries where settlement
incorporated substantial indigenous populations without exterminating them
but at the cost of indigenous cultural traits include Mexico, Peru and South
Africa from the Third World, and New Zealand from the First.

Invariably where there was substantial settlement the settlers displaced the
ruling class and established cultural hegemony. However there was most often
some form of alliance between settlers and the colonial authorities, not a simple forced identity of views. Settlers would come to resent colonial dominance,
and in time they would seek independence, as in the USA, most of Latin
America, South Africa and Zimbabwe (then Southern Rhodesia). The most
important legacy has been the plantation economy. There are essential differences between the farm and the plantation as a basis of economic organisation,
and this is reflected in the social structures that accompany each. Where the
plantation has predominated there has been a strong tendency to horizontal
stratification of ethnic groups.

The post-colonial state has often adjusted incompletely. In Kenya and
Zimbabwe the settlers and/or their naturalised descendants kept their lands
and adjusted to the new post-colonial order; in South Africa, so far, the intention seems to be to take the same course. In Sri Lanka tea plantations were
nationalised and the planters allowed to repatriate only part of their compensation; in Indonesia summary nationalisation took place, but was followed
by extensive corruption (Myrdal 1968). In West Africa plantations were cor-
porately owned and there were few settlers. Only in northern Nigeria and
Senegal did traditional rulers retain their powers, in both cases because the
colonial powers did not seek to control the production of peanuts, and in the

case of Senegal the right of eminent domain was abolished in 1964 (O'Brien 1971: 201–2, see also O'Brien 1978). Traditional rulers retained their powers in Lesotho (formerly Bechuanaland) and Swaziland, and in South Africa under apartheid in the case of the Zulu and Xhosa some limited autonomy within the homeland system as the notional 'states' of KwaZulu and Ciskei (Suzman 1993).

The oligarchy

In place of settlers, in Africa, as earlier in Latin America, there has arisen an indigenous oligarchy. However in Africa only in the case of the Ivory Coast has a local oligarchy emerged that is based on landholding. Elsewhere the new basis for power has been *political office*, which gives access to valuable economic returns. In Asia, where settlers were few and indigenous societies complex, no single oligarchy has emerged: though the dynastic basis of power is often very clear different elites control the basis of economic wealth.

In Africa the alliance between state functionaries and the propertied classes has taken different forms in different countries. Dr Jomo Kenyatta established himself as a chief of chiefs and made fellow Africans socially dominant within independent Kenya, allowing free rein (on conditions) to private entrepreneurs. In neighbouring Tanzania Dr Julius Nyerere established a system in which state enterprise was dominant. Dr Kwame Nkrumah failed to do the same in Ghana and ultimately was unable to retain his power. In Uganda the government of Milton Obote drove out the Kabaka of Buganda, burnt his palace and suspended the Lukiko (traditional assembly), only to be displaced in turn by a military coup led by Idi Amin. In the 1990s the powers of the traditional rulers were partly restored.

The oligarchy has preponderant economic power, generally enhanced by its alliance with key foreign interests. It is the dominant patron–client network, to which all subordinate patron–client networks are attached. Ethnic cleavages, if they exist, are only one amongst a number of ways in which society can be stratified in the interests of maintaining dominance. Wealth can give access to the highest levels in most societies, enabling its holders to exercise influence if not power. Religion and education form alternative axes of stratification. Ethnic allegiances can cut across class differentiation by wealth or power. Hence in Nigeria no single ruling class emerged. Power passed into the hands of the armed forces, whose representatives have continued, despite lip-service to the ideals of democracy, to retain as tight a control over the country as they can.

In Latin America the term 'oligarchy' has strong emotive meaning as a key term in the populist/leftist critique of the landowning elite. Nevertheless the term fits very well the situation that was general in Latin America until the twentieth century, and which continues to some extent in Peru or Colombia. Landowners remain an important element in this section of Latin American society, an element which is so wealthy that it remains undisturbed by domestic economic dislocation and/or political unrest (see Peasantry below).

The bureaucracy

The higher ranks of the civil service form a key part of this elite. They are very well paid compared with both lower civil servants and the general run of the population, especially when other privileges are taken into account. In Nigeria, indeed, a new upper stratum of top civil servants, the 'Perm Secs' (Permanent Secretaries), emerged as a key part of the ruling elite. In Africa generally university teachers and doctors are also very highly regarded and though their advantages have declined with time they can still be regarded as members of the upper class rather than of an intermediate middle class, with the small size of the elite giving them incomes in the top 1 per cent of the population. The importance of a university degree itself has declined with time but is still disproportionate. In an extreme case, the former Belgian Congo, later Zaire, there were only a handful of graduates at independence in a population of over 13 million, and no strong landowning elite to form the core of an indigenous ruling class. In the 1990s South Africa suffered from the consequences of the apartheid system, which by the Extension of University Education Act (1959) deliberately condemned black South Africans to a separate and second-class university education so that they would not challenge white dominance (Sampson 1999: 100).

But in Ghana, as in many other African states, a significant number of senior civil servants who had served the colonial government continued to work for the Nkrumah regime and, on his fall, were retained by the successor governments for precisely the same reason: their specialised knowledge. In addition to senior civil servants a considerable number of expatriate advisers and technicians continued to hold important positions in the former British colonies well after independence; in 1966, for example, 4668 expatriates still worked in the civil service in Zambia. In the former French colonies French *assistants techniques* continued to manage key branches of the economy, justice, interior, agriculture, transport and public works and public health ministries, to say nothing of defence and internal security (Bretton 1973: 189).

Inevitably there are close links between the government of the day and the entrepreneurial or business class. As Bretton emphasises, the economies of African states are so fragile that the public sector elite, both politicians and civil servants, cannot exist independently of their outside earnings:

> For a few among the higher echelons, the payoff from rule or from public office below the level of rule may be satisfaction of lust for power; for the majority, the payoff is personal wealth and economic security or both. Satisfaction of lust for power without substantial material benefit accruing to the powerful is an improbability in the real world. (Bretton 1973: 176)

The National Reformation Council (NRC) report in 1968 on the assets of former government ministers in Sierra Leone is one of a number of such documents produced by successor regimes in Africa that give chapter and verse (Sierra Leone NRC 1968). Such problems continue and under the National Provisional Ruling Council (NPRC) government led by Captain Valentine Strasser considerable publicity has been given to the results of investigations into the financial affairs of high-ranking civil servants and other functionaries who had served under the Momoh regime. *West Africa* (27 September–3 October 1993) reported that the Justice Laura Marcus-Jones Commission of Inquiry had found that the former president himself had acquired 'a sizeable collection of real property' and 'was in control of pecuniary resources and property disproportionate to his past official emoluments'. The NPRC therefore ordered these to be forfeit to the state.

In Latin America public functionaries enjoy considerable prestige and the senior ones are very well paid indeed.

Entrepreneurial/business class

At independence many (though clearly not all) of the colonial civil servants went home. Their business and financial counterparts stayed on, and their role became more important. At the same time, with varying degrees of success, a new indigenous business class began to emerge. The new entrepreneurs, however, are often incomers. In South-east Asia it is the Chinese who perform the role of entrepreneurs, also Indians in the case of Malaysia and Singapore. The emergence of a new Malay business elite has been the objective of the Malaysian government's *bumiputra* policy – a policy of favouritism to the 'native people' or indigenous population, which has proved successful.

In Africa, other than in Zanzibar where they formed the ruling elite, Arabs formed a similar entrepreneurial group, linking Africa North and South of the Sahara. In keeping with this tradition in West Africa a new group has emerged, the Lebanese, to perform the role of traders and entrepreneurs and to be presented as scapegoats for economic failure. In Ghana business partnerships outside the tribe have often tended to founder on mutual suspicions that the other partner was secretly salting away part of the proceeds. There too Lebanese and Indian entrepreneurs have come virtually to monopolise medium-scale trade. In Kenya and Uganda the dominance of trade by Indian immigrants was so much resented that they were summarily expelled by post-independence governments. Friction between traders and government has, however, been commonplace in African states, though until recently it has not taken a markedly ideological form.

In Latin America the traditional structure of a family-owned conglomerate is slowly yielding to a new business elite, among whom recent immigrants, including Italians in Argentina, Germans in Brazil, Japanese in Peru and Lebanese in Ecuador, are prominent. The inability until recently to engage in almost any kind of trade without a multiplicity of forms and permissions has, as ever, ensured that close links with government were essential and has afforded a fertile field for corruption.

Peasantry

In 1970 the majority of inhabitants of the new states were still peasants. The attention of the world at the time was grabbed by occasional insurrection and civil warfare and many in the industrialised world came to regard the peasantry as a revolutionary force (e.g. Wolf 1969, cf. Scutz and O'Slater 1990, Kamrava 1992, Colburn 1994). However, as Marx recognised, the main characteristic of peasants as a class is their extreme conservatism. This is understandable when it is remembered that, living on the margin of subsistence, their entire being is taken up by the need to earn a living (Scott 1976, Bernstein et al. 1992). Foster (1976) calls the cultural expression of this the model of limited good. Peasants, he says, see their environment as a closed system, with insufficient resources. They are aware that there are more resources outside their immediate environment, but they do not see these as being normally available to them.

> To guard against being a loser, peasants in traditional communities have developed an egalitarian, shared-poverty, equilibrium, status-quo style of life, in which by means of overt behavior and symbolic action people are discouraged from attempting major change in their economic and other statuses. (Foster 1976: 35–6)

It is in Latin America that there is the longest tradition of study of the peasantry in Third World states. The most celebrated example is that of the Cornell Peru Project, which was organised in 1951 at Hacienda Vicos, Department of Ancash. The purpose was to engineer rapid social change among indigenous inhabitants by altering the local power structure. Based on the social theories of Harold D. Lasswell and colleagues (Lasswell and Kaplan 1950, Lasswell and Holmberg 1966) it sought to create change through 'participant intervention'. A forerunner of modern efforts to bring about the social empowerment of deprived groups, the project replaced external supervision of work by outside employees with that of indigenous leaders, abolished free services (labour tax) in favour of paid labour, invested the returns from peasant labour in improved agricultural practices, encouraged the setting up of a body of elected leaders to plan further changes, and initiated weekly meetings of the whole labour force to review progress (Holmberg in Dobyns et al. 1971). It is therefore not only one of the most striking examples of the use of the experimental method in social sciences other than psychology, but a pathfinder for 1990s' notions of *empowerment* (see Chapter 8).

The major characteristic of Peruvian peasants was powerlessness. This was not only a characteristic of the group but, because of their position at the bottom of the Peruvian social hierarchy, a determining characteristic of Peruvian society as a whole, where they constituted over 50 per cent of the population. Hence changes on the local and national levels (and indeed on the international level) were interlinked. 'The Vicosinos were not only part of the national society in 1951, they were in their condition essential to it – a necessary subordinated complement to the dominant oligarchy' (Dobyns et al. 1971: 17).

The Vicos peasants wanted one thing above all: land reform. Conservatives blocked local expropriation of land as well as national plans to take over lands of the Cerro de Pasco Corporation, but the elected government of Manuel Prado Ugarteche (1956–61) approved direct sale before being overthrown by a military coup. The Vicos project led to emulation by peasant movements elsewhere in the country, and the government of Fernando Belaúnde Terry (1963–68), under pressure from peasant occupations of land, was able to secure passage of agrarian reform legislation, which however was not implemented. The military government of General Juan Velasco Alvarado (1968–75) however instituted 'Peasant Day' on 24 June 1969 and subsequently expropriated the large coastal estates from which the former oligarchy drew much of their wealth.

In Peru, as elsewhere in Latin America, however, lineages remain strong. Old families have found new outlets for their wealth and have successfully incorporated newcomers. Whether in Mexico, Costa Rica or Colombia, a striking proportion of those holding political power will be descended from or incorporated by marriage into one or other of the ancient lineages, which at the same time show a pronounced tendency to marry amongst themselves. Meanwhile, in the 1980s, in opposition to the intransigence of the old families, many Peruvian peasants took to various forms of action on their own behalf. The Marxist rural insurgent movement *Sendero Luminoso* (Shining Path) sought to capitalise on this unrest, but resorted to coercion when they found that only a minority of peasants were willing to take up arms and subject themselves to outsiders (Palmer 1992, Poole and Rénique 1991, 1992, Taylor 1987, 1998). In Ecuador in January 2000, however, peasant demonstrations in Quito forced the army to topple the government of Jamil Mahuad Witt after it had conspicuously failed to tackle the country's serious economic crisis (*Sunday Telegraph*, 23 January 2000).

In Africa, on the other hand, a striking consequence of the fluidity of the class structure is that many members of the upper and middle classes come from peasant families or themselves started life as peasants (Andreski 1968: 168). The peasantry remain the largest single class in many countries but the African peasantry has been passive on the whole. Since independence peasant organisations have been generally weak. Only in the Portuguese African territories (and, perhaps, in the disputable case of the MauMau in Kenya) did peasants play a major role in movements of national liberation, and then under the leadership of middle-class intellectuals such as Holden Roberto and Eduardo Mondlane. Though Nelson Mandela correctly described himself as 'a country boy' he came from a chiefly family and received a chief's education (Sampson 1999).

Various factors appear to account for the relative powerlessness of the African peasantry. Given strong tribal and kinship ties, it has been difficult for a sense of class identity to develop, and the absence of a traditional landowning elite means that there is no easy focus for their hostility. Africa is relatively sparsely populated compared to other parts of the Third World, hence the struggle for land has not reached the degree of intensity that it has in say Guatemala or Peru. Linguistic divisions and low levels of literacy are also cited as reasons why peasant organisation in Africa has failed to develop. Such divisions make it relatively easy for the elite to divide and rule, by buying off incipient leaders.

Lacking organisation, peasants have tended to resist impositions upon them either by passive resistance or in rare instances by a form of *jacquerie* – a spontaneous, localised revolt against intolerable conditions. Maladministration and tax increases led to such a revolt in Chad in 1965 (Decalo 1980) and similar causes could be seen to lie at the root of the unrest in Kenya in 1998 ('Moi-butu must go!') or Zimbabwe in 2000. Occasionally such revolts have been more organised, but they have similarly been directed towards and focused on local grievances. Peasant revolt has been a repeated feature of life in Congo/Zaire since the outbreak in Kwilu province in 1964. Other African examples range from the Agbekoya rebellion in Nigeria in 1968 (Beer and Williams 1975) to the war between the Sudanese People's Liberation Army (SPLA) and the government in southern Sudan or the so-called 'Ninja militias' in Congo-Brazzaville (*Annual Register 1998*).

Urban workers

Latin America became independent and was urbanised before industrial development arrived. New railways, notably in Argentina, offered a strong base for labour organisation. But movements in Peru, Chile and above all Bolivia centred on mines and so were extremely vulnerable to military repression, leaving the scattered remainder to be subjected to various forms of restriction on their joint action. In practice, therefore, urban workers in Latin America have generally been targeted by populist leaders as one of the main elements in a multi-class alliance (see Chapter 8).

African states, on the other hand, generally had some industry at independence. Though African cities have grown considerably since 1950 the working class remains only a small fraction of the total population. The strength of state power, moreover, has led to incipient trade union movements being either captured by the ruling elite or suppressed by authoritarian governments. In a number of single-party states unions soon became active partners with government in seeking to increase work rates and hold down pay claims and this pattern was repeated in the 1990s. However this has not always been successful. As early as 1961 a major strike broke out amongst the railway and port workers at Sekondi-Takoradi in Ghana, protesting at the corruption of the elite and the increasing authoritarianism of the Nkrumah government. In 1971 a series of strikes in Dar es Salaam showed similar discontent with the authoritarian tendencies of the Tanzanian government. In Nigeria the imposition of military government was strongly resented and in 1971 there was a series of strikes in Lagos and Kano, then the main centres of industrialisation (Williams and Turner in Dunn 1978: 165).

In several former French African colonies, notably Congo (Brazzaville) and Dahomey in 1963 and Upper Volta in 1966, strikes helped to bring about the fall of an unpopular government at the hands of the armed forces. In Senegal, by contrast, external support in the form of French military personnel helped keep Senghor's government in power despite intermittent labour unrest (O'Brien in Dunn 1978: 180). The devaluation of the Communauté Française Africaine (CFA) franc in 1994 took trade unions completely by surprise. 'There were initial protest strikes and demonstrations in Benin, Burkina [Faso], Gabon and Niger. Other unions held meetings and demands for wage increases ranging from 35% in Chad and 50% in Burkina, Mali, Senegal and Togo, to 100% in Gabon' (Percival 1996).

In states already under military government, strikes have been firmly discouraged. Workers have responded by a variety of covert means of resistance, including absenteeism, going slow, sabotage and theft, and sometimes by open rebellion, as in Ghana where the mining industry was in continuous turmoil from 1968 to 1970.

The family

Family, marriage and kinship are basic and universal, though the forms they take vary. The economic basis of marriage, for example, is usually clear, but society specific. Within marriage the division of labour is normally clearly marked. In traditional as opposed to modern societies the central role in social provision falls to the family.

What counts as a family is a difficult and important question. The nuclear family of northern and western Europe is distinctive and rather unusual. It is bilateral and hence forms a rather weak basis for larger structures such as clans and lineages. It is monogamous and related households do not regard themselves in the main as having any special claim to the resources of each other. This pattern is also characteristic of Japan.

The pattern much more characteristic of the Third World is that of the extended family, which is usually unilateral. In India, as in China, a bride makes the physical journey to her husband's house and ceases on marriage to be regarded as a member of her former family. (This can have consequences much more significant than for a family alone: in Pakistan, for example, her mother has attempted to shunt aside Benazir Bhutto from her leadership role in favour of her brother, saying that, after all, she is no longer a Bhutto.) It can be characterised by both forms of polygamy, either polygyny (as in some Arab countries) or polyandry (as in Nepal); neither of which works to the advantage of women. Even where the extended family does not coexist in one household several generations can live together in the same complex and a very carefully graded system of relationships is recognised.

The family is not only the basic organising unit of society, it acts as a basis for all social provision. Mutual obligation in traditional communities is particularly characteristic of the extended family group. A member of the family who acquires wealth is obligated to provide for other family members; yet others can require support. Obviously the effect of this system, as it is among the Gilbertese (now part of the Pacific state of Kiribati), is to prevent any tendency towards hoarding or conspicuous consumption. Among the Tonga of Malawi the family could be relied upon to provide for the wives and children of those seeking contract work in South Africa, and they in turn benefited from the remittances the workers sent home.

Both individuals and families are similarly linked by patterns of dyadic (two-way) exchange. In many cases these obligations are so well developed that they form a very satisfactory way of structuring time and so are not easily surrendered. Brown (1957) found that both Samoans and the Hehe of Tanzania placed such a high value on performing a wide range of social and political obligations that they had a strong resistance to working for money. However a strong solvent of these traditional relationships is to be found in the urban market for cash crops and media images of other consumer goods.

Sociologists have paid particular attention to the tendency for the breakdown of the extended family in the face of modernisation (Goode 1970). Here the dominant influence has been that of the social theorist Talcott Parsons (Parsons 1964), who argued that what he termed the 'isolated nuclear family' was the typical form in modern industrial society because modernisation implied a process of 'structural differentiation'. By this he meant a tendency for institutions progressively to shed functions, so that in the case of the family its economic, political and religious functions have long since, to a greater or lesser extent, been assumed by specialised agencies and latterly the job of caring for the old, the young and the unfit has also been assumed by the state or by commercial enterprises. At the same time the *ascribed* status derived from the traditional family structure is replaced by *achieved* status based on one's own efforts and/or achievement.

Modernisation in the Third World means above all that the family ceases to be the main economic unit of production and is replaced by the workshop or factory. Parsons argued that the demands of factories for labour called for the mobility and flexibility associated with the nuclear family; however in the case of migrant workers into, for example, South Africa, the family unit itself seems in many cases to have disintegrated, the workforce being largely composed of individual young males living together in hostels. Goode (1970) argued that the disintegration of the extended family had in fact been more rapid than could have been expected were Parsonian assumptions correct. He suggested that the spread of the nuclear family had been accelerated by the image presented by the advanced countries that was attractive in Third World countries because of the freedom it appeared to offer. In Africa migrants from the countryside may even have welcomed town life because it freed them from the obligations of the extended family (Little 1965).

It has also been suggested that it was not industrialisation in northern Europe that brought about the decline of the extended family; it was the decline of the extended family that facilitated industrialisation. If this is the case, this decline in the Third World might be expected to have a similar effect.

On the other hand the extended family remains very much part of Indian society and Somjee (1991) argues that the economic success of local elites such as the Patidars of Anand in the state of Gujarat owed much to it. While they were barred by the Indian Land Tenancy Act from increasing the size of their landholding, they were able to gain an increased return from it by growing cash crops such as sugar cane, bananas, cotton and later edible oilseeds, and bene-fited from the absence of tax on agricultural income. However while retaining his interest in agriculture it was also open to a Patidar to leave the cultivation of the land to a brother or cousin and move into Anand itself, to seek work in commerce or industry. The availability of this work came, of course, from other factors stimulating the growth of Anand, especially the rapid development of the transport system that brought into the town a wave of new educational, governmental and other institutions, and with them a wave of professionals wanting new products and services.

> While in undertaking such ventures a Patidar no doubt took some risk, nevertheless he also had his land to fall back upon just in case the commercial or industrial ven-ture did not succeed. The closely knit extended family, together with the facility for absentee agriculture, provided the Patidars with a sense of security for new ventures. (Somjee 1991: 94–5)

Social factors favouring development

The early modernisers thought in traditional terms, in terms of piecemeal change over long periods of time. They recognised that the same land would have to provide food for their children and grandchildren, and they acted accordingly. By contrast the late modernisers have been driven by the urge to create visible results during the brief period of a political mandate. Many Third World countries have significantly changed their economic structures since independence, especially in the cases of Latin America, where independence came early, and Asia, where governmental responses have been particularly flexible. However agriculture is a complex process and it takes a long time for the full consequences of changes to be either felt or understood.

The structure of Third World economies often exhibits glaring divisions, especially those between urban and rural, or between the formal and the informal sectors. The main cause of this has been rapid urbanisation, which may either precede or follow rapid industrial development. Hence urbanisation levels vary a great deal. As noted in Chapter 1, they are high in the Caribbean and Latin America (74 per cent), especially in the Southern Cone. This is in part the result of Latin America's colonial history, where the creation of towns was the key element in the success of Spanish settlement. Many of the world's largest cities are in Latin America – the 24 million who live in metropolitan Mexico City formed some 25 per cent of Mexico's total population of 95,831,000 in 1998 (WHO 1999). Urbanisation, on the other hand, is relatively low in Africa South of the Sahara (32 per cent in 1997).

There is, however, a strong urban bias amongst most Third World policy makers, in Africa as elsewhere (Lipton 1977). Coming as they do from urban or would-be urban backgrounds, they equate urban with modern and prefer urban to rural, favouring strategies of industrial development that result in further urbanisation. Urbanisation hitherto has been seen as essential for rapid economic growth and certainly has always accompanied it, as witness the striking growth of big cities in the NICs and in China. However large cities have to be fed. Bread riots were a feature of life in Mexico City or Lima in the colonial period, when the local hinterland was no longer able to supply the needs of a rising population.

Urbanisation has profound social consequences. Public services tend to be concentrated in urban areas, thus making them even more attractive to rural dwellers. The most able and the most mobile (that is to say, young unmarried adults) migrate to the towns, in the process further disadvantaging the rural areas. But towns are not well adapted to receiving them. Squatter settlements are found on all continents. See Plate 6.

In-migration to the big cities has even wider implications, bringing in its wake an awareness of social change, which gives rise to cultural confusion. Uncertainty creates new tensions while reinforcing existing ones. Informality gives way to formality. A relatively static existence is changed by transport. Extended kinship, as Parsons noted, is replaced by the nuclear family. Social complexity increases, and there is an association between social change and political instability. The problem of unproductive urbanisation arises, and when in-migrants compete for scarce resources and temporary or part-time jobs friction and scarcity lead to 'unregulated petty strife'. At the same time, the other side of the coin is rural poverty. Poverty in the countryside is not a new phenomenon, and it could almost be expected in drought-prone and degraded environments such as those of the Sahel or the Horn of Africa. In fact, as Redclift points out, the problem in both these areas owes much to the structure of landownership. The rich soil of Bangladesh is not a degraded environment. However Bangladesh has an exceedingly unequal distribution of land, such that one-third of the people of this heavily populated country are poor peasants cultivating less than one hectare of land or share-croppers dependent on others for work (Redclift 1984: 74–5).

Maintaining social provision in an evolving society

With rapid social change come also a whole range of problems associated with the provision of housing, health and other social services. Gaps in social provision in the growing towns can be filled in a variety of ways, by: a) a church or sect; b) other voluntary organisations; c) occupational provision; or d) the state.

The effects of migration are felt very differently in town and country. Typically in a plantation economy the main basis for housing provision other than the individual has been occupational: housing for the workforce. The relatively high standard of housing provided by the banana corporations in Honduras, for example, is a significant deterrent to unrest. However such provision is relatively rare in towns, the assumption being that the cost will be picked up by the worker or by the state. In the town the major problems concern housing for young adults, and these can be and are met in a variety of ways by the adults themselves. However unless an agency such as the state steps in to ensure provision there are costs. The need to work impedes both education and training, tending to reinforce low expectations and to create a large semi-skilled labour force. For the individual it results in an unfamiliar (significant word) need to rely on groups other than the family.

For those in towns occupational provision may or may not be made for crèche facilities, education and training schemes. Even if legally required it may well not effectively exist or be capable of being enforced. For those left behind in the country the remoteness of the young adults results in additional problems in the care of both the very young and the aged, which has traditionally devolved on the youngest unmarried daughters of the family, thus reinforcing their dependence on the family unit and leading to very marked differences in the experience of education between men and women. In rural areas provision of schools is much more basic, too, and once children are of an age to work they will be in demand in the fields. Their school attendance becomes spasmodic and soon ends altogether. Authorities on Japan, the most successful non-western society to achieve advanced industrialisation, lay particular emphasis on the distinctive role of education in its economic development. By the end of the First World War Japan had already achieved near-universal literacy – something that is still far from being achieved in Central America, South Africa or Bangladesh, and is already in the decline in Britain and the United States of America (see Table 5.1).

Workers in modern companies often enjoy access to up-to-date health provision, and large cities in the Third World can boast medical facilities that are as good as anything in the world. However in rural areas many peasants and their families still depend on traditional healers, whose services are not only well known and trusted, but who also have the great merit of being relatively cheap. Obviously they cannot cure everything and the reputation of modern medicine for miracle cures has created a demand worldwide for access to modern treatments. But assumptions of health in the Third World can be very different from those in developed societies. Just as the overall figures for the number of people served by each doctor do not reveal the sharp contrast between town and country, they also do not reveal the lack of access amongst the poorest sectors who cannot afford the services provided. In the Mexican village of Tzintzuntzan a government health clinic was accepted in time, despite cultural and other barriers. But the cost of treatment in the neighbouring town of Pátzcuaro, though very low, was noted to be a significant deterrent (Foster 1967).

The need to get social services to those who require them explains why workers in the field of development have been taking increasing interest in the idea of 'empowerment' of local communities. Put simply, empowerment means making it possible for people to take their destinies into their own hands, and this in the Third World means community action. The formation of base communities (*comunidades de base*) within the Catholic Church in Brazil, and the growing impact of the evangelical movement there, has gone along with a much more active political participation amongst the poor, both in the countryside and in the shantytowns. These organisations are not simply religious, although Bible readings and public worship are both central aspects of their activities. They also often establish production cooperatives in the *favelas* and classes to teach basic literacy. They often have close connections with trade unions and with the Workers Party (PT), and this ensures that, despite their religious origins and orientation, they are in conflict with the Catholic church establishment, which sees them as Marxist.

In India, disillusion with the failure of the initial model of state-led economic growth based on the western concept of the individual helped encourage a new emphasis on Gandhian ideas and fresh encouragement for the *panchayat* movement. Obviously there are limits to what such action can achieve unless new resources can be made available, and empowerment is of no value if it simply enables the poor to manage their own poverty.

Conclusion

There are so many things that could be said about the social context of the Third World that any selection will be, to some extent, arbitrary. Stratification systems and institutional structures are the most vital underlying features of society in the Third World, as in the advanced industrial countries. However a consistent pattern is the great gulf that separates the rich from the poor, and the central role of the state in articulating the relationship between them.

CHAPTER 6

The cultural context

Introduction

The term 'culture' has many meanings. For the sociologist, the important thing is that it is the way in which group life is realised. As Hall and Jefferson (1976: 10) put it: 'We understand the word "culture" to refer to that level at which social groups develop distinct patterns of life, and give *expressive form* to their social and material life-experience. Culture is the way, the forms, in which groups "handle" the raw material of their social and material existence.'

As a concept, it has been used to try to determine the relationships between culture, social structure and other aspects of society. However, ironically, there has until recently been no clearly defined 'sociology of culture', and many of the most important contributions to the literature on culture and society have been made by people who did not regard themselves as sociologists. The main debate arises between those who regard culture as the medium within which other developments take place and those who regard it as a residual category in which to group all other aspects of society that are not otherwise accounted for.

Some, with Durkheim, see culture as the method by which social relations are produced and transmitted. The role of ritual and symbols in dramatising and so reinforcing the social order has been a major preoccupation of anthropologists. However Mary Douglas rejects the sharp division Durkheim (in common with many of his age) drew between the primitive and the modern, the former in Durkheim's view being characterised by mechanical solidarity and the latter by organic solidarity. Douglas also rejects the structuralist belief that human thought must necessarily be couched in pairs of opposites. The belief that the anthropologist can confidently determine a single true meaning for any given symbol flies in the face of evidence that symbols are almost always complex and multi-faceted. Hence in any society the reinforcing effect of symbols is felt by their constancy, repetition and familiarity, rather than their precision (Wuthnow et al. 1984).

Some Marxists have in the past argued for a rather simple economic determinism, in which culture forms only part of the superstructure of society resting upon the dominant economic base. However most modern Marxists now accept, and even argue, that the culture of a society (in the sociological sense) also affects and shapes its capacity for economic production, an idea that has antecedents also in the work of the Italian Marxist Antonio Gramsci. They therefore stress the power of ideas to shape events and the way in which some cultures come to dominate others. As Hall and Jefferson put it:

> Groups which exist within the same society and share some of the same material and historical conditions no doubt also understand, and to a certain extent share each others' 'culture'. But just as different groups and classes are unequally ranked in relation to one another, in terms of their productive relations, wealth and power, so *cultures* are differently ranked, and stand in opposition to one another, in relations of domination and subordination, along the scale of 'cultural power'. (1976: 11)

Certainly comparison of, say, the economic history of Argentina with the similar instances of Australia and Canada suggests that a mechanistic economic explanation is inadequate and that cultural differences, in the sociological sense, have to be taken into account if the differences in outcomes are to be adequately explained (Duncan and Fogarty 1986).

Anthropologists generally follow Durkheim in seeking to explain societies in their own terms. To an anthropologist, culture refers to the entire pattern of behaviour of a society. Anthropologists therefore tend to use a very loose definition of the term, following Tylor in defining culture as: 'that complex whole which includes knowledge, belief, art, morals, law, custom and any other capabilities and habits acquired by man (sic) as a member of society' (Tylor 1891: 18, quoted in Billington et al. 1991: 2).

The development of anthropology as a serious academic discipline in the nineteenth century accompanied the involuntary process of encounter with new cultures brought about by colonisation. In one sense this was helpful, since it meant that much was studied and recorded that might otherwise have been lost. In another sense it was not, because the basic assumption behind colonisation – that the culture of the colonisers was in some or all senses 'superior' to that of the colonised – was seldom successfully challenged. Following the path laid down by Lamartine, the French in particular adopted the notion of the *mission civilisatrice*. The justification of colonisation lay in the opportunity it afforded for the colonised to gain access to the dominant culture of France and because of the superior advantages of that culture the French had a right, and indeed a duty, to spread it.

Here we are concerned with the impact of change on culture, 'the common, learned way of life shared by the members of a society, consisting of the totality of tools, techniques, social institutions, attitudes, beliefs, motivations, and systems of value known to the group' (Foster 1973: 11). Colonisation is a drastic change in culture. So too is decolonisation, industrialisation and, for that matter, *globalisation*. Foster notes six characteristics of cultures that are crucial to the understanding of the process of change:

1. Sociocultural forms are learned.
2. A sociocultural system is a logically integrated, functional, sense-making whole.
3. All sociocultural systems are constantly changing: none is completely static.
4. Every culture has a value system.
5. Cultural forms, and the behaviour of individual members of a society, stem from, or are functions of cognitive orientations, of deep-seated premises.
6. Culture makes possible the reasonably efficient, largely automatic interaction between members of a society that is a prerequisite to social life (extracted from Foster 1973: 12–24).

The problem is complicated by the fact that there is a third, very common way in which the term culture is used, and indeed much more commonly and widely used. This is to designate the evidences of specialised forms of self-expression such as art, music, literature, etc. Culture in this sense, sometimes termed 'high culture', is generally seen as being the particular province of intellectuals, who designate what is to be regarded as 'good' or 'bad' within this specialised cultural inheritance. Thus since French culture was admired and copied by other European peoples it seemed obvious both to them and to others that it ought also to be copied by the colonised. Time has shown how successful the policy was.

High culture, therefore, forms part (but only part) of the dominant culture in the sociological sense. But it is a particularly important part, since it embodies in the highest degree the characteristics that differentiate that culture from all other cultures (or subcultures) within that society, and so forms the core of its 'entitlement' to cultural power. This entitlement of the ruling class, and its unconscious recognition by the masses, was called 'hegemony' by Gramsci. It is the distinctive property of culture that the values and norms it conveys are internalised by members of the society in general, enabling rulers the more easily to exercise power over them.

The concept of modernity: competing cultures

In the nineteenth century the development of industrialised society in Europe was increasingly accompanied by a belief in the 'evolution' of cultures – the survival of the fittest. Imperial powers, such as Spain, Portugal, France, Britain, the Netherlands, Belgium, the United States of America and Russia, saw it as their 'duty' to 'civilise' subject peoples and to impose their cultural norms on them.

The main vehicle of transmission was the education system. Utilising both the pedagogy and curriculum of the dominant culture, it subordinated indigenous values by offering those who could take advantage of the system the opportunity to share in the task of government and administration.

Critics call the policy of deliberately propagating a culture of self-defined modernity 'cultural imperialism'. They argue that although formal imperialism, in the old sense of political and military domination, has ended, informal imperialism continues. Imperialism always involved a combination of strategies: it was never simply a matter of superior force, as the history of British involvement in South Africa makes very clear. Obviously the two are closely linked, as Hoogvelt (1978: 109) argues: 'No society can successfully dominate another without the diffusion of its cultural patterns and social institutions, nor can any society successfully diffuse all or most of its cultural patterns and institutions without some degree of domination'.

This process of diffusion could be highly effective. Anthropologists, often inadvertently, helped the process by designating residual indigenous cultures as 'primitive' and so by implication inferior to their own. Even when they did not there were problems. As a social scientist Malinowski (1961) recognised and was concerned about the risk of contamination of cultures by observation. However more recently anthropologists have been criticised for paternalism when they have argued that indigenous peoples should be left alone to evolve at their own rate.

Mere contact with a more powerful culture can certainly be highly traumatic. The impact of an externally driven rapid process of change on whole societies not used to it is potentially even more devastating, since in those circumstances there is no way back to the familiar certainties of the past.

However, rapid adaptation to technological change is likely to be much easier for a society that is already faced with the prospect of rapid change and that has already come to the end of its capacity to adapt than it is for societies which have not been forced to abandon old ways. In *New Lives for Old*, a study of the island of Manus to the north of New Guinea, Margaret Mead argued that it was far more difficult for people to adopt fragments of a culture than to take on board a whole new culture. Toffler quotes her verdict approvingly, but with reservations about the limits to adaptation (Mead 1956 cited in Toffler 1970: 329). Defeat in war afforded Japan and Korea the opportunity to compete on the basis of new technology. Already people are arguing that the collapse of communism may enable large parts of eastern Europe to do the same. But in many Third World states the problem is rather for the future of indigenous cultures surrounded by the modern state.

Certainly various cultures can coexist – if enough space separates them. The Yanomami in Brazil were largely insulated from the outside world until the arrival of the *garimpieros* (gold miners). But cultures are permeable and absorption of new elements is usual. India was simply too large and too complex for its cultures to be swept away. British culture was incorporated but did not supersede indigenous patterns, and in fact with few exceptions (e.g. the

self-immolation of widows) the Raj did not seek to end traditional Indian practices. Given the small numbers of colonisers and the practice of indirect rule
Indians had to collaborate actively in their own domination for the process to
work at all. British culture was admired for its association with power, wealth
and modernity. When these values ceased to be unconditionally admired, and
Indian values came to the fore, the end of the Raj was at hand. Today the survival of the traditional lifestyle of 'tribals' (as indigenous people are known in
India) is now threatened most by the aspirations of other Indians and the quest
for 'modernity' or development.

Relationships established with colonisation do not end at independence. In
his well-known attack on French policy in Algeria Frantz Fanon (1967) argued
that the psyche of black peoples in Africa had been damaged by colonisation
– they had been taught to regard their 'own' culture as inferior. Time has
shown this to be too pessimistic a view, based, no doubt, on his own individual
experience. Fanon himself was born in the French Antilles and brought up in
Martinique but his argument does not appear to have the same resonance in
Africa South of the Sahara as it did in North Africa. Others have yet to explore
fully the impact of the experience of empire on the colonisers themselves.

The global network

The first truly global network was established in the nineteenth century.
However, even though its cables crossed the seas, the electric telegraph operated only on land and its impact was limited. It did, however, enable newspapers throughout the world to carry some international news.

Radio removed the limitation of space. Incredibly, it was first seen merely as
a form of communication between individuals, and it was not until 1920 that
its most obvious defect, the fact that anyone within range could hear it, was
turned into an advantage and the idea of 'broadcasting' became a reality. By
then the cinema had already added the visual element. Together they made a
global culture possible, but not yet a reality, since despite the early lead gained
by Hollywood, USA, language differences and entrenched nationalist attitudes
remained a significant barrier. However there was a foretaste of what was to
come in the role played by All-India radio in unifying the subcontinent.

Television (TV) combined all these experiences in a single medium. It was,
however, initially a very expensive one, limited in its coverage by the need to
transmit along the line of sight. But by the 1960s space technology had
advanced far enough for Arthur C. Clarke's proposal for a network of earth
satellites to begin to become reality (Clarke 1945). Even then there were continuing problems with nationalism and security issues, and the first media event
to achieve anything approaching worldwide coverage on TV was probably
the World Cup of 1986. In 1982 the Falklands War took place under a strict

security blanket on both sides; by 1990 satellite uplinks enabled Cable News Network (CNN) to carry live transmissions during the Gulf War from Baghdad under bombardment and even from allied troops in the desert.

The Internet grew out of links established between computers in California in the late 1960s as a means of communication between government, defence establishments and university researchers. Unlike earlier media it was decentralised and so could not be disabled in the event of war. Its capacity was enormously enhanced in 1989 with the adoption of the universal protocols proposed by Timothy Berners-Lee enabling anyone with access to the system to transmit text, pictures and sound across the World Wide Web. It is this ability for anyone to make use of the net that is its most interesting feature. However its coverage is still not universal. According to the Internet Society in 1996 only 134 countries had full Internet access though a further 52 had limited access, as, for example, to e-mail (Encarta 1999).

Impact of transnational media

To the developed world the ready availability of many channels of information seems a most desirable state of affairs. However there are problems seen from a Third World perspective:

The need to use existing networks of communication

Cables and satellites are very expensive and use of them is controlled by the advanced industrialised countries – though Indonesia and the Philippines have both sought to enter the world of satellite broadcasting by commissioning their own communications satellites. The world's press is largely fed both text and pictures by the US agencies Associated Press and United Press International; the view of the rest of the world is systematically affected by the pro-US bias of agency reporters and editors. British (Reuters), French (Agence France-Presse) and, in the past, Soviet agencies (Tass) have similarly played their part in defining the news agenda. But Third World agencies, with the rather limited exception (for brief periods) of the Cuban Prensa Latina, have not.

The problem of finding a common language

The effort to impose Hindi in India, initiated by Nehru, was only partially successful. Nehru had, after all, to make his independence speech in English. The attempt of S.W.R.D. Bandaranaike in 1956 to impose Sinhalese instead of English as the sole official language of Sri Lanka backfired by alienating the large Tamil minority who had previously made use of English to gain access to the higher ranks of the civil service and other important jobs. His assassination at the hands of a Buddhist extremist was followed within a few years by riots in which Sinhalese sacked and looted the Tamil district of Colombo. Equal status for Tamil was conceded and English continues to be a working language of government, as it is in India and Pakistan.

In North Africa, ironically, Arabic is already available as a common language. Yet unity is elusive and attempts to unite existing states such as Egypt and Syria or Iraq and Kuwait have all failed. Although notions of self-interest are obviously at work here so too has been that elusive perception of difference conveyed by dialect and idiom. Over most of Latin America Spanish serves as a common tongue, though it is resented also for the very fact that makes it universal: the fact that it was imposed from above. The Portuguese speakers of Brazil can understand Spanish. In Africa both Nigeria and South Africa lack a common language and continue to find English invaluable as a working language of communication, though in East Africa Swahili was established as a universal language before the onset of colonisation.

The need for a common language is powerfully reinforced by the universality of radio in the Third World. Radio speaks directly to people over long distances. It is cheap and the modern transistor does not require mains electricity. In Latin America, apart from Cuba, the pattern is one of competing commercial stations. In Africa the service is generally state run. With the gradual economic decline of Sierra Leone the state-owned television transmitter in Freetown broke down and was not repaired; radio, however, continued to function even in the most remote areas.

At the moment the universal language of the Internet is English. Translation programs are already up and running that enable machine translation from one language to another. However ambiguity and the use of idiom render many such translations at best ungrammatical and at worst absurd. Besides, the expense of devising such programs mean that at present they are available in only a few languages; inevitably the less common Third World languages are not available.

The problem of competing with systems of mass cultural production

TV is the most effective of the mass media, since it does not require literacy and, though a low content medium in terms of information, it does have a strong emotive impact through use of visual images. But the very high cost of TV production means that all but the basics of news, weather and talk programmes have until recently been very expensive by Third World standards. Only now have small, lightweight cameras become sufficiently sophisticated to enable companies to compete with imports, especially in the field of drama and serials or, as they are commonly known, 'soap operas'.

The USA sets production standards – viewers come to expect a sophisticated product, even if the content is bland – as well as standards for structure, through the need of products intended originally for the US market to incorporate breaks for advertising. US productions build on the success and reputation of Hollywood and its experience of films (movies). As with movies, which have had a much longer history of exposure in the Third World, TV productions propagate key images of life in the USA, such as universal wealth, which creates a demand for western products, in turn increases dependence on imports and distorts local consumption patterns. This sometimes has specific serious effects, as in the case of the use of infant milk formula, though more usually it works in a more generalised and insidious fashion, propagating the vision of consumerism dubbed 'McWorld' by Jeremy Seabrook ('Return to the Summit', BBC 2, 1997). Another key image available through television is easy violence, from cartoons to *Robocop* and *Terminator III*. Such images may imply that low local standards in this regard are satisfactory because they also exist in the USA, despite the fact that standards in most developed countries, and especially in Japan, are very much higher. Hong Kong is a major producer of films based on proficiency in various spectacular and undoubtedly threatening martial arts, and these are clearly very popular among young viewers.

Major exporters of film in the late twentieth century included, as well as the USA and France, Hong Kong, India and Italy. Among Third World states India and Brazil stand out as major producers of TV. However in general little of their product reaches First World screens, except on cable. *The Mahabarat* has had a major impact in Britain in reawakening pride in Hinduism; in India it is believed to have contributed significantly to the rise of Hindu nationalism. Mexico's state-owned Televisa dominates Mexican programming, but is becoming increasingly important (as is Spain) in productions for the Hispanic-US market, and Brazil's O Globo has grown from a newspaper into the largest TV network in Brazil and the fourth largest in the world.

Opinion formers

Perspectives on the world propagated by the media, etc. are mediated through 'opinion formers', who reinforce stereotypical images. The question of where these opinion formers come from and how they come to perceive the world as they do is an interesting one. Broadly, centre influences periphery, though there remains a special role for churches and sects, teachers, doctors and municipal government officials in the local context.

Education in India is dominated by Brahmins. Though the western-educated elite help shape opinion in towns, in the countryside the traditional elites still hold sway. In Latin America education is skewed by cost towards the well-to-do; the wealthy in turn have traditionally owned/edited newspapers and increasingly dominate radio and TV.

Ideas are carried by people as well as by the media, so travel, for whatever reason, is important in enabling ideas to pass from one place to another. War has a most dramatic influence on all societies, both because it forces people to travel and because of the challenge it presents to traditional notions of leadership and competence. Soldiers returning to Africa (Lloyd 1971) and to India after the Second World War carried with them ideas of independence. When, as in the case of Burma or Indonesia, a country was actually invaded and occupied, the effects were even more powerful. Throughout South-east Asia the Japanese invaders transmitted the electrifying message that colonial rule was not inevitable and that the former colonial powers could in favourable circumstances be challenged and even defeated.

The transmission of ideas works all the time in urbanising societies in a much less spectacular but probably no less efficient fashion. Those who work in towns return to the country with news and gossip about events in the wider world, but also with a certain prestige that makes their ideas more weighty.

In Islamic countries the revival of Islamic fundamentalism has demonstrated both the power of opinion formers and the ability in certain circumstances to bypass them. The power of the mullahs in generating hatred of the Shah in Iran was clearly important. But it was following the revolution that those pressing for the adoption of an Islamic republic were able to use the traditional sermon at Friday prayers to great effect. On the other hand criticism of the ruling elite in Saudi Arabia was not possible in this way. Clandestine sermons have therefore been circulated on audiotape and found a ready market, thus circumventing the ban on public criticism. In both Egypt and Algeria, countries that have been much more directly exposed in the past to influences from western Europe, a similar revival is also very evident, despite strong attempts by the government to prevent it, particularly in the case of Algeria, where the Front Islamique de Salvation (FIS) was prevented from taking power and was then banned from overt activity.

News management and international perception of the Third World

News management does not just affect what is seen in the Third World. It also affects international perception of the Third World. Press agencies, television news and features all combine to present a very selective view.

It is of course natural that people all over the world are concerned with their own local needs and issues. It is also understandable that bad news tends to have a much bigger impact than good. As a result many parts of the Third World get only selective and spasmodic attention from the rest of the world, and then all too often only when some 'natural' disaster hits the headlines. Even the world's first TV station with pretensions of universality, CNN, which has its base in Atlanta, Georgia, is strongly biased towards news from the USA itself.

In 1984 famine in Ethiopia seized public attention in Britain when a BBC news report showed emotive pictures of starving children. In fact the famine had already lasted more than three months, but had not previously caught the public imagination. Government aid (as usual) was slow to emerge; in the mean while, led by a rock star, the public spontaneously put their hands in their pockets to subscribe and increased government aid resulted. However in some ways the manner in which the issue emerged did Ethiopia a disservice. The news coverage was essentially ethnocentric. Ethiopians were underrepresented in such broadcasts and their own relief efforts were minimised, although they were by far the more important. Thus were the traditional stereotypes of helpless Africans and capable and benevolent foreigners confirmed in the public imagination in the advanced industrialised countries. In 1999 the situation was not as much improved as First World television neglect would suggest. Much imported food was still needed, though the rains had come and starvation was much more localised. The government of the Derg had fallen and been replaced by a weak democratic government, hardly able to tackle the country's fundamental problems.

In Somalia in 1989 the main problem was the breakdown of public order. Emphasis on this fact ultimately led to US intervention in 1992–93 and a futile attempt to oust one of the local warlords, General Aideed. Aideed proclaimed himself president in July 1995 but was not recognised by other clan leaders and died in a street battle a year later. His son succeeded him, but repeated efforts to call a conference to restore order had no success. Meanwhile heavy flooding in southern Somalia in 1998 destroyed crops and renewed the threat of famine, though in a large part of the country, former British Somaliland, without publicity, order had successfully been restored and famine was not a problem.

Latterly, with the end of the cold war, US attention has refocused on the security threat allegedly posed by Islamic fundamentalism. This agitation has been given some credence by the view of a leading political scientist, Samuel P. Huntington, that the main threat to US security in the future will come from the clash of 'civilisations' (Huntington 1997).

High culture

A distinctive feature of Europe has been the special role ascribed to the arts and the artist. Each of the arts has defined rules (up to a point) of appreciation, but they vary very much between one art form and another. These rules are established by an elite and subject to the whims of fashion. Breaking the rules may lead to innovation but it can also lead to the artist losing credibility.

Relationships between First and Third World elites are complex, and this is reflected in art as in all else. Though Europe initially provided the first global culture, in the twentieth century the United States of America has come to provide a powerful rival and mass substitute. In the plastic arts the obvious consequence has been a clear trend towards the extension and ultimately glob-alisation of high culture made possible by technology. Since the Middle Ages 'European' culture has incorporated many significant elements from countries that are now relatively underdeveloped – steel from what is now Iraq, carpets from Turkey and Iran, porcelain and stoneware from China, textiles from India, bronze from Thailand. Such objects were first imported and admired, then, more or less successfully, copied, and finally displaced by mass products retaining an eclectic mixture of European and overseas design. In Victorian Britain the severe Gothic of the mid-century contrasts sharply with the riot of interior colour and the use of a spectacular range of elements from (among others) the Indian, Turkish, Arab and Chinese decorative arts.

In recent years there have been other influences. The tomb of Tutankhamun led to a second rediscovery of Ancient Egypt in the United Kingdom and the USA, where its spectacular quality had a powerful influence on Hollywood. The impact of African art on France in the age of art deco is also significant. And if the archaising tendencies in inter-war Mexican art were often awkward, the naive images associated with Diego Rivera, José Clemente Orozco, David Siquieros and others of the Mexican school of muralists spoke far more elo-quently of exploitation and suffering and the need for revolutionary unity than did the Mexican politicians of the generation of the revolution.

It is, of course, the capitalist west that established the idea of an art market, creating a demand for products of the traditions not only of the developed countries but also of the Third World. Art has become an international com-modity. As a commodity, though, it has rather unusual rules, since its value varies very much with the degree of authenticity attributed to it, and this is in most cases much a matter of opinion. The export of large numbers of objects from China and Russia since the fall of the Soviet Union has upset the market, but with the increasing globalisation of trade other traditions have increasingly attracted the attention of collectors.

Music too requires neither language not literacy for comprehension, but here the power of modern mass culture, spread by radio, television, the vinyl disc and audiotape has been overwhelming. African rhythms reappeared at the turn of the twentieth century in US jazz; they have since been reintroduced to Africa along with (disconcertingly) another popular US musical export: coun-try and western.

However literature is not so easily transmitted, and here the relationship between the First and Third Worlds is often confused. Austin (1978: 137) writes of the problem confronting the present-day African writer:

> Whereas African artists can draw on tradition in sculpture or dancing or music, it seems doubtful whether a novelist or poet can write in his mother tongue out of a background of general illiteracy. Where would his audience be? . . . There is said to be a continuing tradition of poetry in the Somali language, and Hausa epics are still recited in northern Nigeria. There have also been local attempts to recast village ceremonies in modern dramatic form, as in the Ogun plays among the Yoruba in

Nigeria, or as Efua Sutherland has tried to do in village theaters among the Akan in Ghana. At every turn, however, the African writer is confronted not simply with illiteracy but with the prevalence of English or French or Portuguese.

There is a problem of the 'cultural hegemony' of the former colonial language that has to be addressed by African writers who do use English or French. They gain access to a wider readership but there is a price to be paid. The first generation of post-independence writers found the transition particularly difficult, as they moved from rejection of colonialism and enthusiastic support for independence leaders to disillusion with and contempt for corrupt and dictatorial regimes. The influence of Marxism on the extent to which writers felt violence was needed for successful liberation is evident throughout; its most famous exponent and advocate, Frantz Fanon, has already been mentioned.

A distinctive feature of the francophone, as opposed to the anglophone writers has been the positive emphasis on Africanness, first termed *négritude* (for which there is no exact equivalent English word) in a poem by the Martiniquais poet Aimé Césaire in 1939. The concept was elaborated in the post-war period by Léopold S. Senghor, former deputy in the French National Assembly under the Fourth Republic and later president of Senegal.

By contrast the notion of pan-Africanism, which originated with Marcus Garvey and W.E.B. DuBois in the United States of America, had in a relatively short time to yield to the political realities of a divided continent. It led to a new emphasis on African identity in the anglophone territories, which was taken up by Nnamdi Azikiwe and Jomo Kenyatta, among others, but expressed in political form by Kwame Nkrumah of Ghana, almost alone among African leaders of the independence generation.

By the end of the decade the first glow of independence was already fading. Wole Soyinka expressed disillusion with new governments: what choice was there but revolution on the one hand or a comfortable symbolic position with the UN or its Educational, Scientific and Cultural Organization (UNESCO) in the other? Chinua Achebe of Nigeria denounced the system of corruption he saw there and foresaw the military coup that was to come. James Ngugi of Kenya Africanised his name to Ngugi wa Thiongo'o and called for revolution. Ironically white South Africa formed the one cause that united a continent.

In the nineteenth century the small elite of Latin American authors similarly rejected their Spanish heritage; in fact the first novel published in Latin America, Fernández de Lizardi's *El periquillo sarniento* (*The Itching Parrot*), published in Mexico in 1816, was a violent condemnation of Spanish colonial rule in all its manifestations. Uniquely at that stage, in Mexico in the latter part of the century Ignacio Altamirano (1834–93) went one stage further. Casting the invading Spaniards as the real savages, he glorified the conquered native peoples as wise and noble. Elsewhere, however, writers ignored both and, despite the advice of Andrés Bello, rejected the challenge to establish a new and typically 'American' literature, choosing instead to try to emulate the highly artificial forms then fashionable in Europe.

This choice reflected both the contemporary cultural dominance of France amongst a cosmopolitan elite and growing disillusion with the actual progress of events in the Americas since independence. The theme of the struggle of human beings against hostile nature came to the fore and has remained a key theme in Latin American writing. Parallel with it was a deep disillusion with human beings and their political achievements. In the age of the dictators the novel was one method by which coded criticism could be made of the established order, and even then such critics often found it necessary to live abroad. One of the earliest and best-known examples of this genre, *Facundo*, was published in 1845 in exile by Domingo Faustino Sarmiento as an attack on the rule of Rosas in Argentina. More recent examples have included the Venezuelan Rómulo Gallegos' *Doña Bárbara* (1919), the Guatemalan Miguel Angel Asturias' *El señor presidente* (1946) and the Argentine Manuel Puig's *Kiss of the Spider Woman* (*El beso de la mujer araña*, 1976). Better known outside the Spanish speaking world is the Mexican Carlos Fuentes, who denounced the betrayal of the Mexican Revolution in *La región más transparente* (1958). This feeling of betrayal of the promise of the region was, however, expressed even more strongly by Alejo Carpentier, who in *El siglo de luces* (1962) rejected the French Revolution itself and all that stemmed from it (by implication including the very existence of Latin America).

However, whereas in the early twentieth century regionalism was the other key feature of a realistic attempt to portray the continent as it was, in the years since 1945 the major trend was away from harsh realism towards fantasy. Yet it is within the strange and exotic rules of what has been termed 'magical realism' that a generation of readers outside Latin America have first perceived and then tried to come to terms with the real social processes at work in its cities and countryside. The Colombia of Gabriel García Márquez is fiction, a product of the imagination of an outstanding writer of world stature. Yet, precisely because of that, his major work, *Cien años de soledad* (*One Hundred Years of Solitude*, 1967), has an aura of reality that still today sends people in search of the 'real' Macondo.

Asia is too big and too diverse for generalisations. In South Asia the use of English as a medium of communication by Indian writers makes their works available to the outside world without translation, and they are increasingly attracting a huge and very appreciative readership in the First World. Examples include Vikram Seth's immense epic *A Suitable Boy* (1993) and Arundhati Roy's Booker Prize-winning *The God of Small Things* (1997). Books by Sri Lankan writers have also received widespread critical acclaim in Britain, though many of the successful such writers deal with controversial matters at home and some may have preferred to live in self-imposed exile at least until the return of the SLFP in 1994.

However the implied criticism of the Muslim attitude towards women in Bangladesh in Taslima Nasreen's novel, *Shame*, led to such a hostile reaction that fundamentalists held an open meeting, wrongly quoted her as condemning the Koran and pronounced a fatwa against her.

The usual punishment for my so-called crime – blasphemy – is hanging. The threat makes me more determined to fight oppression. I nearly went crazy when I was in hiding after the fatwa was pronounced. There are 14 people living in our house in Bangladesh, and only one of them knew I was sheltered there. I wasn't allowed to make a sound, not even a rustle. I didn't know if it was day or night and I couldn't get food regularly. I forgot how to eat and I didn't know when I was hungry. I could only go outside at midnight, as if I was a stray cat. I didn't sleep from worry. (Taslima Nasreen, interview by Marcelle Katz, *The Sunday Times Magazine*, 22 January 1995: 54)

In August 1994 she had to leave her native Bangladesh and seek exile abroad. The hazards facing a creative writer in the Third World are many, since the difference between fact and fiction, though understood, is not always accepted as legitimate.

Indigenous peoples

In 1992 the United Nations responded to the growing indigenous movement by establishing the Working Group on Indigenous Populations and declaring 1993 the International Year of Indigenous People. The end of that year saw the UN launch the Decade of the World's Indigenous People.

It is hard to define indigenous peoples, since from earliest times human beings have been moving about the planet (see Plate 7). However, where such groups are clearly recognised to exist, they:

- tend to have a timeless relationship with their lands
- are descendants of the original inhabitants of the specific lands they relate to although many will not now be living on their original land
- share a common culture, language and ancestry.

Perhaps the simplest definition would stress cultural distinctiveness and suggest that indigenous peoples exist wherever traditional, sustainable lifestyles survive in continued opposition to the encroaching power of the modern, internationalised state. It is precisely this confrontation that brings indigenous peoples to the attention of the outside world. In extreme cases, such as the rising in the southern Mexican state of Chiapas in 1994, it takes the form of physical conflict.

Indigenous peoples probably comprise some 4 per cent of the world's population, an estimated 300 million people in 70 countries, but they are very loosely defined and there is much variety. On the broadest definitions, in the Americas Amerindians still comprise some 70 per cent of the population of Bolivia, 45 per cent in Peru, 40 per cent in Ecuador, 30 per cent in Mexico.

However even where, as in Guatemala, they are substantially in a majority, they are noticeably worse off than the rest of the population. In Guatemala Indian life expectancy is 11 years less than for ladinos (people of part-European descent). Even in Paraguay the infant mortality rate in Guaraní communities is as high as 50 per cent compared with 10 per cent amongst criollos and mestizos (people of whole or part-European descent).

The entry of Mexico into the North American Free Trade Agreement (NAFTA) on 1 January 1994 was accompanied by an unwelcome reminder of Mexico's indigenous past, an uprising by the self-styled Zapatista National Liberation Army (EZLN) in the state of Chiapas. Chiapas, in the extreme south of Mexico on the border with Guatemala beyond the Isthmus of Tehuantepec, is Mexico's poorest state, as was noted by the UNDP *Human Development Report* (1994a). It has an infant mortality rate of 94; 60 per cent of its population is living below the official poverty line; and half the population has no access either to drinking water or to electricity.

The problems of Chiapas stem from two causes: existing inequality and the impact of recent programmes for rapid development. The land reforms of President Lázaro Cárdenas in the 1930s might have had some impact on the traditional pattern of land tenure but the quasi-feudal oligarchy resisted successfully, aided by the local bishop. Since then peasants of Mayan descent who have sought title to their lands have been evicted, forced to occupy the land, faced violence, disappearances and killings at the hands of the local bosses or their *pistoleros* (strong-arm men). Many have been displaced and some 200,000 landless families now work on the coffee and cocoa plantations. In the 1960s the state was linked for the first time to the rest of the country by good roads (Vogt 1969), settlers began to pour in for land colonisation and tensions rose. The PRI government installed corrupt generals to control the province and built an enormous army base in the town of San Cristóbal. Much development funding was given to Chiapas but the oligarchy and the new settlers benefited and the former inhabitants were still deprived.

In Asia too, indigenous peoples are disadvantaged. The Papuan people of Irian Jaya, the eastern province of Indonesia, are being forced to use violence to defend their tribal identities. They confront a well-equipped army only as a simple people with home-made weapons. Their land is the western half of the island of New Guinea (cf. Rappaport 1968), seized in 1963 by Indonesia against the wishes of the native Papuans, who are seen as primitives in Jakarta. Their lifestyles have been marginalised by imported Javanese whom the authorities hoped would speed up the process of change. The case of East Timor, seized by Indonesia after the collapse of the Portuguese Empire in 1975, is similar.

Malaysia exemplifies many of the various pressures threatening indigenous peoples. Paul Harrison cites the case of the Semai of Musoh whose population density is already beyond what is sustainable by hunter-gathering alone. Despite this they still operate a relatively ecofriendly lifestyle, supplementing hunting and gathering with the keeping of chickens and goats. Traditionally the Semai make use of slash-and-burn techniques to grow hill rice and cassava and then shrub crops. The land is then left for 10–20 years before being brought back into cultivation. 'Such forest peoples tread lightly on the earth. They impoverish no soils, destroy no ecosystems. Their survival does not demand the destruction of any other species' (Harrison 1993: 3). But this delicate balance is threatened now. The tribal lands are already surrounded by encroaching Malay and Chinese agriculture. Meanwhile the Semai naturally want the trappings of modern life such as bicycles and radios and to buy them they take (or allow others to take) more from the forest than they need. Semai children supply butterflies for sale in the tourist shops of the nearby Cameron Highlands. Their parents are beginning market gardens to supply urban Malaysia and logging is starting up too (Harrison 1993: 1–6). The former Malaysian Minister of Finance, Anwar Ibrahim, was quite blunt about his attitude towards indigenous peoples: 'the best course for indigenous peoples is to accelerate their integration into the global society'. However the Penan hunter–gatherer tribespeople of the Sarawak rainforest of East Malaysia, who still shoot monkeys and birds with blow-pipes, do not accept this. They have sought to stop foreign logging companies ending their way of life through their so-called policy of 'clear-felling' the mountain forest and have met violence and tear gas for their trouble. Needless to say they were not invited to take part in the Malaysian government's International Seminar on Indigenous Peoples.

The Pergau Dam project would flood some 73,000 hectares of this prime forest and displace 6000 tribal people, who are expected to be relocated to the oil palm plantations in other parts of Sarawak. The local community are not expected to benefit from the electricity produced by the dam, which is expected to be fed 600km under the sea to West (Peninsular) Malaysia.

In Tripura in India secessionist feeling grew as Bengali settlers, fleeing the anti-secessionist violence of the Bangladeshi security forces who drove them from their homes in the Chittagong Hills, were encouraged to settle in tribal areas to the detriment of the identity and culture of the tribal peoples.

In 1979 it was ruled that resettlement and rehabilitation of the tribals displaced by the Narmada River Project must keep in step with the other two aspects: environmental protection and construction. It has not done so and the scheme is being delayed, but for the most part the titles of lands occupied for centuries by the ancestors of those displaced have simply been ignored. Protesting tribals have been fired on by police.

Indigenous peoples' calls for rights are often interpreted as secessionist movements and therefore resisted. Also, indigenous people often occupy resource-rich regions and therefore there is intense outside interest in exploitation of their homelands. However they are also often the world's most fragile environments.

The preservation of indigenous peoples with their way of life intact presents the rest of the world with a moral dilemma. Not everything traditional is desirable. Some elements of modernity, e.g. an expanded trade and protection against imported diseases, may be vital to preserve the traditional. Perhaps the only way forward is some blending together of past and present. Demonstration effect will in any case ensure that indigenous peoples (or at least the youngsters) will crave the trappings of development: the radios, television sets, CD players, bicycles, cars, etc. Those who enjoy such things, or who have experienced them and rejected them, are hardly in a position to argue that such experience should not in principle be available to all who want it. It may be possible to feed that demand in some way that minimises damage to local tradition and cultures as well as to sensitive environments. Blending of the traditional with the modern is certainly possible, as is shown by the locally bottled 'Inca Cola' licensed by the Peruvian government.

Conclusion

Again it is next to impossible to know how to attempt to do justice in outline to the rich cultural variety of the Third World. While a brief summary of the literature of Latin America may serve to illuminate its main themes, because its distinctive characteristic is its common inheritance from Spain from which it has grown, no such summary could ever do more than hint at the diversity of Africa, let alone Asia. Yet there is one thing that all this cultural diversity has in common: an underlying fear that it is threatened by the powerful forces of the North's 'cultural imperialism'. This populist leaders have quite understandably sought to resist. However in their attempt to appropriate cultural symbols for their own personal advantage they have also run the grave risk of stirring up sleeping resentments in the form of nationalism (as will be seen in the next chapter) in a way that can in the end prove politically unmanageable.

PART III

Politics of the Third World

CHAPTER 7

State-building

Introduction

The basic interaction of world politics is the relations of nation-states. Originally the term nation-state was employed to distinguish modern states from earlier forms of political organisation covering relatively small areas, such as tribes or city states. It is true that in modern states the majority of inhabitants generally identify themselves with one another, by the possession of a common language, religion and/or culture. A people with this sense of identity is regarded as a nation. However, the term nation-state is a misleading one, for there is no exact correspondence between state and nation. There are states with more than one nation (Britain), nations with more than one state (ethnic Albanians, Hungarians, Serbs, etc.), states with no definite national identity (Chad) and nations with no definite state (the Palestinian Arabs) (Seton-Watson 1977). The reason why the term is so popular is that in nineteenth century Europe there emerged, with the concept of nationalism (see the next section), the belief that the only appropriate basis for a state was the nation. To this day, therefore, states which lack a sense of national identity try very hard to inculcate it, as for example did the United States of America (Lipset 1979).

As so often with composite terms, over time the newly coined expression comes to have its own meaning which is more (or possibly less, but certainly distinguishable from) the sum of the parts. We can compare the term 'Latin American', which refers to Guaraní-speaking Paraguayans, Welsh-speaking Argentines, German-speaking Chileans, Brazilians of African descent, etc., as well as Colombians from old Spanish families. Similarly 'nation-state' may be seen as simply designating a unit approximating to the ideals of statehood as described by Michael Smith: 'sovereign territoriality, authority and legitimacy, control of citizens and their actions' (Smith in McGrew, Lewis et al. 1992: 256).

These elements express the international as well as the national aspect of nation-statehood. Indeed, at its simplest, full penetration of the national area and the capacity to act as a single unit on the world stage might be taken as a starting point for some kind of definition and/or classification. Even this, however, would be more rigorous than would be wise in certain instances. For example, Sri Lanka would probably fail the first of these two tests: the instruments of the state do not have full penetration of the national area, having been driven out of much of the Jaffna Peninsula by the Liberation Tigers of Tamil Eelam (LTTE – *The Guardian*, 4 May 2000). Nevertheless Sri Lanka, despite its ethnic divisions, remains a nation-state on any meaningful definition. The great danger in seeking precision in such terms as nation-state is that so few countries would fit any reasonably parsimonious definition and a new term seems unlikely to be any more useful or, indeed, accurate.

The rather arbitrary creation of many Third World states raises the issue of nation-building (cf. Kedourie 1971, Golbourne 1979). It is necessary to establish some sense of loyalty to the new state. In the Third World state boundaries do not unite people of common descent, language and customs. This ethnic pluralism has been the source of conflict, the most glaring examples being in Africa. Thus independent Somalia, formed by the union of former British and former Italian Somaliland, has been seeking to extend its borders to embrace ethnic Somalis in Ethiopia. Ex-President Obote slaughtered 300,000 people in his attempts to wipe out the Buganda tribe in Uganda, one of the most ethnically diverse countries in the world. More recently, in tribal slaughter in Burundi in October 1993, 100,000 people were killed and some 600,000 more fled, adding to the already immense and rapidly growing problem of refugees seeking to eke out an existence on marginal lands. Likewise, Tutsi army rebels attacked Hutu in the Rwandan bloodbath of 1994 (see Chapter 2).

The Organization of African Unity (OAU) has sensibly enough taken the view that the colonial boundaries should remain as tinkering would open up Pandora's Box. Hence Igbo independence from Nigeria found little favour and the would-be state of Biafra was not officially recognised by any other power. However in the brief period before it was overwhelmed by the military force of the federal government, General de Gaulle expressed his political support for it and France and some African nations supplied it with arms. Libya's intervention in Chad in turn brought an armed response from Nigeria to preserve the status quo.

To build a state is to institutionalise the need for emotional/ideological penetration of society. Such a link between state and society makes possible the viability of regimes. If there is no dominant group political institutionalisation cannot occur and 'society' remains 'stateless' as in the Lebanon in the 1970s and 1980s. In addition, some peoples have senses of nation but are also stateless, for example the Palestinians until 1993 and the Kurds today; others feel imprisoned in existing states and seek to create independent states, for example the Sikhs in the Punjab and Muslims in Kashmir.

However it is not necessary for secessionist movements to be active for the state to lack authority and efficacy. The reorganisation of Indian states on a linguistic basis in the 1950s has been criticised for intensifying the potential for ethnic violence. Certainly it has weakened state loyalties, though there is no evidence that it has made local politicians any less keen on obtaining the favour of central government.

In such an atmosphere Third World constitutions often seem quite unrelated to reality. Some regard them as foreign impositions, hastily put together and presented to referendum in the hope of enhancing popular legitimacy. But in reality they are compromises, as are constitutions in any other part of the world, between the desire of the central government to exert its will and the determination of peripheral regions to resist it. Hence constitutions often stress democracy and centralism when the reality is of centrifugal forces such as tribalism in Africa and political gangsterism in Asia and parts of Latin America.

Subrata Kumar Mitra (1990: 91) says of India generally:

> the resilience of the state in India can be attributed to its success in incorporating some of the key features of the Indian tradition while retaining the essential features of modernity. Primordial sentiments have been balanced with those of economic interest and ideology. The edge is taken off the potential for authoritarianism through the division of power and widespread participation. By co-opting traditional centres of power and creating new ones the modern state has found a niche for most interests and norms with a support base in society.

Nationalism

National sovereignty has become the core value of international relations, as witness the moral indignation that was generated in response to Iraq's invasion of Kuwait in 1990. It is also the main obstacle to the solution of international problems. Yet in a sense at the national level nationalism looks increasingly obsolete, in the face of the developing importance of local action on the one hand and international interaction on the other. Nation-building involves generating a sense of common will and purpose, which in turn leads to a sense of community, identity, solidarity, loyalty, etc. Without some kind of common political culture the modern nation state is difficult to sustain. Political culture is part of national identity. Yet it is often fragmented in the Third World because of the way in which people feel a lack of legitimacy after independence. There is a certain moral legitimacy to be obtained from the concept of national security, but the fact that there are no accepted rules is a powerful spur to corruption.

The social upheaval connected with independence can be countered with an open appeal to the historic past, especially if, as in the case of Egypt, Iraq, Ghana or Zimbabwe, that past is more glorious than the present (and perhaps the future). An emotional appeal to shared historical experience becomes a means both to acquire legitimacy and to delegitimise the opposition, who become subversive. However states can also suffer harmful effects from an appeal to territorial nationalism, such as the high cost of arms to defend borders often against non-existent threats. This cost has to be seen both in terms of what other things cannot be bought, such as schools or hospitals, but also the 'lock-in' effect that purchases of modern arms entail in terms of the need to maintain weapons systems, to replace ammunition and to buy spare parts from the foreign suppliers.

The colonial practice of 'indirect rule' left a dual legacy. This practice of indirect rule is associated particularly with Lord Lugard, the first governor of Nigeria in 1914, and was given a theoretical justification by him in his *The Dual Mandate in British Tropical Africa* (1922). However it was also used by Britain in East Africa, notably in Uganda, and was employed to some degree by most successful colonising powers. Its effect was to leave the local elites responsible for the collection of taxes and the maintenance of law and order on a day-to-day basis. This maintained to some degree their standing in their own societies. But in the nature of things it also made them potentially very unpopular (see Crow, Thorpe et al. 1988: 28). Generally, indirect rule seems to have been very effective in undermining any general sense of national identity, by reinforcing a specific sense of identity in separate tribal areas.

Religion and ethnicity

As does nationalism, religion penetrates fragmented societies, binds disparate elements, overlooks present problems and establishes future – and past – orientation. Often it is invoked, as in Iran, to present an ideology opposed to that of the west that would suggest a glorious future when compared with so-called decadent advanced societies in decline.

Religion can be a political tool as a mobiliser of masses, a controller of mass action and an excuse for repression. On the other hand religion can also form the ideological basis for dissent. Thus in the Catholic Church in Brazil and Central America 'liberation theology' was a response to repression, and its suppression by the Vatican has left room for the extensive penetration of both Brazilian and Central American society by Protestant fundamentalism.

Ethnic politics is a powerful force challenging the cohesion of states, and in the Third World the challenge is occurring before the state has stabilised. There are four times as many self-defined ethnic groups as states in the world. As a result, ethnic nationalism is responsible for a variety of national and international tensions, such as the revival of communal tension in India.

Ethnicity is often a form of political identity, and where it does not coincide with state boundaries a source of division. Such a coincidence is much less likely to occur in new states established by external intervention. Indeed, as in Nigeria, the establishment of the state itself may threaten ethnicity, and lead to insurgency or even secession.

Ethnicity is not however an exclusively Third World problem. There are ethnic divisions in older states too and, as the history of Europe in the twentieth century has shown, at least as much trouble can arise from trying to eliminate ethnic differences as from having to live with them. Everywhere the problem is compounded by the fact that the nation-state is under increasingly strong attack both from without (international organisations, transnational corporations, regional economic groupings, satellite communications, global environmental concerns) and from within (ethnic nationalism).

Common ancestry is one possible basis for ethnic identity. But the anthropological evidence suggests that from earliest times people have used the notion of common ancestry as a convenient legal fiction, and certainly in the huge multi-ethnic states of today it is in the highest degree unlikely that cultural differences reflect real differences. For example, there is doubt even whether the Tutsi and Hutu of Rwanda and Burundi are, as they believe, different ethnic groups, or whether they merely reflect class differences. Some other factor or factors, most importantly a common language, often a different religion, perceived economic and/or political grievances, usually come into play to differentiate one 'ethnic' group from another. On the basis of such cultural distinctions is a collective ethnic consciousness then made the trigger for a belief in self-determination that may in turn lead to secessionist demands. The aspects of cultural distinctness emphasised may change according to their utility. Religion divides Sinhalese and Tamils as much as language, but it is language that is stressed by the LTTE in Sri Lanka, reflecting the fact that it was the attempt of Sinhalese politicians to deny Tamils the use of their language that triggered the continuing division between the two peoples, but also enabling the LTTE to claim majority status in some areas, including in their 'ethnic' headcounts Tamil-speaking Muslims, who are generally opposed to the LTTE.

In Islamic societies there is much more stress on religion. The tendency to define identity in terms of religion alone had led the Turks in particular to deny the very existence of Kurds as a separate ethnic group, since they, too, are Muslims. Religion is for Muslims the chief source of ethnicity, the means both to mobilise and to contain societies. The consensus on religion stems from the tendency for aspects of Islamic society to be mutually self-supporting. The popular level actions by fundamentalist groups such as the Muslim Brotherhood echo the official level (dogma and law). Moreover there is an important international dimension to Islamic thought and organisation. There are more than 40 Muslim governments, whose agencies are supportive of Islam, wherever it exists. Muslim leaders have a political role by definition, since Islamic thought makes no distinction between the sacred and the secular.

Case study

Sri Lanka

Three-quarters of Sri Lanka's 17 million population are Sinhalese; about 2 million are Tamils. Tamils place great emphasis on education and seek professional jobs in the public services especially in law and medicine. Independence in 1948 'marked no great watershed in Sri Lankan politics' (Moore 1990) and Sri Lanka remained insulated from world politics for nearly three decades. However in the meanwhile the disappearance of colonial rule unleashed Tamil success at obtaining jobs and at the same time promoted the rise of Sinhalese resentment and consequent chauvinism. In 1956 Tamil riots followed the decision of S.W.R.D. Bandaranaike's government to make Sinhala the sole national language in place of English. No allowance was made for Tamil, which would have been a problem anyway, but the exclusion of English as well made it difficult for the Tamils to continue to get jobs in the public sector. By the mid-1970s, with Mrs Sirima Bandaranaike as prime minister, the Tamils felt the government was deliberately loading the dice against them, especially since at the same time they were continuing with the policy begun by the British in the 1930s of resettling Sinhalese peasants from the south and centre in the north and east. See Plate 8.

This was increasing ethnic tensions amongst Tamils, who were beginning to view all Sinhalese in Tamil-dominated areas, whether incomers or not, as intruders. The result was to encourage demands for a separate Tamil state. The LTTE was formed in 1976. In 1977 an electoral landslide overturned the Bandaranaike government and installed one led by J.R. Jayawardene, who took advantage of his victory to introduce a new constitution with himself as executive president.

In 1983 in a Sinhalese backlash a mob rampaged through the market district of Colombo. They killed more than 2000 Tamils and more than 200,000 were made homeless. Within a year a dramatic escalation took place in the number of incidents ascribed to the LTTE, and soon the north and east were in a state of open insurgency. The Indian prime minister, Rajiv Gandhi, feared the spread of separatist demands to the South Indian state of Tamil Nadu. In 1987 he and the Sri Lankan government signed an accord that offered some autonomy to Tamils in the north and east in return for a ceasefire. An Indian Peace-keeping Force (IPKF) was sent to police the agreement.

Two months later the LTTE broke the ceasefire. The Indian presence unleashed the problem of Sinhalese nationalism and Sinhalese left-wing extremists, the JVP, began a campaign of violence intended to stop any concession to the Tamils. The new Sri Lankan president, Ranasinghe Premadasa, negotiated a new ceasefire with the LTTE on condition that the IPKF withdrew, and gave the Indian government notice to go. This they did in 1990 (Saravanamuttu

1990). However 1990 also saw the beginning of armed attacks on the small minority of Muslims. The LTTE claimed the attacks on the Muslims were a government ploy to blacken the name of the LTTE, but the Muslims believed they were the victims of LTTE violence and began retaliatory attacks against Tamil villages.

Then on 21 May 1991 Rajiv Gandhi was assassinated by a suicide bomber at an election rally in Tamil Nadu, one of a series that had appeared to herald his return to power. The LTTE denied responsibility but the method was absolutely characteristic of their suicide squads known as the Black Tigers and there is much evidence that the bomber was a member of such a squad. The LTTE had virtual control of Batticaloa for a while before the government launched an offensive to recapture it. However in early 2000 in a major offensive the LTTE defeated government forces, captured many heavy weapons and gained control of Elephant Pass, the key to the Jaffna Peninsula, which they clearly aimed to recapture (*The Guardian*, 4 May 2000).

Ethnic nationalism is likely to increase in certain specific circumstances – for example where a previously authoritarian state democratises or a formerly democratic one becomes more authoritarian. It is likely to find a sympathetic response given increased international concern for human rights. When it seems likely to work in their favour, emerging regional powers such as India may seek to establish cross-border connections between ethnic groups. As Rajiv Gandhi did not live to find out, they may pay a heavy price for doing so. On the other hand regimes may manipulate ethnicity to their own ends. Where a leader's ethnic base is larger than that of the opposition he or she may strengthen relations with it when threatened. This is exactly what Premadasa did in Sri Lanka. It served to exacerbate ethnic tensions beyond the capacity of the system to manage them and in 1993 it cost him his life in a suicide bomb attack in Colombo. Unfortunately such passions once aroused are not easy to control. President Chandrika Kumaratunga, who was elected in 1994 on a platform of negotiated peace, was unable to achieve it, and though re-elected in 1999 only narrowly escaped death when a suicide bomber blew herself up as the President left a mass rally. The attack killed 21 people and injured 110; among the injured was the president herself, who lost the sight of one eye from a shrapnel wound. The LTTE's battle for an independent Tamil state – which no Sri Lankan government could ever concede – was then estimated to have cost 60,000 lives since 1983 (*Keesing's* 43311).

Personalism

Personalism is a means to bridge the gap between state and society. As Weber himself noted, charismatic authority is an 'ideal type', a tool for comparison rather than something that could exist in its pure form. In practice there is always a tendency for personalistic relations to coexist with a rational–legal framework, Clapham (1982: 48) terms this condition 'neo-patrimonialism'. It is a feature particularly of Latin American polities, but is also found elsewhere. Personalism, therefore, is not just the most spectacular form of charismatic authority, it is closely linked to three related phenomena: patrimonialism, populism and clientelism.

Patrimonialism

This is the most enduring legacy of the pre-colonial society for new states and comes back into its own at independence. Many newly independent Third World states have undergone periods of unstable democracy alternating with military dictatorship. Many would argue that Pakistan, which is a most important example of this phenomenon, came close to becoming the personal fiefdom of the Bhutto family and that politics has degenerated into factional infighting amongst family members. Certainly much of its social structure remains essentially feudal. Two-thirds of the people still live in rural areas where feudal justice is often arbitrarily dispensed by the local landed aristocracy. Eighty per cent of the country's politicians are of aristocratic families such as the Bhuttos themselves and they rely first and foremost on the support of the local people to whom they are patrons.

In Africa indirect rule meant that traditional chiefs were maintained, forming a useful interface between colonial rule and the peasantry. However they were not maintained unaltered. The colonial government frequently merged, promoted or suppressed chiefdoms. Moreover they were not cheap to maintain, though since the costs of 'Native Administration' were borne by the people they helped administer their full cost was not obvious at the time. In Sierra Leone in 1949 46 per cent of the total cost of administration went in payments to hereditary rulers. Comparative figures for Tanganyika, Northern Nigeria and Western Nigeria show a very similar picture, and in Kano in Northern Nigeria the salary of the Emir alone accounted for 13 per cent of expenditure in 1936–37 (Kilson 1966: 31–32, citing Perham 1937: 118).

Max Weber (1964: 132, 324ff.) believed that the authority of government originally stemmed from what he termed charisma; that is to say, the outstanding personality or personal qualities of an individual. In more developed societies charisma was 'routinised', or subjected to legal forms and controls. It could be either traditional – accepted because it had always been accepted – or legal-rational – authority resting in an office, not the individual who occupies it for a finite period of time. Weber therefore distinguished these three types of authority, charismatic, traditional and legal–rational, from one another, while treating them as 'ideal types' that were not found in pure form.

Charisma refers to the possession by the leader of outstanding personal qualities recognised as such by others, and charismatic leadership has often accompanied the emergence of new regimes in the Third World. Thus Mao Zedong was hailed as a prophet, Mustafa Kemal as 'Father of the Turks'

(Atatürk), Ho Chi Minh as 'Father of the Indo-Chinese People', Nkrumah as 'the Saviour, Redeemer and Messiah', Ayatollah Khomeini as Imam. Charisma has been sought by those who lack it. Imelda Marcos, wife of the president of the Philippines, likened herself to Eva Perón (Evita) of Argentina, but the real parallel lay in the use of economic rewards for mass political support as an alternative to the generally much more costly use of force (Bresnan 1986).

Populism

Populism is a rather vague term that refers to the way in which leaders generate support by claiming to speak in the name of those they follow. Appeals for support are direct, expressed by appearances on presidential balconies with arms and voice raised. A classic example would be Juan Domingo Perón removing his jacket and declaring himself also to be a *descamisado* (lit. 'shirtless one' = worker). Personal appearances around the country are important, though radio and television can be and are used to reinforce the leader's image. There is little need to pay much attention to such institutional devices as keynote speeches to Congress, where they are for the most part unheard by 'the people'. Such leaders usually lack strong ideological conviction, seeing the will of the common people as being the determining factor. The key to their success is the way in which they identify issues that call forth the maximum response from their chosen constituency (Canovan 1981). Gamal Abd-el Nasser of Egypt and Saddam Hussein of Iraq are each in very different ways examples of the way in which charismatic leadership can bring forth a strong popular response, and even generate the momentum necessary for war. (See also the section on Populism and democracy in Chapter 8.)

Clientelism

The idea that political office brings with it the duty, as well as the opportunity, to use patronage on behalf of one's family, friends or tribe, which is termed clientelism, is often seen as being the distinctive feature of Third World politics, and is often found in connection with the illegal making of personal gain out of one's office (Clapham 1982). Clientelism is a means to sustain one's political support base during the time in which the rallying force of nationalism declines and classes have not yet developed to provide the bases for political parties. It may be based on ethnicity, as in the tribal society of West African states, where national leaders may go in for 'pyramid buying', by buying up local leaders who can deliver the necessary support at election times. Its strength depends on the fact that the patron–client bond derives from the notion of responsibility to one's family characteristic of traditional society and so is immediately understood by all parties to a transaction, and its dangers from the way in which it lacks the traditional restraints on the individual and as a private relationship is not open to scrutiny by modern state structures.

The key features of the patron–client relationship have been defined by John Duncan Powell (1970) as follows: 'First, the patron–client tie develops between two parties unequal in status, wealth, and influence. . . . Second, the formation and maintenance of the relationship depends on reciprocity in the exchange of goods and services. . . . Third, the development and maintenance of a patron–client relationship rests heavily on face to face contact between the two parties.'

Because of its unequal nature the patron–client relationship is inherently unstable but in the context of traditional village life the fairly simple network of mutual relationships is well known and fully understood. This tendency to instability increases rapidly in the context of urban immigrants, whose desire for jobs makes them vulnerable to recruitment into a much more complex network where any sense of reciprocal obligation is easily lost. At a national level the network is wide open to exploitation by wealthy landowners and entrepreneurs and by foreign interests. Bill (1972) documents how under the Shah's so-called 'White Revolution' the professional middle class of Iran expanded uncontrollably, generating increasing criticism of the failure of the regime to allow it to grow even faster.

State clientelism is also important. The state tends to be the largest employer in Third World countries, hence salaries are generally the state's largest expense. This is most marked in large federal states, such as Brazil, India or Nigeria, where the lower level of regional bureaucracy also has to be maintained. The use of patronage, in the form of appointments to sinecures and posts with parastatals such as Petrobras in Brazil, forms the means by which the state is enabled to intervene in both urban and rural sectors. But there is nothing in this situation which leads us to believe that the government has any interest in reversing it, nor is there any obvious reason why those who benefit from it in the provinces should wish to do so either.

Corruption

Gathering accurate information on corruption is, of course, an impossible task. Even the definition of corruption is problematic. However the boundary is crossed when payment or reward is made directly to government officials to secure a service of some kind. A distinction can be made between payment to expedite a service to which one is entitled anyway and payment to secure a service to which one is not entitled. But in practice both are properly regarded as corrupt. As Williams points out, there is a moral as well as a political meaning to the term corruption. It is 'used . . . to describe a morally repugnant state of affairs and implicit in its use is the desire to eliminate it' (Williams 1987: 13, Wraith and Simpkins 1965, Heidenheimer 1970).

This is implicit in the most widely used definition of corruption in public office, that of Joseph Nye, who describes it as:

behavior which deviates from the formal duties of a public role, because of private-regarding (personal, close family, private clique) pecuniary or status gains; or violates rules against the exercise of certain types of private-regarding influence. This includes such behavior as bribery (use of a reward to pervert the judgement of a person in a position of trust); nepotism (bestowal of patronage by reason of ascriptive relationship rather than merit); and misappropriation (illegal appropriation of public resources for private-regarding uses). (1967: 419)

The dangers of corruption are highest where the divisions between public and private are blurred: 'The morally corrupt society is one where moral life has, so to speak, been privatised' (Dobel 1978). The persistence of traditional culture, where the structure of government is based on reciprocal gift-giving, may contribute to a culture of corruption. Similarly nepotism, the employment of or granting of favours to relatives, is often the logical extension of extended kinship networks. The low salaries paid in the lower echelons of bloated bureaucracies of states such as India, Nigeria and Mexico, and the fact that in all societies status is measured by the conspicuous display of wealth, may contribute too.

It is impossible to tell just how much corruption costs Third World countries. However estimates suggest that corruption in Italy accounts for some 15 per cent of GNP, and it is likely that the rates for Third World states are much higher.

Certainly it is inevitable that under a clientelistic system there will be no hard and fast distinction between public and private and corruption will be endemic. What seems clear is that the effects of clientelism are much more serious in authoritarian or one-party states than they are in competitive systems. Though it is probably impossible to eliminate corruption entirely, the threat of public scrutiny establishes an effective brake on the more outrageous forms. Small-scale corruption may be relatively harmless, indeed it may be redistributive. However on a large scale it can literally undermine the foundations of society. A hospital and other modern buildings collapsed during the Mexican earthquake of 1986 when traditional buildings dating back to the colonial period survived. The ruins disclosed the extent to which the theft of cement and reinforcing bars during construction had compromised the stability of the modern buildings.

In Africa, long spells of military rule have made Nigeria notorious – probably unfairly – for the depth and breadth of public corruption: 'By the mid-1970s, the corruption associated with the Gowon regime, if not with General Gowon himself, had reached amazing proportions and events like the Cement Scandal . . . confirmed popular impressions that the riches of the oil economy were being siphoned off by a parasitic elite at an alarming rate' (Williams 1987: 98). The problem was that it did not end with the return of civilian government and the end of the oil boom. Corruption was a feature of both the 1979 and 1983 elections, and within weeks of the latter the military were back in power, alleging that the main reason for siezing power was the corruption of the Shagari government.

Accusations of corruption have long been standard practice in Latin American elections, but in recent years governments have started to take legal action against particularly flagrant examples. In Venezuela the second term of Carlos Andrés Pérez was brought to a close by his impeachment, followed by his trial on corruption charges. More recently President Collor of Brazil, on the eve of presiding over the Earth Summit at Rio, was accused of corruption by his own brother and subsequently resigned in December 1992 under the imminent threat of impeachment. In December 1994, however, he was cleared by the nation's Supreme Court, though not without criticism of the authorities for having failed to prepare their case properly. And in 1996 Colombia's Chamber of Deputies, many of whose members themselves faced corruption charges, voted by 111 votes to 43 to acquit President Ernesto Samper of all charges of knowingly accepting funds from drug traffickers. This decision not only ended impeachment proceedings but ensured that the charges could not be reopened.

An additional problem of administration in many developing countries is the scale of the bureaucracy and the extent to which it diverges from the 'ideal type' described by Weber and embodied in legislative form by the Northcote-Trevelyan reforms in the UK. In a clientelistic system it is unlikely that personnel will be recruited on merit alone, and pay and promotion alike are dependent on the favour of the ruling elite. Few civil servants have been able to separate themselves convincingly from the political arena. Paradoxically, this situation has been worsened by the attempts of military regimes in countries such as Pakistan and Nigeria to use civil servants in the formation of allegedly 'non-political' governments. In addition, the contempt that military officers tend to have for the police reduces their status and pay, favouring a pervasive culture of low-level corruption in the enforcement of law and order, while in Mexico, as in many other Third World countries, the traffic police enhance their standard of living by arbitrary use of their power to obtain bribes from well-off motorists (*The Guardian*, 22 May 1995).

Certainly the nature and structure of the party system in the single-party states of Africa, Asia and Latin America after 1960 cannot be explained by internal factors alone, but must be sought in the wider context of world politics. For the argument often advanced in defence of these systems was that in the aftermath of colonisation the emerging state simply could not 'afford' the 'luxury' of competitive politics. Hence in these cases, too, the ideological justification for the monopoly of power by the single party was that total control of the economic system was essential for the planning of future development. The trouble was, as events showed, that the silencing of criticism by opposition, far from enhancing efficiency, allowed corruption to become rampant. In an extreme case, Liberia, it led to the violent overthrow of the regime in 1980 and since then its economic base has been virtually destroyed by endemic civil war without any compensating advantage for the bulk of the population.

A Third World state's external connections also feed corruption through the demonstration effect, through the payment of bribes by foreign companies or their agents and through their support of regimes known to be corrupt.

Authoritarianism

As with corruption, the prevalence of authoritarianism is greater where legitimacy is less well developed. Authoritarianism is the belief in the principle of authority as opposed to that of individual freedom. In its most developed form this becomes advocacy of orderly government under military or other dictatorship. Although quite independent of it, it is therefore closely related to militarism (see Chapter 9).

With the rapid decolonisation of the 1960s came disillusion with the allegedly slow processes of democracy, and this in turn led to a wave of military coups in Africa and Asia. In a key study Linz identified the new authoritarian states as 'political systems with limited, not responsible, political pluralism; without elaborate and guiding ideology (but with distinctive mentalities); without intensive nor extensive political mobilization (except at some point in their development); and in which a leader (or occasionally a small group) exercises power within formally ill-defined limits but actually quite predictable ones' (in Allardt and Rokkan 1970: 255).

On the basis of Linz's definition it is possible to distinguish as he does between *new* and *old* authoritarian regimes. The longer established an authoritarian regime is, the less it needs to rely on the overt use of force and the more it tends to develop new forms of legitimacy. However for Linz authoritarian government is always a transitional state, either towards democracy or towards totalitarianism.

In addition, Sahlin (1977) suggests, it is also useful to distinguish between protective authoritarianism and promotional authoritarianism. Protective authoritarianism is the argument of those who intervene by force simply to protect the status quo and the position of those who benefit from it. Following a traditional military coup, which has only the limited aim of displacing the existing government, a period of emergency rule normally follows in which the armed forces emphasise the power available to them, their limited ambitions in making use of it, and their intention to return the country to civilian rule as soon as possible. Some regimes of this type, for example that of Stroessner's Paraguay, do survive for a long period and, Sahlin notes, become 'old' authoritarian regimes in Linz's terms, gaining a degree of legitimacy through force of habit and, generally, needing to depend less on the overt use of force. However their principal aims remain the same: the depoliticisation of issues and the demobilisation of the masses.

Promotional authoritarianism, by contrast, is characterised by a desire to promote change, by supplanting the existing government and establishing one that will stay in power for a period of years to pursue certain stated aims. Chief among these aims is economic development, the desire for which is in itself rooted in a nationalistic belief in the value of a strong state. But this requires a certain degree of mobilisation of the masses in the interests of productivity and this can most safely be achieved by appealing to nationalism. However even this does not resolve, but only postpones, a fundamental conflict between the desire for economic mobilisation and the fear of political mobilisation (Calvert 1994).

Coercive structures

The tendency towards authoritarianism is promoted by the crisis of legitimacy that follows independence or any other serious challenge to the continuity of the state. However it is often in part able to rely on the tradition of paternalism. The masses, generally lacking education, especially so in comparison with the elite, are not seen as being really fit for self-government. Any tendency to revolt is merely seen as confirmation that this judgement is correct. At the same time in the aftermath of a major crisis, such as independence invariably entails, the 'fear of freedom' drives many members of the public to seek refuge in the leadership of a single supposedly wise figure who represents both authority and stability.

Long-serving autocrats with tame military support are noticeably less common now than they were 20 years ago and the move away from military government that began in Latin America in the late 1970s gathered pace and has now affected almost every part of the world, from Haiti to China. Twenty years ago most Third World states were characterised by military governments, personalist dictatorships or one-party rule – or a combination of these. Now in Asia Thailand, South Korea, Bangladesh, Nepal and Indonesia no longer have personalist or military governments. Mongolia and many of the Central Asian republics of the former USSR have adopted democratic forms. However authoritarian rule does remain in Burma (Myanmar) where Aung San Suu Kyi remains under house arrest, despite the fact that as leader of the opposition she successfully won a democratic election organised by the military regime that is still holding her captive. Also, in October 1999 General Pervaiz Musharraf, seemingly reluctantly, assumed power in Pakistan when the Nawaz Sharif government collapsed. China remains authoritarian, as are a number of states in South-west Asia, notably Syria and Iraq. In Africa 25 out of 41 states have held competitive elections in the past five years, and all Latin American and Caribbean states have governments chosen by competitive election, though in Cuba's case the competition is severely restricted.

In liberal democracies, violence in society is controlled through the use of the legal system, but even there behind the legitimate authority of the government lies a very wide range of powers to control and to coerce, all backed by the sanction of force (see *inter alia* Hewitt 1992, Hillyard and Percy-Smith 1988). In the Third World, as in the First, most governments have at their disposal a substantial army, an extensive police system, and some kind of paramilitary reserve or militia that can be called upon in emergencies. However since they tend to identify their own survival with that of the state they rule they are much more likely to make open use of them.

The maintenance of a stable government is the fundamental assurance of the political control of a ruling elite. Losing control of government means at the least that their power will be severely curtailed, at most that it will be lost for good. But maintenance of a government is only part of political control, since it can only operate effectively if the system of relationships around it is maintained also, which is done by the use of both rewards and punishments. Rewards are available both for members and would-be members of the elite, and no less significantly for potentially useful people who might otherwise be political opponents, who may be co-opted into the system. As well as co-option, rewards include promotion, pensions and honours. Punishments include demotion, dismissal, fines, banishment, imprisonment and even execution. In Ghana, Jerry Rawlings had no less than four of his predecessors shot during his first brief term in office, but even military-based governments seldom go quite so far.

Authority is never absolute or unlimited. To have authority to do something is the right to do that thing, and be obeyed. Authority can be, and is, routinely delegated, divided or shared; otherwise complex governments could not work. Hence a government in all but the very smallest states has to depend on the willingness of others to implement its orders. The fact that they do so depends less on a specific act of recognition or legitimacy than on the fact that, on their own, few people regard themselves as having any alternative but to obey. All Weber's forms of authority, therefore, result in the same thing – obedience. The collective habit of obedience gives a tendency to inertia in social systems; once established they will tend to continue unaltered until a cultural shift occurs and society has forgotten any need for them. By extension, the longer a social institution continues in existence the longer it is likely to continue.

Conquest formed the basis of colonial rule. In post-colonial states, however, paradoxically, despite their rejection of colonialism, governments claim their authority by virtue of being successors to the colonial power, notably in Nigeria and Ghana, where force has been used again and again since independence to install a series of military governments. In consequence, for many people in the Third World 'internal colonisation' has simply replaced the traditional external variety. Internal colonisation is a term that has been used occasionally by Marxist writers but not with a very consistent meaning. Here it is used in a very specific sense, to draw attention to the fact that large parts of many Third World states are still in effect colonised by their own ruling elite.

This process has serious consequences, since this elite is generally one of town dwellers who tend both to fear and dislike the countryside and to seek their entertainment in what passes for an urban environment, or abroad in Paris or Las Vegas. The view from the capital involves the colonisation of the countryside by the town. The logical extension of the desire to control is the urbanisation of the countryside, reducing it to orderly, controllable form. The effect of this is the rapid destruction of rural habitat and ecosystems, which has reached an extreme as in the area surrounding Manila in the Philippines. Hence it is this urban perspective that contributes to the environmental crisis of the Third World (see Chapter 13).

Who makes the law?

The symbolism of Third World governments combines traditional elements such as chieftainship, colonial elements derived from the imperial past and modern notions such as the executive presidency. Some rulers, such as Sir Dawda Jawara of The Gambia or Sir Eric Gairy of Grenada retained the knighthoods of colonial governors. The government of India continues to operate from New Delhi designed by Sir Edwin Lutyens to serve as the capital of the Raj, and Indian regiments use bugles, bagpipes and the regimental silver as symbols of continuity. Pakistan is the world's largest manufacturer of bagpipes as well as of cricket bats. Yet the wheel of Asoka on the Indian flag, like the Sinhalese lion of Sri Lanka or the trigrams of Korea, speaks of a much older inheritance. The shield and spears of the flag of Kenya are traditional symbols of military and so of political power, but the fly whisk carried by Jomo Kenyatta (and other East African leaders) was also a symbol of chieftainship, even if the office he held was a modern, constitutional one.

By putting his own head on the coins of Ghana Nkrumah not only demonstrated in the clearest possible way that power had passed to an African but, as earlier rulers had done, confirmed his leadership in enduring form (Clapham 1982: 62). In Kenya, Kenyatta's style was that of an African monarch:

> When Kenyatta moved between State House in Nairobi and his homes in Gatundu, Mombasa and Nakuru, it was less the seat of government that moved, so much as an entire court. Kenyatta became the centre of governmental activity and thus access to him was the *sine qua non* of preferment for politicians, bureaucrats and businessmen alike. As discussed earlier, access to decision-makers is never unlimited and not always free in Africa. The court 'gatekeepers' of Kenya extracted sizeable entry fees and most visitors left with lighter wallets or thinner cheque books after having 'voluntarily' contributed to one of Kenyatta's favourite causes or schemes. (Williams 1987: 83)

What is clear is that in many Third World states, whether as heir of the colonial governor or as heir of the traditional chieftain, the president rules and does not reign. Indeed this is the form of government the citizens understand and (despite some of its obvious shortcomings) are comfortable with. The initiative in legislation lies, inevitably, with the government. Within the government, the adoption of the presidential system has placed great emphasis on the role of presidential leadership.

It has therefore also institutionalised conflict between presidents and legislatures, particularly, but not exclusively, in presidential states. Service as a legislator remains an important rung on the political ladder to preferment and the importance to a would-be Third World politician of a strong local power base in the region/area/tribe can hardly be overstated. In return rewards are expected by the local community as a result of support for the government, even in a one-party state.

In Latin American states institutionalised conflict between presidents and legislatures is compounded by multi-party politics. Factional squabbling was used as an excuse for President Fujimori of Peru to close Congress in 1992 and to rule by decree (Wood 2000). On the other hand the fall of both Carlos Andrés Pérez in Venezuela and Fernando Collor in Brazil was made *easier* by their lack of an effective congressional power base.

However there are limits on the power of other Third World governments to legislate. This is most noticeable in Muslim countries, such as Bangladesh, Pakistan or Sudan, where there has been strong pressure to make the Koran the sole basis of all law and governments have sought to reintroduce punishments such as flogging, amputation and stoning to death, which had been abolished by the former colonial power. In 1995 the government of Benazir Bhutto in Pakistan refused to intervene in the case of a 14-year-old Christian boy sentenced to death under Islamic law for having allegedly daubed walls with anti-Islamic slogans two years earlier. Fortunately for him, on appeal to a higher court, the evidence against him was dismissed as concocted, despite well-organised demonstrations outside the courtroom calling for the sentence to be upheld. In the long run the thing that may cause the greatest problem for these governments is the Koranic prohibition against charging interest on the use of money, since if it too is implemented it means either that banking systems will not function at all, or that they will be wholly in the hands of foreigners.

The problem of the weak state

Many of the problems of the Third World, therefore, come down to what can be called the problem of the weak state. Populist campaigning and the emotional aspects of television are used to reinforce the illusion that choice of a single candidate or party will solve all (or at least some) of the personal difficulties of the voter. But this is just not possible.

Even if it was possible to fund the overnight improvement in the distribution of wealth envisaged (for example) at the time of the election of President Mandela of South Africa, it is hard to see how he (or any other leader in a similar position) could be in a position to deliver. And the fact is that the Third World leader is rarely in a position to ensure policies become practice, not only because s/he lacks the resources, but because s/he does not have the power to see that those resources are actually allocated to the purpose for which they are intended. Even in relatively sophisticated states like Iran in the last years of the Shah, or Mexico under Gustavo López Portillo (1976–82), large sums were expended for work that was not carried out, government inspectors being bribed to ignore the obvious fact that the buildings and roads did not exist.

Conclusion

State-building is the most vital process in any newly independent Third World country. It is intimately linked to the development process because without an adequate perception of the country as its own state the dynamism and ambitions of the population (and in particular the entrepreneurial elite) will not be directed constructively. An identity must be forged at the collective level, just as it must for individuals. Nationalism, religion, ethnicity can either strengthen or weaken state identity, depending on how they are used. Clientelism, corruption and military intervention all act to undermine both authority and legitimacy, and in extreme circumstances can contribute to the collapse of regimes and the disintegration of the economic order. Because for a modern government to survive it must be supported by a healthy civil society, in which individuals and groups are able to exist openly and pursue their interests free from the fear of arbitrary power.

CHAPTER 8

Democratisation

Introduction

There has been much criticism of the fact that few of the constitutions of the newly emerging states in Africa or Asia long survived independence. Much of this criticism, in English-speaking countries, was directed at the 'Westminster model' of parliamentary democracy. Although the governments of both Sri Lanka and Pakistan seemed to be reconsidering reintroducing it, parliamentary democracy was alive and well in a number of Third World countries. Jamaica, Trinidad & Tobago, Botswana, Mauritius, India and Papua New Guinea and some smaller island states, together with Costa Rica in Central America, have all had stable democratic systems since 1948 (Pinkney 1993: 83). We could add to these Sri Lanka, which has had constitutional government since 1948, and Malaysia since 1957. Both have been independent longer than Jamaica. In Latin America, Mexico has had a stable constitutional government continuously since 1948; in fact, since 1920. On the other hand, though smaller island developing states are a better bet for democracy than their mainland counterparts, there is no guarantee of this: the Comoros (1975, 1978) and the Seychelles (1977) in the Indian Ocean, Fiji (1987, 2000) in the Pacific and Grenada (1979, 1983) in the Caribbean have all suffered from armed intervention in the political process. In 1994 the government of Sir Dawda Jawara in The Gambia succumbed, at the second attempt, to a military coup; in 1999 Melchior Ndadaye, its first Hutu head of state, was killed in a coup in Burundi. The 'Third Wave' of democratisation (Huntington 1993), which began in the later 1970s, has had setbacks. However the overall trend remains towards the spread and consolidation of democracy in the Third World.

Obviously, as the inclusion of Costa Rica makes clear, the absence of military forces or, alternatively, their weakness, is a major factor in safeguarding democracy (see Chapter 9). Other reasons for the survival (or otherwise) of democracy can be grouped as political, economic and social. Among the political reasons are: the existence of a widely accepted constitution for government, the

ability of major interest groups to influence decision making and the emergence
of broadly based and well-organised political parties.

Constitutions

It is certainly doubtful if many of the constitutions of independence would have
survived for long anyway. However their main problem was that they were
drafted by lawyers with a lawyer's concern for the *output* of government. Hence
the way in which democracy was to function was left to a series of assumptions
about the uses of power that were not widely shared and not necessarily understood. The result was a democracy for the elite, at best; at worst a system in
which smooth-tongued demagogues manipulated unsophisticated masses to
give electoral support to an essentially authoritarian system.

Naturally, too, in different ways the various colonial powers sought to ensure
as far as possible the continuing protection of their own interests. The documents
therefore took little or no account of the *input* side, especially the relationship
of business and financial interests to government. Business is often inimical to
democracy in its need to strike bargains and gain advantages over rivals, especially when armed with the financial resources of transnational corporations.
The precursors of independence were in a particularly strong position. They
could use their historical position to negotiate with the former colonial power
a settlement that left them in control of the key resources. Hence in many cases
the new government was dominated by a single tribe or regional faction. As
long as it had the necessary resources it was then in a position to generate political support through clientelism. Where such systems have survived, therefore,
there seem to have been at least two preconditions: that the resources available should be sufficient and that they be spent in a way that enhanced social
satisfaction and not frittered away on the self-indulgence of those in power.

Interest groups

Demands on the political system originate in the minds of individual citizens,
often in a quite unformed state. They may well not be immediately recognised
as political, and whether they are seen as such will depend on the nature of the
society concerned. However, except in a very local sense, the voice of one individual in a modern society will normally carry little weight unless the demands
which that individual articulates come from within the central elite and its
decision-making body – what Easton (1957, 1965) calls 'withinputs' or 'intra-
puts' – or until those concerned get together with others who share a common
interest and aggregate their demands into a programme for action. In liberal

democracies, typically, demands are articulated by interest groups and aggreg-
ated by political parties. However this model is by no means always applicable elsewhere.

It is now recognised that interest groups – people sharing a common interest – exist in all societies, though usually in a *latent* rather than an *active* state,
waiting to be activated by a relevant issue. In a sense they cover the entire field
of political interest articulation other than that of the individual, for the family
itself can be regarded as an interest group. Many groups, especially those with
better formal organisation, aggregate interests also into a common action programme. But the interest group differs from the political party, to which it is
closely related, by not seeking political power for itself; it seeks merely, when
it acts at all, to influence decisions taken by others.

In Third World countries interest groups are distrusted, and when they take
the form of ethnic or community groups there is great fear that they endanger
national unity. In India where a caste, ethnic group or region dominates the
politics of a state that group will benefit disproportionately in the allocation of
appointments and contracts. Many government officials, as Weiner (1962)
noted, tended initially to decry this tendency as a violation of democratic principles. They had, he suggests, a rather idealistic picture in their minds, not of
the way that the British system of democracy actually works, but of how it was
supposed to work, and nor were they well informed about the politics of the
United States of America.

Most Third World states are still characterised by a predominance of non-
associational interest groups (groups people are born into) and a relative
scarcity of formally organised associational groups (groups that people choose
to join – Almond in Almond and Coleman 1960: 33ff.). Theorists of democracy have identified a number of factors that appear to facilitate the emergence
and/or maintenance of democracy. Two relate to the expression of interests.
On the one hand, a relatively wealthy society is better able to fulfil all the
demands made upon it than a poor one. By definition, therefore, many Third
World states, lacking such resources, will find it difficult to satisfy these
demands. On the other, the development of powerful opposition coalitions is
much less likely where interests are diverse in nature and base, creating cross-
cutting cleavages within society, such that no one tribe or group is able to dominate the whole. The problem is how to secure this state of affairs.

The device of the separation of powers (or the division of powers between
federal and state governments in a federal system) is only effective where
enough interests pull in both directions.

Political parties and elections

A political party is a formal organisation of people seeking to achieve or to
retain political power.

Some writers on political parties find it hard to see many Third World political groupings as parties and regard them only as factions. While all political parties derive ultimately from factions, factions are temporary and their future always uncertain. Parties, on the other hand, are characterised by permanence of structure, a deliberate attempt to win recruits and regular procedures for recruitment of political leaders. Possession of these attributes can and does lead to the formal acceptance of their right to exist in law. For this reason Sartori believes that personalist parties, which often have a very short life with little or no institutional continuity, do not really deserve the title of party at all (Sartori 1976: 254–5). Since such parties are inevitably rather common in new states, where, that is, they are allowed to exist, this presents something of a problem. It is certainly also possible for them to institutionalise over time. Such is the case with the Peronist (or, more properly, Justicialist) Party in Argentina.

It is important to distinguish, too, between political parties and party systems. The most important distinctions are those between competitive systems, in which a number of parties compete for power, and non-competitive systems, where there is only one party. Where there is more than one party, parties shape not only themselves but one another. Hence the number of parties active is certainly significant, though unfortunately it is very difficult to define.

Competitive systems are the ideal of democratic theorists. However the public display of dissension that democracy requires comes as an unpleasant surprise to those brought up under the enforced stability of a colonial government or traditional regime. It is also true that in many democracies, perhaps the majority, elections are often accompanied by a high level of violence, and sadly more people may be killed in the quarrels that accompany an election than in the course of a military coup. Three-quarters of all military coups in Latin America in recent years have resulted in no casualties at all.

Hence, especially in the years immediately following independence, many Third World states sought to control internal rivalries by creating what is often loosely called a 'one-party state'. There are in fact three distinct types:

1. those systems where no party is allowed
2. single party systems
3. one-party (dominant) systems.

It is arguable all are clearly separable from competitive multi-party systems, but in very different ways.

Rise and fall of the 'one-party state'

Apologists for authoritarian rule paved the way for military intervention, especially but not exclusively in Africa. Abroad many who might otherwise have been more suspicious were influenced by enthusiasm for specific leaders, notably Julius Nyerere and his model of Tanzanian socialism.

From the 1960s onwards the idea that only one state-sponsored party was sufficient and indeed desirable was repeatedly justified by Third World leaders on the grounds that it overcame divisions damaging to an emergent nation. The one-party state may be seen as replacing tribal loyalties and identifications in holding together a fragmented society such as that of Zaire. However coalition building is always vital even under single-party rule or military dictatorship. Opposition elements, such as newspapers or trades unions, may be and frequently are co-opted by government by a not very subtle combination of inducement and threat.

The weakness of authoritarian government is that it rarely meets the aspirations of the population at large. Exceptions include both Brazil and South Korea where rapid economic growth was experienced under military government. However there are very many cases in which the reverse happens. The development boom of the 1970s was accompanied by growth of grassroots organisations. These were often seen as subversive by Third World governments, and every effort was made to limit their effectiveness. However in Brazil, where the number and importance of these 'base communities' is very marked, they were (and remain) strongly connected with the informal structure of the Catholic Church (see Chapter 6).

In modern times political parties are so widespread that it is usually only under a military dictatorship, when they are forbidden to organise, that they are entirely absent. Recent examples include Chile under General Pinochet after 1973 and Burma (Myanmar) at the present time. However there have been other cases. A noteworthy example was that of Afghanistan after the introduction by the king of parliamentary government in 1964. Since there were no political parties candidates ran as individuals, and very few eligible voters bothered to turn out. With no basis for organisation the parliament's proceedings were chaotic. This, as was possibly intended, enabled the king and the court clique to continue to run the country without effective interference, but in the end it helped create the conditions for the Soviet-backed military coup that overthrew the king and his parliament in 1973 (Weinbaum 1972).

By contrast, the Shah of Iran in 1963 had sponsored the organisation of one 'official' party, the Rastakhiz (New Iran) Party. Other parties were not banned, but strong pressure was brought to bear on members of the elite to show their loyalty to throne and country by becoming active members of the new organisation (Bill 1972: 44–51). Protected at least to some extent by the complex network of family influence many did not do so, but initially the new party seemed to be very successful; it was only later that it was shown how far its introduction had broken up the traditional structure of loyalties and so helped focus opposition on the regime and on the Shah personally.

A variant of the one-party system is to be found in Morocco, where officially there are a number of political parties but it is known which one at any one time enjoys the favour of the king, without which nothing can be done.

The party in such cases serves merely to identify the political elite and to enable them to continue to control the political process behind a façade of democracy. The pretence is the more convincing if the government does not formally create a one-party state, and encourages the emergence of an official opposition party that it can continue to control. Such states create an illusion of democratic participation while ensuring as far as possible that it does not become a reality. S.E. Finer termed them 'façade democracies'. As shown above, the mere existence of elections and parties does not guarantee that a system will give genuine and effective participation. It is essential to look closely enough to determine how the system works in practice, and especially what other political or social structures exist to control nominally 'democratic' activity.

Between one-party (dominant) systems and single-party systems the difference in theory is great but in practice there is a grey area. In some states one party can obtain overwhelming dominance of the political system without restraints being placed on opposition parties. Once in power it then becomes very difficult to dislodge. See Plate 9.

A striking example, as the opposition has found in recent years, was Mexico. When the Mexican Party of the National Revolution (PNR) was founded in 1929 no one was in doubt about its 'official' status. All key interests were required to form part of it and it was financed by a levy on the salaries of state employees. However other parties did function and in the period after the Second World War there seemed a genuine possibility that the system would evolve into a two-party system such as that of Colombia or Venezuela. However since 1964 it has become increasingly clear that every step in that evolution so far was being strenuously and, on the whole, successfully resisted. Even under President Salinas (1988–94) the opposition found it virtually impossible to succeed, if only at state level, and it was not until May 1995 that an opposition party succeeded in winning the governorship of a key state, Guanjuato.

India in the years immediately following independence is another obvious example. The Congress enjoyed its initial hegemony owing both to its leadership of the struggle for Indian independence and the presence of Pakistan. Nehru himself strengthened this position through the international good will and attention India obtained as the result of advocating, on behalf of smaller and less influential countries, a theory of their place in the world that they found congenial. But at home the supremacy of the Congress Party was maintained as the result of its success in monopolising patronage and being able to 'deliver' on its political promises. When excluded groups decided that they were not going to obtain access to patronage through the system, they were able through the democratic process to mount successful regional and ultimately national challenges. Their suspicions were confirmed by the autocratic style of Indira Gandhi and her willingness to use any means, including force, to maintain her leadership of a divided Congress. Still with the assistance of her land reform campaign, the dominant faction, Congress (I), retained sufficient credibility to recover from the disaster of the State of Emergency and its defeat at the polls in 1977. Though the party's hegemony has since been broken, following the breach in its dynastic leadership with the assassination of Rajiv Gandhi, the example of the Congress Party in India seems to illustrate both the strength of one-party politics and its most obvious limitations.

Such one-party systems, on the other hand, are quite different in principle from single-party systems, where opposition parties are either banned or persuaded by a variety of means, including if necessary force, to disband themselves. In single-party states elections are held. In the modern world there is no other universally accepted way of showing that a government is legitimate. But such elections (really plebiscites) merely act to confirm the continuity of a regime. There is no real chance of changing the office holders. The problem is, of course, that this situation is unstable. The creation of a single party does not really end competitition for power or office; it merely creates a pretence that it does not exist, while at the same time allowing resentment to build up against the existing office holders.

Two (and more) party systems do not guarantee rotation in office, but they do make it possible. Theorists of democracy regard the ability of the voters to change their rulers as one of the most important advantages of the system. The amount of harm they can do is limited to their elected term and rival groups are given a turn in managing the affairs of the state. Of course there is a cost. Holding elections is expensive and competitive politics leads to a great deal of money being spent to win votes, though the history of the spoils system in the United States of America (and Japan) suggests that clientelism in itself is not a barrier to economic or political development. The short timespan of an elected government, however, may also operate against long-term development planning. However opposition builds up over time and giving up political power is better than facing the firing squad.

Presidential vs. parliamentary government

Parallel with the move to institute one-party states was the tendency in the years after 1960 to abandon the parliamentary constitutions inherited from the colonial period and replace them with presidential systems. Of course almost all republics use the term 'president' to designate their head of state, the official who represents the state on formal occasions receives ambassadors and performs a range of ceremonial duties. A presidential system is one in which the president does not merely carry out the formal duties as head of state but also acts as head of government, chief executive and (at least in theory) commander-in-chief of the armed forces.

The system of government in which power is concentrated in the hands of an executive president was a regional curiosity before 1946. In the first three decades of the nineteenth century presidential systems were adopted by most of the newly independent states of the Americas, with the exception of part of Haiti and of Brazil, which remained a parliamentary monarchy until 1889

(Needler 1963). Only one other presidential state dates from this period: Liberia, a colony for freed American slaves, independent in 1847. After that there was a long gap, until the rising power of the United States of America created Hawaii (1892; annexed by the USA 1898) and Cuba (1901).

It was only after 1946 when the Philippines, under US tutelage from 1898 onwards, became independent, that the presidential system came to sweep the rest of the Third World, beginning with the Middle East and North Africa, and spreading throughout Africa South of the Sahara in the wake of the dissolution of the British, French and Portuguese colonial empires after 1960. So powerful was the urge to imitate it that even established parliamentary systems such as those of Pakistan and Sri Lanka were modified in the direction of presidentialism.

But few of the systems that have resulted are true presidential systems in the constitutional sense. Since there is no focus of power presidential systems are dynamically unstable. The invariable tendency has been for the president to assume, often with the aid of force, control over all functions of government. To be a true presidential state three conditions have all to be observed. The president must be elected directly by the people according to agreed rules generally regarded as fair and for a definite term. There is a subtle difference between being elected for a series of definite terms and being in power indefinitely, but in practice one tends to lead to the other. Consequently constitutional provisions limiting presidential terms are normal, though they are often abused, if necessary by the systematic rewriting of the constitution. The president must not be able to dissolve the assembly, or suspend its powers during its fixed term of office. In practice this is often done, as in Uruguay in 1973, by the leaders of military or military-backed regimes, making use, in most if not all cases, of emergency powers (Weinstein 1975: 132–3).

Though there must, if government is to function at all, be a close relationship between the two areas of competence, executive and legislature, summed up in the American phrase 'checks and balances', they must be reciprocal and there must be limits on the president's ability to influence the assembly. The balance is perhaps easier to attain when, as usually happens, the president is elected at the same time as the assembly. Even then different political parties may, as in Brazil since 1990 or in Venezuela in 1994, be chosen to represent the people in each of the branches of government.

Populism and democracy

The term arises from its use by the People's Party, which achieved some electoral success in the USA of the early 1890s for its Omaha Platform, but was eventually swallowed up in the Democratic Party (Hicks 1961). Slightly earlier, a group of intellectuals in Russia had called themselves the *narodniki* – a term usually translated as 'populist'. They, like their very different US counterparts, believed in the proposition that 'virtue resides in the simple people, who are the overwhelming majority, and in their collective traditions' (Wiles in Ionescu and Gellner 1969: 166).

Populist movements have received particular attention in the Latin American context, where they are associated with the early stages of industrialisation. There a populist movement has been defined as: 'A political movement which enjoys the support of the mass of the working class and/or peasantry, but which does not result from the autonomous organizational power of either of these two sectors. It is also supported by non-working class sectors upholding an anti-status quo ideology' (Di Tella 1965).

Dix (1985) has argued that there are two distinct forms of populism: authoritarian and democratic. For him the authoritarian form is characterised by leadership from the military, the upper middle class, landowners and industry, support from a 'disposable mass' of urban/unskilled workers and a short-term, diffuse, nationalist, status-quo-oriented ideological base. The democratic form is led by professionals and intellectuals, its support comes from organised labour and/or peasants, and its ideological base is more concrete and reformist, with its nationalism more articulate. Yet in practice populist movements are both democratic and authoritarian in differing degrees.

Latin American populism, therefore, is 'urban, multiclass, electoral, expansive, "popular," and led by charismatic figures' (Conniff 1982: 13). However, as di Tella implies, it is stretching matters to suggest that populism is urban rather than rural, and in practice the term has come to refer to any movement characterised by three things:

1. an assertion that the people are always right
2. a broad, non-ideological coalition of support
3. a charismatic leader, often lacking any specific ideological commitment.

Canovan (1981: 13) derives from actual examples a typology of no less than seven types of populism. These, too, are 'ideal types', and actual movements may well overlap more than one of her categories. The importance of them is precisely how clearly they demonstrate both how widespread populism is and how its main characteristic is its *fluidity*. It was this that provided a vehicle for leaders such as Gamal Abd-el Nasser of Egypt and Saddam Hussein of Iraq to mobilise the masses in support of their governments. The key to their success is the way in which they identify issues that call forth the maximum response from their chosen constituency (Canovan 1981).

The populist leader, however, speaks on behalf of the masses and seeks to control them for his or her own purposes. S/he finds out what they want, only to be able to offer it to them. To that extent, therefore, the successful populist leader takes responsibility off the shoulders of the people, whereas if they are to participate in a fully democratic society they have to avoid the temptation to abandon the cares of responsibility to others.

Empowerment and democratisation

Empowerment, on the other hand, lies in encouraging individuals and groups actually to make their own decisions and to take part in shaping their own future.

This is not a new idea in the Third World. It lies at the root of the panchayat system in India, and in the island states of Oceania the tradition is so strong that decisions concerning the whole community are made collectively by a Council of Elders.

Empowerment, if it is to mean anything, means that people must be able to participate effectively in the making of decisions affecting them. In other words it is not enough for them to be told what the government is going to do for them. They have to be able to initiate policies and to shape the development of policies initiated by others.

This means having the ability to participate in decision making at all relevant levels and through a variety of channels. In most states significant decisions are made on at least two levels: local and national; in federal states at least three. It is also true that certain important decisions relating to the national and local economy of Third World states are taken abroad, outside the state boundaries, whether by banks, aid agencies, transnational corporations or otherwise. Nevertheless the first step in empowerment is learning how things work on the local level. External influences are only effective when they work with local interests.

Democratisation in the Third World has certainly been encouraged by the fall of communism in eastern Europe. However the pressure for democratisation already existed in the Third World before 1989, by which time most of the countries in Latin America had returned to constitutional government and more than half the countries in Africa had held competitive multi-party elections.

Democratisation movements have in the recent past been seriously hampered by their identification with anti-state activity, and in many cases concessions have been made that on closer examination often turn out to be more apparent than real. Hence the mere existence of multi-party elections does not guarantee that truly competitive politics will operate.

Singapore illustrates some of the ambiguities of the democratisation process. Before 1991 the ruling People's Action Party held all the seats in Parliament. Since the election of 1991 there have been four opposition members in the 81-member unicameral Parliament but they hardly add up to an effective opposition. Although he had had the support of the vast majority of his people since he came to power in 1959 with a programme of social reform/economic development that has been very successful for most of the population, Singapore's first prime minister, Lee Kuan Yew, who led the country into independence from Malaysia in 1965, had been in effect an autocrat for more than 30 years when he decided to retire. He continued to watch over his creation, a remarkably disciplined city-state, from the post of senior minister in the prime minister's office.

In consequence the impulse to democratisation may produce a system where democracy is defined in very limited terms (Arat 1991). For example, equal political rights may exist on paper but social and economic inequality may be protected from political interference. Third World democracies often have quite restrictive politics with considerable coercive power, for example India and Kenya. The more adept regimes arrange for a public display of the trappings of democracy and may allow semi-official opposition parties to participate in doctored elections, as in Mexico.

A third possibility is illustrated by Brazil, where a mass electorate is influenced by the enormous power and highly questionable role in the Third World context of the media. Some 18 million people in Brazil get their news from the O Globo TV station each evening and O Globo sees part of its role as manufacturing presidential candidates. But for Brazil, as for some other Third World countries, the replacement of formal military government with formal 'democratic' government conceals the continuing (and possibly enhanced) importance of some groups in society, including (and perhaps especially) the military establishment. If the military have ceased to intervene it can be because they really do not need to do so. In 1994 President Cardoso, elected with the support of O Globo, sent troops into the *favelas* (shantytowns) of Rio de Janeiro in search of drug dealers. Ever since these depressed neighbourhoods have echoed to the sound of gunfire, but the drug problem gets no better, since the methods that are being used to counter it are entirely inappropriate.

The growth of civil society

'Civil society' is defined by Rueschemeyer et al. (1992) as: 'The totality of social institutions and associations, both formal and informal, that are not strictly production-related nor governmental nor familial in character'. Walzer (1995: 7) uses a slightly wider definition: 'The space of uncoerced human association and also the set of relational networks – formed for the sake of family, faith, interests and ideology – that fill this space'. This space cannot exist unless civil and political rights are effective and organisations formed by individuals and groups enjoy associational autonomy.

Modernisation and transition theorists argue that a 'vibrant' civil society is essential to successful democratisation, because it:

1. is an essential bulwark against the power of the state, concentrating people into groups and increasing interaction between them so that a protest against authoritarian rule is more likely (Diamond 1992);
2. mobilises previously excluded classes (Rueschemeyer et al. 1992);
3. enables a *political culture* favourable to democracy to emerge and to become consolidated (Dahl 1989, Almond and Verba 1963, 1980).

Conclusion

With the fall of communism in eastern Europe there have since 1989 been signs of a new interest amongst international funding and lending agencies in promoting 'good government' in developing countries. Hence political conditions are attached to loans. These conditions may encourage formal democratic procedures rather than substantive democratic gains for the majority in the recipient countries.

Certainly many more Third World countries enjoy ostensibly democratic structures today than was the case, say, 20 years ago. However there are factors that militate against real participation whatever the theoretical arrangements. First, democracy cannot be imposed from above, and it takes time to establish itself even in the most favourable circumstances. Second, democracy, as does the market, functions less effectively in conditions of poverty, and where, for example, it means freedom to sell your vote to a corrupt local politician, it has little substance. Third, even for many genuinely newly democratised countries, much energy has first to be consumed in trying to come to terms with an undemocratic past.

For the increasingly secular societies of the non-Islamic world there is no other basis for legitimate authority than some form of democracy. How then can national history be satisfactorily explained? Democracy is no longer a decorative ideological overlay on a functional authoritarian base, it is the essence of that functioning. As Brundtland so rightly points out (WCED 1987), without participation development will not happen and the environment will be destroyed.

CHAPTER 9

The armed forces and politics

Introduction

There are nearly 200 countries in the world but only three (Costa Rica, Iceland and Luxembourg) have no military forces. In general, where there are military forces there will be military intervention, though usually of a limited kind. Even in the advanced industrialised countries, where armed military intervention is a rarity, the armed forces are a major spending department of government and with the advantage of inside knowledge constitute a most formidable lobby in defence of their privileges and their budget, though this is not usually regarded as intervention. For that the armed forces have to show that they are ready and willing to make use of their unique resource, the ability to use force.

And in Third World states armies are of very great importance indeed. During the 1980s they not only assumed and/or retained political power throughout the Third World, they spent at the same time an ever increasing proportion of their countries' wealth on arms. The consequence was arrested development and (in some places) accelerated environmental degradation.

Military intervention

Finer (1975) regards military intervention, in the more active sense usually implied by the term, as being the product of both the ability and the disposition to intervene. Virtually all armies, however, have the ability to intervene; the question is why and how they choose to do so.

Military intervention in politics in Third World states results both from push (propensity/disposition to intervene) and pull (stimulation/provocation) factors. Both may be needed to trigger an actual intervention, as for example when the breakdown of legitimate civilian government is accompanied by changes in the military institution.

Push factors for military intervention include the ambitions of individual officers, factional disaffection and institutional activity said or believed to be in the 'national interest'. Pull factors include the association of the armed forces with military victories, a general perception of a lack of cohesion, discipline or stability in society, and a specific perception by the armed forces of threats to the military institution or to the officer class, or to the dignity or security of the nation.

The ambitions of individual officers undoubtedly do play a part in military coups. However their idiosyncratic nature makes it plain that they cannot of themselves be regarded as a general cause of coups. Some individual leaders, such as General Sani Abacha in Nigeria in 1993, have seized power in their own names. But, on the other hand, some coups have resulted in the choice as leader of personnel who did not take part at all in the coup itself. Examples from Africa are the choice by his fellow officers of Captain Valentine Strasser as head of state of Sierra Leone in April 1992 and the release of Major Johhny Paul Koroma from prison to head the new junta that siezed power in Sierra Leone in May 1997 (*Annual Register*, 1992: 261, 1997: 253–4; see also Wiking 1983: 134–5).

Factional disaffection is a serious problem when poorer Third World states are unable or unwilling to reward their armed forces at the level they have come to expect. The former was clearly the case in the mutiny of ordinary soldiers led by Sergeant Doe that overthrew and killed the president of Liberia in 1980, and the latter in the fall of Busia in Ghana in 1972. Both are exemplified by the episode in January 1994 in Lesotho when the capital Maseru was shelled by opposing army factions ostensibly seeking OAU mediation of a pay dispute. Behind this claim, however, lay the fear of both factions that they would lose both power and perquisites following the landslide defeat in Lesotho's first free elections of the military-supported Basotho National Party, which had ruled since 1966. On the other hand in an army mutiny in June 1998 President Viera of Guinea Bissau received support from both Senegal and Guinea.

Institutional activity, the most important of these factors, rests on military ethos, socialisation of officers, the social standing of the military in Third World states and the organisational strengths of the military relative to other institutions. The armed forces intervened in Ghana in 1966 to put an end to the government of President Nkrumah that they regarded as 'interfering' with the army (Austin 1978: 51, Afrifa 1966).

The contagion theory of military intervention, that coups in neighbouring states contribute to the will to intervene, and the habituation theory, that coups are fostered by the tradition of past coups by the same military institution, are also aspects of military explanations. However though neither is necessarily simply military, and the latter in particular obviously reflects the weak legitimacy accorded to civilian institutions, both are supported by statistics which show clearly that coups tend to be particularly common in certain countries and do seem to be imitated within regions (Brier and Calvert 1975).

In a number of military takeovers external influence and encouragement can be inferred, though rarely proved. As Ruth First pointed out, even if foreign influence did play a part in African coups in the 1960s, internal factors were also at work and were at least equally important (First 1972: 17, Decalo 1976).

However, despite the argument of Samuel P. Huntington that military aid and assistance has no political effect (1968: 192), the wave of military coups that occurred in Africa in the 1960s did receive significant foreign encouragement both before and after the event by the way in which foreign powers, especially the United States of America and France, provided support for military governments, military aid and training missions. Britain, too, welcomed the fall of Milton Obote, whose aircraft had been unaccountably delayed in returning to Uganda, enabling Idi Amin to seize power in his absence (Wiking 1983: 28). At the same time post-1961 counter-insurgency training by the USA both in the United States of America itself and in the School of the Americas in Panama promoted the development of a virulent anti-communism and the 'national security ideology' amongst the armed forces of Latin America. The latter was later summed up by the Argentine General (later President) Leopoldo Galtieri in the phrase, 'The Third World War is one of ideology against ideology', and it was to lead in that country to the atrocities of the 'dirty war'.

Civilian explanations rest on pull factors such as the weakness of civilian institutions, participation overload, lack of political legitimacy and economic instability.

The first three of these undoubtedly played a part in shaping the military assumptions of power in both Africa and Latin America during the 1960s. However Jenkins and Kposowa (1992) found that the African military coups they studied had their roots in military centrality and ethnic competition, not in participation overload or economic dependency causing social unrest. In Latin America, following encouragement from the Carter administration in the USA, civilian institutions successfully reasserted themselves during the 1980s.

The economic failure of a civilian government affects the armed forces both directly, by leaving less money for them, and indirectly, by alienating popular support for the government (Nordlinger 1977). The impact of economic instability on the social groups of which officers are members, rather than on the military institution itself, may be important in encouraging them to take action. True, economic failure is seldom cited as a major reason for a military coup, and more often than not it has been given as a reason for the replacement of one military government by another (Wiking 1983: 116). However the fall of Jamail Mahuad Witt in Ecuador in January 2000 did follow many months of unrest and rioting at the economic failure of his government.

Sometimes the military assumption of power results from a civilian government shooting itself, metaphorically speaking, in the foot. The *autogolpe*, or 'self-coup', led by an elected leader against his own government, continues to be a problem in Latin America. Even President Fujimori of Peru has referred to his illegal assumption of additional powers in 1992 as an *autogolpe*. President Itamar Franco was still being urged to close Brazil's Congress in January 1994.

However he wisely resisted the temptation to try to do so and the Presidential elections scheduled for later in the year went ahead as planned.

Structure of armed forces

Obviously the military role in the politics of any given country does depend crucially on the nature and origins of the armed forces themselves and their relationship to the society in which they serve. In Nigeria, for example, the military takeover of 1966 owed much to the persistence of tribal consciousness in the army amongst the northerners who felt excluded by the commercially active and politically dominant Igbo (Ibo). The first coup, in January 1966, was directed not only against the civilian government but also the military leadership of Major-General Ironsi. The killing of senior officers that accompanied it significantly altered the composition of the officer corps, leaving Ibo officers holding nearly every senior position. The second coup, in April 1966, led to a massacre of both Ibo soldiers and civilians (Luckham 1971a: 76).

The coup which killed William V. Tubman in Liberia in 1980 was born of resentment by the dominant tribe of the interior, the Vai, of their exclusion from power by the True Whig Party and Americanised settlers on the coast. The assassination on 6 April 1994 of President Habyarimana, first Hutu president of Rwanda, triggered the wholesale massacres of the dominant Tutsi that had been promised for some months by Radio Mille Collines.

However it does not follow that the military act only as the armed wing of a tribe, or indeed of a class. Even weak Third World armies are highly organised and hierarchically structured organisations, and the profound importance of the army as an institution to soldiers should never be underestimated. This is compounded by the fact that the majority of armies are dominated by a relatively small, professionally trained officer corps (Howard 1957). Its recruits are in terms of their respective societies largely middle class. Though in a number of African states they tend overwhelmingly to be drawn from a single tribe or region this is not always the case, and anyway once recruited and trained they are bound together by important institutional ties. It is through the service as an institution, moreover, that they obtain access to a system of substantial personal privileges, such as pensions, mortgages, credit, cheap goods, clubs and free medical attention. Most importantly, it is membership of the institution that guarantees at one and the same time a high standard of living relative to that of the societies they are supposed to serve, and also the opportunity through promotion to gain access to much greater rewards in various government positions.

Military intervention in politics is guaranteed by the need to maintain this institutional structure in the face of competing civilian interests. Its persistence is due to the complex interrelationship between the three levels of the social, institutional and personal interest of the intervenors, such that no one of them can be singled out as the cause, nor wholly disentangled from the others (Calvert 1990: 42–4).

Competing roles of armed forces: military, social, political

The principal role of the armed forces is, of course, to fight the armed forces of other countries. However for a variety of reasons this role is relatively unlikely to be dominant in many Third World states. In Latin America distance, formidable natural barriers and relatively small armies have helped prevent all but a handful of major conflicts. In Africa at decolonisation, armies were often no more than token forces. The decision of the OAU to respect colonial boundaries has meant that despite a very considerable build-up of potential trouble actual conflicts have been few. In both cases the majority of armed forces are too small and too dependent on supplies from abroad to present serious resistance to the armed forces of a major power. However, as noted above, the 1980s saw a very rapid arms build-up in Third World states, especially in Africa SSA.

In South Asia, on the other hand, the long-standing feud between India and Pakistan has resulted in four wars since 1947, and the loss to Pakistan, not only of part of Kashmir but more seriously of its former eastern part, now Bangladesh. The Soviet Union invaded Afghanistan in 1979 but was unable to defeat its ill-organised, tribal armies. China's army has mounted a punitive expedition against Vietnam and its navy disputes with both Vietnam and the Philippines the sovereignty of the Spratly Islands. Significantly in each of these cases the armed forces seem for the most part to be highly professional and to have been brought in recent years under civilian control. Only in South-west Asia do large fighting forces operate under the command of authoritarian military governments, notably those of Syria and Iraq.

Governments may also be challenged from within, by insurgent movements. In Latin America such challenges have been a major reason (some would say excuse) why armies have intervened in politics. The wave of military coups that began in 1961 initially formed a limited response to the Cuban Revolution and to local circumstances (Lieuwen 1964). By 1965 the challenge of guerrilla-type movements had been effectively contained, and the attempt by some movements to switch their tactics into what was loosely and incorrectly termed 'urban guerrilla warfare' was to prove equally unsuccessful. Part of the reason was the intrinsic weakness of the movements themselves, criticised by Gérard Chaliand (1977: 48–9):

A certain number of other sociological traits common to most Latin American societies also need to be mentioned. While these would be secondary in a major war, with the revolution held together by a central revolutionary ideology, these traits weigh against successful action in other circumstances: verbal inflation, accompanied by a slight ability to keep secrets; lack of group cohesiveness, worsened by an obsession with authority (what Latin American in charge of a dozen others resists proclaiming himself *comandante*?); machismo and fascination with death (largely products of the Hispanic tradition).

However it was perhaps inevitable that Latin American armies, encouraged by fresh supplies of arms from the USA, should have taken the credit for defeating subversion. Hence, during the transition from the first to the second phase, in the mid-1960s the doctrine took root that the only way to cope with armed insurgency was through military government, beginning in 1964 with Brazil (Philip 1984, 1985, Black 1976, cf. O'Brien and Cammack 1985).

With the return to civilian government over most of the Americas the two major states in Latin America in which combating guerrillas remained a major task for the armed forces in the 1990s were Colombia and Peru, the former under civilian government, the latter at least nominally so. However in other parts of the Third World governments are also faced with widespread insurgency. In Asia, insurgency and subversion are still the major concerns of the government of Burma (Myanmar) and despite the nominal victory of Taliban much of Afghanistan remains effectively outside the control of the government in Kabul. In Africa, the peace settlement between the government of Mozambique and Renamo meant that in 1999 the latter, initially organised as a guerrilla movement by the settler government of Rhodesia and supplied by South Africa, continued to control most of the core of the country, drawing their support (as did the government) from specific ethnic groups (*Annual Register*, 1998: 297).

Military training may however, even in broadly civilian societies, be a valuable path to social preferment. In Latin America compulsory military training was introduced towards the end of the nineteenth century, enabling the armed forces to promote themselves as one of the major pillars of the national identity.

Historically soldiers have played a major role in geographical surveying and the establishment of communications in remote regions. In Third World states these tasks too are still of considerable significance in the development of, *inter alia*, North-west India and modern Pakistan, Iraq and Egypt. In Amazonia the Brazilian army maintains communications, surveys geographical formations, watches for infiltrators, and teaches civics classes. In the remoter regions of Ecuador, Bolivia and Peru too, the army has historically often been the sole agency of government that is actually effective over large areas (see Bourricaud 1970: 313–15).

Miltary developmentalism

Not surprisingly, armies that have assumed such tasks are easily persuaded that they have a wider mission to bring about the development of their countries. In

Latin America in the 'developmentalist' era of the 1960s a new phenomenon emerged, starting with Brazil in 1964, by which the armed forces seized power with the open intention of staying in power for an indefinite period, long enough to bring about the forced development of their societies. This phenomenon is often termed 'bureaucratic authoritarianism', a term originally invented by the Argentine Guillermo O'Donnell (1988), whose views derive from Marxism and more particularly from dependency theory.

O'Donnell's theory envisages three stages of development of political systems. In the oligarchic stage the popular sector is not yet politicised, and so is neither mobilised nor incorporated in the state structure. In the populist stage the popular sector is mobilised and incorporated. In the bureaucratic-authoritarian stage it is then demobilised and excluded. For O'Donnell the bureaucratic-authoritarian state 'guarantees and organizes the domination exercised through a class structure subordinated to the upper fractions of a highly oligopolized and transnationalized bourgeoisie' (1988: 31). Within the state structure two groups have decisive weight: specialists in coercion (the armed forces), whose job it is to exclude the 'popular sector' from power, and finance capitalists, whose role is to obtain the 'normalisation' of the economy, which performs the dual purpose of excluding the popular sector from economic power and promoting the interests of large oligopolistic interests. As part of the exclusion policy social issues are depoliticised by being treated as a matter of narrow economic rationality, and direct access to government is limited to the armed forces, the state bureaucracy and leading industrialists and financiers.

However the term bureaucratic-authoritarianism seems rather to be designed to distract from its key feature, the fact that the process was directed by the army and gained its distinctive features from the army's ability to make use of force. For this reason the present writers use the term 'military developmentalism', a term that stresses its analogies with the military regimes of Egypt under Nasser, Pakistan under Zia ul-Haq or even Thailand, where a succession of military leaders have held office within a strongly formalised system of public administration deriving legitimacy from the charismatic and traditional authority of the monarchy.

Military and civilian militarism

There are two types of militarism: 'military' militarism – militarism amongst the military personnel themselves, and 'civilian' militarism – militarism among the civilian population (Vagts 1959).

Military militarism is a caste pride, a pride in the glory, honour, power and prestige of the military forces. This type of militarism, however, goes well beyond the normal pride of belonging to a well-organised force, resulting in extreme cases in an exaggerated sense of remoteness and of superiority over the outside world in all aspects, so that those functions that the military does not undertake are considered to be not worthwhile for society as a whole. Military militarism, then, tends to arise in one of two sets of circumstances.

The first is when, for whatever reason, the whole end, existence and pride of the state is seen by them to be the concern of the army and the army alone. In modern Third World states this condition in its extreme form is fortunately rather rare, if only because few Third World armies can convincingly see themselves as an effective fighting force against all possible opponents. However the Chinese army, which re-emerged as a distinct political force during the chaos that followed the Great Proletarian Cultural Revolution, has shown in its handling of the Tiananmen Square demonstrations that in the last analysis it was prepared to intervene to safeguard the state structure that it has established. There is also some evidence of military militarism as a factor in North Korea.

However a lower level of military militarism is widespread in Third World states. The forces in such countries – whether in Asia, Latin America or Africa – have a pride in their prowess that does not necessarily derive from recent combat, as, in many cases, for geographical or other extraneous reasons the opportunity has not arisen. Until recently, however, the fact of independence implied an important historic role for the forces. They had the role of guardians of the state thrust upon them, in their opinion, because they saw themselves as the ones who had given birth to it. Second, the forces in those countries are relatively well educated compared with their fellow-citizens and in addition have a significant capacity for the use of force.

The alternative situation is when the military feel that they have been betrayed by their own civilians. The most striking Third World example may well still be Egypt after the humiliation of 1948, when the government of King Farouk accepted the Anglo-Egyptian Treaty. The fact that Egyptian forces were so conspicuously outclassed by the apparently amateur Israeli army (Neguib 1955) led to a process of military politicisation and ultimately to the revolution of 1952. Throughout the Middle East, in Libya, Iraq and elsewhere, the military have continued to see the confrontation with Israel as justification for their continued rule, a situation deftly exploited by leaders such as Gadaffi in Libya or Saddam Hussein in Iraq.

Civilian militarism is the other side of the same coin. It may afflict either the elite or the mass of the society, or in extreme cases both. It is a feeling amongst civilians that the army should be rewarded with the unconditional support of the population on whose behalf it fights. In extreme cases it then becomes a nationalist pride in crude power and can lead, again in Vagts's words, to 'self-immolation on the altar of violence' (1959: 22). In weak states, relying for the effective use of force on inadequately trained and equipped armies, this can lead to catastrophe. Thus the intervention by West African states in the civil war in Liberia did not succeed in arresting the slide of that country into chaos, but it did succeed in destabilising neighbouring Sierra Leone. Military rule is often seen as an efficient and therefore acceptable substitute for weak and divided civilian government. Unfortunately the reality is often very different.

Table 9.1 Expenditure on defence in excess of 12% of budget in 1990 with 1992 percentage (high income countries in italics)

Country	1990	1992
United Arab Emirates	*41.9*	*na*
Oman	41.0	35.8
Syria	40.7	42.3
Pakistan	30.9	27.9
South Korea	25.8	22.1
Israel	*25.4*	*22.1*
Burma (Myanmar)	24.7	22.0
El Salvador	24.5	16.0
Jordan	23.1	26.7
United States of America	*22.6*	*20.6*
Kuwait	*19.9*	*na*
Thailand	17.3	17.2
India	17.0	15.0
Zimbabwe	16.5	na
Bolivia	14.1	9.8
Iran	13.6	10.3
Guatemala	13.3	na
Paraguay	13.3	13.3
Ecuador	12.9	12.9
Egypt	12.7	na
United Kingdom	*12.2*	*11.3*

Source: World Bank, *World Development Report*, 1992

Arms procurement

Independence is often accompanied, as we have already noted, by a rise in nationalism that in turn promotes enhanced arms expenditure (Table 9.1). Since then the costs have escalated and in most cases faster than income.

The quest for 'security' has three aspects for both politicians and military. The importance of each kind varies between these two groups, but also within them too. The three aspects are:

1. defence of territory from invasion/occupation
2. defence of raw materials and markets
3. defence of political and social values.

The fact that military budgets are remarkably constant over time as a percentage of GNP suggests they are not responsive to actual threats but reflect aspects of the national political culture, such as how much the people will endure, the degree of paranoia or the salience of the presumed threat. Likewise, in the rare cases in which Third World states have significant navies or air forces, the allocation of resources between the services seems to be more a consequence of their lobbying power than of a real estimate of a strategic or tactical threat.

Vested interests include not just military establishments and the arms industry, but also scientists and engineers, diplomats and other civil servants who administer the defence establishments of their countries. Though this is more obvious in the weapons-producing countries it is no less true of those that are buying. Thus the perception of national 'security' contributes to economic and environmental insecurity. As Brundtland says in *Our Common Future*: 'Competitive arms races breed insecurity among nations through spirals of reciprocal fears. Nations need to muster resources to combat environmental degradation and poverty. By misdirecting scarce resources, arms races contribute further to insecurity' (World Commission on Environment and Development 1987). This was echoed in 1989 by Paul Shaw, a UN adviser on population and development: 'No amount of deforestation in Brazil, desertification in the Sahel, or water pollution in the Nile can compare with the cumulative effects of war' (quoted in *New Internationalist*, September 1992: 14).

It is hardly surprising that heterogeneous new states experience internal conflicts, sometimes even civil wars. These were during the cold war period sometimes exacerbated by 'great power' intervention. When this takes place on opposite sides the risk of escalation increases dramatically.

Since 1945 there have been over 120 international and civil conflicts in the South. More than 20 million people have died as a consequence. There have been hundreds of attempted coups, some much bloodier than others. There are countless refugees from conflict both directly because of fear and indirectly from the environmental degradation it causes and the consequent loss of livelihood.

However at the same time developed countries have lost no opportunity to promote profitable arms sales to the South. Four out of five of the largest arms dealers: the United States of America, the United Kingdom, France and Russia, are in the North and all are members of the UN Security (sic) Council. Credits for such purchases are generally easy to get and it is left to future generations to pay the bill. As it is, the military expenditure of developing countries is some 25 per cent of the world total, and even in 1986, ironically designated the International Year of Peace, this amounted to more than $900 billion. Of course the Third World's contribution to the arms trade specifically is proportionately much greater, accounting for some 60 per cent of the $21 billion trade by 1990. These figures represent a colossal transfer of funds from the South to the North and are estimated to have added some 40 per cent to the Third World debt burden.

Third World military expenditure is highly concentrated in a few countries, but even so it is rarely proportionate to the potential threat or to the resources available. Developing countries spend more as proportions of their budgets on military activity than developed countries. Their spending on arms for example is three times as much as would be needed to provide healthcare, sanitation and clean water to all their populations. One of the most glaring examples of this obsession is Ethiopia, where under the Derg the armed forces consumed some 10 per cent of the country's GNP, while only some 1.5 per cent was spent on health. Moreover the diversion of resources to arms is only the direct cost to development. There are also indirect costs associated with the distortion of the political culture, including the decline of democracy and participation, the growth of corruption and popular alienation from the government and society. In the late 1990s the government of President Mugabe of Zimbabwe spent so much on military intervention in the Democratic Republic of Congo that it destabilised the Zimbabwean economy and resulted in the defeat of his proposals for constitutional reform (*Financial Times*, 9–10 April 2000).

Third World arms production also exists and is in fact becoming an increasingly significant, although a far from desirable South–South linkage. There is already generally a redistribution of funds within the Third World from the poorer to the richer and more powerful states. Brazil stands out as the leading arms manufacturer and exporter in the Third World, with more than a million people employed in arms production. The future role of South Africa, where the African National Congress (ANC) government has inherited a strong indigenous arms industry, has yet to be determined.

Nuclear weapons in the Third World

The idea of deterrence due to the threat of mutual annihilation is really a product of a bipolar world and relies on the rationality and stability of the actors concerned. But as Keith Colquhoun has put it (1993: 210): 'The problem of North Korea is that the government is widely perceived to be insane'.

In 1945 only the USA had nuclear weapons. During much of the cold war era the nuclear 'club' remained limited to the USA, USSR, UK, France and China. Moreover, the power blocs gave rise to an ideological line-up and only China could be said to have an independent nuclear capability. By the end of the cold war a further six countries, including Pakistan, were on the verge of acquiring nuclear weapons and ten more, including India, Brazil and South Africa, had the capacity to do so.

It is clear that the original US strategy of non-proliferation has failed. This is not surprising, since successive summits were aimed primarily at reducing the inherent risks of superpower confrontation and the United States of America felt it necessary to connive at the acquisition of nuclear capability by friendly countries such as Britain, France and Israel rather than risk its overall strategic dominance. The Non-proliferation Treaty was negotiated to try to limit superpower activity and was not really aimed at the Third World.

Since 1989 there has been a sharp move away from bipolar confrontation but the world is still littered with the debris of the cold war; literally so in the case of the conventional and nuclear weapons of the former Soviet Union. Week by week the news of the interception of smuggled uranium consignments compounds the uncertainty about the future intentions of middle-range states such as Iraq and Iran. The US post-cold war strategy is to keep enough nuclear weapons to confront 'any possible adversary', and this continued nuclear hegemony is thought by some to be a means to prevent proliferation. The assumption is that we have moved into an era of an interdependent world military order that is both established and hierarchical. The problem, it has often been suggested from a First World perspective, is that nuclear capacity does not necessarily follow this hierarchy.

The spread of nuclear weapons to more countries is generally termed horizontal proliferation, and was inherent in the nuclear game from the outset owing to the diffusion of knowledge about nuclear processes. The spread of civil nuclear technology cannot be stopped and indeed was actively encouraged by the capitalist countries as a way of building up their own nuclear capability. The inherent tendency for scientific knowledge to diffuse did the rest. Hence Argentina and Pakistan both have uranium enrichment plants that could produce nuclear weapons material rather than reactor fuel, but they have developed these capabilities themselves, having been unable to purchase such sensitive technology on the world market, and Pakistan has therefore been in a position to match India's decision to 'go nuclear'. On the other hand, happily Argentina and Brazil have been able to forge a new relationship and to move decisively away from confrontation.

The whole world is now a single strategic arena, and military deployment of nuclear weapons in any future confrontation would be global. However this does not mean that horizontal proliferation does in fact present serious dangers. It is not clear what the use of nuclear weapons could achieve for a Third World state that happened to possess them given their likely political objectives. The obvious reason would be to enhance their power in relation to surrounding states. For this purpose a mere bluff may suffice and some argue this is the case of North Korea. On the other hand the normal response to fear of a nuclear attack seems to be to respond in kind, as in the case of India and Pakistan, whose relative position has not changed as a result. Third, the acquisition of nuclear weapons might be sought to empower a southern state in face of a threat from the North. It has been argued that customers always have some leverage against their suppliers so they can gain a degree of empowerment through purchase. On the other hand a more realistic perception is that any advantage gained is offset by the weakness of needing spare parts and support services in the form of technological advice and periodic updates. If new standards are set by technology, striving to achieve them is a treadmill, and certainly does not constitute empowerment.

Chemical weapons

Chemical weapons are sometimes called 'poor man's atom bombs'. They are much cheaper, they use much more readily available and more easily disguised technology, and the major powers (officially at least) have chosen not to have them. They are for these reasons the weapons of mass destruction most obviously inclined to proliferation in the Third World. In view of the rapidly blurring boundaries between the destructiveness and grossness of nuclear and conventional weapons the distinction no longer really makes sense.

The manufacture of chemical weapons is an offshoot of the civil chemical industry and therefore the potential exists in many moderately industrialised countries. In the Third World the most notorious example is Iraq under Saddam Hussein, who used them against his own citizens at Halabjah and so breached what had been becoming an unwritten norm of international conduct, unbroken since the 1930s.

Chemical weapons exist in countries other than Iraq. They are known to exist in the USA, France and somewhere in the former USSR. But more worrying is the extent of their probable existence in the Third World. Argentina, Chile, Cuba, Guatemala, Peru, Angola, Chad, Ethiopia, Libya, South Africa, Afghanistan, China, India, Burma (Myanmar), Pakistan, Thailand and are Vietnam all believed to have a chemical capability. Perhaps Iran does also – it is believed to have been very active in seeking supplies in 1993–94 and is unlikely to have ceased trying to do so.

The problem with chemical weapons as weapons of mass destruction is that the manufacturing processes involved are relatively simple, so that an Iraqi plant could be easily disguised as a factory producing infant milk formula, for example. Detecting breaches of international agreements is therefore much more difficult than with nuclear weapons, where the telltale signs of reprocessing and storage facilities are hard to conceal from the circling spy satellites.

Regional powers

The role of regional powers in Asia has been much complicated by the fragmentation of the former Soviet Union. However one thing remains certain: in East Asia the massive size of China outweighs all others, although in many ways it is still very much a Third World state with a Third World army.

In South Asia India has naturally assumed the regional role that its size and population seemed to indicate. However, despite a string of successes in the early years following independence, it received a severe setback when Chinese forces entered Ladakh in 1962. Even if the actual loss of territory was insignificant the blow to its security and even more to its morale was considerable. Its confidence revived considerably after its successful intervention in former East Pakistan in 1971, which resulted in the independence of Bangladesh. At the end of the 1980s, however, the mission of the IPKF in Sri Lanka was not accepted either by the insurgents or by the Sri Lankan government, which took the first convenient opportunity to invite it to withdraw. In return, in 2000, the

Indian government refused to come to the aid of the Sri Lankan army when they were faced with a major offensive in Jaffna (*The Guardian*, 5 May 2000).

In South-east Asia Vietnam has been unable to avoid involvement in its neighbouring countries since the end of war in 1975. The brief Third Indo-China War resulted from Chinese concern about its growing military strength, and tension remains between the two countries over control of the Spratly Islands, which are also claimed by Malaysia and the Philippines. Vietnamese intervention expelled the Khmer Rouge from Cambodia in 1979, but cut short the opening to the west begun in 1976 and halted its economic recovery. It was followed by a ruthless campaign to force Vietnamese withdrawal.

In 1962 the creation of Malaysia by the incorporation of the former British North Borneo (Sabah) and Sarawak led to 'confrontation' (*konfrontasi*) with Sukarno's Indonesia. The effects of Indonesian incursions into East Malaysia were sufficiently serious to require a substantial deployment of British troops and resulted in the loss of 114 British servicemen before the abortive coup of October 1965 that led to the death of perhaps up to half a million Indonesians, the ending of confrontation and eventually the deposition of Sukarno himself (Hughes 1968). With the collapse of the Portuguese Empire in 1974 General Suharto ordered the seizure of East Timor, where tens of thousands of Timorese have since died resisting the new colonialism of Djakarta. The annexation was never recognised by the rest of the world, but the western powers, fearful as they were of communist influence gaining a foothold, were not prepared in the cold war days to do anything about it.

In South-west Asia the most active regional powers have been Israel, a military power, and Iran, an oil-rich state with substantial economic resources. Iran may perceive itself as both a regional power and a leader of Islam against the rest of the world – certainly many have sensed a desire to export the revolution to the secular states of Central Asia that have Muslim majorities. Sir Anthony Parsons, former British ambassador to Iran, saw the West as fearful of a resurgent Iran and suggested that this is due to the perception of Iran as behaving differently from the rest of the world. Iran's geographical position, controlling access to the Persian Gulf and therefore to half of the world's known oil reserves, is at once a strength and a weakness, in that it makes Iran vulnerable. The eight-year Iran–Iraq War (1980–88) cost Iran a generation.

In Africa the most important regional role has been played by South Africa (an economic and military power). Nigeria (which gains its standing both from its size and from its considerable oil revenues) has also shown by its actions that it aspires to a significant regional role. In their different ways so too have Egypt, Guinea, Senegal and Tanzania.

As a regional power South Africa intervened in Mozambique after it had become independent from Portugal in 1975. Civil strife has continued at some level ever since. Of the rival guerrilla groups one, the National Revolutionary Movement, had South African backing. This group deliberately disrupted food production, causing the 1983 famine in which more than 100,000 people died; they also poisoned wells and burned villages. Together these measures contributed to the displacement of more than half the rural population of the country, after the infrastructure on which they relied, including health clinics and schools, had been callously destroyed.

The ability of the South African apartheid regime to exercise regional power was considerably enhanced by its control of Namibia. Originally allocated to the South African government under a League of Nations Mandate, the apartheid government refused to recognise the authority of the United Nations and treated it as a de facto territory of South Africa. This extended the reach of that government to the borders of Angola and, angered at the support given by the Angolan government to the South West Africa People's Organization (Swapo), the armed Namibian liberation movement, they had no hesitation in supporting the National Union for the Total Independence of Angola (UNITA), a guerrilla force dedicated to overthrowing the government in Angola.

In Latin America the dominance of the USA has tended to overshadow that of all other regional powers, including that of the world's most populous Spanish-speaking country, Mexico. Brazil, however, can be considered a regional power in South America, as since at least the 1920s it has been seen as an ally by the United States of America, which country has been prepared to let it act as a surrogate.

Conclusion

Third World states, therefore, have taken an increasingly active role in regional, if not in world politics. This activity extends to armed confrontation and, in a number of specific cases, of armed conflict. Taking into account also civil wars and insurgencies, at any one time over the past decade there have been at least 15 wars in progress, and of those the overwhelming majority have involved Third World states.

Though fewer Third World countries are now under formal military government the tendency for armed forces to exercise a political role has been much enhanced since the beginning of the 1980s by the militarisation of the Third World. Third World countries have been the major target of the arms salespersons from the advanced industrialised countries. In many cases, notably in Britain, France and the United States of America, these efforts have had the vigorous support of government. However the evidence is that arms sales of this kind, though they create a certain sense of dependence and lock the recipient country into a continuing sales drive, have won few friends and, as the Gulf War demonstrated, those that are gained in this way are all too liable to turn on their former supporters if the political situation should change.

CHAPTER 10

The international dimension

Introduction

Until 1991 the cold war was the main factor affecting relations between the Third World and the superpowers. Not only did the superpowers evaluate everything that happened in the Third World in terms of how it would affect the global balance of power, but the Third World states themselves entered actively into the game of winning superpower support. In the process a great many people were to get hurt, but it could be argued that a certain element of discipline was thus imposed on the international community.

Whatever the cold war may have meant for Europe or for the USA, for the Third World it meant one thing: foreign intervention. The forms of intervention varied from place to place and from time to time: sometimes overt, as in Lebanon in 1958 or the Dominican Republic in 1965; sometimes covert, as in Iran in 1953 or in Nicaragua after 1981; sometimes formal, as in Vietnam in the 1960s, sometimes informal, as in Honduras in the 1980s.

Intervention

Intervention means coming between contending parties in such a way as to alter the balance between them (Little 1975). Hence the usual meaning in international relations is support for opposition movements or insurgents or even the direct use of armed force to overthrow an existing government or regime. Strictly speaking support for an incumbent government that has been formally recognised by the international community is not only not intervention but is something that every friendly government should be prepared to give. However, support for an unpopular government to protect it against the anger of its own people does constitute intervention in the eyes of many Third World countries. In addition there can be a number of ways in which indirect pressure can be exerted to affect the political, economic or social stability of a target state.

We must therefore distinguish between different modes of intervention:

- **Military intervention.** When other forms of intervention are not specified, use of the term 'intervention' will be understood as meaning military intervention. Sending troops to support an incumbent government is legitimate in international law if their presence is requested and hence is not strictly speaking intervention. Direct military intervention against a government, on the other hand, is an act of war unless sanctioned by UN or regional bodies, and not necessarily even then. Invasion, bombardment or armed blockade of a country's ports are all acts of war and may invite retaliation as well as criticism by third parties. Since the 1950s therefore both the USA and the former Soviet Union have used indirect military intervention, including support to insurgents, military training for friendly personnel and support for military governments.

- **Economic intervention.** This can be carried out though a variety of institutional devices. Pressure can be brought to bear either directly through increasing or decreasing bilateral aid, or indirectly (in the case of the United States of America, which has a preponderant say) through international lending bodies such as the IMF. Pressure can be exercised less effectively though trade restrictions such as blockades, sanctions or the imposition of tariffs, since the ideal of free trade is embodied in a series of international agreements. It is difficult in many cases to determine how far a national agenda is pursued by transnational corporations or whether they follow their own. The US corporation International Telephone & Telegraph (ITT) was eager for US intervention in Chile in 1970 but the Administration response was limited.

- **Diplomatic (psychological) intervention.** Major powers can influence events by suggesting action rather than by direct intervention. They do this by developing contacts and building friendships that enable them to discourage or to encourage specific political outcomes.

- **Cultural intervention.** It is doubtful whether this constitutes intervention at all, since cultural influences are so slow and it is often impossible to point to any one moment at which they take effect. However since aid and trade distribute the culture of industrialised nations (see Chapter 6) along with its products it also assists the far more pervasive force of ideological penetration by CNN and the major news agencies.

Sensitive as they inevitably were to any violation of their newly won sovereignty, Third World states generally regarded all forms of intervention as illegitimate and were inclined to extend the meaning of the term to include all actions of which they disapproved. They pressed for the norm of non-intervention enshrined in the Charter of the United Nations to be taken literally. In practice, the question of how far (if at all) intervention was legitimate was determined not by the Third World state but by external powers such as the USA, the Soviet Union, Britain, France or Israel.

For the Third World the problem of the cold war was that it complicated their desire for independence by presenting them with the need to choose a position in the international arena for reasons they felt were not of their making. In Asia independence was substantially complete by the 1970s and by 1975 the United States of America had withdrawn from direct involvement. In Latin America the experience of Cuba meant that with the rather idiosyncratic exception of Grenada between 1979 and 1983 there was no serious attempt after 1962 for an American 'state' to choose the Soviet Union as a partner.

In Africa all internal crises of independence, however, were externalised when states called on the outside world for help. The UN operation in the Congo/Zaire in 1960 was complicated by US and French intervention and before the decade was out the French, Russians, Americans and Chinese were all involved in various ways. In 1963 the French intervened in Gabon to reverse a military coup and to restore the government of President M'ba. In 1964 Britain sent help when the armies of Kenya, Uganda and Tanzania mutinied. It was reluctant to do the same when in the following year the European settlers of Rhodesia made a unilateral declaration of independence. Soon it became clear that the new government was receiving the tacit support of both Britain and the USA, to say nothing of South Africa. The British, French and Soviets all became involved in the Nigerian civil war after 1967. In 1975 under *Operación Carlota* Cuban troops arrived to support the Marxist government of Angola just as large consignments of weapons began arriving from eastern Europe, and later the same year more Cuban troops were flown into Ethiopia to support the Ethiopians against the US-backed communist (sic) government of Somalia.

Such unity as there was resulted from the fact of western tolerance and covert support for the white South African regime. Protected as it was behind the UN mandate territory of Namibia (former German South-west Africa, administered by South Africa as an integral part of its territory) and a screen of what were later to become the 'front-line states', namely Angola, Botswana, Mozambique, Tanzania, Zambia and Rhodesia (until 1980, then Zimbabwe), the apartheid regime proved very difficult indeed to dislodge. Then revolution in Portugal in 1974 broke up the Portuguese Empire from within, much as the invasion of Spain in 1808 had led ultimately to the independence of Spanish America. Marxist governments obtained international recognition in Angola, Mozambique, Guinea Bissau and Cabo Verde. This sudden unexpected 'success' of Marxist liberation movements and the subsequent revolution in Ethiopia led to a dramatic transformation of the scene in Africa. It was followed by Soviet interventions in Angola, Mozambique and Ethiopia, seeking to support friendly governments and extend their influence in a region where the Soviet Union previously had had rather limited success in winning friends.

A number of armed conflicts were soon in progress. The Soviet Union, finding itself faced with confrontation between its former ally Somalia and the Derg in Ethiopia, had no hesitation about supporting Ethiopia, which was seen as strategically far more important. Cuban troops, serving under Soviet command, successfully recovered the Ogaden for Ethiopia, while the Somali government turned to its former antagonist the USA for help. Meanwhile the USA, hesitant about direct intervention after the fiasco of Vietnam, countered the threat of a communist takeover in Southern Africa by enlisting African groups to help undermine the Soviet-sponsored states of Angola and Mozambique, and offered indirect support to South Africa's intervention in Angola through the organisation, training and supply of Jonas Savimbi and UNITA. Proxy conflicts provided an outlet for hostilities and ideological revitalisation.

US politicians of all parties had been wary of intervention ever since the hurried end of the Vietnam War. Direct intervention in Africa was unthinkable. However, quite legally in terms of international law, the USA propped up pro-western states such as Kenya and Zaire. Here as elsewhere the value of development aid was far exceeded by military assistance. Arms exports were seen by some as the chief instrument of US and Soviet foreign policy towards Africa in the 1970s/1980s.

Ronald Reagan, president of the United States 1981–89, saw all crises in the South as the product of East–West divisions. The radicalisation of much of the Third World and US failure to penetrate ideologically many former European colonies was taken hard by the New Right. Reagan's State of the Union message in December 1985, with an eye specifically on Nicaragua and El Salvador, pledged US support for Third World anti-communist guerrillas. This policy became known as the Reagan Doctrine. A major consequence was that economic aid was withdrawn and/or replaced to some extent by military aid. However both the burden of military spending and Reaganite free market economic policy, with the accompanying interest rises necessary to counteract US overspending, contributed to the debt crisis that broke at the beginning of the 1980s and continued to be a problem for Third World states throughout the decade.

Despite its rhetoric, by the late 1980s the Reagan administration, fragmented and discredited by the Iran–Contra scandal, had rediscovered the necessity of superpower cooperation. Bilateral talks at all levels focused on the twin problems of stopping the growth of nuclear arsenals and limiting the spread of nuclear weapons. At the same time the superpowers increasingly found themselves with a common interest in joint diplomatic action to resolve Third World crisis points. In Washington observers began to talk about the emergence of a superpower condominium.

After the high human, financial and diplomatic costs of the invasion of Afghanistan in 1979, and the consequent loss of Third World support, the 1980s saw the rethinking of Soviet policy to the Third World. The high cost of intervention did not sit well with the economic problems facing the USSR at home. There was a movement away from support for 'wars of national liberation' and the maintenance of client states to the acceptance tacitly of diplomatic and economic expediency. Soviet aid was in any case very limited compared to that of the USA and larger OECD nations owing to the inconvertibility of the Soviet currency and its lack of purchase on the world economic system. Soviet military capacity was very limited at levels 'useful' in the Third World. (For example, when the USSR sent humanitarian aid to Peru following the earthquake of 1970, the mission had to be cut short when one of the AN-25 transports was lost in the sea off Iceland.) In addition, Third World allies were ideologically untrained and not very reliable. Allende was overthrown in Chile in 1973 and Guinea began to move away from association with the USSR after the death of Sekou Toure in 1984. With three heads of government in four years the USSR itself had also become very unpredictable! The Gorbachev government, even more than its predecessors, made good relations with the USA its top priority in foreign affairs. Faced with gathering crises at home, it withdrew from Afghanistan, yielded to the pressure for change in eastern Europe (which had repercussions in Central Asia) and limited its intervention. It did not seek to stop the US-led UN response to the Gulf Crisis in 1990.

With both North-east and North-west seeking to resolve Third World conflicts and limit arms supplies to the Third World (at least in public), both sides came to recognise the value of the United Nations as a potential peacekeeper.

Non-alignment

The Non-aligned Movement had its origins in the Afro-Asian Conference at Bandung in 1955 and has met triennially since 1961 (with the exception of 1967). It includes all the African states, which belong automatically as members of the OAU, most of the Asian countries and some of the Latin American republics. The original thinking behind non-alignment was to create an association sufficiently strong to avoid association with either of the two blocs. However from the beginning the concept was regarded with great suspicion by both sides, and this suspicion was at times well justified as, in particular, when Fidel Castro as president of the Non-aligned Movement abused his position to call on the non-aligned at the Havana Summit of 1979 to accept the Soviet Union as their natural ally. The invitation was not well received and the Soviet invasion of Afghanistan later the same year put an abrupt stop to any further moves to revive it.

The collapse of communism ended the moral justification for much US intervention. The change was not immediate: the new public vocabulary included phrases such as 'ensuring international stability' or 'the worldwide crusade for democracy'. But the new US administration of George Bush did not show much respect either for national sovereignty or for democracy. Its intervention in Panama in December 1989, claimed to be enhancing the cause of democracy, was carried out in breach of the charters of both the UN and the Organization of American States (OAS), and was censured by the OAS. Then in 1991 the decision (after a long period of delay) to launch Operation Desert Storm on Iraq was justified as defending what Bush claimed was 'the legitimate government' of Kuwait. Though Saddam Hussein had few friends even amongst Arab states, and his own government had formally recognised that Kuwait was not the nineteenth province of Iraq, the Emir's government was certainly not democratic. In fact the decision to go to war had much less to do with defending democracy than with ensuring that the combined oil output of Iraq and Kuwait did not pass out of western control, while the unilateral US decision to end the war after only 100 hours has had long-lasting consequences for the stability of of other smaller oil-producing states in this key region.

The USA is now a 'lonely superpower', constrained by its own internal divisions to tread a much more cautious course. Other countries have different agendas and in groups could be powerful, but Russia too is torn by internal dissension and the decision of Chancellor Kohl to recognise Bosnia has left the European Union divided and apparently impotent. The end of the cold war may well mean that in the future there will be no superpowers present to restrain their former client states when local conflicts threaten to get out of hand. In a bipolar world in a sense every conflict matters to the two camps, as victory for one is defeat for the other. In an era of multipolarity most Third World conflicts will not matter to the First World at all. If regional leaders do not intervene no one may do so, and this may be even more undesirable.

Third World conflicts

Among Third World 'hotspots', where intervention has continued into the post-cold war era, are Cambodia, Cuba, Angola, Ethiopia, Liberia and Somalia.

The withdrawal of the United States of America from Cambodia in 1975 left the country to the Khmer Rouge. Hardened by their long and bitter struggle, the guerrillas marched into Pnom Penh and immediately instituted a reign of terror against the town dwellers, and especially the intellectuals, whom they regarded as having collaborated first with the French and later with the Americans. Tens of thousands of skulls testify still to the ruthlessness with which the process was carried out. However when reunified Vietnam sent troops into Cambodia to remove the Khmer Rouge and institute a Soviet-style government the western powers, with breathtaking cynicism, switched their support to any group that could get rid of the Vietnamese, including the Khmer Rouge. Then, with the changing world balance, the Vietnamese, seeking to better relations with the USA, decided to withdraw from Cambodia and the

Table 10.1 Third World conflicts 1990–2000

Country	Dates	Cause
Afghanistan	1979–92	War of *mujahidin* guerrillas against Soviet-backed government
	1992–	Fighting between rival groups continues
Algeria	1992–	Coordinated anti-government activity
Angola	1975–91	South African-backed insurrection (UNITA)
Azerbaijan	1991–94	Armenian secessionist movement in Nagorny Karabakh
Burma	1949–	Armed ethnic opposition
Burundi	1993–94	Ethnic violence
Cambodia	1978–91	Civil war
Chad	1975–93	Insurrection
	1971–94	Part occupied by Libya
Djibouti	1991–94	Afar insurrection
Ecuador	1995	War with Peru over boundary delimitation
Egypt	1992–	Coordinated anti-government activity
El Salvador	1979–91	Civil war; government backed by USA
Eritrea	1994–2000	Insurrection backed by Sudan; war with Ethiopia
Gambia	1994	Coup and counter-coup
Georgia	1991–94	Secessionist movement in Abkhasia
Ghana	1994	Insurrection in Northern Region
Guatemala	1960–94	Guerrilla operations
Guinea	1994	Armed clashes with opposition forces
Haiti	1994	US intervention to restore President Aristide
India	1947–	Armed Kashmiri resistance
Indonesia	1976–99	Resistance to annexation of East Timor
Iraq	1990–91	Invasion of Kuwait
	1991	Gulf War
Kenya	1994	Ethnic violence
Kuwait	1990–91	Occupied by Iraq
	1991	Gulf War
Lebanon	1982–2000	Part occupied by Israel and allies
Lesotho	1993–94	Fighting between rival army factions
Liberia	1990–	Civil war
Libya	1973–94	Occupation of disputed territory in Chad
Mali	1992–	Continued clashes with Tuaregs
Mexico	1994–	Agrarian insurrection in Chiapas
Morocco	1976–91	War against Polisario Front of Western Sahara
Mozambique	1986–94	South African-backed insurrection (Renamo)
Nicaragua	1981–91	US-backed insurrection ('contras')
Peru	1995	War with Ecuador over boundary delimitation
Rwanda	1990–	Insurrection by Rwandan Patriotic Front (FPR)
	1994	Ethnic violence following death of President
Sierra Leone	1991–	Insurrection backed by National Patriotic Front of Liberia (NPFL)
Somalia	1991–	Ousting of Siad Barre followed by civil war
South Africa	1990–94	Inkatha/ANC clashes
Sri Lanka	1983–	Separatist war led by Liberation Tigers of Tamil Eelam
Sudan	1983–	Separatist guerrillas in South
Togo	1994	Insurrection against President Eyadema

Sources: Instituto del Tercer Mundo (1992) *Third World Guide 93/94 Uruguay*; *Keesing's Record of World Events*, Longman

successful UN supervision of elections in 1993 paved the way for a coalition government to assume power under the nominal authority of King Norodom Sihanouk, deposed in a US-backed military coup in 1970. Sadly, since 1993 Khmer Rouge activity has increased once more, and the future of the settlement looks extremely problematic (see Table 10.1).

Another casualty of changing international alignments has been the Soviet-backed regime in Cuba. Since the end of the cold war the government of President Fidel Castro has lost its superpower patron and come under much external pressure from the USA, which has tightened its embargo on trade with the beleaguered island. The most serious blow was the withdrawal in 1991 of its guaranteed supply of Russian oil, which had not only fuelled its agriculture and industry but provided a considerable surplus that could be sold abroad for hard currency. However, despite increasing diplomatic isolation and a serious economic crisis, the Cuban government survives and the US government has so far not risked direct intervention.

Even before the crisis in eastern Europe in 1989 Soviet military support for the Popular Movement for the Liberation of Angola (MPLA) had dried up and the Cuban troops that had been supporting the internationally recognised government of the country were withdrawn. Meanwhile US material and strategic support to the South African-sponsored UNITA continued unabated, and Zairian troops arrived to lend them material support. Early in 1993 UNITA held some two-thirds of the country. Though the US ambassador to the UN, Margaret Anstee, described the situation in Angola as full-scale civil war, she still argued that there was nothing the UN could do. Nevertheless by the end of the year the UN was sponsoring peace talks.

Ethiopia received the most military 'aid' of all the African states from both the USA and the Soviet Union. However, despite all their efforts, the government of General Mengistu Haile Mariam was unable to suppress the secessionist movements in Tigray and Eritrea. When their support for him became too embarrassing Soviet and Cuban support for Mengistu was withdrawn and he was overthrown and forced to seek political asylum in Zimbabwe in May 1991.

It was noted in Chapter 9 (p. 170) that for a century Liberia, a state for freed slaves on the west coast of Africa, had been dominated by the settler elite at the expense of the tribes of the interior. In September 1990 the government of Samuel Doe was ousted by a military coup and the deposed president and much of the political elite hacked to death. The USA, which had sponsored the formation of Liberia, and which benefited from the rubber produced there for the Firestone Tire Co., refused to intervene, though President Bush did send a small team of marines to rescue US citizens. The civil war that followed led to a joint military intervention by the Economic Community of West African States (ECOWAS), and was apparently ended by a peace agreement signed in Benin in July 1993. However the UN remains concerned that the armed forces appear to be still out of control and it continues to receive reports of refugees being massacred.

The role of the United Nations

Since the ending of the cold war the USA has reverted to its 1945 policy of supporting the United Nations. During the cold war the UN's capacity for action was little used, but it is now the northern-dominated instrument of intervention. Vetoes of substantive issues in the Security Council have all but ceased, the USA and other major powers act together and their actions are legitimised as they are UN sponsored. Since only the decisions of the Security Council are binding on member states, this means that in practice the organisation continues to be dominated by the advanced industrialised countries.

The UN is an international rather than a supranational organisation. 'International' means between nations, with the implication of theoretical if not actual equality; while 'supranational' means something above nations that in some way limits sovereignty. However in reality international, supranational and transnational links all act to reduce not only sovereignty (which is an old-fashioned, impractical concept anyway) but also to reduce the autonomy of all but (or perhaps even) the largest states.

The UN represents states, not non-governmental organisations. Though the latter may be bigger and of more service to the UN they have no votes, though they may be represented and speak at major international conferences. The member countries of the UN are organised politically into groups that frequently take up common positions to enhance their clout. Groups of organisations, other than regional conferences, include the Non-aligned Movement and the Group of 77.

The most striking feature of UN activity in the past ten years has been the dramatic extension of UN peacekeeping activity. More UN intervention has taken place since 1989 than in the whole of the previous 44 years of the organisation's history. Since UN peacekeeping operations are not funded out of the UN budget, but from precepts on member states, the situation has been viewed with increasing concern by both supporters and opponents of the UN role.

It was the unusual case of Somalia that seems in the end to have brought this problem to a head. A military revolt in Somalia in January 1991 that deposed the tyrannical government of General Siad Barre had been almost universally welcomed. However, as time went on, no new government was able to gain power and the country relapsed into tribal conflict between factions led by contending warlords. At the end of 1992, following his defeat in the presidential elections, President Bush sent US marines to Mogadishu nominally to protect food aid to the starving people. Soon they were embroiled instead in a futile attempt to eliminate one of these warlords, General Aideed, whom the USA accused of interfering with the aid convoys. Then in October 1993 both US and UN policy changed away from seeking to oust General Aideed to seeking a peaceful settlement with some new government that could obtain control, and the UN proceeded to halve its troops to 15,000 when US troops eventually left the country in March 1994.

The significance of this rather tangled story is that UN Resolution 794 makes no pretence that UN forces were invited into Somalia in the first place. Its justification for intervention is that its objectives were reconstruction and disarmament and not just peacekeeping, but that in the course of active pursuit of these objectives subsequent resolutions reconfirmed both the objectives and the role of UN troops. The conclusion is that UN intentions may have been worthy enough but the extension of its powers that this implied conflicted with the norm of non-intervention and was bound to raise doubts. Additionally, the fact that the Somalis soon started complaining of human rights abuses did it no credit and set back the cause of so-called humanitarian intervention. Early in 1995 the new Republican majority in the US House of Representatives passed legislation that will effectively end UN intervention, since it requires the president to subtract from the cost of any contribution to UN peacekeeping budgets the cost of UN forces and will effectively transform the US contribution into a negative balance.

Regional alignments

One obvious way to avoid excessive dependence on or influence by great powers was to create regional organisations. However the oldest such organisation, the Organization of American States, founded in 1948 as a regional organisation within the UN system, is not clearly a Third World organisation. Since its foundation, as a development of the old Pan-American Union, it has been dominated by the regional and world superpower, the United States of America; and the parallel military alliance, the Inter-American Treaty of Reciprocal Assistance (commonly known in English as the Rio Pact) was specifically created in 1947 to form one of a network of alliances supporting the USA against the Soviet Union.

The OAS was largely bypassed in the confrontation between the United States of America and Cuba, which led to the exclusion of the latter from the working of the organisation in 1962. In the 1960s and 1970s its numbers were swollen by the accession of Suriname and the former British colonies in the region. Two, Belize and Guyana, were excluded because they had frontier disputes with existing members. However both were admitted at the beginning of the 1990s together with Canada, which had previously chosen to stand aloof. Hence the organisation, which was reorganised along UN lines by the Protocol of Buenos Aires in 1970, reproduces many of the conflicts that characterise the working of the UN itself.

The Organization of African Unity was formed in 1963, in the first flush of independence. Despite the hopes expressed at the time by Kwame Nkrumah of Ghana it did not aim so high as to create some form of pan-African superstate. Its three main aims were the eradication of colonialism, the promotion of economic cooperation and the resolution of disputes among member states.

Originally annual meetings were held in different capitals, which nearly bank-rupted the host government; since 1970 there has been an established perman-ent centre in Addis Ababa.

At its inception the OAU created an African Liberation Committee to chan-nel aid to liberation movements. However most African governments have given little and in the major case, that of South Africa, the strategy of armed confrontation destabilised the so-called 'front-line' states without any obvious effect on apartheid. The Lusaka Declaration of 1970 was a belated admission that negotiation might be a more effective way to secure the desired objection of decolonisation. The collapse of Portuguese colonial rule in 1974 was fol-lowed by the alliance of the front-line states to give support to the liberation of Rhodesia/Zimbabwe, but in the years that followed the South African gov-ernment successfully organised guerrilla forces to destabilise both Angola and Mozambique. In its major confrontation with South Africa the main instru-ments of the OAU were a combination of sanctions and economic boycotts, but once again a significant number of African states failed effectively to implement sanctions. A few, notably Malawi under Dr Hastings Banda, openly rejected them; and Dr Kenneth Kaunda of Zambia, who consistently pressed for a peaceful transition of power in Rhodesia/Zimbabwe, was prepared to meet South African leaders and even to support their action in intervening against the Marxist government of Angola (Tangri 1985: 142).

The OAU's Economic and Social Council was set up to promote economic collaboration, but with a few small exceptions it has been notably unsuccess-ful. Most African states have only slowly lost their trade and other economic links with their former colonial powers.

It is as a political organisation seeking to maintain the defence of the sover-eignty of existing national territories that the OAU has been most successful. An early and important decision was to recognise the existing colonial boundaries of member states. Since then it has had to deal with conflicts of three main kinds:

1. challenges to state integrity
2. challenges to regime integrity
3. ideological/personality disputes.

The three great achievements of the OAU have been the settlement of the 1967 frontier dispute between Kenya and Somalia, the independence of Zimbabwe (formerly Rhodesia) and the collapse of apartheid in South Africa. However on most of the major post-colonial issues it has shown itself weak and divided, failing to contribute effectively to the settlement of the Congo/Zaire crisis, the Nigerian civil war, the Angolan crisis and the dispute between Morocco and Mauritania over the Western Sahara. In 1982 the member states were so divided that it was unable initially to obtain a quorum to hold its annual summit.

Meanwhile a steady build-up of arms in the region led to an increasing willingness to use force. Significantly this tended to be on an individual state or subregional level. Armed support for incumbents was given when Guinean troops were sent to support Siaka Stevens in Sierra Leone in 1971 and Senegalese forces to The Gambia in 1981. Armed intervention to end a state of anarchy and civil war included Tanzania's intervention in Uganda in 1979 to expel Idi Amin and the ECOWAS intervention in Liberia in 1989, which led to the destabilisation of Sierra Leone and the fall of President Momoh. Armed aggression to obtain additional territory has been rarer. Libya's intervention in Chad in 1983, which led to the virtual annexation of one-third of its territory, was countered, ultimately successfully, by US and French intervention. Only in this last case did the OAU act to set up a peacekeeping force (largely Nigerian), which was withdrawn after a few weeks for lack of support.

Its main weaknesses as an organisation are nationalism, the problems it faces in getting member states to pay their contributions and the fears of African heads of state and heads of government that they will be deposed while they are out of their country preventing their attendance at conferences. The end of apartheid in South Africa has taken away the one cause that motivated the desire for unity.

Asia is too big to have a clear existence as a continent so there is no regional equivalent to the OAU or the OAS. Western attempts to set up regional alliances in the Middle East and South-east Asia foundered on the realities of local politics. Subregional organisations in the 1990s included:

- The **Commonwealth of Independent States** (CIS), founded in 1991, the ghost of the former Soviet Union. Though rivalry between the Russian Federation and the Ukraine over the Crimea and the Black Sea fleet seems to have died down, regional rivalries seem for the time being to be sufficiently strong to forestall any greater degree of unity.

- The **Arab League**, founded in 1945, which is effectively a regional organisation for South-west Asia and North Africa. The League displays vast political differences between member states despite their religious and ethnic bonds. However its members dominate the more recently formed Islamic Conference, which with 41 members is now the most powerful regional bloc in UN politics.

- The **Association of South East Asian Nations** (ASEAN), founded in 1967, which has only six members: Brunei, Indonesia, Malaysia, the Philippines, Singapore and Thailand.

- The **South Asian Association for Regional Cooperation** (SAARC), founded in 1985, with eight member states: Bangladesh, Bhutan, India, the Maldives, Nepal, Pakistan and Sri Lanka.

- The **South Pacific Forum** (SPF), founded in 1971 as an association of the self-governing states in the Pacific, which meets annually. It has gradually superseded the older (1948) South Pacific Commission (SPC), consisting of representatives of the non-self-governing Pacific territories and their administering powers.

To some, the extraordinary survival of the Commonwealth owes much to the relatively peaceful transition to independence of many of its members and to the informality of its organisation. With the accession of Namibia and the return to membership of South Africa it now has 51 members; Fiji remaining self-excluded by its refusal to accord equal treatment to its citizens of Indian origin. Hence despite the inclusion in its membership of two of the G7 nations (Canada and the UK) as well as Australia, it is very much a Third World organisation, which helps account for the fact that the former British Prime Minister Margaret Thatcher so obviously had little or no time for it. The Commonwealth however is not a federation but a club. Its effectiveness, which is often underrated, lies precisely in the fact that it operates through informal meetings and relies on shared understandings that do not have to be put into words.

Globalisation

For the past century or more we have been witnessing a process of globalisation, 'the process by which events, decisions, and activities in one part of the world can come to have significant consequences for individuals and communities in quite distant parts of the globe' (McGrew, Lewis et al. 1992: 23). Globalisation is the key characteristic of the modern economic system and even, it has been argued, of modernity itself (Giddens 1990). As a result theorists of international relations have come increasingly to emphasise the systemic factors affecting state behaviour rather than the individual decisions of states themselves. See Plate 10.

The notion of systemic factors, however, implies the existence of an international system. By system we mean an enduring set of interactions between individuals or, in this case, states (Nye and Keohane 1971, Keohane and Nye 1977). States are in themselves functional systems, and can be viewed either as such or as subsystems within the larger international context. Despite the formal absence of authority in the world system states have in general behaved in an orderly way, which presupposes some notion of international order (Bull 1977). The world is a very complex place and with the speeding up of communications during the present century we have all come to interact with one another, across national boundaries, to a much greater extent than was ever before possible. Hence despite the formal absence of global political authority, states do act together cooperatively, with each other and with a whole variety of non-governmental organisations and international organisations (IOs) to make decisions that for the most part are effective. Indeed, in some areas such as TV broadcasting or air traffic control, they have no practical alternative.

The concept of system, though, is inappropriate to the Third World as such. Indeed it is not always of much use in a regional context. There is one obvious exception: the western hemisphere. Not only is it isolated by water from the main arena of world politics (Calvert 1988), but it is even conceptualised by those who live there in system terms, and the notion of an 'inter-American system' has actually been embodied in a regional international organisation. But few would concede the same degree of identity, for example, to South Asia. Differences of perception are easily illustrated:

> The open invitation by Pakistan to 'foreign powers' in the early 1950s led to an Indian condemnation that has never really stopped. Yet Pakistan has argued that India's subsequent policy of non-alignment, and the need for cold war rivalry to be kept out of the South Asia region, was a rather purple Indian version of simple power politics, a cunning disguise of Indian expansionist interests dressed up in the language of moral virtues. This belief is still held to this day. A recent Pakistani commentator has pointed out that: 'It is significant that many Indians, when they speak of the *Indian* land mass cannot refrain from making it clear that what they are really talking about is the entire South Asian region'. (Hewitt 1992: 27, quoting Khan 1990)

Otherwise we are left with the rather vague concept of a world system, and the problem with this is that while it may in some sense be true that everything and everyone in the world influences to some degree everyone else, in practice we have to establish some sorts of limits on our inquiry if we are to make any sort of sense. What then are the sort of transnational links that transcend the nation state? How far are they actually able to avoid the power of the national state to regulate and to control them?

Transnational links

Theorists of international relations no longer accept the classical view of their discipline as being concerned only with relations between states – the so-called 'billiard ball' model. However many other links there are between people and organisations, though, the fact remains that the state system, originally evolved in Europe at the Treaty of Westphalia, continues and is likely to continue to structure all such relationships.

The first problem begins with the notion of citizenship and the requirement of an individual to have a passport and permission to enter another country. Citizens of Third World states do not enjoy the same freedom of movement as citizens of the advanced industrialised countries, and their governments are unable to give them even the same limited degree of protection that most of the industrialised countries can arrange. If they have to flee from persecution, in theory they have to be received wherever they go. In practice the industrialised countries have made matters very difficult for refugees, and by classifying all other potential immigrants as 'economic migrants' they have absolved themselves from any obligation to receive them. Only the universal human institution of the family, to a limited extent, transcends these barriers: in some, but not all cases successful immigrants are allowed to sponsor their relatives as immigrants also.

The second problem comes from the multiplicity of currencies and the lack of an agreed world standard of value. It is true that this has in recent years been supplied to some extent by the US dollar. However since the devaluation of the dollar by the Nixon administration in 1971 its pre-eminence has no longer been taken for granted, although it is still more widely available and more widely accepted than any other currency. In recent years a growing difficulty has been the growth of global currency dealing on a scale that makes even the currencies of the advanced industrialised countries vulnerable to sudden attack on the financial markets. The fact that billions can be moved in seconds renders the currencies of smaller states even more vulnerable than those of larger ones. And the global market is all too prone to sudden alarms, on the principle that it is better to be safe than sorry. The devaluation of the Mexican peso in December 1994 not only smashed the illusion of financial stability in Mexico itself but immediately threatened the stability of the financial systems of other Latin American states, especially Brazil and Argentina, and the governments of those countries found it very difficult indeed to counter the impression that they too were in some way affected. The private citizen of a Third World state lives with this perpetual instability, which gets greater the more open his or her country is to the world market.

The third problem concerns the availability of information. As we have already noted (see Chapter 6) the provision of world news has long been dominated by the advanced industrialised countries and their news organisations. Only in the last 15 years has the spread of the Internet, which celebrated its 30th anniversary in 1999, begun to erode this control. The irony is that although the computers that have made this possible are actually manufactured and assembled in the Third World, it is the inhabitants of the developed countries who benefit from the new freedom of communication.

Similarly, it is they who have benefited most from the rapid decline of sea travel in favour of air, and of rail travel in favour of the private car. The explosion in long-haul holidays has turned Thailand into a major tourist destination for Europeans and is in the process of doing the same to the Indian state of Goa.

Tourism

In 1950 about 25 million people travelled abroad as tourists, by the mid-1990s this figure had risen to 550 million and that market is increasing. As Urry (1990) has it, tourism is a vital part of a 'modern' lifestyle. Its international form reflects time–space compression and other aspects of globalisation. It is also a part of that process or, more accurately, set of processes. Since it is necessary to be able to afford a modern lifestyle to be a tourist, most of these tourists travel from developed countries. Most also prefer to experience that 'modernity' while on holiday and they travel to other developed countries, but there is a growing interest in travelling to the developing countries. Tourism employs one-ninth of the world's population. It is the fastest growing industry in the world and according to the World Tourism Organisation it will soon be the largest. It is labour intensive and a massive source of employment. Further, as a potential foreign currency earner it is obviously an attractive aspect of a development strategy for southern states that are touristically well endowed or just heavily indebted.

The mass tourism that developed after the Second World War was originally between North America and western Europe, but by the mid-1970s 8 per cent of tourists were North Americans and West Europeans travelling to the Third World, and by the mid-1980s this figure had risen to 17 per cent. Tourism has replaced sugar as the Dominican Republic's main foreign exchange earner, and bauxite as that of Jamaica. In Barbados tourism employs 10–20 per cent of the workforce and accounts for more than 60 per cent foreign exchange. There are more than 10 million visitors to the Caribbean each year. But this could suggest that a new dependency has developed, as Cynthia Enloe (1989: 32) puts it: 'Countries such as Puerto Rico, Haiti, Nepal, Gambia and Mexico have put their development eggs in one basket, spending millions of dollars from public funds to build the sorts of facilities that foreign tourists demand'.

Although tourism implies a redistribution of resources, the tourist relationship is essentially one of purchaser and servant (some have gone further and suggested master and slave (see Pattullo 1996: 63–5); it is essentially an unequal one in a way and to a degree that other trading relationships do not have to be. But on the other hand it puts First World people into the Third World, inducing culture contact in a way that other industry does not.

Many would see tourism as a means to development, indeed it was recognised as such by the 1963 UN Conference on Tourism and International Travel. Tourism generates employment, and money flowing into a tourist area is at least partly respent there, creating further indirect developmental effects. The West Indian Commission established by the Caribbean Community (Caricom) in the early 1990s recognised this in their 1992 Report *Time for Action* (106, cited in Pattullo 1996: 6): 'Out of the tourist industry radiates stimuli for a wide range of industries producing goods and services; this is the concept of tourism as an axial product. Viewed in this light, the tourism sector can play an important role in the diversification and transformation of the region.'

It is at once a modernising and conserving process. Preservation of the environment is a key aspect of tourism in a way it is not of other industries precisely because a damaged environment would be less saleable. Further, tourists provide new markets for traditional and threatened activities. Infrastructural developments benefit tourists and locals alike. Not only is it a means whereby

First World wealth can be transmitted to the Third World, but also a means by which modern values can be diffused. This process would imply, for example, integration and empowerment of women, whose status and standard of living is expected to be enhanced. (See Levy and Lerch 1991 for a powerful critique of this position.) However the clash of modernity and tradition is unresolved in the tourist relationship with developing countries. As Lanfant, Allcock and Bruner recognise (1995: ix, Preface):

> A fundamental contradiction is that from the inside, from the native point of view, tourism is a route to economic development; but from the outside view, the natives are a traditional object of desire. From the inside, tourism means modernity and change; but from the outside, the tourist object is seen as exotic, primitive and immutable. The locals are called upon to preserve a purity that never existed.

Critics of tourism as development have argued that it does not produce the benefits claimed for it, indeed it may promote an essentially unbalanced development. It tends to confirm existing local class/gender relations along with existing international economic and power relations. It can be actively harmful, increasing vulnerability. The social, cultural and environmental costs are seen as outweighing any benefits. These costs include:

- Enclave development with most benefit going to TNCs involved in global tourism. Less than 25 per cent of the cost of a package holiday reaches the host country.
- Damage to local economies and social dislocation caused by people leaving their homes and families to work in tourist enclaves.
- The best sites being taken for hotel complexes and the price of land in such areas rising beyond the means of locals.
- The need to import consumables for the tourists, for example some islands have to import vast quantities of water and in the most extreme case tourism constitutes a cost.
- Money spent on infrastructure is geared to tourism and tourist areas, not to the needs of local people, for example in terms of health, education, housing.
- Local culture gets preserved as a spectacle, local people as a sort of human zoo – it may even be reconstructed or mythologised to suit tourist tastes, but at the same time tourism as one source of 'demonstration effect' disenchants locals and instils alien values such as materialism which damage local cultures; see Paul Harrison *The Third Revolution* (1993).

Those who explain the problems of developing nations in terms of core/periphery would tend to argue the high costs of tourism as a development strategy. As with all such strategies it is doomed to failure because the inherent power imbalance between the core and the periphery ensures the continuance and increase of that inequality. Tourists from the core visit peripheral countries, but they do so through travel companies located in and repatriating profits to the core. Enclaves with First World advantages develop within the peripheral countries that receive these tourists. These outposts of the core draw resources, human and otherwise, from the surrounding areas.

Despite expecting many of the comforts of home the long-haul traveller is looking for a different experience, otherwise there is no point in the expense and inconvenience of long-distance travel. Thus some of the most vulnerable societies, located in the global South, are targets for tourist attention. In the case of the most fragile such areas the 'carrying capacity' is already strained without the added impact of tourists. In most places this is not a particular problem and a well-managed tourist industry could enhance the conditions of local people. Unfortunately these places often lack precisely the administrative and managerial expertise that could make tourism beneficial to the local community. Moreover, the relative strength of foreign stakeholders in the tourist industry ensures that they, not local interests, benefit. Local people often lack an effectively organised voice and are unable to assert their interests against those of foreign hotel chains and travel companies along with the national governmental interests they have persuaded to take their part.

Case studies

Goa

Goa is a small state on the west coast of India with about 1.2 million people. It is a relatively healthy place compared with some parts of India, and culturally interesting. It was a Portuguese colony from 1510 to 1961 but the Portuguese influence is mainly limited to coastal areas and it is to these areas that European visitors go. International tourism started to take off in the 1960s with youths from the First World who rejected western materialism seeking enlightenment. In the mid-1980s the Indian government drew up a Tourist Development Plan designating Goa a national centre of tourism along with the beaches of Kerala and Orissa.

The Goan tourist industry is not popular with all sections of the local community. There has developed an opposition, mainly informal but exemplified by the Goan Foundation. Concern is that development has been too large scale and too rapid. Problems have arisen that threaten the livelihoods and lifestyles of locals. These include the pollution of the coastline, visually damaged by high-rise hotels, through discharges of sewerage from the hotels, pesticide/fertiliser run-off from the gardens and golf courses surrounding those hotels and by pleasure boating in the inshore fishing grounds. There is much resentment of the profligate use of water for the tourist industry when locals often lack domestic running water. Further there is the perception that much of the financial benefit of the development has accrued to foreign stakeholders, the rest to national interests and very little to Goans.

Belize

There is much debate about precisely what 'ecotourism' is, but here it will be taken to imply tourism primarily aimed at experiencing aspects of the natural and social environments without necessarily implying the sustainability of this tourism. There is, it is argued, a built-in tendency to sustainability in such tourism because its attraction will cease if it develops into a mass tourist industry and thus despoils its purpose. Despite this it is the fastest growing form of tourism and Belize is a perfect place for ecotourism with dense forests in the interior and a barrier reef along its coast. It only became amicably independent from Britain in 1981. Independence was so late because Belizeans were not particularly bothered to achieve it but were subject to an unwelcome claim by Guatemala. Only a small proportion of its land area is cultivated. It is clearly a country looking for ways of increasing its foreign exchange earnings.

Tourism is growing in importance and the tourism strategy is official government policy. It recognises Belize's unique attractions and has devised government actions to take account of the nature of ecotourism. Certain potential tourist groups are directly targeted and indigenous problems that might put off such tourists are addressed. The tourist potential is thought to be balanced against the needs of Belizean society present and future in a strategy of conservation and wise use. Belize is very anxious to avoid the problems associated with mass tourism, overdevelopment of tourist areas, pollution and damage to the natural environment. Just as it has a major market nearby in the United States of America so it is also located very close to some of the busiest tourist areas, for example Miami and Cancun in Mexico. And tourist numbers are growing at an accelerating pace, targeting two-centre tourists wanting to combine the mass package resorts with a week in Belize. Tourism is hitting the developmental activities of Belizeans, though it is possible to argue this is not necessarily a bad thing. Over 30 per cent of the national area has been set aside as reserves in which no traditional slash-and-burn cultivation is permitted and traditional subsistence farmers are rerouted into tourist-related activities. Some ecological damage is inevitable and some has already occurred. For example, some mangrove swamps have been cleared for hotel development in the north, a loss in terms of breeding grounds for fish and as a protection against coastal erosion.

Costa Rica

Another haven of relative calm in Latin America also noted for the rapid development of ecotourism is Costa Rica. The country's government recognised its rich potential and planned its marketing of Costa Rica as a product and foreign exchange earnings from tourism have overtaken those from banana production. Although there is greater diversity in Costa Rican tourism, with only a minority of tourists attracted primarily by the rich flora and fauna, others by the more usual sun and sea, most want to visit the extensive areas of national park. There is clearly a tension between the original protected status of the national parks and the recognition of their attractions to visitors evident in the National Tourist Board's large-scale tourism strategy (Weaver 1999: 85–98).

The Caribbean Islands

Other parts of the Caribbean have also experienced the growth of large-scale tourism. This is an obvious strategy for an area caught between the emergent trading blocs of the EU and NAFTA, which has sought to protect Latin American producers at a cost to EU traditional Caribbean suppliers. This remains a small percentage of global tourism, but it is far greater than that experienced in other parts of the Third World. The number of visitors to the Caribbean each year is in excess of the total population of the region. This anomaly is most marked in the cases of the longer-standing tourist destinations, the Bahamas and Bermuda, but other islands are catching up. By the 1990s the Dominican Republic was the most popular destination in the Caribbean with 1.9 million stopover visitors in 1994. In a region where unemployment is a key problem tourism is a major source of jobs on many of the islands. The most extreme case is the Bahamas where more than a third of the official labour force are directly employed in the tourist industry. Direct employment of locals is for the most part low paid, unskilled and seasonal. Many more work in the informal sector in activities connected with tourism such as providing transport or selling souvenirs.

Development in the islands is primarily by foreign stakeholders, such as the British company Airtours and the Dutch airline KLM, and relatively little of the benefits accrue to the locals. This is especially true where the all-inclusive package is being developed to ensure that tourist expenditure remains in the enclave resort facilities. The dependency and vulnerability of the Caribbean economies is being perpetuated in these new external linkages. (See Monbiot's attacks on the Dominican Republic's tourist industry June 1998 in *The Guardian*.) Tourist development, because its purpose was not primarily developmental and it was not therefore planned, is also uneven. In some parts of the region there is just too much supply and too little demand. The number of visitors is limited by the relatively high costs of provision in the region, especially the costs of imports of goods and services that hits foreign currency earnings very hard. There are also other ongoing costs that fall not to the tourist industry itself but to the governments of the islands. Maintaining international airports is probably the greatest such cost in financial terms. For locals, tourist consumption of scarce water supplies could be still more important (Pattullo 1996).

Kenya

Africa South of the Sahara as a region has relatively little international tourism, largely due to the perception of Africa as poor, unsafe and unhealthy.

Sea and sun tourism has been concentrated in Kenya, The Gambia and South Africa; wildlife tourism in Kenya and Southern Africa. An ability to offer a combination of these two kinds of tourist activity in a two-centre package has been a terrific advantage to Kenya. Wildlife tourism in Kenya is an obvious development given the rich biodiversity of the game parks of the Kenyan interior. Its known mammal and bird species (what most wildlife tourists want to see) are outnumbered only by the Congo, a much less pleasant place for the northern tourist. The recognition of the actual and potential importance of this diverse fauna led to the creation in 1991 of the Kenya Wildlife Service.

The sheer quantity of tourist activity in Kenya constitutes a distortion of development and a vulnerability to changes of circumstances in the tourist-sending countries as well as in the host country itself. Tourism is Kenya's largest foreign currency earner and has contributed as much as 11 per cent of GNP before domestic problems in the mid-1990s caused a falling off in tourist numbers. Government policy has encouraged foreign investment in the tourist industry and the majority of Kenyan hotels are foreign owned. They are also concentrated in the coastal area, around Nairobi and near the game parks. Development in these areas has not been planned and tourist numbers have not been controlled. This concentration can present problems in protected areas simultaneously charged with the preservation of biodiversity and the accommodation of tourists. Very little of the funds raised through tourism are spent on conserving the protected areas (Weaver 1999: 109–25).

The Gambia

The Gambia's problems resulting from its tourist industry are not so much the problems of conserving its natural resources as coping with its distorted development. The tourist industry has been developed with the support of UNDP and the International Development Agency since the late 1960s. Most tourists are from northern Europe and some two-thirds are British. This makes The Gambia highly dependent on the UK and tourism contributes more than 10 per cent of The Gambia's GNP.

Further The Gambian tourist industry is dominated by international hotel chains. This foreign investment was encouraged by a government policy of tax breaks and preferential land allocations. Although for The Gambia tourist industry receipts are vital, most of the profit generated accrues to foreign interests. Tourists book their seats on foreign-owned airlines, through foreign tour operators and stay in foreign-owned hotels, built with imported foreign materials, and during their stay they consume imported products because there is relatively little local production that could meet their needs. Clearly tourism provides an important source of both direct and tourist-related employ-ment, but The Gambia is at the top end of the range for the seasonal compon-ent of employment in the tourist industry (Weaver 1999: 55). Two-thirds of those employed in the tourist industry are laid off in the low season from April to October. It is also highly localised, being concentrated in the area around Banjul. Thus tourism may be seen as exacerbating inequalities within The Gambia.

Southern Africa

Much of Southern Africa is experiencing the rapid development of ecotourism. Again it is the diverse fauna that attracts visitors. Wildlife tourism is a major source of income for Africa. In 1995 the chairman of the National Parks Board of South Africa estimated that within only a few years tourism would earn enough to fund the entire National Programme of Reconstruction and Development. The year 1996 was declared 'The Year Of Ecotourism'. The game reserves are booked up months in advance and there are too few flights to meet demand. International and local hotel groups have cornered the mar-ket at present and most provision is in the top price bracket. There is a need for smaller-scale, lower-priced provision if South Africa is to open up a mass market in order to integrate the wider local community in accordance with the expressed intentions of the National Programme of Reconstruction and Development, which aims to boost jobs and welfare in rural areas. Zimbabwe earns more than $200m p.a. from tourism.

But there is a conflict between what tourists want to see and the aspirations of the poor. In Zimbabwe conservation areas for endangered wildlife threat-ened by poachers are perceived as a means for large landowners to avoid the post-colonial redistribution of land. Further, in some areas, the traditional ways of life are being sidelined for the tourist industry. The establishment of national parks in some parts of Africa has been damaging for the hunting or nomadic lifestyles of the local populations. George Monbiot points out that the Khwe Bushmen of Botswana have been pushed out of their traditional home-lands that now form part of the Central Kalahari Game Reserve despite being supported by international human rights groups. They are considered a threat to the wildlife that tourists travel to see (Monbiot 1998).

Sex tourism

As Enloe (1989: 36) notes: 'To succeed, sex tourism requires Third World women to be economically desperate enough to enter prostitution; having done so it is difficult to leave'. Although there are newer centres such as Cuba and the Dominican Republic, sex tourism has developed often as an extension of the 'Rest and Recreation' (R & R) facilities expected by US troops in the past. It is no accident therefore that some of the centres are former R & R locations

– Thailand, South Korea and the Philippines; others, such as Indonesia and Sri Lanka, are relatively nearby. Having said that, historical/cultural factors also contribute to the degree of acceptance of this exploitation. In Thailand, for example, prostitution expanded in the nineteenth century and child prostitution predates the arrival of foreign troops in 1962 and the growth of the mass tourist industry (Lee 1991: 79; Kent 1995: 55).

But the connection of economic inequality and child prostitution in countries such as India, Brazil and Thailand is no coincidence. The UN estimates that there are 700,000 female prostitutes in Thailand alone, most of whom are aged 17–24. Young girls are drawn to the cities such as Bangkok looking for work and are then unable to find formal employment. Male tourists outnumber female visitors to Bangkok by 3 : 1. Thailand has an increasing problem with AIDS cases and more than half a million Thais (of 59 million) are HIV positive. The Thai government deliberately moderated its restrictions on prostitution in the Entertainment Places Act of 1966 and thus encouraged the development of the sex tourist industry. It was only the emerging evidence of the extent of HIV infection that led to a change of policy in the late 1980s. Laws against prostitution elsewhere in South Asia may long have been stricter in theory, but they were and are often not imposed by police and tourist officials who turn a blind eye. This is true in Goa, one of the newer sex tourist areas.

Sex tourism is often the means to satisfy unusual sexual preferences because most people would not pay to travel somewhere far away to get something available at home. As Julia O'Connell Davidson (1996) points out, those with these preferences include paedophiles, men who want multiple anonymous encounters with teenagers and those who have racialised fantasies. Different places cater for different prefences. Cuba for example does not really yet cater for paedophiles, the main market is for men from Italy, Canada and Germany who seek teenage girls.

A unique set of historical circumstances has led to the development of the sex tourist industry in Cuba. The continuing US blockade and the collapse of Soviet support have meant a desperate need for foreign exchange and hence the development of tourism generally. For ordinary Cubans the blockade means food rationing and shortages of basics such as clothing, soap, cooking oil and painkillers. Tourists obviously expect better hence the development of tourist enclaves. The Cuban government has sought to keep the tourist economy separate but this has been unsuccessful and a thriving black market in currency and goods meant for tourists has developed. Cubans are anxious to get hold of dollars to buy the basics that are only available for hard currency on the black market. Cuban girls and women are therefore more than willing to sell sexual favours to tourists for dollars (Davidson 1996).

It is not just the growing awareness of HIV/AIDS that is leading to demands for curbs on sex tourism from the supply side in parts of the Third World. A moral backlash from Islamic fundamentalist groups has grown, but so too has opposition from Third World nationalists and feminists alike.

Business and politics: taxation, tariffs and privatisation

The problem for Third World states of the links between transnational corporations and local interests have already been mentioned. The main issues between such corporations and governments revolve around three main issues: taxation, tariffs and privatisation.

International law accepts that companies are subject to local taxation wherever they operate. However it is quite a different matter for a weak Third World government actually to obtain the revenues to which it feels entitled. The fact that the country needs the company more than the company needs the country weakens its bargaining position. The practice of 'transfer pricing', by which goods are sold internally by one branch of a company to another can, if judiciously employed, result in a much reduced tax bill. In extreme cases a company can, if it has sufficient resources, simply buy the outcome that it wants, preferably in a weak, undervalued local currency.

One thing at least has changed. It is no longer acceptable practice for a company that feels hard done-by to appeal to its home government for military force to be used in its defence. It is also true that they seldom need to do so.

Much economic growth in the Third World has taken place behind protective tariff barriers. The conclusion of the Uruguay Round, and the creation of the World Trade Organization, if taken literally, rules out such a strategy and leaves Third World countries vulnerable to strong selling pressures from the advanced industrialised countries. However common sense suggests that both tariff barriers and non-tariff barriers will be employed for some time yet. The fact is that for major transnational corporations they have always been manipulable by a variety of devices, even if the country concerned has not, as in many cases it has, been so keen to invite in foreign investment that it has been prepared to waive all tariffs on imported capital goods for a substantial period, typically ten years.

In the current economic climate the nationalisation of foreign-owned enterprises is unlikely to be an issue in the immediate future. Its place as a problem area has been taken by privatisation.

'Privatisation' now generally refers to the process by which state assets are transferred to private ownership. In this sense it is a new term, originally popularised in Britain when, following its successful re-election in 1983, the Thatcher government embarked on a crusade to divest the state of its ownership of profit-making enterprises. The sale of public enterprises has however gone on for many years – as long, perhaps, as public enterprises have existed. In Argentina, for example, a report by Raúl Prebisch for the interim military government of 1955–58 recommended the sale of all state enterprises except the railways and the oil industry, but no action was taken (di Tella and Rodríguez Braun 1990: 7). Under President Frondizi, however, in order to reduce public expenditure the government sold off 40 companies previously German owned that had been expropriated at the end of the Second World

War and privatised the urban bus transport network in Buenos Aires with, the then Minister of Economy claims, 'excellent results' (Roberto T. Alemann, in di Tella and Rodríguez Braun 1990: 69). At the same time private participation was invited both by Argentina's state oil corporation Yacimientos Petrolíferos Fiscales (YPF) and by Petróleos Mexicanos (PEMEX) in Mexico, where in an act widely hailed at the time as a declaration of economic independence British and American oil companies had been nationalised in 1938.

Despite vigorous US propaganda for private enterprise the real shift towards privatisation in Latin America did not get under way until the 1970s, when it was associated with the policies of the 'Chicago boys' in Chile. It is only since the early 1980s that it has become a major theme of Latin American economic policies (Glade 1991: 2). Its spread to the rest of the Third World has been slower, the obvious reason being that many of the poorer Third World countries have few if any major assets that a buyer would find attractive. Additionally it is one of the ironies of privatisation programmes that, by the law of supply and demand, a government keen to privatise national assets can be expected to receive the *lowest* possible price for them, and many Third World governments that were originally keen to sell have at least hesitated when they found that they might end up paying out more in inducements than they were going to receive from the sale.

Were the choice of either nationalisation or privatisation purely a matter of economics the question of which to adopt would be a purely technical one. Unfortunately, however, both the acts themselves, and the way in which they are executed, involve significant and complex ethical questions. For a Third World state a major problem is presented by potential foreign-owned monopolies. The desire of foreign corporations to bid for former public enterprises is much enhanced when a successful bid will give them exclusive economic control. However turning state monopolies into private monopolies is likely at the least to breed nationalist resentment. Alternatively, where two or more companies are bidding for a key asset, the question of which bid to choose may well be determined as much by political (or even personal) considerations as by economic ones.

Conclusion

Economic weakness makes Third World countries politically powerless. Opening up their economies to investment and trade promises wealth, but brings with it a greater vulnerability to outside influences. Because of this purely Third World organisations have not been particularly successful at influencing world affairs, while regional organisations incorporating a substantial power are inclined to come under the influence of that power. The OAS has not for long been able to avoid the influence of the USA, and through the

francophone states France has exercised and continues to exercise a disproportionate influence within the OAU.

Though interactions between the citizens of different countries are becoming technically easier, money and political influence combine to ensure that the
globalisation of world politics tends to strengthen the power of the major states
and/or the advanced industrialised countries, not of the Third World.

PART IV

Policy issues

CHAPTER 11

The right to development

Introduction

The meaning that you attach to the term 'development' depends on where you start from. It means different things to different people, even at its most mundane and practical level. For example, a resident of rural Senegal might see development as the availability of very basic services such as a reliable source of potable water; someone living in the suburbs of Greater Buenos Aires would expect rather more. Certainly both would associate the term with some sort of improvement in the quality of their lives.

In its earliest form development was seen in terms of economic changes that would seek to counter the problem of global poverty, which was being addressed for the first time in the post-war era. Poverty was believed to be measurable in economic terms, simply as the amount by which per capita income fell short of the US level, and so was easily solvable by economic changes. Today development is seen as a much more complex concept, involving consideration not only of the crude increase in production but the nature of that production and the range of social facilities that accompany it. It is this stress on quality rather than simply quantity that separates development from growth.

But this still does not answer the often-asked question of whether the concept is properly an economic or a political one. Development agendas change over time (see the discussion on poverty and basic needs in Chapter 3). A decisive response laying strong emphasis on political or economic aspects of development usually reflects strong attachment to a particular perspective.

It would be hard to criticise the scope and range of the definition given by Michael Todaro (1994: 16):

Development must therefore be conceived of as a multidimensional process involving major changes in social structures, popular attitudes and national institutions, as well as the acceleration of economic growth, the reduction of inequality, and the eradication of poverty. Development, in its essence, must represent the whole gamut of change by which an entire social system, tuned to the diverse basic needs and desires of individuals and social groups within that system, moves away from a condition of life widely perceived as unsatisfactory toward a situation or condition of life regarded as materially and spiritually 'better'.

At its simplest and most cogent the term may be best expressed as in the work of Amartya Sen (Sen 1981) as a reduction in vulnerability and as increased strength to counter problems consequent upon an enhancement of the options available. For Sen development involves the increased freedom of the population. There is in this a validity that other definitions do not so adequately express, since income as measured by purchasing power gives freedom, but the freedom it gives also embraces a series of needs within society, for participation, health, education, etc.

Ghana: the desire for economic independence

The early history of independent Ghana illustrates the hopes and failures associated with the 'take-off' model of development. Ghana's future leader, Kwame Nkrumah, returned in 1947 to the Gold Coast, as it was then known, from the USA where he had been a postgraduate student and taken his doctorate. By 1949 he had formed his own political party the Convention People's Party (CPP) seeking immediate independence from Britain, which had been the colonial power for more than a century.

In 1951 the Gold Coast held its first elections. Nearly a million people voted. Although Nkrumah himself was still in gaol, his party swept to power and he became prime minister in an elected government that had full internal self-government though Britain still controlled foreign and defence policy. In 1957 he became the first leader of a newly independent black African state and set out to turn Ghana into a modern industrial utopia.

The British had planned the Volta dam to provide hydroelectric power to smelt aluminium, but in 1956 cancelled the project, saying it was too expensive. Nkrumah saw the Volta dam as a means to the power needed to fuel the modernisation of Ghana. It would be a source of power for comprehensive development as well as the means to irrigate the Accra plains. Eisenhower, anxious that Ghana should be pro-USA in the cold war, suggested US aluminium manufacturers might be interested in supporting the Volta scheme. In 1958 Kaiser Industries agreed to build a smelter in Ghana and to buy the electricity generated by the scheme. Nkrumah asked the World Bank for $30 million, the largest loan ever requested up to that time.

In accordance with the prevailing take-off model of development popularised by W.W. Rostow, power on a massive scale was seen as the means to industrialisation and therefore to development. In 1960 the World Bank approved the scheme in principle but expressed some reservations about the prices Kaiser had agreed to pay to Ghana for energy to run the smelter. The World Bank took the view that these prices must be higher if Ghana was to have a chance of realising the development plans that were an integral part of the Volta River scheme. Kaiser was determined not to pay more than the lowest rates available anywhere in the world. Nkrumah had little option but to agree to Kaiser's price or it would pull out and the dam would not be built.

Nkrumah wanted to keep Ghana out of the cold war tensions, but the United States of America saw the dam and his developmental aspirations as the means to win him over. The USA had agreed to lend millions to the scheme and used these loans to pressure Nkrumah into accepting US policies. Hence the Volta River scheme was shaped by political and economic pressures, not by Nkrumah's idealism. As an investment Ghana was initially seen as an excellent prospect. The colonial power, Britain, had left it a good infrastructure and an educated population. Thus the dam got built.

Construction of the Volta dam took four years. The process came to illustrate the high levels of corruption in Ghana. It was not just that there were corrupt government officials, but also corrupt foreign suppliers who would do anything to make a sale. European industrialists seeking to sell their products in Ghana found that the easy way was to offer a bribe, and bribery soon became the business culture of Accra. One result was a rush to sell Ghana anything, no matter how inappropriate. The most grandiose development schemes were encouraged by foreign suppliers and domestic vested interests and taken up by local politicians eager to win popular support. Most proved expensive and some unviable.

The key to Ghana's strong economic position was cocoa. However in 1964 cocoa prices collapsed and since cocoa was Ghana's main source of foreign exchange the country, which had been one of the richest in Africa, slid into debt. Nkrumah's vision was now beginning to be seen as megalomania. Only one month after the dam was finished in 1966 the armed forces took over the government while Nkrumah was abroad. Nkrumah fled to Guinea where he died in 1972.

Significantly, the post-Nkrumah years were also a period of economic failure. The Kaiser aluminium plant flourished and the World Bank loan was paid off with the money paid for power, but as electricity prices rose everywhere in the 1970s Kaiser still paid very little. In 1979 Flt Lt Jerry Rawlings took power in the seventh coup since Nkrumah and he was determined to get more from the Kaiser smelter. In 1983 the Ghanaian government tried to get Kaiser to renegotiate prices by allowing rumours of nationalisation to circulate and by keeping the dam shut down until Kaiser agreed, and two years later, in 1985, a new agreement was signed that raised prices threefold ('Pandora's Box', *Assignment* BBC Television, 1993).

The right to development?

The World Conference on Human Rights (June 1993) revealed once more the extent of the North–South divide on the issue of the 'right to develop'. However this is only a particular example of the fact that human rights are defined differently the world over. These arguments can be divided into two main groups.

Developing countries argue that political and civil rights are not separable from and certainly not more important than economic, social and cultural rights. The industrial West argues that political and civil liberties should come first. Some thinkers believe that economic, social and cultural rights cannot be regarded as true human rights, since they depend on the ability to make economic resources available.

A further question is whether collective (i.e. developmental) rights should outrank individual rights. The question is complicated by the fact that, as so often in international politics, countries have put their names to high-sounding statements of general principles that they are not always prepared to put into practice.

As early as 1948 the UN confirmed development as a right in Article 28 of the Universal Declaration of Human Rights. This commitment has been reiterated and deepened on many subsequent occasions. The 1960s were proclaimed as the UN 'Decade of Development'. The results for many Third World countries were so disappointing that a second Decade was proclaimed for the 1970s. Any hope that this might be more successful was to be abruptly cut short by the first 'oil shock' of 1973.

This was enormously ironic since the oil crises of the 1970s were initially seen by both oil-rich and oil-poor states as an opportunity to redress the balance between the First and the Third Worlds. However in practice it was the Third World countries that did not have access to their own oil reserves and lacked the leverage to gain preferential access on the world market that came off worst. In 1979 the Brandt Commission proposed a formal redistribution of wealth from the First to the Third World states by way of a 'global income tax' (Brandt 1980). However the 1980s were a decade of neo-liberal 'solutions' and high interest rates and by 1990 the majority of Third World countries were actually worse off than they had been in 1979. See Plate 11.

Meanwhile with the enlargement of the United Nations came in 1964 a response to western domination of trade in the holding of the United Nations Conference on Trade and Development. That first meeting of UNCTAD, UNCTAD I, stressed the need for structural reforms in world trade if rapid development was to be achieved by the South. But although UNCTAD became a permanent organisation, holding a sequence of major conferences, it had no real power, as the northern states were unwilling to consider more than minor tinkering with the existing system.

At UNCTAD III at Santiago de Chile the president of Mexico, Luis Echeverría Alvarez, called for the creation of a New International Economic

Order (NIEO). The Mexicans voiced the feelings of most Third World governments when they criticised the prevailing terms of trade. They saw themselves as being condemned by the existing system to export large quantities of primary products at low prices, and to import the manufactured goods they needed at very high ones; hence the demand for an arrangement that would link producer prices to changes in the price of manufactured goods. They were backed by the president of Venezuela, Carlos Andrés Pérez, and by most of the other states that were members of the Organization of Petroleum Exporting Countries (OPEC). In April 1974 the UN General Assembly, which was then heavily dominated by Third World states, endorsed the idea of the NIEO.

This resulted in the adoption by the United Nations General Assembly in December 1974 of the Charter of Economic Rights and Duties of States (CERDS). Its main planks were:

• fair terms of trade for developing countries
• a new world currency linked to the price of primary materials
• the abolition of IMF conditionality as a requirement for new loans.

Though the resolution to adopt CERDS was carried by 120 votes to 6 with 10 abstentions, the programme it represented was in fact, though acknowledged by President Carter, totally opposed by the governments of the United States of America and the advanced industrialised countries and so was effectively a dead letter (Thomas 1985: 65–6). CERDS might, on paper, have been agreed, but not surprisingly it was never implemented. For example, it was intended that prices of primary products would be pegged to prices of manufactured goods, but this proved to be unrealistic. Manufacturers were unwilling to pay more, and competition between Third World suppliers kept prices down. OPEC had for a time been successful in driving up the price of petroleum, but similar cartels for other products failed for a variety of reasons (see Chapter 4). The United Nations called the Cancun Conference of 1981 to promote global negotiations on the NIEO but it came to nothing.

The problem was not just economic but political. In general the USA does not feel itself bound by UN decisions with which it does not agree. The fact that it foots 25 per cent of the bill for the UN is the most powerful argument for this. The agreement by Japan in September 1994 to become the UN's second-largest supporter and pay 15 per cent of the costs of maintaining the organisation is likely to give Japan almost as much leverage if it chooses to use it. Not only did the USA under Ronald Reagan withdraw from UNESCO and constantly chivvy other agencies into accepting its wishes, but on the first occasion when it was confronted with a legal challenge before the World Court to its clandestine war on Nicaragua it refused to accept that body's jurisdiction. At the same time by choosing to work through other groupings such as G7 it is able to bypass many of the constraints that the Third World domination of the UN General Assembly would otherwise impose on its freedom of action.

A New International Economic Order would depend on stability. To achieve this, many argue that what would first be needed is a democratisation of international relations, just as democracy and participation must accompany development at a local or national level (see WCED 1987: 297). The restoration of superpower hegemony could restore stability, but that state of affairs would be unlikely to meet the *economic* aspirations of Third World countries.

Development strategies

Different Third World states have devised their own strategies for development. These routes have varied with starting point, location, tradition and ideology. For example, while some states such as Zambia have continued to rely on exporting primary products and some, such as Cuba, have been forced to do so, others have chosen (or perhaps chosen is too strong, given the constraints) more unusual directions such as India's quest for self-sufficiency or Singapore's investment in technology and education. Some have favoured export-led growth as in Taiwan or South Korea, taking advantage of, if not actively embracing, a free market ideology premised on the assumption that benefits will trickle down to the poorest sectors. This latter strategy is illustrated by the cases of Brazil, Chile and other countries of Latin America.

Development relies on availability of funds for infrastructural and other capital investment. Third World states generally get such funds as revenues from import/export duties, fees and taxes on transnational corporations, the profits made by state agencies for the import or export of products, foreign loans or aid and manipulation of exchange rates. Domestic revenues are much more difficult to extract, since local elites resist (often successfully) any attempt of the state to set realistic levels of personal taxation. Hence Third World regimes must necessarily be reluctant to contemplate any development strategy that hits international trade relations, and certainly their relatively small size in the main precludes the realistic possibility of economic autarky.

In some cases there may be a conflict between a Third World state's development strategy and the interests of transnational corporations. Although a state must be fairly small for TNCs still to have a great degree of national power, a number of them are still in that position, particularly in Africa SSA. Generally speaking the two parties, the state and the corporations, need each other, but the relationship is often unequal and the increasing globalisation of the world economy and deregulation of transnational activities are enhancing linkages between transnational corporations and thus increasingly marginalising the weaker South.

Development strategies vary but usually stress either import-substitution-industrialisation (ISI) or enhancement of exports. Often Third World governments develop medium-term (five to seven years) comprehensive development plans and/or a national development ideology such as South Korea's New Community Movement. These are assertions of government control of the economy that is not always capable of being realised in practice. Diversification is perhaps the most important part of any development strategy. It is vital to most Third World states owing to variations in the prices of commodities on the world market. However the grandiose plans of the developmentalists often fail. The process of ISI can easily be hijacked by transnational corporations, as is the case in Brazil, where some 85 per cent of the pharmaceuticals industry is owned by TNCs. But some countries have succeeded with ISI. In South Korea it has been transformed into an exporting success as corporations such as Hyundai, though some argue that such development can only be achieved if repression is used to channel resources from consumption to investment.

Third World countries often target their exports on to other Third World countries. A striking example is the Brazilian arms industry. But since much of the technology needed for development, and especially that needed to get beyond ISI, must come from the developed countries and often from their transnational corporations, their capacity for independent action is limited.

Development of stronger First World regional economic groupings, for example the EU and NAFTA, is also marginalising the Third World. While North–North interdependence is strengthening, as yet South–South bonds have not been much developed. The 1950s and 1960s did see the establishment of regional and subregional links in the South, some of which were political and some economic. Regional and subregional development banks were founded. Despite this, South–South trade and communications often pass through northern facilities en route. South–South linkages without northern intervention would strengthen the southern bargaining position in relation to the North. At present the South's organisations and structures do present a common front and these can be effective, but not usually in economic matters where individual countries short of skilled negotiators can be easily 'picked off' one by one. Often this is done by the North meeting some pressing short-term need, as in the case of the Pergau Dam in Malaysia. Economies of scale for countries trying to meet broadly similar needs and facing similar problems should be possible. Further, in one sense, newer and poorer Third World states may have more choice in development strategies in that they have fewer vested interests to placate.

Development directions may be influenced either externally or internally or both. Externally they are shaped by advice and pressure from the US Agency for International Development (USAID), the World Bank, the IMF, etc. The combined effects of these powerful bodies is striking, and the example of the Caribbean Basin Initiative (CBI) is instructive. During the 1980s, when the United States of America moved from being the world's largest creditor to being the world's largest debtor, its economy was booming as a result and the CBI was supposed to enable it to benefit its smallest neighbours, allowing them preferential access to the US market for selected products. But at the same time the small nations of the Caribbean, which faced a declining price for their few commodities, were being told by the international lending agencies to stop 'living beyond their means'. The combined effects of structural adjustment on their economies was to export capital to the advanced industrial economies, a situation made much worse by prevailing high dollar interest rates, which had increased so much that they significantly worsened the terms of borrowing and hence the debts that the countries concerned had been forced to assume.

> In 1987, the Caribbean as a whole paid out US$207 million more to the foreign governments, banks and multilateral agencies that are 'aiding' the region than it received from all of them combined in the same year. This net outflow of funds was mainly in the form of interest and principal payments on the region's foreign debt, which totalled US$20.9 billion in 1988. The removal of funds from the Caribbean would have been even greater had not a major portion of official debt bills been repeatedly postponed; Jamaica's debt payments, for example have been rescheduled every year since 1979. The consequence is accumulation of arrears and even higher bills to be paid in the future. (McAfee 1991: 13)

However no less significant are internal political considerations such as who must be consulted and who must be bought off. Vested interests are just one indigenous obstacle to development. Others may include: a lack of industry and infrastructure at independence, especially in Africa; low literacy, poor education, low school enrolment; rapid population growth and urbanisation; little administrative capacity; poor financial institutions; archaic social structures; and internal conflicts. External assistance is important but the key requirement is for self-directed development using human and material resources to satisfy local needs.

Transnational corporations

Because the majority of TNCs are small companies with headquarters in one country and often only one other branch abroad, the term transnational corporation is preferred both here and by the World Bank to 'multinational' corporation, which implies a large enterprise with regional or even worldwide reach and many foreign subsidiaries.

Transnational corporations are responsible for 40 per cent of world trade, 90 per cent of world trade in commodities and 30 per cent of world food production. The largest TNCs are responsible for most of the world's foreign investment. The USA provides most such investment, with the UK second and Japan third. The largest firms are household names such as IBM, Exxon, General Electric and General Motors.

Although more than three-quarters of transnational corporations are based in the United States of America or in Europe, TNCs are also based in LDCs and hence some LDC-transnational corporation involvement in other less developed countries. Brazilian companies are involved in West Africa, Indian companies in Indonesia and Malaysia and the Argentine corporation Bunge y Born in Brazil and Uruguay. The United Nations estimates that transnational corporations employ more than 60 million people worldwide. The figures are sobering. The annual turnover of Nestlé is more than seven times the GNP of Ghana. In 1984 no African state had an annual turnover as big as Exxon. Only South Africa, Nigeria, Egypt, Morocco and the Ivory Coast had GNPs big enough to get them places amongst the top 100 corporations. Transnational corporations now control more than 40 per cent of world output and as much as 30 per cent of world trade takes place not between but within large corporations (Thrift in Johnston and Taylor 1986).

Why is this so? A major reason is the number of states and the relatively limited number of major corporations. There is keen rivalry between less developed countries to attract transnational corporations. Once they have chosen to set up operations the governments concerned find that they cannot effectively regulate them as it is so easy for large corporations to switch production to another Third World state. Sometimes TNCs transfer dangerous or polluting operations to the South. But there are always countries available to allow them to do so, in view of the very large legal and illegal returns that they expect to obtain.

In some states there have been attempts to develop different development strategies and eliminate the involvement of transnational corporations. The Bolsheviks in Russia seized their oil fields in 1917. The oil companies were slow to realise that the change was permanent, but by 1924 they were ready to compete both openly and secretly with one another to market Soviet oil abroad. However as Stalin consolidated his grip foreign participation in the Russian economy was ended and did not return until after the collapse of the Soviet Union in 1991. Later transnational corporations were squeezed out of the oil industry in the 1930s in Bolivia and Mexico, in the 1940s in Romania, in the 1950s in Brazil, in the 1960s in Peru and in the 1970s in Algeria, Libya, Iraq and Venezuela. However the key to the oil industry, as John D. Rockefeller was the first to realise, is not production but distribution and marketing, and by 2000 the 'Seven Sisters' (Sampson 1975) who for so long dominated the industry were only five: BP-Amoco, Chevron, Exxon-Mobil, Texaco, and Royal Dutch-Shell.

By the 1970s Third World countries were finding that nationalisation was a strategy fraught with dangers. In Jamaica the ownership of sugar production was taken out of the hands of Tate & Lyle and the plantations nationalised. Twenty-three cooperatives were established by the People's National Party (PNP) led by Michael Manley from 1976 on; with the plantation workers in charge of production they succeeded in producing one-half of the country's sugar. However several factors worked against them: plant diseases, the hostility of the USA and the IMF and a drop in sugar prices. In 1980 the PNP lost the elections, the cooperatives were shut down and Tate & Lyle was invited back in.

Supporters of transnational corporations use arguments associated with free market economic theories. They claim that TNCs fill gaps of various kinds that exist in local economies. Such corporations, they argue, enhance the earning capacity of host states and generate foreign exchange. They see them as being risk takers, which are exceptionally dynamic in promoting growth. They argue that transnational corporation investment may reduce the need of a host country to borrow abroad or may fill a need not met by borrowing. Notably, when bank lending declined during the debt crisis of the 1980s transnational corporation investment became still more important. Company investment not only supplements local savings but also increases saving by increasing local income and stimulating domestic investment to provide inputs to transnational corporations.

Manufacturing output is seen as the motor of development and some 30 per cent of LDC manufacturing output comes from transnational corporations. Some of the most successful emerging economies are to be found in the regions that have been most penetrated by TNCs; in Singapore more than 60 per cent of manufacturing output is generated by transnational corporations. Such organisations enhance the earning capacity of host states and generate foreign exchange. Local individuals and companies are paid for their part in production. While some profits are repatriated, some are reinvested in local plant and supplies and much flows into the local economy by way of wages and salaries. Transnationals are also responsible for generating substantial additional tax revenues.

Several other aspects of TNC activity can be seen as positive. Some technical knowledge is transmitted to local employees and contractors along with managerial skills, resulting in new products becoming available locally and a more efficient use of local labour. In particular transnational corporations are often seen as a major force in modernising agriculture, the sector traditionally most resistant to change. TNCs frequently pay well above the going market rate in salaries and wages. Additionally they often provide social services for their workforces, contributing to local health and education and minimising any drain on local provision.

Some even argue that they act as buffers, insulating the host economy from the full harshness of the international system. There is widespread agreement that they tend to have a generally liberalising effect in the developed economies in which they are based. One of the results is they have a strong incentive to lobby against quotas and tariffs that would limit entry of their Third World products to the advanced industrialised countries.

Opponents of TNCs take a very different view of both the economic and political processes involved. They note that most transnational corporation investment occurs in countries that have been in a position to promote export-led growth, such as Brazil and Malaysia. Transnational corporations are conspicuously absent from many parts of Africa South of the Sahara. Zambia's economy, 70 per cent controlled by transnationals, has collapsed since 1991 as a result of a combination of structural adjustment and trade liberalisation.

The critics cast doubt on the real rate of return a country can expect from attracting TNCs. The inducements offered, such as tax concessions and stable exchange rates, can be very expensive to the host government and in business terms hardly justify their use.

Far from adding to local capital resources, critics argue, transnationals consume them. Through their presence foreign investment is made easy for the local foreign-oriented elite. They do not promote domestic development but seek only to invest where they can maximise their profits. Agricultural transnational corporations do even more harm by buying up high-quality land that could better be used for domestic food production, and so indirectly increase the need to import food. Such corporations hit local economies by repatriating an excessive level of profit, at the same time minimising their real rate of return to local economies through devices such as transfer pricing. This involves the undervaluing of transnational products in the host country, but their revaluing by the time they reach the home base of the corporation by being sold on through the company's subsidiaries. As with transfer pricing, the high cost of imported inputs, whether real or as an exercise in accounting, reduces the profits that can be locally taxed.

Transnational corporations go abroad to find new sources of inputs that are declining or becoming more expensive at home. This includes labour. Skilled labour is to be found in middle income rather than poor Third World states, so the more technical operations are located there.

Transnationals use the protection of LDC import-substitution-industrialisation strategies but tend to go where new markets open up in order to exploit those temporary advantages. Hence they are more likely to invest in the top and middle-income countries of the Third World.

As for them transferring technology to the local economy, they do often use superior technology, but this can be quite inappropriate to local conditions and invariably much more capital intensive. LDC transnational corporations are often thought to provide more labour-intensive technologies and therefore to be more acceptable. However in both cases the sharp end of advanced technology may be kept under wraps at home to prevent transfer, in order to preserve the corporation's competitive advantage.

Lastly, wherever they operate, transnationals may enhance the unevenness of development. Manufacturing companies charge the local population premium prices for local products carrying popular brand names. They may displace local firms. They often produce inappropriate products intended originally for the First World and stimulate local consumption of products such as cigarettes, baby milk formula and brand-name drugs. This is the technique of 'cocacolonisation'. On the other hand mining companies and plantations worsen the rural/urban imbalance, use up natural resources much faster than otherwise would be the case and bring about environmental degradation.

An open question following the Bhopal disaster has been the question of safety. Certainly in that case the standards maintained by a local subsidiary of a transnational corporation were found to be very inadequate, and there are serious doubts as to whether such a dangerous process should have been located so close to a centre of population. However in their defence it can be argued that generally transnational corporation standards of environmental protection and safety are higher than those of small local companies that can afford less.

The prejudice against TNCs in many Third World countries is very great. Times of crisis weaken Third World states in the face of transnational corporations and the debt crisis of the 1980s made them more vital to Third World states and enabled them to rebuild their position. On the other hand, transnational corporations are mainly involved in the more autarkic sections of the Third World, because middle-income countries offer them diversified economic structures, sophisticated and substantial markets and the skilled labour these corporations most often need. The 1960s and 1970s saw the development of a variety of controls on their activities. States prescribed the degree of local investment required, the maximum length of time an activity could be left under transnational corporation control before transfer to local interests, etc. Such restraints on freedom of manoeuvre caused IBM and Coca-Cola to leave India in the 1970s. The ultimate weapon was expropriation, but this has been very rare outside the oil industry. There was some use of nationalisation in emerging states in the 1960s and 1970s, but the number of countries prepared to confront transnational corporations was always small and amongst the most

Table 11.1   Countries receiving most overseas development aid 1990

Country	Aid US$millions	US$ per capita
Egypt	5,604	107.60
Bangladesh	2,103	19.70
China	2,076	1.80
Indonesia	1,724	9.70
India	1,586	1.90
Israel	1,374	295.00
Philippines	1,277	20.80
Turkey	1,264	22.50
Tanzania	1,155	47.10
Pakistan	1,152	10.30
Kenya	1,000	41.40
Morocco	970	38.60
Mozambique	946	60.20
Jordan	891	282.50
Ethiopia	888	17.40
Zaire	823	22.10
Thailand	805	14.40
Sudan	792	31.50
Senegal	739	99.80
Côte d'Ivoire	689	57.90

Source: World Bank (1992) *World Development Report*, Oxford, Oxford University Press.

notable were Chile, Cuba, Uganda, Zaire and Zambia. Generally, where nationalisation has taken place, output has fallen and the expected benefits have not been for the most part realised. Most such Third World weapons against the power of TNCs have disappeared under the new WTO regime.

Aid

Foreign aid is a very new concept. It was virtually unknown before 1945. The use of economic aid as a tool of superpower competition in the cold war established the practice, but it took much longer than that for the concept that rich countries had a duty to help poor ones to become accepted.

With the ending of the cold war much of the self-interest that generated aid flows between 1950 and 1980 has come to an end. The Third World is likely to be the main victim of the change. Already there is in human terms far too little economic aid, and despite their professions of good intentions at the Rio Summit and elsewhere, the budgets the advanced industrial countries devote to aid are minimal (see Table 11.1). To put the figures in perspective, the European Union uses two-thirds of its budget to subsidise European farmers through the Common Agricultural Policy and spends only about 3 per cent of its budget on food aid.

Much excellent work is done, especially in emergency situations such as famine and earthquake, by NGOs such as Oxfam and Save the Children. But it is state action that is vital, the role of individuals and NGOs being minimal in comparison. For a variety of reasons government aid is however often of very little value for development purposes.

It is very difficult to decide where aid stops and other forms of financial transactions take place but broadly aid refers to a transfer of resources at non-commercial rates. It may be official, that is collected from tax-payers and transferred by governments themselves or international agencies, or it may be voluntary, that is raised and administered by NGOs. But this distinction is becoming more blurred as NGOs are increasingly being used to administer official funds. Likewise it varies in purpose, but what is usually meant by the term foreign aid is official development assistance (ODA). It is possible to make the case that aid has a much broader generic meaning and that non-ODA transfers may in some circumstances carry far greater entitlement to the term.

The term ODA comes from the 1969 redefinition of aid by the Development Assistance Committee of the OECD. This redefinition was a recognition that the term should exclude money collected and administered by NGOs, should exclude assistance not intended for developmental purposes such as military aid and should exclude loans available only at commercial rates that conferred no concessions on the recipients (White and Woestman 1994).

But, as Burnell notes, many authors suggest a broader definition of aid reflecting more strongly the donor intentions. To qualify for the name 'aid', transfers should not be self-interested: 'Foreign aid can be construed as inter-societal transfers of resources that are intended by all relevant parties, especially the provider, to serve first and foremost the recipients' needs, interests or wants' (Burnell 1997: 3). But he recognises the problems with such a definition. Transfers given for non-charitable reasons may have more benefit to the recipients than those given with good intentions that have adverse unintended consequences. There is also a question surrounding the coherence of the 'needs, interests or wants' of the recipient. These are not necessarily the same, and will certainly not be identically experienced by all within a recipient state. Aid varies according to recipients, donors, purposes and forms, or alternatively to whom it is given, who gives it, what it is given for and whether it consists of money, material benefits, advice, etc.

Definitional problems reflect the variety of forms aid takes. Aid in its broadest sense is contributed by intergovernmental organisations such as the International Development Agency, a specialised section of the World Bank established in 1960, and UNICEF, as well as by states and their governmental organisations, charities and private individuals. Aid from international organisations is termed multilateral, compared to aid from one specific donor country that is called bilateral aid. These two kinds of aid differ in why they are given and in what they are given for.

Aid then is increasingly multinational and is increasingly channelled through international organisations and international non-governmental organisations. Recipients also vary and they include states, would-be states, governments, oppositional elements and subnational groups.

Why is aid given?

Aid is at its most high profile and least contentious when it is a response to an emergency. Crisis aid may take the form of humanitarian aid from UN agencies or private disaster relief organised by pre-existing charities, such as Oxfam, or specially convened organisations such as Bandaid.

Some counties give aid for idealistic reasons. These are countries, including the Scandinavian States, Belgium, the Netherlands and Canada, which take the view that the present level of global inequality is unjustified and ought to be rectified. But there is of course a less charitable view of the good intentions of donors in that aid may be seen as a legitimation of the very inequality it purports to address. Further, there may be, as some authors suggest, a First World collective interest here: 'If the international economic system is incapable of providing the wherewithal for an effective reduction of inequality within the community of nations, the LDCs will feel justified in their attempts to destroy the political and economic system which perpetuates international inequalities' (Singer and Ansari 1997: 139).

But the big aid givers take a much more nationally self-interested and pragmatic line that can at times make aid seem to be little more than another branch of foreign policy. In the 1980s for example US aid increasingly tended to supporting private enterprise and the restructuring of economies and was channelled to areas where the USA perceived a threat to economic and political stability. These funds were whole country subsidies and not targeted on the poor, thus they could be used to free up funds for military purposes.

It is not entirely clear where aid stops and loans or trade begin. Much that is not really aid is termed so to make it sound better and to confer status on the donor(s). Aid is often seen as being 'given' by the international financial institutions (IFIs), that is by the IMF, the main body of the World Bank and the regional development banks, but in reality these organisations for the most part make loans at not particularly favourable rates and it is therefore difficult to percieve this funding (to which the recipients contribute) as aid. The same can be said of some loans from national institutions.

There is a strong connection between aid and trade in many instances, as is illustrated by the interconnections between the work of the British Overseas Development Agency and the Department of Trade and Industry, whereby the giving of aid and the winning of contracts for British companies are frequently dealt with in conjunction.

Such close connections are part of the generalised problem of conditionality with regard to aid. Aid may be given to secure contracts, to boost exports through the tying of what it may be spent on or, as indicated above, to exert an ideological influence in favour of democratisation, human rights, environmental considerations or economic liberalisation (see also p. 227). Even where such influence may be considered desirable questions of cultural imperialism have been raised.

What is it given for?

Despite all these uncertainties, there are clear trends in the patterns of aid. Food aid for example has diminished a good deal, and is now only around 10 per cent of ODA. Technical assistance and cooperation is a growing part of aid, worth up to $15 billion p.a. Programme aid is growing, as is debt relief.

Military aid remains one of the biggest items on the aid agenda despite the ending of the cold war. It sometimes involves arms transfers, sometimes military education and training, as in the notorious School of the Americas in Panama, where the USA trained many Latin American officers in counter-insurgency techniques and thus equipped them to coup more effectively. The military aid received by the developing countries in the late 1980s was in excess of the combined health and education budgets in one-fifth of cases. During President Reagan's second term (1984–88), direct military aid comprised more than one-third of all US aid and almost two-thirds of all US aid was military related. Such aid is given for ideological reasons not only by the wealthy western nations but also by developing countries themselves; for example, Saudi Arabia and Iran both supplied arms to the Bosnian Muslims in the 1994–95 fighting in the former Yugoslavia.

With the end of the cold war and the collapse of the USSR Eastern Bloc aid, which was often military aid (as can be seen by its concentration on recipients such as Vietnam and Cuba), effectively ended. Certainly this has led to a decline in conflict in some areas, e.g. Central America. Also it has helped donor agencies such as the IMF/World Bank to employ a policy of considering a recipient's military spending when deciding whether to make a loan. There have been massive decreases in arms imports to Africa, but this just reflects the dire economic situation in the region.

The decline of military aid, relative to its 1980s' highpoint, has been accompanied by a growth of political aid. As we have already noted good governance, political pluralism and democratic consolidation are actively sought by donors to recipient countries in transition (Burnell 1997: 8). These are aims rather than specific objectives. British ODA has emphasised seven specific priority objectives, to:

1. promote economic liberalisation
2. promote enhanced productive capacity
3. promote good government
4. reduce poverty
5. promote human development especially education and health
6. enhance the position of women
7. assist in tackling environmental problems (Eyben 1995).

As can readily be observed, these priorities may not sit comfortably together and in any case such a list does not address the question of what aid is directly given for. Apart from short-term disaster relief, what aid actually funds can be divided into particular projects and generalised development programmes.

In what form is it given?

This is not just a question of whether aid is given in the form of money or some other form, it is also about the form that the transfer of funds takes. Grants are generally seen as more likely to comprise aid than loans, but loans have their supporters too. Loans are thought to encourage self-reliance rather than dependence. Start-up costs are preferred to aid to meet ongoing maintenance costs. This is better publicity for the donor nation, but it may also mean that projects get started but then fail through lack of continuing support. Alternatively recipient countries get lumbered with the maintenance costs, they get locked into the purchase of expensive replacement parts from the 'donor' country. This is frequently the case with military aid.

Whose aid is it anyway?

As Cassen points out, the precise degree of effectiveness of aid is essentially 'unknowable', but it is vital that it is considered from the point of view of donors and also in order to enhance aid management (1994: 1–6). Clearly the form in which aid is given will impinge on its effectiveness, and the fact that donors and recipients will see aid differently contributes to the difficulty of assessing its effectiveness. There is an unusual degree of consensus between left-wing and conservative economists on the negative effects of aid for the recipient country. Both perceive domestic economic policy as becoming politicised in the search for aid to the detriment of developmental activity. Though it tends to be conservative economists who emphasise the growing culture of dependence in aid recipients, both sides acknowledge the capacity of aid to feed the consumption patterns of elites and promote a culture of corruption rather than meet the needs of the poor for economic growth and development. It is mainly radical economists who point to the distortion of local production patterns and markets as a consequence of aid.

A particularly glaring example of how aid can work for donors but distort recipient economies is tied aid, which requires recipients to directly spend the funds received on the products of the donor country or alternatively to agree to projects that for some reason can only be undertaken by donor country companies. Tied aid is increasing and may now constitute more than two-thirds of bilateral aid. It is essentially a protectionist measure for northern industry against which the WTO cannot act. The tying of aid means that aid recipients are not free to take advantage of global competition, to buy really appropriate products and to support local production.

Multilateral aid is much less likely to be self-interested and is therefore increasingly preferred, and it has now reached more than one-third of all aid transfers. Multilateral aid is also much more likely to go to the poorest countries because it is related more to need than other considerations and it does not create the same direct obligation on the part of the recipient. It can also offer some degree of coordination for the myriad different projects underway in some developing nations. However it is also true that not all members are equal partners in multilateral agencies and that 'aid' from the Bretton Woods institutions has been highly conditional, inflexible and has produced extensive environmental damage.

Donors are generally the wealthiest nations so they have a vested interest in stabilising the existing global economy and that is precisely what the Bretton Woods System was set up to do. Perceptions of how this stability may be achieved have changed with time and the demise of the former eastern bloc. The 'first generation' conditionalities of the 1980s, fiscal stabilisation and macroeconomic liberalisation, have given way to the 'second generation' conditionalities of the 1990s – good governance, democratisation and human rights.

Too frequently, therefore, aid is given to further the aims (whether these be national economic or ideological aims) of the donor rather than to address the needs of the recipient. Flexibility is required for an aid programme to be effective, aid must have the capacity to respond to local conditions. Where it is donor needs that are being met by aid this is not the case, aid is for the most part tied to specific projects and worse still donor country inputs often must be used. Much food aid is not a response to local needs at all but rather dumping of surplus production by the 'donor' countries as part of domestic price-support programmes that help to maintain global prices. Food aid has some peculiar problems all its own and is particularly controversial, partly for the reasons outlined by Sen (1981), that in a well-organised and less selfish world it should not be necessary, but also for other reasons. Food aid may avert disaster in the short term in the particular local area where it is distributed if it is targeted on those in need, but it does nothing to change the conditions that gave rise to the problem in the first place. It quite simply does not meet local needs beyond the very short term, in fact it may even contribute to them by depressing local prices and thus reducing incentives to increase local food production. There have been glaring examples of food aid being used as a political weapon, for example by the USA during the 1974 famine in Bangladesh in refusing to release food aid due to political disagreements with the recipient government.

Aid as an asymmetrical power relationship frequently reflects historical connections with donor nations rather than need on the part of recipients. This skewing of the aid process means that most aid does not go to the poorest countries where need is greatest. It may be given for strategic reasons or because the ex-colonial powers prefer to support their remaining colonies and to swing this support on to their aid budgets. Donors become trapped in the aid relationship too because they have so much invested in the recipients of their aid. The aid relationship is not a static one and recipients may well wish to enhance their power *vis-à-vis* the donor(s) of their aid by reducing their dependence, possibly by building up trade relationships with non-donor countries or by increasing self-sufficiency.

The most obvious failure of aid to address recipient country 'needs' in any real sense is military aid. It is possible to argue that all aid ultimately ends up as military expenditure because it frees up other funds for military purposes. But more directly there are notorious examples of tying of aid to military purchases, for example British support for the Pergau Dam in the late 1980s 'coincided' with Malaysia's proposed purchase of Tornado fighters.

Aid requiring structural adjustment has been charged with not only environmental degradation but also negative impact on human rights and especially on women. The adjustment may be a temporary process, as optimists suggest, but much of what would be termed 'development', that is the better quality of life for the majority of the population, is being lost. Aid is being used to reverse development in any meaningful sense of the word. The very existence of an external creditor/donor applying unpopular conditions may be destabilising, promoting a nationalist backlash/popular unrest as in Peru under Fujishock.

Perhaps the most devastating critique of aid is that in an increasingly globalised world economy aid is small beer and declining. US aid was 2 per cent of GNP during the years of the Marshall Plan but is now only one-eighth of that. Jan Hogendorn (1996) writes: 'total aid from all sources is equal to less than 18 days' worth of military expenditure or two months' worth of rich-country alcohol and tobacco consumption'. From the donor countries' points of view aid is usually fairly minimal but even that may be difficult to get past an increasingly unequal and hostile tax base at home. For the recipients, net inflows from aid do not compensate for net outflows as debt service charges. Wayne Ellwood argues that in 1998 developing countries received $30 billion of official aid but repaid $250 billion in debt. The anomaly is most striking where aid is most needed. In 1996 Africa SSA paid $2.5 billion more in debt service charges than it received as new loans and credits. The IMF alone has taken more than $3 billion out of Africa since the mid-1980s (Various 2000).

NGOs and aid

NGOs have been increasingly active as development agencies working in the distribution and administration of aid, both voluntary and official. The funds available to northern NGOs increased massively in the 1980s through media portrayal of their role in crises such as the 1984–85 famine in the Horn of Africa. This level of funding further ensured that such NGOs were taken seriously by intergovernmental organisations (IGOs) such as the World Bank and UN agencies (UNDP, UNHCR, WHO, UNICEF).

Official aid such as that of the EU is increasingly channelled through NGOs for practical reasons. Inappropriate aid-funded development projects have frequently failed completely or at least failed to serve the intended beneficiaries. The outcome for aid has been negative as such failures have sapped the goodwill of First World taxpayers who suffer from 'aid (or donor) fatigue'. Aid is seen as having failed especially in the case of Africa where crises are more frequent, but also in other places such as India where inequality is increasing.

The recognition that an aid establishment exists that talks to Third World elites and keeps them sweet has led to the development of a new anti-aid movement as well as a more pragmatic recognition of the need to use aid to bolster grassroots, local, municipal and provincial involvement in development projects. NGOs are seen as having the capacity to target the poor and use local expertise via fieldworkers in ways that official agencies cannot. Also they are seen as being less wasteful, having relatively lower administration costs. The costs related to aid greatly reduce its value. These include administration for all types of aid and transport costs for aid such as food that necessitates distribution.

But even if aid is administered and distributed through NGOs there are logistical problems. Large northern NGOs have been less successful than had been hoped. They tend to be bureaucratic and, in some cases, are indulging in their own millennial turf wars. They may even be seen as having been coopted into the aid establishment. Southern NGOs are burgeoning. They often have the real grassroots expertise, though their importance in international relief work is often overlooked by the media. They are often fragmentary and difficult to coordinate, with different interests and approaches to the northern groups that aim to harness their energies.

It is hard to discern how effective NGOs are in their role as disseminators of aid. Processes of accountability are missing from the activities of most NGOs and there is very little information available. Resources are not expended on evaluations and, where evaluations of projects have been done, the results are often not published except in an edited form designed to win further funding from the public. What little evidence there is suggests that they are not very cost effective and their services often miss the poorest and also fail to extend participation to women. Provision is reactive and therefore tends to be patchy.

The importance of aid

As Bob Hammond has pointed out, the problems of aid are not necessarily inherent in the process itself, but may be the results of the ways in which it has been operated (1994: 210–21). This does not just refer to the way it is perceived by donors, but also to the obstacles to success in the recipient countries. Cassen (1994: 7) writes that 'the relief of poverty depends both on aid and the policies of the recipient countries – a collaboration in which aid is definitely the junior partner'.

Perhaps this weakness reflects the fact that aid involves very small sums in comparison with direct investment and trade, but nevertheless these sums can be vital in moments of real crisis and are important to the very poorest states, which do not receive private investment anyway. For such countries aid is a major capital inflow. Aid can address problems that private investment cannot or will not address. It may provide the boost to infrastructural development that leads to a country being perceived as viable and thus to private foreign investment. In other words aid may be a sprat to catch a mackerel, it may be a catalyst for development by private enterprise. Further it may finance projects where the pay-off is not tangible, such as health and education schemes, or is too long term to interest private investors, such as agricultural research. Aid can be and has been a spur to growth in specific cases, Korea obviously, Brazil, Colombia and Thailand (Cassen 1994: 10). There have been real benefits as a result of official aid:

- an increase in Third World food production, without which the crisis of global hunger would be much more widespread;
- extension of primary health care and support for UN agency health programmes;
- scholarships for study in the First World and other educational programmes through institutions such as the British Council (Hammond 1994: 216–17).

Further there has been over the past 20 years a conscious effort on the part of aid givers to target the least developed countries, to give them aid as grants (grants now comprise two-thirds of all ODA) rather than loans and to write off their debts at intervals. Even where, as in the Sahel, there has been no obvious economic achievement, in that aid has failed to stimulate growth or reduce poverty, it has certainly contributed to tangible social improvements that have been achieved against a barrage of obstacles, not least the massive increase in population. Food security has increased, as has educational provision (Naudet and Pradelle 1997).

The future of aid

Many have questioned whether aid has a future given the power of the criticisms levelled against it. As Burnell (1997: 232) puts it, 'as people look increasingly to the next millennium, aid is being talked about more and more as a transitory phenomenon of the twentieth century'. However there is much evidence that the increasing role of the UN in the post-cold war world will more and more involve the administration of aid. This role is increasingly to address complex emergencies involving humanitarian issues, such as peacekeeping, the protection and resettlement of refugees through the UNHCR, and the distribution of food aid, the majority of which is now a UN responsibility. In fact, much ODA is now channelled through the UN and 45 per cent of it is spent on emergencies.

It is uncertain whether aid donors can expect any clear leadership from anywhere other than the UN as the USA as an aid giver is in decline, Japan is just recovering from a severe economic crisis and the EU is more concerned with the the problems of the euro and its territorial expansion. But the UN is not perceived as a total success in its international role (see the role of the UN in Rwanda, Chapter 2). The World Bank might have wished to provide leadership in the sphere of aid, but its role is increasingly being questioned from within and without and it lacks the political leadership to coordinate the diverse agencies involved. The emergence of regional banks and the growing importance of private capital flows, which sit more comfortably with the dominant neo-liberal discourse, have reduced its role.

South–South trade

South–South cooperation can provide important new opportunities for development based on geographical proximity, on similarities in demand and tastes, on relevance of respective development experience, know-how, and skills, and on availability of complementary natural and financial skills. . . . South–South cooperation offers developing countries a strategic means for pursuing relatively autonomous paths to development suited to the needs and aspirations of their people. (South Commission 1990: 16)

The assumption behind the stress on South–South trade is that, if widespread, South–South trade relations would break the stranglehold of dependency. Dependency on the North would be ended if the North could no longer control the terms of trade. However some would argue that there is an infrastructure of northern domination, that the global institutions, the monetary system and the transport system are dominated by the North, and that in consequence dependency would not come to an end with the ending of the conditions that gave rise to it in the first place.

As well as enhancing the South's bargaining power against that of the North, South–South cooperation would possibly enable the South to benefit from economies of scale. Complementary and supportive neighbours would enhance the possibilities of development. However, working against the development of South–South linkages is the existing preoccupation of the LDCs with North–South negotiations. The greater the concern with relations with the North the greater the tendency to place South–South cooperation on the back-burner. A second cluster of causes is to be found in the disagreements, hostilities and sometimes even wars that reduce cooperation between Third World states. These become much more likely where very similar economies see themselves as being in competition; single or very limited product economies force their members to be constantly aware of their dependency on the goodwill of their northern customers.

The diversity of the South at once militates against South–South cooperation and makes for economic complementarity with the North. Some LDCs have capital (Brunei, Saudi Arabia, the United Arab Emirates) and/or energy surpluses. Indeed these and other OPEC members such as Kuwait have made development loans available at preferential rates to less fortunate Third World states. Others, such as Mexico and Brazil, are technologically advanced relative to their neighbours and their technology may be more accessible and more appropriate to other LDCs than that of the North.

Some countries rich in capital but lacking technical skills have made good this deficit by importing LDC nationals. Examples are Iraq and Kuwait. China has numerous technical and scientific exchange programmes with a variety of countries all over the world and has undertaken thousands of development projects in LDCs. Some countries, for example India, have enormous manufacturing capability; others, such as Congo or Namibia, are rich in various natural resources. Collectively they have the components for a bright future if only the many political difficulties that stand in the way of cooperation can be overcome.

In the 20 years between 1955 and 1975 trade amongst developed countries grew faster than either trade amongst LDCs or between developed countries and LDCs. But LDC exports to developed countries increased much faster than developed countries' exports to LDCs, suggesting that interdependence has been enhanced. Yet it remains true that the main developed country market is other developed countries and that they also provide the main market for LDC products. The character of developed country imports from less developed countries is more vital than in the reverse case. They are either mainly non-renewable or developed countries cannot produce them due to their properties of climate, etc. This gives less developed countries strength in the long term through import-substitution-industrialisation. Japan and the EU are more dependent on LDC imports than the United States of America, which is the most self-sufficient of all developed countries, but projections suggest US import dependence will increase with time.

Another possibility, already tried in some cases, is cartelisation. To create a producer cartel in some products is possible, but the very poverty of Third World nations and their need for funds to tide them over in the short term works against success. Oil is the best-known case. But oil was an exception in that it is the essence of modern production, it would cost a great deal to substitute and a high proportion of supplies were held by OPEC members who had surplus resources that strengthened their position. There are few if any other products that would qualify under all these headings. And indeed since the beginning of the 1980s many of the best-known producer cartels have collapsed, not least the International Tin Agreement (ITA) (Crabtree 1987). OPEC itself no longer controls the greatest share of traded oil and is nothing like as powerful as it was in the 1970s, though as it showed at the end of 1999 it still had the capacity to raise oil prices if its members were prepared to act in concert.

Conclusion

No one in their senses would want to stop the development of the Third World, nor could anyone make a moral case for people elsewhere in the world being denied the material things First World people take for granted. But the pattern of development that has been established over the years is not sustainable and has certain very obvious disadvantages. The problem of rapidly expanding populations has been met by encouraging uncontrolled and unplanned development. Those countries that have been successful in making the breakthrough into long-term growth have made industrialisation a prime target and invested heavily in education to provide a skilled workforce. Unfortunately at the same time they have degraded the environment and made their societies overreliant on the continued expansion of production. Where plantation agriculture exists, and it is widespread, it has had serious effects on the capacity of a country to feed its own people. This mode of development, therefore, is not sustainable in its present form (Jackson 1990).

Foreign investment and the growth of transnational corporations are features of development in the Third World about which there is considerable controversy. To the proponents of the free market, they have been largely beneficial. To their critics, they have at the least produced significant negative effects, and there is reason to suspect that both act to widen the gap between rich and poor countries, and between rich and poor in any one country.

CHAPTER 12

Women

Good Stuff !

Women and development

To understand our unequal world we have to give special consideration to women. Women comprise half of the world's adult population, constitute one-third of the world's official labour force, perform two-thirds of all working hours, get one-third of world income and own 1 per cent of the world's property. Between 60 and 100 million women are missing altogether from the world's population as a result of son-preference. Development is about social change and women are disproportionately subject to the effects of social change. In the distorted way development has largely been perceived, modernisation has emphasised capital accumulation. However the move away from artisan production tends to disadvantage women, since as employees they are not in a position to accumulate meaningful amounts of capital, and industrialising makes them part of the labour force in a way not previously the case. If they are married women their earnings essentially become the property of their husbands and contribute to his standing rather than their own. Such inequitable distributions of work and benefits are obviously topics that social scientists would wish to probe. Essentially over the years approaches to the understanding of the situation of Third World women have reflected the changing perception of the development agenda.

The 'modernisation' approach quite simply ignored women. It was assumed that what benefited men also benefited 'their' women. Women were not recognised as constituting a distinct – and particularly disadvantaged – group.

The 'basic needs' or anti-poverty approach to development in the early 1970s, expressed, for example, through UN Conferences on Food and Population held in 1974, for the first time drew attention to the fact that social policies, developmental or otherwise, have not been gender neutral. It was recognised that a disproportionate number of the world's poor are women and that, if considered with the dependent children for whom these poor women carry responsibility, they constitute the vast majority of the poorest people on earth. Hence their well-being is a primary ethical question for developmental schemes.

The effects of development on women and its corollary, the role of women in the development process, were therefore opened up to research and the UN declared 1975 International Women's Year, with a major conference held in Mexico City. However in Mexico the majority of women are still poor and still work extremely hard. They may do so out of economic necessity or because of social expectation. They do not do so because of legal bonds, since though the population are nominally Catholic the majority of poor people are not formally married (Lewis 1962).

The period 1976–85 was decreed the UN Decade for the Advancement of Women. The position of women, together with that of indigenous peoples, was established as a key human rights issue for the World Conference on Human Rights (June 1993), and at the UN's Fourth World Conference on Women, in Beijing, China, in 1995 governments made solemn undertakings to protect and promote the human rights of women and girl-children; promises that in many cases have yet to be fulfilled.

Apart from moral and ethical questions concerning their rights as human beings, women form a vital part of the development process and their contributions to a sustainable form of development are integral. Environmental degradation is increased by inappropriate development that is a consequence of poverty and it then in turn increases the poverty from which it arises. It is most painfully experienced by the poorest elements of society. These usually include women and children. More radical approaches also stress that women are a separate issue on the development agenda, but they do so for functional as well as moral reasons. They argue either:

a)   that the involvement of women is vital for the efficiency of any developmental scheme; or
b)   that the empowerment of women is *the* motor force for development of any meaningful kind.

Empowerment, a concept deriving from the work of Brazilian educationalist Paulo Freire, means acquiring the awareness and the skills to take charge of one's own environment. This perspective, combining as it does elements from radical and Marxist feminist thought, often also takes on board other poor sections who suffered under colonialism and now continue to do so under a form of development perceived as distorted and exploitative of both people and of nature (Shiva 1988: 2).

Gender and society

Women constitute a majority in most societies. Yet stratification by gender is to be found in most Third World societies and separate organisations for men and women exist in most, if not all, societies. There are two main reasons for this. First, stratification by gender occurs in the first instance within the family and involves personal relationships between individuals and groups; it is therefore resistant not only to change but even to study and research. Second, because of the central importance of personal relationships, women are the only major group that actively collaborate in their own exploitation.

Though in some societies these are tighter and more formal groupings, in Africa secret societies play a major role in gender differentiation. In Sierra Leone, where male secret societies were the dominant organisations before colonisation, the Poro still operates and retains considerable power today, especially among the Mende tribe, where it originated, and the Sherbro Bullom and the Temne, to which it later spread. Significantly, female secret societies also exist, and are known to be central to training girls in the social roles they are to assume as women.

Many religious traditions, too, separate men and women from one another. This is frequently defended as being both divinely ordained and socially necessary if public morality is to be maintained. Where women have been admitted, either in the past or as a result of recent changes, to the priesthood, men continue to hold the key posts and interpret religious teaching in a fashion that both requires women to accept male dominance in their daily lives and encourages them to believe that it is right that they should do so. In Saudi Arabia, in the name of Islam, women are required to veil themselves in public, their freedom of movement is severely restricted, they are not allowed to be educated with or work alongside men, and they may be subject to violence and even sexual abuse by police without any hope of redress.

In Papua New Guinea women are subordinated in public affairs through the clan system and may be excluded from public discussion entirely. Clans are male dominant; their leadership is exercised by a chief (*bigman*), who presides over village meetings and as such has the power to interpret the law. Among the rights commonly assumed by men is that of wife beating. Ironically, before colonisation, women did have control over their own earnings and autonomy in economic affairs, but this has been lost as European influence reinforced male dominance (Black 1999: 232).

In modern societies, however, the most common factor placing women at a disadvantage to men in making their views felt and sharing their skills is lack of formal education. There are estimated to be a billion adult illiterates in the world, of which 60 per cent are women. The education of women, their capacity to control their fertility and their economic independence are not just concessions to a disadvantaged group – the Third World cannot afford sops. Women are functional parts of the process of development that the Third World cannot afford not to encourage. Women must play a fuller part in development in this generation and in future through their care and education of their children. Their lack of education damages their capacities as primary health carers and educators. Education for women has repeatedly been shown, moreover, to be the single major factor leading to limitation on family size and a fall in the otherwise inexorable rate of population growth.

Economic

Women and work

The tradition of 'bride price' in Africa reflects the traditional attitude of male society to women as a commodity – though a commodity that does retain some rights and in some tribes can attain positions of considerable power. It is part of the role of women in rural society to cultivate land to provide food, and this tradition survives, modified, in the urban context. Andreski notes that in urban Ghana an artisan will typically provide his wife with capital to trade on her own account, and, while not expecting her to feed him, does expect her to feed herself and her children (1968: 50–1). Two traditional occupations for urban women are market trading and prostitution, though the latter did not originally carry the social stigma it does in Europe and often does not do so today, despite the efforts of both Christian and Muslim missionaries to change this perception.

Colonisation in West Africa as in other places distorted the traditional role of women. Colonialism brought foreign-owned large estates growing cash crops for an external market. Women's labour remained important, indeed essential to the large-scale production of cotton and tea, but the land was owned by men who received the profits from it and imports hit craft production. Hence development brought new forms of exploitation. There were benefits, for example education, but in Muslim areas women were often excluded from the benefits colonialism brought and cultural norms have been powerful enough to resist legal changes for the benefit of women. This was the case, for example, when after the end of the colonial period female circumcision was officially banned in Sierra Leone by the government of Milton Margai.

The post-colonial era has brought jobs in electronics and other skilled assembly work, where some 80–90 per cent of workers are women. Women form the bulk of the labour force in the *maquiladoras* (mills of gold) of Mexico and Central America (see e.g. Petersen 1992). They work long hours for very low wages and return to families where they are still expected to do all the housework. In China male dominance continues in some key urban aspects, especially in heavy industry, skilled trades, management and secondary education. It is largely unquestioned in traditional rural areas where women's activities are generally restricted to the household, which is that of the husband's family anyway. Despite legal rights the real situation is that Chinese women do not have property, and lack the resources for independence. The 1982 census showed that 70 per cent of China's 200 million illiterates were female. During the 1980s high unemployment rates gave employers more choice in selecting workers, and women were perceived as more expensive owing to the requirement to provide for childcare, maternity leave and earlier retirement. Employers were only required to make the rather cheaper provision of accommodation to male employees.

In the 'Asian Tigers' women make up the bulk of the workforce in the so-called Economic Processing Zones (EPZs):

The EPZ economy is based on employing cheap labour for the assembly of high-volume standardised components. Such work is seen as particularly suited to women. Since the 1960s young women have been employed in EPZ factories on a large scale. They comprise the majority of child labour, often spending most of their teenage years in sweatshops making plastic toys or garments. By the 1970s they had moved on to the more sophisticated assembly lines – particularly electronics and pharmaceuticals. By 1982, of the 62,617 workers employed in EPZs in Taiwan 85 per cent were women. (*New Internationalist*, 263, January 1995)

Such workers are recruited in the countryside under false promises, often that they will gain valuable education as well as make a useful contribution to the marginal existence of the family group. While in work they live in dormitories under strict control and supervision. However safety at work is not much of a consideration – in South Korea, for example, 10 or 12 hours' work a day is still normal and the country has one of the highest rates of industrial accidents in the world. If recession comes the women workers are often unaware of any rights they may possess under employment legislation and can be speedily laid off.

Such occupations, even at the beginning of the twenty-first century, are not however typical. Some 90 per cent of the world's women still depend directly on the land for survival. In fact women produce most of the food in developing countries, and between 60–80 per cent in Africa South of the Sahara. They work longer hours and do heavier work than men. Ester Boserup (1981) popularised the view 'that African agriculture exhibited a dualism based on gender: a cash crops sector in which *men* grow highly productive income-earning export crops, and a food crop sector in which *women* use traditional methods to produce food for their families to consume' (Boserup 1989). This view has now been shown to be wrong, as it understates the involvement of women in the modern sector of the economy and ignores the fact that food crops are also grown as cash crops (Whitehead in Bernstein et al. 1990: 55). But it still leaves women responsible for the bulk of food production.

The reasons women's productivity is so often underestimated are:

- The assumption that they are less strong and their work is therefore in some sense 'light'. This clearly is not the case and anyway women usually work far longer hours than men.

- The fact that domestic labour is not accorded its proper value. Domestic labour is still not counted in the calculation of GNP, although common sense suggests that it must account for a very high proportion of it in less developed countries.

- The fact that local economies are largely ignored in favour of urban and export markets and it is men who own the land on which cash crops are grown or who manage the factories in which women work.

Though women's roles are often marginal, not to say invisible, women, like men, are basic economic units. They are often wrongly perceived as dependents when in reality they are producers. Much of their time and energies have been squandered on the least productive domestic concerns from which it should have been possible to begin liberating them. In China on marriage a woman ceases to be part of her birth family, symbolised by the physical removal of herself and her possessions to her husband's home, but she does not cease to work. In rural areas the planting and cultivation of wet rice is regarded as women's work and on any building site in China and Vietnam the bulk of the unskilled labour is provided by women.

It is also assumed that work done in or about the home and not for pay can be disregarded. Domestic labour, even if on the farm, is not accorded its proper value; production for subsistence or of chickens, ducks and vegetables for the local market does not have the same status as the production of cash crops. Further, women have not received support for their agricultural production in the form of loans, technology or training. They have not had a say in the decision making that affects them, so irrigation is not available for subsistence farming, only for cash crops. This is a major contributory factor to the decline of food production for local consumption in most Third World countries. In the Amazon basin women who for whatever reason find themselves without male partners or mature sons cannot, according to colonisation agencies, constitute 'families', so they lose their right to land. The widespread rural poverty of women has led to their out-migration as agricultural labourers in plantations, as export workers in entrepôt enclaves or as domestic help at home or abroad. Women are also responsible for overseeing the considerable additional contribution that children make to the domestic economy. Women and the children under their direction are usually exclusively responsible for domestic access to water. Policy makers (who are usually male) often perceive women as burdens and do not take their needs on board. See Plate 12.

Energy in the rural Third World is mainly biomass (fuelwood, crop residues and manure), which is collected by women and children. Biomass accounts for 75 per cent of fuel used in the Third World generally and 90 per cent of fuel consumed in Africa SSA. Fuelwood collection is often blamed for deforestation. However rural women traditionally use fallen dead wood. Fuelwood from cut trees is usually for commercial sale to urban areas. Burning dung is of course a contribution to agricultural underproduction, but not a very great one. Women have well-developed skills in managing resources and, as Agenda 21 specifically recognised, probably know more about sustainable development than men as they live it more directly. But while women look after their men and the environment, they pay a price. The burning of biomass in the cooking process in rural dwellings, for example, has now been recognised as having devastating effects on female and child health. It is the major, but most forgotten form of air pollution, because it occurs out of sight in the home, where it causes all manner of respiratory ailments. It is hard not to conclude that it is a problem overlooked because it almost invariably affects only Third World women.

Women's participation in development requires that they receive increased access to land, credit, skills, primary health care, water, sanitation and education. There is of course also an ethical question as well as practical ones. It must be clear that, if development is a right, equal opportunities to achieve development should be available to all nations and also to all individuals (cf. Chapter 11). Without full participation in the development process, as recommended by *The Brundtland Report* (WCED 1987), there cannot be the peace and stability in which development can occur.

Women and children

Half a million women still die in childbirth each year, but African women are 200 times as likely to die from pregnancy-related causes as women in industrialised countries, where perinatal mortality is now very low owing to professional attendants, good hospital resources and advanced medical techniques. Even within the Third World there are very considerable differences in the standard causes of death. The main avoidable risk is specific to women and is pregnancy. In the Third World pregnancy still carries a significant hazard of potentially fatal infection for the mother. WHO figures show that of 500,000 maternal deaths each year (deaths during or within 42 days of pregnancy from causes specific to the pregnancy), only 3000 now occur in the industrialised countries. As with other diseases, the prevalence of neonatal diseases is now greater in the Third World than it was a century ago. The avoidance of pregnancy through birth control is therefore an important factor in enabling women to live longer, while by reducing the burdens of looking after large families it has important additional social benefit, especially for the children of the smaller families.

In China the establishment of the Republic in 1911 meant the end of the appalling abuse of foot binding, which was, in any case, a Manchurian custom introduced by the Ching Dynasty. After 1949 equality was a prime goal of the new communist regime and many improvements were made in the position of women, such as the introduction of a 48-hour week, maternity leave and childcare. However, after Mao Zedong's death in 1976 there was a tendency for pragmatic economic goals to push out ideological political goals. Officially the one-child policy stresses child health, good parenting and care for the elderly. The policy has been very successful in urban areas where the vast majority of children under 12 are the only children of their families. However in rural areas where the first child is female there are fears of high levels of female infanticide, and a second or even third child may be permitted ostensibly to help provide labour on the homestead. This may be seen as official government endorsement of traditional assumptions of male superiority. In urban areas a second child may lead to loss of benefits including the advantage of nursery care for the first child. A subsequent illegal child may mean compulsory sterilisation for the woman, not for the man.

Mahatma Gandhi said that to understand India one should study its villages and its women. The respect Gandhi accorded Indian women is not necessarily echoed in Indian society as a whole. Since 1911 there has been a steady decline in the ratio of women to men with the steepest fall in the decade 1961–71. There are now 929 women to every 1000 men (in the UK, by comparison, the ratio is 1060 : 1000).

In India the killing of baby girls was once associated mainly with isolated rural communities. In Rajasthan female infanticide was a military custom. Only boys could become warriors so girls were often killed. 'Devdasis' was the offering to God of female children as a ritual sacrifice, usually to get a son. Now that India is at peace the practice should be dying out, but it is actually spreading. Female infanticide was outlawed in India more than a century ago by the British Raj, but in India, as elsewhere, laws do not necessarily change social customs and in recent years there have been reports of the continuance of the practice in South India, where it is usually carried out by the grandmother. The local authorities often collude in the slaughter of baby girls. It is just not possible not to notice that perhaps up to four out of ten baby girls are being killed soon after birth; it shows in the sex ratio of the children in the villages.

Women go on childbearing in the hope of having a son who will bring a dowry to the family, look after his parents in their old age, preserve the family name, keep the family property intact, attend to his parents' funeral rites and light their funeral pyre. Cradle schemes now exist so that 'unwanted' girl babies may be deposited and cared for, but they are not really unwanted in this sense and fatalism about death means that many mothers prefer to kill their girl babies, and such schemes have few takers. Girls who are not killed at birth sometimes die of neglect while their brothers thrive – it is often boys who are taken to hospital when ill, girls are in some areas considered to be very lucky if they receive any medical treatment at all. Girls suffer a 30–60 per cent higher rate of mortality simply because they less often receive medical treatment when sick.

Meanwhile modern technology has offered an alternative. Millions of women in India are now using ultrasonic scans to decide on terminations. The Indian government has recently prohibited the selective use of scans to determine the sex of babies, but in the nature of things it may be difficult to prove. There is no shortage of ultra-sound equipment even though India suffers a huge deficit in medical technology. More than 1 million female foetuses are destroyed after scans in India each year. Sex determination has become big business and science has become a tool of a traditional prejudice. Scientists have made it easier not to give birth to girls and it has therefore also become less acceptable to do so. There is a shortage of some 25 million women in India already and the use of selective abortion will increase this imbalance – the sex ratio of newborn children is now 100 girls : 116 boys. Sex determination tests have been banned in one state but to little effect; there are proposals to extend this ban, but it will not work without a change in attitudes.

The main problem is the rising cost of dowries, or rather the high costs of 'gifts' on marriage now that dowries are no longer legal, since there is now much less restraint on the parties involved. Girls are a very expensive liability for their parents and to have even one in a family can mean financial ruin in the future. In Tamil Nadu, where expensive rituals accompany the growing-up of girls, a 'dowry' can cost as much as 15 years' income and the daughter of parents who cannot pay may be outcast. Dowries were made illegal 30 years ago and were in any case largely confined to the upper castes, but the institution has now spread to the poorest villages. With the demonstration effect of western television programmes, families are making demands for still bigger dowries to meet their aspirations to western luxuries. Where marriages are arranged dowries often represent a simple transfer of capital from one family to another. The dowry may be used as an ongoing form of blackmail and daughters may be returned unwanted to their parents when their husbands' further financial demands are not met. Worst of all, some women are extremely cruelly treated for not bringing larger dowries, or to extort more money from their families. The extreme case is bride-burning, where the bride is set on fire with paraffin, to simulate an accidental fire in the cooking area. Officially bride-burning claimed 2449 women's lives in 1991, but the real figures are undoubtedly much higher (*Assignment*, 'Let Her Die', BBC Television 1993). The custom of paying dowry has even spread to non-Hindu communities. In parts of Muslim Bangladesh young women have been disfigured and even blinded in acid attacks after they had rejected suitors or were the innocent victims of dowry disputes with their former families (McKean 2000).

Deliberate cruelty of this kind is of course relatively rare. Much more common is the impact of cultural norms promoting inequality. These norms are sustained as much by the women who are disadvantaged by them as by the men who might be perceived as benefiting. It is women who struggle to feed their families, even actually eating afterwards in many cultures. As it is women who generally organise food in any household it seems natural to them to feed their families first and more adequately than they do themselves. Seventy per cent of pregnant women suffer anaemia caused by malnutrition. This is not really surprising as even early studies (e.g. Sinha 1976: 13) show the extent of inequality – in Hyderabad the calorie intake for pregnant and lactating women was only 1400 per day against the average Indian requirement of 2200 calories per day.

Women and political power

It was through her membership of the Sande (*bundu*) society that Madam Yoko (*c.*1850–1906), later to be chief of Moyamba and ally of the British in the Hut Tax War, acquired her initial fame which led to an influential marriage (Foray 1977). As this example shows, in pre-colonial times women could and did hold political power in West Africa, and indeed were to take an important role in asserting the right to retain African dress and their African identity, but marriage formed an important key to their possibility of social advancement. In post-independence Africa, however, women have yet to reach the highest political positions, and this ironically despite the survival of traditional matriarchal features in some societies. The best-known example is Swaziland, where on the death of the King, the Queen Mother acts as Regent (with the title of 'Great She-Elephant') until a new King is formally selected.

In Asia the political position of women varies greatly. In China women notionally have complete equality, but in practice the ageing government of the People's Republic is unusual today for the almost total absence of women in high office. In Thailand and the Philippines, on the other hand, women retain their identity and in recent decades have emerged into important managerial and political positions. In Burma (Myanmar), Aung San Suu Kyi has been denied by the armed forces the position of leadership to which she had been elected. However in South Asia, where Mrs Bandaranaike became the world's first woman prime minister in Sri Lanka in 1960, she again held that office under her daughter, now president. Meanwhile India, Pakistan and Bangladesh have all had women leaders.

In other parts of the Third World the situation is very different. In Latin America only one woman held political office in some 300 years of colonial rule and that for only three days. Nevertheless since women obtained the franchise, beginning in Ecuador in 1929, the situation in the region has steadily improved. In Mexico and Chile today the status of middle-class women can be very high. In Argentina María Estela (Isabel) Martínez de Perón became the world's first woman executive president in succession to her husband in 1974. Since then Lidia Gueiler Tejada has served as interim president of Bolivia (1979–80), and Violeta Barrios de Chamorro, Janet Jagan and Mireya Elisa Moscoso de Gruber have been elected president of Nicaragua (1990), Guyana (1998–99) and Panama (1999) respectively. In the Caribbean Eugenia Charles, Jennifer Smith and Suzy Camelia Römer have been prime ministers of Dominica (1980), the Bahamas (1998) and Curaçao. In 1999, it was Panama's first woman president, Mireya Elisa Moscoso de Gruber, who received the Panama Canal from former US President Jimmy Carter, representing the United States of America (which has yet to have a woman as president).

Research by UNICEF, however, shows that women's representation in national assemblies is still dismayingly small. Only in a few advanced industrialised countries does it exceed 25 per cent, and the world average actually *fell* from 15 per cent to 9 per cent in the ten years from 1985 to 1995 (*The Guardian*, 9 June 1995). According to the UNDP *Human Development Report 1995* only 10 per cent of seats in the world's legislatures were held by women and only 6 per cent of the posts in national executives. Women are much more effective in local and grassroots organisations, but in a still state-centric world women are missing out at the levels that count. Policy makers often perceive women as burdens and do not take their needs on board even when asked to do so.

An exception is where women band together in organisations to run base communities. For example, in Brazil they have been able to overcome some of the misconceptions that govern official dealings with them, because their contribution as an organised group requires a political response from elected officials and civil servants. Tamil Nadu in India had 25,000 registered grass-roots organisations in 1993 and women play a major role in the setting up and running of such groups.

Women and the neo-liberal ideology

International relations has until recently not paid any special attention to the position of women. There are three reasons for this. Relations between states have traditionally been seen as primarily concerned with military security, a reserve area for men. The clannish nature of foreign services has ensured that senior diplomats and policy makers have also been mostly male. The language of international relations itself is gendered, with Darwinian overtones of the survival of the fittest.

However 'international policies and processes, far from being gender-neutral, in practice play an important role in determining women's place in society and in structuring economic, political and social relations between the sexes' (Halliday 1994: 153). In the event of war women may be and frequently are called on to do 'men's' jobs, but when peace comes they are again excluded. While the war lasts they are its prime victims, not just as civilians but as objects of rape, which in ethnic wars in the 1990s was repeatedly employed to enforce in the most brutal fashion imaginable the dominance of one ethnic group over another.

In peacetime it is the economic consequences of international decisions that bear most heavily on women. As the IMF sought to maintain stable exchange rates in the 1980s, in a world afflicted by rising oil prices and accelerating inflation, structural adjustment packages were oriented to markets and in particular to the removal of what were considered to be distortions in them. This had a detrimental effect on the standing of women. Women were largely excluded from national markets and the food subsidies, and other support for the poorest sectors from which they might hope to benefit were precisely the 'distortions' to development identified by the market liberal approach, and their removal the main target of such adjustments. In addition, when SAPs require cuts in Third World expenditure (male) vested interests and (male) national pride ensure that disproportionately large military budgets are protected. In turn, since protection for military personnel is built into those budgets, social services are hit hardest. There are a few exceptions, e.g. Uruguay, but in general a reluctance to cut social services is seen by international lending agencies as unwillingness to comply with the terms of loans and can lead to serious consequences for the credit rating of the governments that try to evade these requirements.

Women are an 'adjustment variable' on whom SAPs impact particularly hard. The problem is that austerity measures intensify as they pass down social structures. The semi-autonomous and wholly privately funded UN agency with responsibility for the children of the world, UNICEF, estimates that a 2–3 per cent decline in national income in developing countries hits the poorest sections to the tune of 10–15 per cent (UNICEF 1990). At the same time SAPs hit the public sector and women are disproportionately likely to be employed as teachers, nurses, etc. This was especially true of Nigeria in the 1980s. There women had moved into a rapidly expanding public sector during the petroleum bonanza of the late 1960s and the early 1970s. When negotiations with the IMF broke down a World Bank-backed indigenous SAP was devised. This aimed, amongst other things, to reduce the public sector, and the immediate result was the loss of many of these new public sector jobs.

SAPs also raise food costs. Between 1980 and 1983, 76 per cent of IMF-supported programmes included increased indirect taxation, 46 per cent increased tariffs and only 13 per cent involved increases in direct personal or corporation taxes, the least regressive of the alternatives available.

SAPs have diverted women from their families to marginal economic activities and thus have contributed to social problems such as child abandonment and delinquency, as in Brazil. Both directly and indirectly, therefore, they have lowered standards of health care and nutrition for mothers and children causing lower birthweights, poor child health and lower intelligence, building up problems for the future. In Chile child mortality was increased by cutbacks in the child-feeding programme in 1983, though these have since been reversed. And the long-term effects are also significant: SAPs hit education budgets and girls' secondary education is generally seen as the area most easily sacrificed.

The sad thing is that it would not cost much to protect the living standards of the poorest sectors from the impact of economic fashions. They have so little to protect. But they do not make the decisions. Because of the impact of SAPs on most disadvantaged groups UNICEF has recommended changes: more medium-term financial support and less shock, the encouragement of policies that do not hit vulnerable groups, sectoral policies confining adjustment to the productive sectors, policies to enhance efficiency and equity of the social sector, compensatory programmes and the monitoring of living standards. The World Bank is now well aware of the impact of SAPs on women and other vulnerable groups. In April 1987 it issued *Protecting the Poor during Periods of Adjustment*, but argued for compensatory measures to be added on rather than changing the basic nature of SAPs.

Environmental issues

Environmental politics

All our basic needs have sources in the natural world. The natural world, however, is finite. Human beings are, therefore, now faced with a two-pronged crisis. On the one hand in the near future more and more resources that we now take for granted are going to start to run out. On the other our environment is becoming increasingly contaminated by the waste we produce (Thomas 1992).

The combined pressures of the increasing awareness of coming scarcity and the build up of toxicity has increased the salience of the environment as an issue. Even more, it has given rise to ecopolitics, defined by Guimaraes (1991) as 'the study of political systems from an ecological perspective'. Social, cultural and political understanding is as important as natural science when considering ecosystems and their capacities.

Environmental degradation

The late 1980s saw the change from the environment as a local and regional issue to a global one (Tolba 1988, Hurrell and Kingsbury 1992). Initially this formed part of the globalisation of security concerns. Security had historically always been defined primarily in military terms.

Jessica Tuchman Matthews (in Prins 1993) says: 'Global environmental trends shift the balance [of power]. . . . No more basic threat to national security exists.' However though interest coalitions straddle the North–South divide on some environmental issues the politics of the environment still mainly reflects a North versus South division. It is, sadly, not the spectacle of human misery as much as potential threats to global stability consequent on resource scarcity that invoke the concern of the First World. At the same time national economic advantage gets in the way of a coherent world policy. Agreements tend to be compromises between vested interests. They are not intended to save the world and they will not do so.

The 1972 Stockholm Intergovernmental Conference on the Human Environment established that the problems of the environment were urgent and sought to identify those that were global. The work of the conference resulted in two documents: the Stockholm Declaration of basic environmental principles that should govern policy and a detailed Action Plan. This in turn led to the creation of the United Nations Environment Programme (UNEP), whose director, Maurice F. Strong of Canada, who had been secretary-general of the Stockholm Conference, was in due course to become secretary-general of the United Nations Conference on Environment and Development (UNCED), which met at Rio de Janeiro in 1992.

The message that the environment was too big and too important to be dealt with by national governments was unwelcome to many of those governments, and in the ten years that followed the majority were very slow to accept that it had any relevance. However some progress was made. In 1972 the Convention on International Trade in Endangered Species of Wild Fauna and Flora (CITES) was concluded and a World Heritage Convention was held. But a potential setback to the cause of the environment came in 1974 with the adoption by the General Assembly of the otherwise welcome Charter of Economic Rights and Duties of States. It laid heavy emphasis on the 'rights' of states to development but lacked any reference to environmental criteria. This was paralleled in the late 1970s and early 1980s by increased emphasis on free market 'solutions' in the advanced industrialised countries, accompanied by their abdication of responsibility for the outcomes of economic processes. At this stage the trend was away from international consensus.

The crucial turning point came in 1983 when the secretary-general of the UN asked the prime minister of Norway, Gro Harlem Brundtland, to form a commission to investigate how a planet with a rapidly accelerating population growth could continue to meet basic needs. The Brundtland Commission (properly the World Commission on Environment and Development) was charged with formulating realistic proposals linking development issues to the care and conservation of the environment and raising the level of public awareness of the issues involved. With the publication in 1987 of its report, *Our Common Future*, the concept of 'sustainable development' became central to future thinking. It was the realisation of the extent to which matters had worsened since 1973 that was to lead directly to the Earth Summit.

The biggest shock to world public opinion had come from the discovery of the 'ozone hole' over Antarctica, which led in 1987 to the conclusion of the Montreal Protocol to the Vienna Convention on the Protection of the Ozone Layer, with the aim of regulating the use and release of ozone-depleting substances such as chlorofluorocarbons (CFCs) and halons. The belated realisation both that ozone depletion was accelerating and that it was also taking place, though at a slower rate, in the Arctic, where it posed a much greater threat to major concentrations of the world's population, led to urgent measures to extend the Montreal Protocol. As a result the problem of the ozone layer was not directly addressed at Rio, though it was very much a matter of concern to delegates from the southern hemisphere.

Many other developments, however, did contribute to the agenda for the Earth Summit. In 1987 UNEP called attention to the alarming rate of extinction of species. It was estimated that if the current rate of extinction continued up to one-third of all species could be lost for good within 40 years. The international nature of the trade that was leading to extinction called for an international convention on biological diversity (biodiversity), and in 1988 the General Assembly established an ad hoc working group on biodiversity. In 1990 the Committee of Experts became the Intergovernmental Negotiating Committee (INC) on Biological Diversity.

In 1988 the Intergovernmental Panel on Climate Change (IPCC), which had been set up by the World Meteorological Association and UNEP, reported that if nothing was done to arrest the rising level of 'greenhouse gases' in the atmosphere the global mean temperature would continue to rise by about 0.3°C per decade. A global temperature rise of 1°C by 2025 would place serious strains on the capacity of agriculture to modify its procedures and risk flooding by the melting of the polar ice caps of lowlying areas and small islands. At the Second World Climate Conference in 1990, 137 countries called for negotiations for a framework convention on climate change and by Resolution 43/53 the United Nations General Assembly established an INC on Climate Change to prepare a draft.

Both climate change and biodiversity were linked to a third major area of concern, the accelerating rate of destruction of forests. Forests act both as 'carbon sinks', returning to the earth the carbon dioxide liberated by the burning of fossil fuels (Leggett 1990) and so acting naturally to arrest global warming, and as a rich habitat for a diversity of species. Their destruction, on the other hand, releases significant additional volumes of carbon dioxide. In addition their sustainable management could in time prove to be of immense and increasing value to the rising populations of the developing states. Sadly, their governments have been unable or unwilling to act to prevent their hasty destruction for short-term gain or ground clearance. In the early 1980s it was estimated that some 27–40 million hectares were being lost annually; by the late 1980s this figure had doubled.

Several other areas of concern were sidetracked along the way. Notably, the poorer African states of the Sahel had been calling for global action on desertification. There was no doubt about its importance to Africa: television had beamed pictures of starving children in Ethiopia, Sudan and Somalia on to TV screens throughout the developed world. What was at issue was its urgency as a global question. The UN Plan of Action to Combat Desertification (PACD) instituted by UNEP and approved by the General Assembly in 1977 had never been effectively implemented, largely because of the lack of effective resources. However reluctance to support it had recently been reinforced by new satellite pictures that proved conclusively that the general advance of deserts, though widely accepted, was a myth (Pearce 1992).

Sustainable development

The suggestion that there is a choice between environment or development is, like many political arguments, a false alternative. It is no longer possible (if it ever was) to have one without the other. The world is a closed system and everything affects everything else. In short, what is needed is sustainable development.

The Brundtland Report defined sustainable development as: 'development that meets the needs of the present without compromising the ability of future generations to meet their own needs' (WCED 1987: 43). Sustainable development does not use non-renewable resources faster than substitutes can be found, nor renewable resources faster than they can be replaced, nor does it emit pollutants faster than natural processes can render them harmless.

It was the WCED that first popularised the term sustainable development. They defined it in terms of two criteria: intra- and intergenerational equity. The next generation must be left a stock of quality assets, and not simply left to scrabble amongst the scraps. It was hardly surprising, given the numerical majority of the Third World states in the UN, that when the WCED was established, with commissioners from 21 countries, most of them were from the Third World. In the words of Gro Harlem Brundtland: 'the "environment" is where we all live; and "development" is what we all do in attempting to improve our lot within that abode' (WCED 1987: xi).

At the moment, however, unbalanced development is a major cause of the destruction of the environment. The poor can hardly be blamed for exploiting their environment in a way that destroys its long-term potential when the rich, including transnational corporations, are doing the same thing on a much more massive and destructive scale. Deteriorating terms of trade and the burden of debt on the Third World states increase pressure for exploitation by making short-term returns the most urgent consideration. The implication is that in any plan for sustainable development the future development needs of the South must be allowed for. Development cannot be sacrificed for environment any more than the other way round. The North–South gap cannot be perpetuated if the world is to remain stable. Therefore sustainable development must meet the economic, social and environmental needs of all the world's peoples.

Brundtland's call for sustainable development is now an article of faith in the First World but too often it has been seen as open to a much more limited interpretation, that of growth as usual but slower. *The Brundtland Report* itself is a compromise. It is weak on the subject of population growth and does not really suggest a solution to the problem of rich world resource consumption.

At present the depreciation of natural resources is not taken into account in calculating GNP, etc. Economists have already been able to demonstrate 'the physical dependency of economic activity on the sustainability of crucial natural-resource systems and ecological functions, and to indicate the economic costs, or trade-offs, resulting from the failure to preserve sustainability and environmental quality' (Barbier 1989: xiv). If new measures were to be devised it would be easier to see where sustainability was attainable and where not.

Following the Earth Summit in 1992 the UN created a new Commission on Sustainable Development in December 1992 to oversee implementation of its most radical document, Agenda 21, a plan for the twenty-first century. Introducing the proposal to the General Assembly, the secretary-general, Boutros Boutros-Ghali, said in November 1992: 'The challenge after Rio is to maintain the momentum to sustainable development, to transform it into policies and practice, and to give it effective and coordinated organisational support. . . . The UN must put its development objectives on a par with its political and social commitments'.

The Prince of Wales (1993) argues that the Third World needs for sustainable development to be possible:

- developed countries to put their own houses in order on pollution
- a reversal of the flow of funds from South to North
- different terms of trade that allow the South to sell more expensive goods to the North
- the end of subsidies on agriculture, etc., which make Third World products uncompetitive
- shared technology.

The technology that will most benefit the Third World (and the First) need not be complicated – in fact, the simpler and more trouble free the better. The Prince, for example, recommends the use of photovoltaic cell technology as a non-polluting source of electricity to run 'the five great liberators of development':

- cookers (which conserve fuelwood resources)
- refrigerators (which keep food from spoiling)
- water pumps (which avoid diseases associated with scarce surface water supplies and saves so much female time)
- radios (which provide cheap links to the outside world)
- lights.

Michael Grubb (1992) says: 'With the continuing pressure of public opinion and steady penetration of environmental concerns into governmental thinking sustainable development is on the agenda to stay.' However the inertia shown by First World governments since that time suggests that his optimism was rather premature (see also Grubb 2000, Carroll 1990).

Global warming

During the last glaciation, which ended only some 12,000 years ago, the average temperature was only 4°C lower than it is today. An increase of 2.5–5.5°C on the present figure it is believed now would raise sea levels initially only due to the expansion of water at higher temperatures. Although the temperature increase from global warming is expected to be greatest at the poles the vast ice sheets of Antarctica will take a long while to melt.

The main 'greenhouse gases', the increased emissions of which cause this rise in temperature, are:

1. Carbon dioxide from burning fossil fuels and burning off of the world's forest cover, especially in the tropics. Some 8.2 billion tons of CO_2 is being given off into the atmosphere each year. This is thought to contribute more than half of the global warming effect.

2. Methane from the decomposition of organic matter. Rice (paddy) fields are a major source. So too are cattle, so the conversion of tropical rainforest to poor quality ranching land, as in Costa Rica, has a double effect. Cattle, being ruminants, generate far more methane than goats, pigs – or human beings. A great deal of methane is held in suspension in the permafrost and the seabed and is likely to be liberated if global warming takes place, thus accelerating the effect.

3. Nitrous oxide, especially from motor vehicles but also from the overuse of chemical fertilisers.

4. Low-level ozone mainly from reaction of sunlight and pollution from motor vehicles (high-level ozone molecules, in the outer atmosphere, form an essential shield against radiation and are therefore crucial to our survival).

5. CFCs synthesised by human endeavour. Although 'thoroughly' tested when discovered in the 1930s, nobody dreamt then that they would contribute disproportionately to the Earth's warming, let alone that they would have damaging effects on the upper atmosphere.

Governments signing the Climate Convention at Rio numbered 157. Of these one country, the United States of America, is responsible for no less than 23 per cent of global CO_2 emissions. Other major contributors are the former USSR (19 per cent) and Europe (15 per cent). Their responses have been particularly disappointing, and it is not just political neurosis that has led some Third World countries to feel that they are being required to conserve their rainforest (Guimaraes 1991, Hall 1991) to allow the rich countries to go on burning fossil fuels.

For the fact is that more than two-thirds of the global production of greenhouse gases is due to burning of fossil fuels. Only six countries agreed to cuts in their emissions of CO_2. The maximum was Germany's target of a reduction of 25–30 per cent by 2005, which will be partly met in any case by phasing out inefficient plant in the former East. For the USA, similar cuts in CO_2 would mean cuts in GNP of the order of 3 per cent p.a. – less than the military budget. However the USA did not agree to sign the Framework Convention until it had succeeded in weakening it to the point of meaninglessness. The Berlin Conference of 1995 showed that even the relatively weak targets established by the major states had not been achieved, except where (as in the case of the UK) economic recession had fortuitously cut back emissions.

As things stand, a sea level rise of only $c.20$ cm is expected to take place by 2030. However floods and storms can be confidently expected to make matters worse. The Maldives, to take an extreme case, have no land more than 2 metres above sea level. A 1 metre rise in sea level would cost the Maldives $10,000 per person to defend against. Even their situation, however, could be better than that of the populations of the world's great river deltas in the South that are home to, and rich food production areas for, millions of people in the Third World. They will not have the means to defend their land against even small rises. Some 95 per cent of Bangladesh is already at risk from flooding. Monsoon shifts may be catastrophic for it as for some other tropical areas, although they are unlikely to experience much temperature increase.

An awkward problem is that environmental degradation will not affect all countries equally. Global warming will actually benefit some in the short term, since rainfall increases will not be uniform. Climatic zonal shift will be devastating for many animal and plant species owing to the lag between climatic change and species evolution. Even the most conservative estimates of the likely effects of global warming imply a rate of change that would be at the limits of what species have hitherto found it possible to accept.

Deforestation

In 1950 just over 100 million hectares of forest had been cleared. By 1975 this had more than doubled. Between 1950 and 1975 120 million hectares of tropical forest were destroyed in South and South-east Asia alone. In India 1.3 million hectares are lost each year to commercial plantations, river valley and mining projects. Each year 12–20 million hectares disappear and losses sustained at this level would mean total destruction of the rainforest well before 2050. Globally ten trees are cut down for every one planted.

Central America and Amazonia are losing more than 2.5 million hectares of forest each year to cattle-ranching (even without small-scale slash and burn that may clear an even greater area). The fact that Brazil is the largest Third World debtor and one of the fastest-growing economies in the world has been a dangerous combination for its rainforest. Successive Brazilian governments

have not sought to protect Brazil's forests. They have been much more concerned with northern markets – the Amazon has been seen as a huge resource
available to large-scale enterprise and extraction has accelerated. It has also
been viewed as somewhere to relocate millions of displaced people who then
slash and burn the forest to gain two or three years of crops. Sadly the red lat-
erite soils of southern Brazil, northern Argentina, Paraguay and West Africa on
which some of the richest forest resource grows are very thin and particularly
vulnerable. Once uncovered they soon bake hard and, where not washed away
into the rivers first, become impervious to rain. Soon the disappointed settlers
begin the trek back to the big cities that they were heading for in the first place.

The loss of trees results in:

- loss of soil nutrients
- loss of biodiversity – some 50 per cent of species live in the rainforest
- fuelwood shortages
- soil erosion and thus river silting, which results in flooding and droughts,
  and damage to dams, HEP installations, etc.

Deforestation and consequent soil damage add every year to the numbers of
refugees on the move, for example from Haiti. Its most dramatic consequence
is drought. The moisture given off by forests actually helps precipitate rain
clouds. Drought is not new to countries like Sudan and Ethiopia, but massive
recurring famine in their newly treeless wastes is. Every year 12 million
hectares of land become desert.

Forest is frequently the most accessible aspect of the environment to debt-
equity swaps. The World Wide Fund for Nature (WWF) buys up Third World
debt that is then paid to WWF in local currency and the funds used on local
environmental schemes such as those in Ecuador. The activities of NGOs
must however overcome nationalistic and selfish First World responses. For
example, Japan protects her own rainforest while importing hardwoods from
South-east Asia.

Biodiversity

The problem of biological diversity (Wilson 1988) affects all of us on three levels:

1. there are different types of ecosystems
2. there are a multitude of different species
3. there is a great deal of genetic variation of individuals within species.

With extinction running at between 1000 and 10,000 times the 'natural' rate,
species losses are estimated at somewhere around 50,000 a year. Certainly

more than 100 species a day, or four per hour, are being lost forever. There is no return from extinction – and ultimately that applies as much to human beings as to any other living creatures.

Though these are 'conservative' guesses it is quite clear that extinction rates are not constant but are actually accelerating. A loss of between 2 per cent and 8 per cent of currently existing species can be expected over the next 25 years. Much of what is lost in this time will never have been 'discovered' by human beings.

Biological diversity is not an optional extra but a matter of sheer self-interest. Biodiversity is an essential feature of the natural world, which enables species to respond to challenge. It is biodiversity, ironically enough, that enables the malaria parasite to survive the onslaught of the so-called 'wonder drugs'. At the same time the variety of the natural world offers us all sorts of medicinal and biochemical possibilities to combat disease. Quinine, still an effective drug against some kinds of malaria, was first introduced to Europeans by the Jesuits in the tropical rainforest of Paraguay.

For similar reasons we need to conserve the wild relatives of major food crops, such as wheat or maize, in case, as happened with the potato in Europe in the years 1846–48, our cultivated varieties should suddenly succumb to an attack from a new pest or disease.

These varieties are to be found mainly in what is now the Third World. But biodiversity is big business for the transnational corporations based in the developed countries. At the Earth Summit President Bush of the USA failed to sign the Convention on the Conservation of Biological Diversity (which President Clinton has since signed), arguing that there was no agreement on what biodiversity was or how its benefits should be shared. The United States of America took the view that anything enhanced by human endeavour should be patentable *and indeed the WTO appears to make it so*. The states of the South disagreed, believing that the countries where new discoveries are made have a right to the lion's share of the rewards of development. But though they have the biodiversity many of them have neither the will nor the strength to conserve it, with the result that some at least of it will be lost to the whole world.

Democracy and the environment

The Brundtland Report rightly saw democracy and participation as integral parts of sustainable development. Without the active participation of every member of the community sustainability cannot be achieved. Rio was a reminder that the environment cannot be safeguarded without development and justice for the South. The relationship between the three can be represented by a triangle, each influencing the other two, see Figure 13.1.

Figure 13.1   Environment, development and democracy

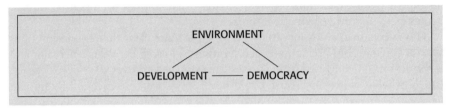

Democracy, often taken for granted in the industrialised countries, has in the Third World both a local and a global meaning.

The Mexican novelist Carlos Fuentes has pointed to the Zapatista insurrection in Chiapas as indicative of what could be expected without full participation and democratic rights (*The Guardian*, 15 January 1994). Base communities need incentives to improve their local environments. Security of land tenure gives the peasantry a stake in the long-term future.

On the global level, it is salutary to remember that the ratio of the per capita wealth of Europe to that of India in 1890 was about 2 : 1. Today it is 70 : 1. Hence global solutions to the environmental crisis have to be sought in a democratic atmosphere through global institutions. But the decision making required is very complex and at every stage it interacts with national and local politics.

The UN and the environment

The Earth Summit or 'Eco 92', the United Nations Conference on Environment and Development, held in Rio de Janeiro from 3–14 June 1992, was the largest high-level conference ever staged. Over 120 heads of state and heads of government took part in the 'summit segment' presided over personally for much of the time by President Fernando Collor de Mello, and some 20,000 people in all were involved in the preparation, planning and administration of the event. Its purpose was of appropriate importance: to concert measures to save the planet for future generations.

The publicity surrounding the Earth Summit aroused unrealistic expectations. Being an international conference it could not and did not fulfil the hopes of those – probably the majority of the world public – who expected it to produce concrete results. It is hard for the general public not to believe that, given many of the world's leaders are powerful separately, they will be even more powerful together. But the Earth Summit was not an 'Earth Senate'. Both the constitutional position of international decision making and the way in which decisions are arrived at are significantly different from the way in which things are done in a national context. The very fact that the Summit took place was itself significant. Beyond that, anything that could be achieved in the way of agreement was positive.

It was back in 1989 that the UN General Assembly, in resolution 44/228, had decided to convene UNCED, and urged the nations of the world to send representation at head of state or head of government level. However it is a well-established principle of international conferences that as little as possible must be left to chance and the Declaration of Rio would be a key statement of intent. The European Community favoured the idea of an Earth Charter, a relatively brief statement of principles. Four in particular were suggested:

1. The **precautionary principle** was that action to arrest the causes of environmental damage should not be delayed to wait for full scientific knowledge.

2. The **principle of prior assessment** called, on the other hand, for full assessment of the risks before any activity likely significantly to damage the environment was allowed to proceed.

3. The **principle that the polluter pays** focused on the need for individuals or companies polluting the environment to meet the public costs of cleaning it up.

4. The **principle of non-discriminatory public participation** called for all people to be fully informed about potential interference with their environment and a right to have their views taken into account in the making of policy.

Decision making within the UN system, however, is characterised by three factors:

1. **The juridical equality of sovereign states.** Each state has to be treated exactly the same as each other state. Hence each delegate who speaks is thanked for his/her 'important' statement, even if, as in at least one case at Rio, the delegate concerned simply reads out a civil service brief on the history of environmental politics since 1972.

2. **One state one vote.** Decisions of all bodies other than the Security Council, where the five permanent members continue to exercise the veto, reflect the desires and wishes of the developing South rather than the developed North.

3. **Voluntary consensus.** However wide the consensus, no decision (other than of the Security Council) is mandatory, unless the states concerned freely enter into a treaty obligation by signing and ratifying a convention or other agreement.

In practice, therefore, the politics of UNCED reflected the basic world divisions between North and South. Some optimism was generated by agreement on the

Rio Declaration and on the formidable list of further problems to be investigated, termed Agenda 21. Both represented a massive step forward in public awareness of the underlying problems. Both, however, were above all the product of compromise. Even the two formal treaties that survived the preliminary discussions, the Framework Convention on Climate Change and the Convention on Biological Diversity, though formally binding, lacked specific deadlines and so fell far short of what might have been hoped.

Worse still, the United States of America signed the Framework Convention on Climate Change only because it had first been watered down and all binding commitments removed. Malaysia refused to sign it, asserting its right to 'exploit' (i.e. destroy) its remaining tropical rainforest if it chose. Hence there was no agreement on a forestry convention that would check the destruction in time to forestall irrevocable loss on a massive scale (it was forecast that Malaysia would have successfully destroyed all the rainforest in Sabah and Sarawak in just eight years, by the end of the century). Instead there was a vague Statement on Forest principles and a call for governments to meet again to iron out the remaining difficulties. The Group of 77 wanted a public recognition of their specific concerns, especially:

> their sovereign right to development, acknowledgment that the industrialised countries were primarily responsible for current environmental problems, and the need for new financing and technology to enable developing countries to avoid taking the same polluting route to development as did the developing [sic] countries. (United Nations 1992)

President Collor had of course taken the opportunity to tell the world just how much Brazil (and by implication its president) was doing about the environment (Collor 1992). However his own 'green' credentials were rather dubious. Although no longer official policy, the destruction of the Amazon rainforest at the hands of would-be settlers continued, while the *garimpeiros* (gold prospectors) invaded Indian lands, carrying with them disease and other problems. The spectacle of the burning of the rainforest diverted attention from some very uncomfortable arithmetic. It was the 23 per cent of the world's population that consumed 77 per cent of the world's energy resources that had created and was continuing to accelerate the problem of global warming. Left to themselves the world's own ecosystems could have coped with emissions of greenhouse gases from the countries of the South. However if these countries were, in the coming 30 years, to maintain a reasonable standard of living for their populations, it was all but certain that they would have to do so by burning fossil fuels. Even if they were to do so, however, they would not attain the limits recommended by the IPCC for the maintenance of climatic stability. Hence there was nothing that the developing countries could do, or not do, on their own to prevent the onset of catastrophic instability. Only by a substantial reduction in greenhouse emissions from the developed North could that risk be postponed and/or averted.

There were two obvious weaknesses in the position of the South at Rio, neither of which is likely to be solved. First, there were a wide range of special interests to be served amongst the very large number of states that might (or might not) be counted in that category. Second, the strong tendency in the UN for states to caucus by region was replicated at UNCED. For example, only a few of the new island states of the Caribbean voiced the fears of their Pacific and Indian Ocean counterparts, that within a generation the rising sea level caused by global warming could threaten their livelihoods if not their actual existence as states. The president of the Republic of the Maldives, Maumoon Abdul Gayoom, said that he expected his country to be seriously damaged by 2030 and to cease to exist altogether by 2100. However Michael Manley of Jamaica had been succeeded in March by his former deputy, Percival Patterson, thus depriving the Commonwealth Caribbean of their most experienced radical voice, and their contribution to the public debate was muted. Patterson, who had been forced out of Manley's cabinet for alleged corruption as recently as December 1991, made a good plea for the implementation of the Law of the Sea Convention, but predictably placed the responsibility for global warming on the developed countries. The prime minister of Barbados, Erskine Sandiford, treated the assembled delegates to an ode in honour of the occasion composed entirely by himself.

Africa South of the Sahara was universally recognised as the world's most seriously deprived region. As noted above, its main preoccupation, drought and the issue of desertification, was sidelined at UNCED, despite being the subject of Chapter 12 of Agenda 21, 'Management of fragile ecosystems: combating desertification and drought'. A Convention to Combat Desertification was finally concluded in June 1994 and received the necessary 50 ratifications by 1997. However a Convention that is limited to the world's poorest countries and lacks adequate means of financial support is unlikely to be any more effective than its predecessor (Manu 1993).

The Earth Summit can fairly be evaluated not as an event in itself but the beginning of a much longer process of global self-education. One of its most important results was the provision by each country of a report on the state of its own environment. Often these were the first reports of their kind and so of immense value in establishing the dimensions of the problem. Its importance, however, will in the end have to be measured in terms of the willingness or otherwise of the world's powers to recognise their own problems and to implement the programme so clearly set out for them. The first signs have been far from encouraging.

No one at Rio, least of all the authors of the numerous drafts of Agenda 21, thought that the 'major shift in priorities' it called for would be either easy or quick; involving as it did 'the full integration of the environmental dimension into economic and sectoral policies, decision-making in every sphere of economic and environmental activity and a major redeployment of human and financial resources at both national and international level' (Strong 1992: 19).

Critics argue that no real action resulted. Basic policy differences were highlighted, especially those between the USA and the Third World, but they were not resolved. The same patterns of production and consumption continue and in any case commitments made were not in proportion to the size and severity of the problems we face. Up to $2.5 billion in additional finance to begin funding the $400–600 billion estimated price of Agenda 21 may have been pledged as a result of Rio, but a minimum of $10 billion extra would be needed to reckon it a success. The debate over how to fund it was, as we have seen, split along North–South lines with the Third World seeking, but not getting, assurances that official development assistance funding would not simply be diverted for the purpose. As UNCED Secretary-General Maurice Strong said of the possibilities of implementing Agenda 21: 'The real question is political will'. See Plate 13.

Agenda 21 is above all a social programme. Social programmes take time and money to implement.

> The priority actions of Agenda 21 are grouped within the context of principal substantive social themes, including a prospering (revitalization of Growth with Sustainability), a just (Sustainable Living for All) and a habitable (Human Settlements Development) world. They entail promotion of a fertile (Efficient Resource Use), a shared (Global and Regional Resources) and clean (Managing Chemicals and Waste) world, through wide and responsible participation at local, national and global levels. (Strong 1992: 19)

To deal with the obvious question first, the new and additional cost of implementing Agenda 21, if all activities had begun at once and were fully implemented between 1993 and 2000, was estimated at an average annual figure of $125 billion. Although this looks a large amount, in relation to the current expenditure of the developed countries it is in fact minimal – less than 1 per cent of GNP (Strong 1992: 17).

Unfortunately it was already clear before the delegates left Rio that the developed countries, led by the USA, were simply not prepared to pay up. Worse still, the economic ideas that they were advocating were only likely to make things worse. Advocacy of the 'free market' was in practice accompanied by a clear tendency to try to define the parameters of the market in a way that sacrificed long-term stability to short-term returns.

Conclusion

The problem for Third World countries was not so much that the so-called 'free market', which they had embraced so enthusiastically, would not work, but that it would not work in the way that they hoped. Specifically, the beneficiaries were likely to be the larger, low-cost producers; the losers, the smaller, weaker economies. The result would be the further erosion of their already dubious ability to resist short-term demand for environmental degradation. Second, the action of the market promised to be much too slow to prevent irrevocable damage to the environment – the extinction of species, in particular, could not be averted once their numbers had declined below a critical level, and until that level was reached there was insufficient motivation, under the unchecked market system, to halt the decline. In the last year before the formal implementation of CITES, South Korea imported 300 *tons* of tiger bones, representing the death of half of all the known Siberian tigers left in the wild. In March 1994 the UN Food and Agriculture Organization reported that 'severe' political and economic consequences could be expected to follow the potentially catastrophic decline of species in nine of the world's 17 main fishing grounds. Given the importance of fish, both fresh and dried, in Third World diets, this warning came not a moment too soon.

Some hope remained for the Commission on Sustainable Development proposed to monitor the implementation of Agenda 21. This was established by the UN Economic and Social Council (ECOSOC) on 12 February 1993. It consists of 53 members chaired by Razali Ismail of Malaysia and meets annually for two to three weeks. The first session was held in New York in June 1993 (*UN Chronicle* June 1993).

CHAPTER 14

Conclusion

The future

The old order is changing, although as yet the nationalist perception of the world survives to continue recognition of obsolete categories and to obscure the real inequalities, such as those between the rich of India and the poor of the southern USA. Nigel Harris (1986: 200) exemplifies this view:

> Thirdworldism began as a critique of an unequal world, a programme for economic development and justice, a type of national reformism dedicated to the creation of new societies and a new world. It ends with its leading protagonists either dead, defeated or satisfied to settle simply for national power rather than international equality; the rhetoric remains, now toothless, the decoration for squabbles over the pricing of commodities or flows of capital.

Last but not least, the very economic criteria that once seemed to unite them seem no longer to apply. Economic systems are seen to be constantly changing, in particular with the rise of the NICs and the 1980s 'pulling apart' of the Third World. There have been massive gains in East Asia, some gains in South Asia, some loss of development in Latin America, and near total disaster for many countries of Africa South of the Sahara.

The view of the future of the Third World can be either optimistic or pessimistic. The optimistic view is that:

- Third World economic growth is good if we compare such countries with the condition of the now developed nations when they were at the same stage of development.
- Third World manufacturers are increasing their share of the developed world's markets.
- Third World countries are experiencing rising life expectancy, literacy, etc.

The pessimistic view is that:

- The income gap between the Third World and the First World is still colossal. GNP per capita of Switzerland in 1994 was $36,080 per year. This was 13 times that of Brazil but 601 times that of Mozambique (UNDP 1994a, 1992 figures). But though the economy of Brazil has been growing rapidly, so that by 1997 the GNP per capita of Switzerland ($43,060) was only 9 times that of Brazil ($4790) it was still 307 times that of Mozambique ($140), so Mozambique seems to have little hope of catching up even with Brazil, let alone Switzerland (UNDP 1999, 1997 figures). The irony is that the best Third World growth rates are to be found in the richest Third World countries and in all the major regions of the world there are the same huge variations. In Africa, for example, Botswana has one of the fastest growth rates in the world while much of the rest of the region falls into the 'least developed' category and has stagnant or declining economies. This is without the striking variations within countries; for example in Indonesia Java is rich and Sumatra poor.

- The energy gap between the rich countries and the poor ones is vast.

- The social gap, whether in life expectancy/health, education/literacy or otherwise, is increasing within the Third World if not between the average of Third World and First World states.

This pulling apart has contributed to the idea that the concept of the Third World no longer has any value. However, as we have seen, it continues to be used because it is familiar and serves a need.

The collapse of the 'Second' World

Some writers, as we have seen, reject the concept of the Third World simply because, with the collapse of the 'Second', the term now seems odd. However the most worrying thing about the changes in eastern Europe and North Asia is precisely that they are tending to reinforce, not reduce, the yawning gap between the rich countries and the poor ones.

Some of the east-central European countries seem likely to find their common European home within the European Union. Obvious candidates are the Baltic states, the Czech Republic, Hungary and Slovenia. However outside the boundaries of the former Austro-Hungarian Empire the picture is rather of a precipitate decline into the Third World status that the poorest country in Europe, Albania, already holds. In fact Richard Perle's sarcastic description of the former Soviet Union as 'Upper Volta with rockets' seems now to have been uncomfortably close to the truth.

The interesting and worrying thing is, therefore, that within the territories of the former Soviet Union and its satellites, we seem already to be witnessing the same process of pulling apart that is characteristic of the Third World. The same economic and social problems are also already developing. So, despite some encouraging signs, are the political ones.

Modernisation in Asia

Other writers argue that the emergence of the NICs (or NIEs) is an Asian phenomenon, based on a very special combination of local circumstances, and not easily replicable elsewhere. Far-reaching land reform in the 1950s in Taiwan and South Korea created a loyal class of small farmers and at the same time a substantial pool of industrial labour. Autocratic government, a large public sector controlling key industries and a command economy directing heavy subsidies into the manufacture of goods for export are distinctive features of the Asian NICs. So too are long working hours at low rates of pay for millions of workers and heavy costs borne both by individuals and by the local environment. South Korea has the highest rate of industrial accidents in the world.

Some of these features are shared by other Asian developing countries. India, Malaysia, Thailand and the Philippines are much less autocratic, but in their different ways they have all encouraged the emergence of a low wage, export-oriented economy.

However, as we have seen, where there is a reasonably equal distribution of wealth the society as a whole does benefit and the general standard of living improves. It is quite possible that in the twenty-first century Asia will again become what it once was, the most advanced region of the world in economic terms. However much depends on the continued progress of India, soon to become the largest nation in the world in terms of population.

The decline of Africa

In Africa the situation is bleak and has deteriorated significantly in the past ten years. North of the Sahara Islamic fundamentalism has been threatening economic progress in Egypt and Algeria. It is possible that this could result in improved conditions for some of the poorest sectors, but so far it looks more likely to mean a retreat to insularity and isolationism that damages whole societies. Any attempt at bloc-building by Muslim countries would undoubtedly provoke similar responses elsewhere. It would certainly provide a convenient excuse to pander to the increasingly inward-oriented perspective of key sectors in the United States of America, for example.

South of the Sahara the HIV/AIDS epidemic continues to spread and there has been no significant economic advance over the last ten years. War and insurrection have blighted the hopes of some of the poorest nations on earth. One bright spot is in the far south, where the independence of Namibia and the relative stability of South Africa offers that possibility of cooperative economic development which had for so long been denied by political considerations.

The deindustrialisation of Europe

The problem with the assumption that export-led growth is the route to economic development is that there has to be a market big enough to absorb the products. In the nineteenth century Britain prospered on free trade. When other industrialised countries put up tariff barriers the markets of the Empire were big enough to allow trade to continue, at least for a time. The USA created a single internal market as early as 1791 and from that time on was able to develop behind the shelter of tariff protection. However the industrialisation of the Third World in recent years has been accompanied by the deindustrialisation of Europe. As transnational corporations have moved production out into Third World countries, to profit from their low wages, unemployment in Europe has risen to levels that have not been sustained for so long a period in recent times. At the same time wages have become depressed, to the point at which Timex watches were assembled in Scotland and not in a Third World country, as long as labour costs were low enough to make the operation profitable, because the workforce was skilled enough to make sure that the work was done to a sufficient standard.

Such development hardly suggests that Europe will be able to offer a big enough market for all the new goods that the Third World plans to put on sale. In fact, the markets of the developed world seem to have become saturated for some products already. People only need so many washing machines, refrigerators, vacuum cleaners, cars and television sets. Already the market for personal computers is getting very crowded. Prices are falling, quality and reliability has gone up to very acceptable levels, and after the first flush of enthusiasm for new electronic gadgetry it is clear that customers are becoming much more choosy. Hence newly industrialising countries face the unpalatable truth that if they are going to succeed they are going to have to sell their goods to the Third World itself. Whether they can succeed in doing so does not merely depend on their own efforts, but on the creation of markets for those goods consequent upon development on a scale probably immensely damaging to the global environment we all have to share.

The future of the Pacific Rim

With the emergence of the USA as a world superpower in 1945 Americans recalled the old belief that the major centre of world civilisation tends to move in a westerly direction. At the beginning of the 1990s this interesting, but fallacious, historical notion received a new twist with the emergence of the concept of the Pacific Rim as the new centre of world economic activity.

It is true that the United States of America, Japan, China and the NICs are all situated on the edge of the Pacific. So too are Mexico and Chile, which have both at different times been tipped for future NIC status. Given the size of the Pacific, a great many of the world's countries are bound to be found on its shores. However it is not the fact that they are on the edge of the Pacific that is the common factor amongst the most rapidly developing of these states, but the fact that they are attached closely to the mainland of Asia.

First World and 'Fourth' World

Finally we have to recall that the poorer countries of the Third World are slipping behind, not catching up. The pulling apart of the Third World is continuing. Yet the boundary between the Third World and the Fourth does not always run between countries. Often it forms a series of invisible barriers between the rich and the poor of a single country, or of a group of countries.

Those of us who have the good fortune to live in the First World have to some extent relied on the disparate and in many cases powerless nature of countries of the Third World. The reality of encroaching environmental problems, if not catastrophe, changes this situation. It is no longer possible to remain unconcerned about the plight of other people because their existence does not really impinge on ours. The futures of their children and of ours are now clearly recognisably bound together.

It is of course true that many people in First World countries have more pressing problems than the apparently rather remote dilemmas that surround our relationships with other parts of the world and they have in many cases too little to be expected to make any significant contribution to a more equal world by giving up material possessions. Nevertheless the quality of all our lives ultimately depends on our recognising our interdependence. Above all, the First World must acknowledge the special responsibility it now has for helping the Third World to achieve a quality of life appropriate for *all* human beings at the beginning of the twenty-first century.

References

Adams, Nassau (1993), *Worlds Apart: the North–South divide and the evolution of the international economic system*, London, Zed Press.

Adams, Patricia (1991), *Odious Debts: loose lending, corruption, and the Third World's environmental legacy*, London, Earthscan.

Afrifa, Col. A.A. (1966), *The Ghana Coup 24th February 1966*, London, Frank Cass.

Almond, Gabriel A. (1960), 'Introduction: a functional approach to comparative politics' in Almond, Gabriel A. and Coleman, James S., *The Politics of the Developing Areas*, Princeton, NJ, Princeton University Press.

Almond, Gabriel A. and Verba, Sidney (1963), *The Civic Culture*, Princeton, NJ, Princeton University Press.

Almond, Gabriel A. and Verba, Sidney (1980), *The Civic Culture Revisited*, Princeton, NJ, Princeton University Press.

Amin, Samir (1990a), *Delinking: towards a polycentric world*, London, Zed Press.

Amin, Samir (1990b), *Maldevelopment: anatomy of a global failure*, London, Zed Press.

Andreski, Stanislav (1968), *The African Predicament: a study in the pathology of modernisation*, London, Michael Joseph.

Arat, Zehra F. (1991), *Democracy and Human Rights in Developing Countries*, Boulder, CO, Rienner.

Austin, Dennis (1978), *Politics in Africa,* Manchester, Manchester University Press.

Australian Broadcasting Company (1998), 'Oil production begins in Timor Gap', 21 July.

Baran, Paul A. (1957), *The Political Economy of Growth*, New York, Monthly Review Press.

Barbier, Edward B. (1989), *Economics, Natural-resource Scarcity and Development: conventional and alternative views*, London, Earthscan.

Beer, Christopher E.F. and Williams, Gavin (1975), 'The politics of the Ibadan peasantry', *The African Review*, 5 (3): 235–56.

Bernstein, Henry, Crow, Ben and Johnson, Hazel, eds (1992), *Rural Livelihoods: crises and responses*, Oxford, Oxford University Press.

Bill, James Alban (1972), *The Politics of Iran: groups, classes, and modernization.* Columbus, OH, Merrill.

Billington, Rosamund, Strawbridge, Sheelagh, Greensides, Lenore and Fitzsimons, Annette (1991), *Culture and Society: a sociology of culture*, Basingstoke, Macmillan Education.

Black, Cyril E. (1976), *Comparative Modernization: a reader*, New York, The Free Press.

Black, Jan Knippers (1999), *Inequity in the Global Village: recycled rhetoric and disposable people*, West Hartfort, CT, Kumarian Press.

Bonilla, Frank, and Girling, Robert, eds (1973), *The Structures of Dependency*, Stanford, CA, Institute of Political Studies.

Boserup, Ester (1981), *Population and Technology*, Oxford, Basil Blackwell.

Boserup, Ester (1989), *Woman's Role in Economic Development*, London, Allen & Unwin, 1970; new edn, London, Earthscan.

Bourricaud, François (1970), *Power and Society in Contemporary Peru*, New York, Praeger.

Bradley, P.N. (1986), 'Food production and distribution – and hunger' in R.J. Johnston and P.J. Taylor, eds, *A World in Crisis? geographical perspectives*, Oxford, Basil Blackwell: 89–106.

Brandt, Willy (1980), *North–South: a programme for survival. The Report of the Independent Commission on International Development Issues under the Chairmanship of Willy Brandt*, London, Pan Books.

Bresnan, John, ed. (1986), *Crisis in the Philippines: the Marcos era and beyond*, Princeton, NJ, Princeton University Press.

Bretton, Henry L. (1973), *Power and Politics in Africa*, London, Longman.

Brier, Alan and Calvert, Peter (1975), 'Revolution in the 1960s', *Political Studies*, **32** (1): 1–11.

Brown, G. Gordon (1957), 'Some problems of culture contact with illustrations from East Africa and Samoa', *Human Organization*, **16** (3): 11–14.

Bull, Hedley (1977), *The Anarchical Society*, London, Macmillan.

Burnell, Peter (1997), *Foreign Aid in a Changing World*, Milton Keynes, Open University Press.

Cairncross, Alec (1994), 'Forget Bretton Woods – recovery was born in the USA', *The Guardian*, 22 July.

Calvert, Peter (1985), *Guatemala: a nation in turmoil*, Boulder, CO, Westview.

Calvert, Peter (1990), *Revolution and Counter-revolution*, Milton Keynes, Open University Press.

Calvert, Peter (1994), *The International Politics of Latin America*, Manchester, Manchester University Press.

Calvert, Peter, ed. (1988), *The Central American Security System: North/South or East/West?* Cambridge, Cambridge University Press.

Canovan, Margaret (1981), *Populism*, London, Junction Books.

Cardoso, Fernando Henrique (1972), 'Dependency and development in Latin America', *New Left Review*, **74**: 83–95.

Cardoso, Fernando Henrique, and Faletto, Enzo (1979), *Dependency and Development in Latin America*, Berkeley, CA, University of California Press.

Carroll, John E. (1990), *International Enviromental Diplomacy: the management and resolution of transfrontier environmental problems*, Cambridge, Cambridge University Press.

Cassen, Robert (1994), *Does Aid Work? Report to an intergovernmental task force*, Oxford, Clarendon Press.

Chaliand, Gérard (1977), *Revolution in the Third World: myths and prospects*, Hassocks, Sussex, Harvester Press.

Chilcote, Ronald H. (1978), 'A question of dependency', *Latin American Research Review*, 12 (2): 55–68.

Chilcote, Ronald H. and Edelstein, Joel C., eds (1974), *Latin America: the Struggle with Dependency and Beyond*, Cambridge, MA, Schenkman.

Chossudovsky, Michel (1994), 'IMF–World Bank policies and the Rwandan holocaust', *Third World Resurgence*, 52: 27–31.

Clapham, Christopher, ed. (1982), *Private Patronage and Public Power: political clientelism in the modern state*, London, Frances Pinter.

Clapham, Christopher (1985), *Third World Politics; an introduction*, London, Routledge.

Clarke, Arthur C. (1945), 'Extra-terrestrial relays', *Wireless World*, October 1945: 305–8.

Colburn, Forrest D. (1994), *The Vogue of Revolution in Poor Countries*, Princeton, NJ, Princeton University Press.

Collor, Fernando (1992), *Agenda for Consensus: a social–liberal proposal*, Brasília, Governo do Brasil.

Colquhoun, Keith Colquhoun (1993), 'North Korea, the dangerous outsider', *World Today*, November 1993: 210.

Conniff, Michael L., ed. (1982), *Latin American Populism in Comparative Perspective*, Albuquerque, NM, University of New Mexico Press.

Crabtree, John (1987), *The Great Tin Crash: Bolivia and the world tin market*, London, Latin American Bureau.

Crow, Ben, Thorpe, Mary et al. (1988), *Survival and Change in the Third World*, Cambridge, Polity Press.

Crowder, Michael (1967), *Senegal*, London, Methuen.

Dahl, Robert A. (1989), *Democracy and its Critics*, New Haven, CT, Yale University Press.

Danida (1989), *Environmental Issues and Human Health*, Copenhagen, Department of International Development Cooperation.

Davidson, Julia O'Connell (1996), 'Sex tourism in Cuba', *Race and Class*, 38 (1).

Decalo, Samuel (1976), *Coups and Army Rule in Africa*, New Haven, CT, Yale University Press.

Decalo, Samuel (1980), 'Regionalism, political decay, and civil strife in Chad', *Journal of Modern African Studies*, 18 (1): 23–56.

Dicken, Peter (1986), *Global Shift: industrial change in a tubulent world*, London, Harper & Row.

Dickenson, J.P., Clarke, C.G., Gould, W.T.S., Prothero, R.M., Siddle, D.J., Smith, C.T., Thomas-Hope, E.M. and Hodgkiss, A.G. (1983), *A Geography of the Third World*, London, Methuen.

Di Tella, Guido and Rodríguez Braun, Carlos, eds (1990), *Argentina, 1946–83: the economic ministers speak*, London, Macmillan with St Antony's College, Oxford.

Di Tella, Torcuato (1965), 'Populism and reform in Latin America' in Claudio Véliz, ed., *Obstacles to Change in Latin America*, London, Oxford University Press: 48–51.

Dix, Robert (1985), 'Populism: authoritarian and democratic', *Latin American Research Review*, 20 (2): 29–52.

Dobel, J.P. (1978), 'The corruption of a state', *American Political Science Review*, 72 (3): 958–73.

Dorman, Sara Rich (2000), 'Change now?' *The World Today*, 56 (4), April: 25–27.

Dos Santos, Theotonio (1969), 'The crisis of development theory and the problem of dependence in Latin America', in Henry Bernstein, ed., *Underdevelopment and Development: the Third World today*, Harmondsworth, Penguin Books, 1973: 55–60.

Dos Santos, Theotonio (1970), 'The structure of dependence', *American Economic Review*, 60, May: 291–336.

Dreze, Jean and Sen, Amartya (1989), *Hunger and Public Action*, Oxford, Clarendon Press.

Duncan, Tim, and Fogarty, John (1986), *Australia and Argentina: on parallel paths*, Carlton, Victoria, Melbourne University Press.

Easton, David (1957), 'An approach to the analysis of political systems', *World Politics*, 10: 383–400.

Easton, David (1965), *A Systems Analysis of Political Life*, New York, John Wiley.

Encarta (1999), Microsoft.

Enloe, Cynthia (1989), *Making Feminist Sense of International Politics*, London, Pandora Press.

Eyben, Rosalind (1995), 'What can aid do for social development?' *Development in Practice*, 5 (1).

Fanon, Frantz (1967), *The Wretched of the Earth*, Harmondsworth, Penguin Books.

Finer, Samuel (1975), *The Man on Horseback: the role of the military in politics*, 2nd edn, Harmondsworth, Penguin Books.

First, Ruth (1972), *The Barrel of a Gun*, Harmondsworth, Penguin African Library.

Foray, Cyril P. (1977), *Historical Dictionary of Sierra Leone*, Metuchen, NJ, Scarecrow Press.

Foster, George M. (1967), *Tzintzuntzan: Mexican peasants in a changing world*, Boston, Little, Brown.

Foster, George M. (1973), *Traditional Societies and Technological Change*, New York, Harper & Row.

Foster, George M. (1976), *Traditional Societies and Technological Change*, 2nd edn, New York, Harper and Row.

Frank, André Gunder (1966), 'The development of underdevelopment', *Monthly Review*, 18 (4): 17–31.

Frank, André Gunder (1967), *Capitalism and Underdevelopment in Latin America*, Harmondsworth, Penguin Books.

Frank, André Gunder (1969), *Lumpenbourgeoisie: lumpendevelopment, dependence, class, and politics in Latin America*, New York, Monthly Review Press.

Frank, André Gunder (1970), *Latin America: underdevelopment or revolution*, New York, Monthly Review Press.

Frank, André Gunder (1974), 'Dependence is dead, long live dependence and the class struggle: a reply to critiques', *Latin American Perspectives*, 1 (1): 87–106.

Frank, André Gunder (1981), *Crisis: in the Third World*, London, Heinemann.

Fukuyama, Francis (1992), *The End of History and the Last Man*, London, Hamish Hamilton.

Furtado, Celso (1970), *The Economic Development of Latin America: a survey from colonial times to the Cuban Revolution*, Cambridge, Cambridge University Press.

Gamer, Robert E. (1976), *The Developing Nations: a comparative perspective*, Boston, MA, Allyn & Bacon.

George, Susan (1993), 'The debt boomerang', *New Internationalist*, May.

Ghosh, Jayati and Bharadwaj, Krishna (1992), 'Poverty and development in India' in Bernstein, Henry, Crow, Ben and Johnson, Hazel, eds, *Rural Livelihoods: crises and responses*, Oxford, Oxford University Press: 139–64.

Giddens, Anthony (1990), *The Consequences of Modernity*, Cambridge, Polity Press.

Glade, William (1991), 'The contexts of privatization', in Glade, William, ed., *Privatization of Public Enterprises in Latin America*, San Francisco, CA, International Center for Economic Growth, Institute of the Americas and Center for US–Mexican Studies.

Golbourne, Harry, ed. (1979), *Politics and State in the Third World*, London, Macmillan.

Goldthorpe, John (1975), *The Sociology of the Third World: disparity and involvement*, Cambridge, Cambridge University Press.

Goode, W.J. (1970), *World Revolution and Family Patterns*, Glencoe, IL, The Free Press.

Grubb, Michael (1992), *The World Today*, 48 (8/9), August/September: 140–2.

Grubb, Michael (2000), 'Protecting the planet', *The World Today*, 56 (5), May: 8–11.

Grugel, Jean (1995), *Politics and Development in the Caribbean basin: Central America and the Caribbean in the new world order*, Basingstoke, Macmillan.

Guimaraes, R.P. (1991), *The Ecopolitics of Development in the Third World: politics and environment in Brazil*, London, Rienner.

Hall, Anthony L. (1991), *Developing Amazonia: deforestation and social conflict in Brazil's Carajás programme*, Manchester, Manchester University Press.

Hall, Stuart, and Jefferson, Tony, eds (1976), *Resistance through Rituals: youth subcultures in post-war Britain*, London, Hutchinson in association with the Centre for Contemporary Cultural Studies, University of Birmingham.

Halliday, Fred (1994), *Rethinking International Relations*, Basingstoke: Macmillan.

Hammond, Bob (1994), 'A geography of overseas aid', *Geography*, 79 (3), 174: 210–21.

Hardoy, Jorge E., Mitlin, Diana and Satterthwaite, David (1992), *Environmental Problems in Third World Cities*, London, Earthscan.

Harris, Nigel (1986), *The End of the Third World? newly industrialising countries and the decline of an ideology*, London, I.B. Tauris.

Harrison, Paul (1993), *The Third Revolution: population, environment and a sustainable world*, Harmondsworth, Penguin Books.

Hayter, Teresa (1983), *The Creation of World Poverty: an alternative view to the Brandt Report*, London, Pluto Press.

Heidenheimer, A.J. (1970), *Political Corruption*, New York, Holt Rinehart.

Hewitt, Vernon Marston (1992), *The International Politics of South Asia*, Manchester, Manchester University Press.

Hicks, John D. (1961), *The Populist Revolt*, Lincoln, NB, University of Nebraska Press.

Higgins, Graham et al. (1982), *Potential Population Supporting Capacities of Lands in the Developing World*, Rome, FAO.

Hilling, David (1978), 'The infrastructure gap' in Mountjoy, Alan B., ed., *The Third World: problems and perspectives*, London, Macmillan.

Hillyard, Paddy and Percy-Smith, Janie (1988), *The Coercive State*, London, Pinter.

Hogendorn, Jan S. (1996), *Economic Development*, London, Longman.

Holmberg, Allan R. (1971), 'Experimental intervention in the field' in Henry F. Dobyns, Paul L. Doughty and Harold D. Lasswell, *Peasants, Power, and Applied Social Change: Vicos as a model*, London, Sage Publications: 21–32.

Hoogvelt, Ankie (1978), *The Sociology of Developing Societies*, London, Macmillan.

Horowitz, Donald L. (1971), 'Three dimensions of ethnic politics', *World Politics*, **23** (2): 232.

Howard, Michael, ed. (1957), *Soldiers and Governments*, London, Eyre & Spottiswode.

Hughes, John (1968), *The End of Sukarno: a coup that misfired: a purge that ran wild*, London, Angus & Robertson.

Huntington, Samuel P. (1965), 'Political development and political decay', *World Politics*, **17** (3): 386–430.

Huntington, Samuel P. (1968), *Political Order in Changing Societies*, New Haven, CT, Yale University Press.

Huntington, Samuel P. (1976), 'The change to change: modernization, development, and politics', in Cyril E. Black, ed., *Comparative Modernization: a reader*, New York, The Free Press.

Huntington, Samuel P. (1993), *The Third Wave: democratization in the late twentieth century*, Norman, OK, University of Oklahoma Press.

Huntington, Samuel P. (1997), *The Clash of Civilizations and the Remaking of World Order*, New York, Simon & Schuster.

Hurrell, Andrew, and Kingsbury, Benedict, eds (1992), *The International Politics of the Environment*, Oxford, Clarendon Press.

Ianni, Otávio (1975), *A formaçao do estado populista na América Latina*, Rio de Janeiro, Civilizaçao Brasiliera.

Jackson, Ben (1990), *Poverty and the Planet: a question of survival*, Harmondsworth, Penguin Books.

Jaguaribe, Helio (1967), *Problems do desenvolvimiento Latino-Americano*, Rio de Janeiro, Ed. Civilizaçao Brasiliera.

Jenkins, J. Craig and Kposowa, Augustine J. (1992), 'Political origins of African military coups: ethnic competition, military centrality and the struggle over the postcolonialist state', *International Studies Quarterly*, **36** (3): 271–91.

Johnson, John J. (1964), *The Military and Society in Latin America*, Stanford, CA, Stanford University Press.

Kamrava, Mehran (1992), *Revolutionary Politics*, London, Pinter.

Kamrava, Mehran (1993), *Politics and Society in the Third World*, London, Routledge.

Kedourie, Elie (1971), *Nationalism in Asia and Africa*, London, Heinemann.

Kent, George (1995), *Children in the International Political Economy*, Basingstoke, Macmillan.

Keohane, Robert O. and Nye, Joseph S. (1977), *Power and Interdependence: world politics in transition*, Boston, Little, Brown & Co.

Keesing's Record of World Events, Harlow, Longman, 1990–93; London, Cartermill International, 1994–95; Bethesda, MD, Keesing's Worldwide, 1996–2000.

Kerr, Clark, Dunop, John T., Harbison, Frederick H. and Myers, Charles A. (1960), *Industrialism and Industrial Man; the problems of labour and management in economic growth*, London, Heinemann.

Kilson, Martin (1966), *Political Change in a West African State: a study of the modernization process in Sierra Leone*, Cambridge, MA, Harvard University Press.

Kitching, G. (1982), *Development and underdevelopment in historical perspective: populism, nationalism and industrialization*, London, Methuen.

Krugman, Paul (1995), 'Dutch tulips and emerging markets', *Foreign Affairs*, **74**, 28–9.

Laclau, Ernesto (1977), *Politics and Ideology in Marxist Theory: capitalism–fascism–populism*, London, NLB.

Lanfant, Marie-Françoise, Allcock, John B. and Bruner, Edward M., eds (1995), *International Tourism, Identity and Change*, London, Sage for International Sociological Association.

Lasswell, Harold D. and Kaplan, A. (1950), *Power and Society: a framework for political inquiry*, New Haven, Yale University Press.

Lasswell, Harold D. and Holmberg, Allan R. (1966), 'Toward a general theory of directed value accumulation and institutional development' in H.W. Peter, ed., *Comparative Theories of Social Change*, Ann Arbor, Mich., Foundation for Research on Human Behavior.

Lee, Wendy (1991), 'Prostitution and tourism in South-East Asia' in Nanneke Redclift and M. Thea Sinclair, eds, *Working Women: international perspectives on labour and gender ideology*, London, Routledge.

Leggett, Jeremy, ed. (1990), *Global Warming: the Greenpeace report*, Oxford, Oxford University Press.

Levy, Diane E. and Lerch, Patricia B. (1991), 'Tourism as a factor in development: implications for gender and work in Barbados', *Gender and Society*, 5 (1): 67–85.

Lewis, Oscar (1962), *The Children of Sánchez: autobiography of a Mexican family*, London: Secker & Warburg.

Lieuwen, Edwin (1964), *Generals versus Presidents: neomilitarism in Latin America*, London, Pall Mall.

Linz, Juan J. (1970), 'An authoritarian regime: Spain' in E. Allardt and S. Rokkan, eds, *Mass Politics: studies in political sociology*: 254.

Lipset, Seymour Martin (1979), *The First New Nation: the United States in historical and comparative perspective*, New York, W.W. Norton.

Lipton, M. (1977), *Why Poor People Stay Poor: urban bias in world development*, London, Temple Smith.

Little, K. (1965), *West African Urbanisation*, Cambridge, Cambridge University Press.

Little, Richard (1975), *Intervention: external involvement in civil wars*, London, Martin Robertson.

Lloyd, Peter C. (1971), *Classes, Crises and Coups: themes in the sociology of developing countries*, London, Paladin.

Luckham, Robin (1971a), *The Nigerian Military 1960–67*, Cambridge, Cambridge University Press.

Lugard, Sir Frederick D. (1922), *The Dual Mandate in British Tropical Africa*, Edinburgh, William Blackwood & Sons.

McAfee, Kathy (1991), *Storm Signals: structural adjustment and development alternatives in the Caribbean*, Boston, MA, South End Press in association with Oxfam America.

McGrew, Anthony G. and Lewis, Paul G. et al. (1992), *Global Politics: globalization and the nation-state*, Cambridge, Polity Press.

McKean, Liz (2000), 'Women 2000: the struggle for their rights persists', *Amnesty*, 100, March/April: 12–13.

Malinowski, B. (1961), *The Dynamics of Culture Change*, New Haven, CT, Yale University Press.

Manu, Christopher (1993), 'The road to the Desertification Convention', *Resources*, 4 (2): 7–10.

Matthews, Jessica Tuchman (1993) in Glyn Prins, ed., *Threats Without Enemies; facing environmental insecurity*, London, Earthscan.

Mead, Margaret (1956), *New Lives for Old*, New York, New American Library.

Mehta, Gita (1990), *Raj* (a novel), London, Mandarin Paperbacks.

Mitra, Subrata Kumar, ed. (1990), *The Post-colonial State in Asia: dialectics of politics and culture*, New York, Harvester-Wheatsheaf.

Monbiot, George (1992), in Oxfam/*Guardian Supplement*, June.

Monbiot, George (1998), 'Whose wildlife is it anyway?' *The Guardian*, 20 June.

Moore, Mick (1990), 'Sri Lanka: the contradictions of the social democratic state' in Subrata Kumar Mitra, ed., *The Post-colonial State in Asia: dialectics of politics and culture*, New York, Harvester-Wheatsheaf: 155–91.

Myrdal, Gunnar (1968), *Asian Drama: an enquiry into the poverty of nations*, Harmondsworth, Penguin Books.

National Council for Science and the Environment (2000), *Sustaining Water: population and the future of renewable water supplies*, Washington, DC: Population Action International, http://www.cnie.org/pop/pai/water-14.html

Naudet, David and Pradelle, Jean-Marc (1997), 'A verdict on aid to the Sahel', *The OECD Observer*, 205, April/May: 15–18.

Needler, Martin C. (1963), *Latin American Power in Perspective*, Princeton, NJ, Van Nostrand.

Neguib (Naguib), Muhammad (1955), *Egypt's Destiny*, Garden City, NY, Doubleday.

Nordlinger, Eric A. (1977), *Soldiers in Politics: military coups and governments*, Englewood Cliffs, NJ, Prentice Hall.

Nye, Joseph S. (1967), *Pan-Africanism and East African Integration*, Cambridge, MA, Harvard University Press.

Nye, J.S. and Keohane, R.O. (1971), *Transnational Relations and World Politics*, Cambridge, Cambridge University Press.

O'Brien, Donal B. (1971), *The Mourides of Senegal*, Oxford, Oxford University Press.

O'Brien, Donal B. Cruise (1978), 'Senegal', in John Dunn, ed., *West African States: failure and promise; a study in comparative politics*, Cambridge, Cambridge University Press: 173–88.

O'Brien, Philip and Cammack, Paul, eds (1985), *Generals in Retreat: the crisis of military rule in Latin America*, Manchester, Manchester University Press.

O'Donnell, Guillermo (1988), *Bureaucratic Authoritarianism: Argentina, 1966–1973, in comparative perspective*, Berkeley, CA, University of California Press.

Oneworld (1998), http://www.oneworld.org/ips2/oct98/21_32_090.html

Palmer, David Scott, ed. (1992), *Shining Path of Peru*, London, Hurst & Company.

Parsons, Talcott (1964), *Essays in Sociological Theory*, New York, The Free Press.

Patullo, Polly (1996), *Last Resorts: the cost of tourism in the Caribbean*, London: Cassell with Latin American Bureau.

Pearce, Fred (1992), 'Last chance to save the planet?', *New Scientist*, 30 May.

Percival, Debra (1996), 'The changing face of trade unionism in Africa', *The Courier ACP-EU*, 156, March–April: 76–77, http://www.oneworld.org/euforic/courier/156e_pet.htm

Perham, Margery (1937), *Native Administration in Nigeria*, Oxford, Oxford University Press.

Petersen, Kurt (1992), *The Maquiladora Revolution in Guatemala*, Occasional Paper Series 2, Orville H. Schell, Jr., Center for International Human Rights at Yale Law School.

Philip, George (1984), 'Military-authoritarianism in South America: Brazil, Chile, Uruguay and Argentina', *Political Studies*, 32 (1): 1–20.

Philip, George (1985), *The Military and South American Politics*, London, Croom Helm.

Pinkney, Robert (1993), *Democracy in the Third World*, Buckingham, Open University Press.

Poole, Deborah and Rénique, Gerardo (1991), 'The new chroniclers of Peru: US scholars and the "shining path" of peasant rebellion', *Bulletin of Latin American Research*, **10** (2): 133–91.

Poole, Deborah and Rénique, Gerardo (1992), *Peru: Time of Fear*, London, Latin American Bureau.

Postel, Sandra (1989), *Water for Agriculture*, Washington, DC, Worldwatch Institute, Worldwatch Paper 93.

Powell, John Duncan (1970), 'Peasant society and clientelist politics', *American Political Science Review*, **64**: 411–25.

Prebisch, Raúl (1950), *Economic Development of Latin America and its Principal Problems*, New York, United Nations Department of Economic Affairs, ECLA document E/CN 12/89/Rev.1.

Prescott, J.R.V. (1965), *The Geography of Frontiers and Boundaries*, London, Hutchinson.

Prince of Wales (1993), 'Introduction' in Gwyn Prins, ed., *Threats without Enemies: facing environmental insecurity*, London, Earthscan.

Randall, V. and Theobald, R. (1985), *Political Change and Underdevelopment*, London, Macmillan.

Rappaport, Roy A. (1968), *Pigs for the Ancestors: ritual in the ecology of a New Guinea people*, New Haven, CT, Yale University Press.

Redclift, Michael (1984), *Development and the Environmental Crisis: red or green alternatives?*, London, Methuen.

Roett, Riordan (1985), 'Latin America's response to the debt crisis', *Third World Quarterly*, **7** (2), April.

Rostow, W.W. (1960), *The Stages of Economic Growth*, Cambridge, MA, Harvard University Press.

Rostow, W.W. (1971), *Politics and the Stages of Growth*, Cambridge, Cambridge University Press.

Roxborough, Ian (1979), *Theories of Underdevelopment*, London, Macmillan.

Rueschemeyer, Dietrich, Huber Stephens, Evelyne and Stephens, John D. (1992), *Capitalist Development and Democracy*, Chicago, IL, University of Chicago Press.

Sahlin, Michael (1977), *Neo-authoritarianism and the Problem of Legitimacy: a general study and a Nigerian example*, Stockholm, Reben & Sjögren.

Sampson, Anthony (1975), *The Seven Sisters: the great oil companies and the world they made*, London, Coronet.

Sampson, Anthony (1999), *Mandela, the Authorised Biography*, London, HarperCollins.

Saravanamuttu, P. (1990), 'Instability in Sri Lanka', *Survival*, **32** (5): 455–68.

Sartori, Giovanni (1976), *Parties and Party Systems, a framework for analysis*, Cambridge, Cambridge University Press.

Schmandt, Jurgen (1994), 'Water and development in semi-arid regions', Paper presented to the XVI World Congress of the International Political Science Association, Berlin, Germany, 21–25 August.

Schmitter, Phillippe, ed. (1979), *Trends towards Corporate Intermediation*, Beverly Hills, CA, Sage.

Scott, J.C. (1976), *The Moral Economy of the Peasant: rebellion and subsistence in Southeast Asia*, New Haven, CT, Yale University Press.

Scutz, Barry M. and O'Slater, Robert, eds (1990), *Revolution and Political Change in the Third World*, London, Adamantine.

Sen, Amartya (1981), *Poverty and Famines: an essay on entitlement and deprivation*, Oxford, Clarendon Press.

Seton-Watson, Hugh (1977), *Nations and States: an inquiry into the origins of nations and the politics of nationalism*, London, Methuen.

Shaw, Paul (1992), quoted in *New Internationalist*, September: 14.

Shiva, Vandana (1988), *Staying Alive: women, ecology and development in India*, London, Zed Books.

Sierra Leone National Reformation Council (1968), *Report of the Forster Commission of Inquiry on Assets of Ex-Ministers and Ex-deputy Ministers*, Freetown, Government Printer.

Singer, H.W. and Ansari, Javed A. (1992), *Rich and Poor Countries*, 4th edn, London, Routledge.

Sinha, R. (1976), *Food and Poverty*, London, Croom Helm.

Smith, Michael (1992), 'Modernization, globalization and the nation-state' in Anthony McGrew, Paul G. Lewis et al. (1992), *Global Politics: globalization and the nation-state*, Cambridge, Polity Press.

Smith, Tony (1979), 'The underdevelopment of development literature: the case of dependency theory', *World Politics*, 31 (2): 247–88.

Somjee, A.H. (1991), *Development Theory: critiques and explorations*, Basingstoke, Macmillan.

South Commission (1990), *The Challenge to the South: the report of the South Commission*, London, Oxford University Press.

Staley, Eugene (1954), *Political Implications of Economic Development*, New York, Harper.

Stepan, Alfred, ed. (1973), *Authoritarian Brazil*, New Haven, CT, Yale University Press.

Stepan, Alfred (1978), *The State and Society: Peru in comparative perspective*, Princeton, NJ, Princeton University Press.

Strong, Maurice F. (1992), Foreword to *The Global Partnership for Environment and Development: a guide to Agenda 21*, Geneva, UNCED, April 1992.

Sunkel, Osvaldo (1969), 'National development policy and external dependence in Latin America', *Journal of Development Studies*, 6 (1): 23–48.

Suzman, Helen (1993), *In No Uncertain Terms: memoirs*, London, Sinclair-Stevenson.

Tangri, Roger (1985), *Politics in Sub-Saharan Africa*, London, James Currey.

Taylor, Lewis (1987), 'Agrarian unrest and political conflict in Puno, 1985–1987', *Bulletin of Latin American Research*, 6 (2): 135–62.

Taylor, Lewis (1998), 'Counter-insurgency strategy, the PCP-Sendero Luminoso and the civil war in Peru, 1980–1996', *Bulletin of Latin American Research*, 17 (1): 35–58.

Thomas, Caroline (1985), *New States, Sovereignty and Intervention*, Aldershot, Gower.

Thomas, Caroline (1987), *In Search of Security: the Third World in international relations*, Boulder, CO, Rienner.

Thomas, Caroline (1992), *The Environment in International Relations*, London, The Royal Institute of International Affairs.

Thomas, Caroline (1999), 'Where is the Third World now?', *Review of International Studies*, 25 (4): 225–44.

Thomas, Caroline and Howlett, Darryl (1992), *Resource Politics: freshwater and regional relations*, Buckingham, Open University Press.

Thrift, Nigel (1986), 'The geography of international economic disorder', in R.J. Johnston and P.J. Taylor, eds, *A World in Crisis: geographical perspectives*, Oxford, Basil Blackwell.

Timberlake, L. (1985), *Africa in Crisis*, London, Earthscan.

Todaro, Michael (1994), *Economic Development*, London, Longman.

Toffler, Alvin (1970), *Future Shock*, London: The Bodley Head.

Tolba, Mostafa, ed. (1988), *Evolving Environmental Perceptions: from Stockholm to Nairobi*, London, Butterworth.

Toma, Hideko (1999), Displaced persons and international human rights with reference to Rwanda and Cambodia, unpublished PhD thesis, University of Southampton.

Tylor, E. (1891), 'Culture defined' in L.A. Coser and B. Rosenberg, eds (1964), *Sociological Theory: a book of readings*, London, Collier-Macmillan.

UNICEF (1990), *State of the World's Children*, London, Oxford University Press.

United Nations (1992), *Earth Summit: Press Summaries*, New York, United Nations.

UN Chronicle (1993), June, **30** (2): 66.

United Nations Development Programme (1994a), *Human Development Report, 1994*, New York, Oxford University Press.

United Nations Development Programme (1994b), *World Urbanization Prospects: the 1994 revision*. United Nations Population Division, gopher://gopher.undp.org:70/00/ungophers/popin/wdtrends/urban

United Nations Development Programme (1995), *Human Development Report, 1995*, New York, Oxford University Press.

United Nations Development Programme (1999), *Human Development Report, 1999*, New York, Oxford University Press.

United Nations Development Programme (1998), *World Population 1998*, UN Department of Economic and Social Affairs, http://www.undp.org/popin/wdtrends/p98/fp98toc.htm

United Nations Development Programme (2000), *Population Distribution, Urbanization and Internal Migration*. United Nations Population Information Network, http://www.undp.org/popin/icpd/prepcomm/official/rap/RAP8.html

United Nations Food and Agriculture Organization (1999), *The State of Food Insecurity in the World 1999*, http://www.fao.org/FOCUS?E?SOFI?Count-e.htm

United Nations Population Fund (UNFPA 1992), *The State of World Population, 1992*, New York, United Nations.

Urry, John (1990), *The Tourist Gaze: leisure and travel in contemporary societies*, London, Sage.

Vagts, Alfred (1959), *A History of Militarism, Civilian and Military*, London, Hollis & Carter.

Vajpeyi, Dhirendra (1994), 'To dam or not to dam? Social, economic and political impact of large hydro-electric projects: case studies of China, India and Brazil', Paper presented to the XVI World Congress of the International Political Science Association, Berlin, Germany, 21–25 August.

Various (2000), 'Solving insolvency', *New Internationalist*, January/February: 32–3.

Vogt, Evon Z. (1969), *Zinacantan: a Maya community in the highlands of Chiapas*, Cambridge, MA, The Belknap Press.

Wallerstein, Immanuel (1974), *The Modern World System*, New York, Academic Press.

Walzer, Michael (1995), 'The concept of civil society' in Walzer, Michael, ed. *Toward a Global Civil Society*, Providence, RI, Berghahn: 7–27.

Warren, Bill (1977), *Inflation and Wages in Underdeveloped Countries: India, Peru and Turkey, 1939–1960*, London, Frank Cass.

Weaver, D.B. (1999), *Ecotourism in the Less Developed World*, Wallingford, Oxon., CAB International.

Weber, Max (1964), *The Theory of Social and Economic Organization*, New York, The Free Press, trans. by A.M. Henderson and Talcott Parsons.

Weinbaum, Marvin G. (1972), 'Afghanistan: nonparty parliamentary democracy', *Journal of Developing Areas*, **7** (1): 57–64.

Weiner, Myron (1962), *The Politics of Scarcity: public pressure and political response in India*, Chicago, IL, University of Chicago Press.

Weinstein, Martin (1975), *Uruguay, the Politics of Failure*, Westport, Conn., Greenwood Press.

White, Howard and Woestman, Lois (1994), 'The quality of aid: measuring trends in donor performance', *Development and Change*, **25**: 527–54.

Whitehead, Ann (1990), 'Food crisis and gender conflict in the African countryside', in Bernstein, Henry, Crow, Ben, Mackintosh, Maureen and Martin, Charlotte, eds, *The Food Question: profits versus people?*, London, Earthscan: 54–68.

Wijkman, Anders and Timberlake, Lloyd (1984), *Natural Disasters: acts of God or acts of Man?*, London, Earthscan.

Wiking, Staffan (1983), *Military Coups in Sub-Saharan Africa: how to justify illegal assumptions of power*, Uppsala, Scandinavian Institute of African Studies.

Wiles, Peter (1969), 'A syndrome, not a doctrine: some elementary theses on populism' in Ghita Ionescu and Ernest Gellner, eds, *Populism: its meaning and national characteristics*, New York, The Macmillan Co.

Williams, Gavin and Turner, Terisa (1978), 'Nigeria' in Dunn, John, ed., *West African States: failure and promise: a study in comparative politics*, Cambridge, Cambridge University Press.

Williams, Robert (1987), *Political Corruption in Africa*, Aldershot, Gower.

Wilson, E.O., ed. (1988), *Biodiversity*, Washington, DC, National Academy Press.

Wolf, E.R. (1969), *Peasant Wars of the Twentieth Century*, New York, Harper & Row.

Wood, David (2000), 'The Peruvian press under recent authoritarian regimes, with special reference to the *autogolpe* of President Fujimori', *Bulletin of Latin American Research*, **19** (1): 17–32.

World Bank (1987), *Protecting the Poor during Periods of Adjustment*, Washington DC, World Bank.

World Bank (1992), *World Development Report 1992*, Oxford, Oxford University Press.

World Bank (1994), *World Development Report 1994*, Oxford, Oxford University Press.

World Bank (1997), *World Development Report 1997*, Oxford, Oxford University Press.

World Bank (1999), *World Development Report 1999*, Oxford, Oxford University Press.

World Commission on Environment and Development (WCED) (1987), *Our Common Future (The Brundtland Report)*, Oxford, Oxford University Press.

World Health Organization (1993), *World Health Statistics Annual 1993*.

World Health Organization (1999), *World Health Statistics Annual 1999*.

Worsley, Peter (1967), *The Third World*, London, Weidenfeld & Nicolson, 2nd edn.

Wraith, Ronald and Simpkins, Edgar (1965), *Corruption in Developing Countries*, London, Allen & Unwin.

Wuthnow, Robert, Hunter, James Davison, Bergesen, Albert and Kurzweil, Edith (1984) *Cultural Analysis: the work of Peter L. Berger, Mary Douglas, Michel Foucault and Jürgen Habermas*, London, Routledge & Kegan Paul.

Index

militarism 149, 173–4
military aid 223, 225–6
military developmentalism 78, 172–3
military expenditure 85, 175–7, 229, 245
military intervention 11, 154, 158, 167–8, 170–1, 183
military security 175–6
mineral resources 45, 48
Moldova 21
modernisation 72–3, 165, 235
modernity 120–2
Monserrat 26
Montreal Protocol 248–9
Morocco 6, 159, 192, 219
Mozambique 11, 60, 172, 180–1, 184–5, 192, 263
Myanmar 103, 150; *see also* Burma

Namibia 28, 63, 181, 194, 232, 265
nation-state
  defined 137
nationalism 6, 75, 79, 91, 125, 134, 139–40, 143, 149–50, 154, 204, 206, 262
Nauru 46
neo-liberalism 17, 19, 50, 73, 214, 231, 245–6
Nepal 58, 113, 150, 193, 197
Netherlands 6, 7, 31, 41, 67, 120, 224
New International Economic Order (NIEO) 214–16
New Zealand 21, 22, 25, 35, 105
newly industrialising countries (NICs) 4, 5, 16, 32, 77, 79, 80, 82, 84, 99, 115, 262, 264, 265, 266
Nicaragua 182, 185, 215, 244
Niger 112
Nigeria 6, 28, 35, 36, 85, 94, 104, 105, 106, 107, 111, 112, 124, 128–9, 138, 140, 141, 144, 146, 147, 151, 168, 170, 180, 192, 193, 219, 246
Non-Aligned Movement (NAM) 7, 16, 17, 186–7, 190
non-governmental organisations (NGOs) 36, 50, 89, 223, 229–30
Non-Proliferation Treaty (NPT) 177
North Africa 122, 124, 162, 193, 265
North America 35, 41, 66, 74, 79, 197

North American Free Trade Agreement (NAFTA) 201, 217
North Asia 263
North Korea 174, 177, 178

Oceania 22, 27, 35, 164
oil 23, 37, 80, 147, 187, 205–6, 215, 219, 222, 233
  first oil shock 80, 85, 214
oligarchy 106–7
opinion formers 125–6
Organization of African Unity (OAU) 138, 171, 186, 191–2, 207
Organization of American States (OAS) 187, 191, 206
Organization for Economic Cooperation and Development (OECD) 18, 82, 83, 186, 223
Organization of Petroleum Exporting Countries (OPEC) 215, 232, 233
Outer Mongolia 23, 150
overseas development assistance (ODA) 223, 226, 231; *see also* aid
'ozone hole' 248

Pacific Ocean 25, 46–7, 155, 259, 266
Pacific Rim 266
Pakistan 7, 35, 38, 105, 112–13, 124, 144, 148, 150, 152, 153, 155, 160, 162, 171, 172, 173, 177, 178, 179, 193, 195, 244
Palestinians 137, 138
Panama 187, 225, 244
Papua New Guinea 61, 121, 155, 237
Paraguay 132, 149, 254, 255
patrimonialism 144–5
peasants 28–9, 52, 78, 108–11, 116, 132, 163
  'peasantariat' 78
personalism 143, 158
Peru 25, 27, 33, 55, 62, 87, 94, 102, 105, 106, 108, 109–11, 131, 134, 153, 169, 172, 179, 186, 219, 228
Philippines 6, 25, 26, 30, 43, 45, 53, 63, 79, 104, 123, 145, 152, 162, 171, 180, 193, 204, 244, 264
plantation economy 105
political parties 157–61
  defined 157